Additional praise for *The Open Secret*

"For much of the twentieth century natural theology was regarded as intellectually moribund and theologically suspect. In this splendid new book, bestselling author and distinguished theologian Alister McGrath issues a vigorous challenge to the old prejudices. Building on the foundation of the classical triad of truth, beauty, and goodness, he constructs an impressive case for a new and revitalized natural theology. This is a well-conceived, timely, and thought-provoking volume."

Peter Harrison, Harris Manchester College, Oxford

The Open Secret

A New Vision for Natural Theology

Alister E. McGrath

Blackwell Publishing

© 2008 by Alister E. McGrath

BLACKWELL PUBLISHING
350 Main Street, Malden, MA 02148-5020, USA
9600 Garsington Road, Oxford OX4 2DQ, UK
550 Swanston Street, Carlton, Victoria 3053, Australia

First published 2008 by Blackwell Publishing Ltd

1   2008

Library of Congress Cataloging-in-Publication Data

McGrath, Alister E., 1953–
   The open secret : a new vision for natural theology / Alister E.
McGrath.
      p. cm.
   Includes bibliographical references and index.
   ISBN 978-1-4051-2692-2 (hardcover : alk. paper)—ISBN 978-1-4051-2691-5
(pbk. : alk. paper)   1. Theism.   2. Natural theology.   3. Nature—Religious
aspects—Christianity.   I. Title.

   BL200.M35 2008
   211′.3—dc22
                                                                      2007041410

A catalogue record for this title is available from the British Library.

Set in 10.5/12.5pt Sabon
by Graphicraft Limited, Hong Kong
Printed and bound in Singapore
by Markono Print Media Pte Ltd

The publisher's policy is to use permanent paper from mills that operate a
sustainable forestry policy, and which has been manufactured from pulp
processed using acid-free and elementary chlorine-free practices. Furthermore,
the publisher ensures that the text paper and cover board used have met
acceptable environmental accreditation standards.

For further information on
Blackwell Publishing, visit our website at
www.blackwellpublishing.com

Contents

CONTENTS

CONTENTS

Acknowledgments

It is a pleasure to be able to acknowledge those who have contributed to the writing of this volume. My greatest debt by far is to Joanna Collicutt, who was my research assistant on this project, and is now lecturer in the psychology of religion at Heythrop College, London University. Her research for this work focused on John Ruskin, John Dewey, and the biblical material, particularly the call of Samuel, the parables of Jesus, and the Johannine "I am" sayings. She provided expert advice on the psychology of religion, and authored chapter 5, dealing with the cognitive neuropsychology of perception, and some portions of other chapters. She also proposed the title of this work.

I also acknowledge financial support from the John Templeton Foundation, without which this work could never have been written. The argument and approach of this book have been shaped, in part, through significant conversations with Justin Barrett, John Barrow, John Hedley Brooke, Simon Conway Morris, Paul Davies, Daniel Dennett, Robert McCauley, and Thomas F. Torrance. While these scholars may not agree with the approach I have taken in this work, it is appropriate to acknowledge their kindness in discussing some key issues relating to natural theology, and the significance of their views in shaping my analysis of critical questions. I remain completely responsible for errors of fact or judgment in this work.

This work represents a substantially expanded version of the 2008 Riddell Memorial Lectures at Newcastle University, England. It also includes material originally delivered as the 2005 Mulligan Sermon at

Gray's Inn, and the 2006 Warburton Lecture at Lincoln's Inn. I am grateful to both these ancient London Inns of Court for their invitations to speak on the theme of theology and the law, and their kind hospitality. My thanks also to Michelle Edmonds, who suggested the cover illustration for the book; to Jenny Roberts, for her skill as a copyeditor; and to Rebecca Harkin of Blackwell Publishing, for her encouragement and patience as this work gradually took shape.

Alister McGrath
Oxford, June 2007

I seem to have been only like a boy playing on the sea-shore, and diverting myself in now and then finding a smoother pebble or a prettier shell than ordinary, whilst the great ocean of truth lay all undiscovered before me.

Isaac Newton (1643–1727)

The greatest thing a human soul ever does in this world is to see something, and tell what it saw in a plain way . . . To see clearly is poetry, prophecy, and religion – all in one.

John Ruskin (1819–1900)

CHAPTER 1

Natural Theology:
Introducing an Approach

The heavens are telling the glory of God;
    and the firmament proclaims his handiwork.
Day to day pours forth speech,
    and night to night declares knowledge.
        (Psalm 19: 1)

When I look at your heavens, the work of your fingers,
    the moon and the stars that you have established;
what are human beings that you are mindful of them,
    mortals that you care for them?
        (Psalm 8: 3–4)

For as the heavens are higher than the earth,
    so are my ways higher than your ways
    and my thoughts than your thoughts.
        (Isaiah 55: 9)

These familiar words from the Hebrew Scriptures characterize the entire enterprise of natural theology: they affirm its possibility, while pointing to the fundamental contradictions and tensions that this possibility creates. If the heavens really are "telling the glory of God,"[1] this implies

---

[1] The Hebrew term in Psalm 19: 1 here translated as "tell" can bear such meanings as "declare," "set forth," and "enumerate." See further James Barr, "Do We

that something of God can be known through them, that the natural order is capable of disclosing something of the divine. But it does not automatically follow from this that *human beings*, situated as we are within nature, are capable unaided, or indeed capable under any conditions, of perceiving the divine through the natural order. What if the heavens are "telling the glory of God" in a language that we cannot understand? What if the glory of God really is there in nature, but we cannot discern it?

Natural theology can broadly be understood as the systematic exploration of a proposed link between the everyday world of our experience[2] and another asserted transcendent reality,[3] an ancient and pervasive idea that achieved significant elaboration in the thought of the early Christian fathers,[4] and continues to be the subject of much discussion today. Yet it is essential to appreciate that serious engagement with natural theology in the twenty-first century is hindered both by a definitional miasma, and the lingering memories of past controversies, which have created a climate of suspicion concerning this enterprise within many quarters. As Christoph Kock points out in his excellent recent study of the fortunes of natural theology within Protestantism, there almost seems

---

Perceive the Speech of the Heavens? A Question in Psalm 19," in Jack C. Knight and Lawrence A. Sinclair (eds), *The Psalms and Other Studies on the Old Testament*, pp. 11–17, Nashotah, WI: Nashotah House Seminary, 1990. Some medieval Christian writers interpreted this psalm allegorically, holding that Paul's citation of the psalm in Romans 10: 18 implied that the whole psalm was a prophecy of the apostolic preaching under the allegory or image of the created heavens. This view was rejected by Martin Bucer, who regarded this as exegetically implausible: see R. Gerald Hobbs, "How Firm a Foundation: Martin Bucer's Historical Exegesis of the Psalms," *Church History* 53 (1984): 477–91.

[2] Throughout this work, we shall assume – without presenting a detailed defense of – a realist worldview. For a defense of this assumption, see Alister E. McGrath, *A Scientific Theology: 2 – Reality*, London: T&T Clark, 2002, pp. 121–313.

[3] The existence of such a transcendent reality is not universally accepted: see, for example, the position set out by Bertrand Russell, "On Denoting," *Mind* 14 (1905): 479–93.

[4] See especially Jaroslav Pelikan, *Christianity and Classical Culture: The Metamorphosis of Natural Theology in the Christian Encounter with Hellenism*, New Haven, CT: Yale University Press, 1993.

to be a presumption in some circles that "natural theology" represents some kind of heresy.[5]

The lengthening shadows of half-forgotten historical debates and cultural circumstances have shaped preconceptions and forged situation-specific approaches to natural theology that have proved singularly ill-adapted to the contemporary theological situation. The notion of "natural theology" has proved so conceptually fluid, resistant to precise definition, that its critics can easily present it as a subversion of divine revelation, and its supporters, with equal ease, as its obvious outcome. Instead of perpetuating this unsatisfactory situation, there is much to be said for beginning all over again, in effect setting aside past definitions, preconceptions, judgments, and prejudices, in order to allow a fresh examination of this fascinating and significant notion.

This book sets out to develop a distinctively Christian approach to natural theology, which retrieves and reformulates older approaches that have been marginalized or regarded as outmoded in recent years, establishing them on more secure intellectual foundations. We argue that if nature is to disclose the transcendent, it must be "seen" or "read" in certain specific ways – ways that are not themselves necessarily mandated by nature itself. It is argued that Christian theology provides an interpretative framework by which nature may be "seen" in a way that connects with the transcendent. The enterprise of natural theology is thus one of discernment, of seeing nature in a certain way, of viewing it through a particular and specific set of spectacles.

There are many styles of "natural theology," and the long history of Christian theological reflection bears witness to a rich diversity of approaches, with none achieving dominance – until the rise of the Enlightenment. As we shall see, the rise of the "Age of Reason" gave rise to a family of approaches to natural theology which asserted its capacity to demonstrate the existence of God without recourse to any religious beliefs or presuppositions. This development, which reflects the Enlightenment's emphasis upon the autonomy and sovereignty of unaided human reason, has had a highly significant impact on shaping Christian attitudes to

---

[5] Christoph Kock, *Natürliche Theologie: Ein evangelischer Streitbegriff*, Neukirchen-Vluyn: Neukirchener, 2001, pp. 392–5. Before any reconstruction of the discipline is possible, he suggests, there is a need to bring about "die Enthäretisierung natürlicher Theologie" (p. 392), a somewhat clumsy and artificial phrase which is probably best paraphrased as "the removal of the stigma of heresy from natural theology."

natural theology. Such has been its influence that, for many Christians, there is now an automatic presumption that "natural theology" designates the enterprise of arguing directly from the observation of nature to demonstrate the existence of God.

This work opposes this approach, arguing for a conceptual redefinition and methodological relocation of natural theology. Contrary to the Enlightenment's aspirations for a universal natural theology, based on common human reason and experience of nature, we hold that a Christian natural theology is grounded in and informed by a characteristic Christian theological foundation. A Christian understanding of nature is the intellectual prerequisite for a natural theology which discloses the Christian God.

Christianity brings about a redefinition of the "natural," with highly significant implications for a "natural theology." The definitive "Christ event" as interpreted by the distinctive and characteristic Christian doctrine of the incarnation can be said to redeem the category of the "natural," allowing it to be seen in a new way. In our sense, a viable "natural theology" is actually a "natural Christian theology," in that it is shaped and made possible by the normative ideas of the Christian faith. A properly Christian natural theology points to the God of the Christian faith, not some generalized notion of divinity detached from the life and witness of the church.[6]

The notion of Christian *discernment* – of seeing things in the light of Christ – is frequently encountered throughout the New Testament. Paul urges his readers not to "be conformed to this world," but rather to "be transformed by the renewing of your minds" (Romans 12: 2) – thus affirming the capacity of the Christian faith to bring about a radical change in the way in which we understand and inhabit the world.[7]

---

[6] This point was stressed by Stanley Hauerwas in his recent Gifford Lectures: Stanley Hauerwas, *With the Grain of the Universe: The Church's Witness and Natural Theology*, London: SCM Press, 2002, pp. 15–16: "Natural theology divorced from a full [Christian] doctrine of God cannot help but distort the character of God and, accordingly, of the world in which we find ourselves . . . I must maintain that the God who moves the sun and the stars is the same God who was *incarnate* in Jesus of Nazareth" (emphasis added).

[7] This is about more than cognitive or intellectual change. Thus John Chrysostom argues (in *Homilies on Romans*, 20) that Paul's meaning is not that Christians ought to see the world in a new manner, but that their transformation by grace leads to their seeing the world in such a manner. See the excellent analysis in Demetrios Trakatellis, "Being Transformed: Chrysostom's Exegesis of the Epistle to the Romans," *Greek Orthodox Theological Review* 36 (1991): 211–29.

The New Testament uses a wide range of images to describe this change, many of which suggest a change in the way in which we see things: our eyes are opened, and a veil is removed (Acts 9: 9–19; 2 Corinthians 3: 13–16). This "transformation through the renewing of the mind" makes it possible to see and interpret things in a new way. For example, the Hebrew Scriptures came to be understood as pointing beyond their immediate historical context to their ultimate fulfillment in Christ.[8] In a similar way the world comes to be seen as pointing beyond the sphere of everyday experience to Christ its ultimate creator.[9]

A Christian natural theology is thus about seeing nature in a specific manner, which enables the truth, beauty, and goodness of God to be discerned, and which acknowledges nature as a legitimate, authorized, and limited pointer to the divine. There is no question of such a natural theology "proving" the existence of God or a transcendent realm on the basis of pure reason, or seeing nature as a gateway to a fully orbed theistic system.[10] Rather, natural theology addresses fundamental questions about divine disclosure and human cognition and perception. In what way can human beings, reflecting on *nature* by means of *natural* processes, discern the transcendent?

This book represents an essay – in the classic French sense of *essai*, "an attempt" – to lay the ground for the renewal and revalidation of natural theology, fundamentally as a legitimate aspect of Christian theology, but also as a contribution to a wider cultural discussion. Natural theology

---

[8]   See Gordon J. Hamilton, "Augustine's Methods of Biblical Interpretation," in H. A. Meynell (ed.), *Grace, Politics and Desire: Essays on Augustine*, pp. 103–19, Calgary, AB: University of Calgary Press, 1990; John Barton, "The Messiah in Old Testament Theology," in John Day (ed.), *King and Messiah in Israel and the Ancient Near East*, pp. 365–79, Sheffield: Sheffield Academic Press, 1998, especially pp. 371–2.

[9]   John 1: 14–18; Colossians 1: 15–19; Hebrews 1: 1–8. There are important parallels here with the Renaissance quest for a "natural language," itself grounded in the natural order, capable of representing "that which is" rather than merely "that which is said." See Allison Coudert, "Some Theories of a Natural Language from the Renaissance to the Seventeenth Century," in Albert Heinekamp and Dieter Mettler (eds), *Magia Naturalis und die Entstehung der modernen Naturwissenschaften*, pp. 56–118, Wiesbaden: Steiner, 1978.

[10]   See Barr's comments on the scope of biblical conceptions of natural theology: James Barr, *Biblical Faith and Natural Theology*, Oxford: Clarendon Press, 1993, p. 138.

touches some of the great questions of philosophy, and hence of life. What can we know? What does what we know suggest about reality itself? How does this affect the way we behave and what we can become? These questions refuse to be restricted to the realms of academic inquiry, in that they are of relevance to culture as a whole.

The book thus sets out to re-examine the entire question of the intellectual foundations, spiritual utility, and conceptual limits of natural theology. Such a task entails a critical examination of the present state of the debate, but also rests on a historical analysis. Crucial to this is the observation that the definition of natural theology was modified in the eighteenth century in order to conform to the Enlightenment agenda. As a result, natural theology has come to be understood primarily as a somewhat unsuccessful attempt to prove the existence of God on the basis of nonreligious considerations, above all through an appeal to "nature."

The book is broken down into three major parts. It opens by considering the perennial human interest in the transcendent, illustrating its persistence in supposedly secular times, and describing the methods and techniques that have emerged as humanity has attempted to rise above its mundane existence, encountering something that is perceived to be of lasting significance and value. This is correlated with contemporary understandings of the psychology of perception.

The second part moves beyond the general human quest for the transcendent, and sets this in the context of an engagement with the natural realm that is sustained and informed by the specific ideas of the Christian tradition. Natural theology is here interpreted, not as a general search for divinity on terms of our own choosing, but as an engagement with nature that is conducted in the light of a Christian vision of reality, resting on a trinitarian, incarnational ontology. This part includes a detailed exploration of the historical origins and conceptual flaws of the family of natural theologies which arose in response to the Enlightenment, which dominated twentieth-century discussion of the matter.

The third and final part moves beyond the concept of natural theology as an enterprise of sense-making, offering a wider and richer vision of its tasks and possibilities. It is argued that rationalist approaches to natural theology represent an attenuation of its scope, reflecting the lingering influence of the agendas and concerns of the "Age of Reason." Natural theology is to be reconceived as involving every aspect of the human encounter with nature – rational, imaginative, and moral.

In that this volume offers a new approach which poses a challenge to many existing conceptions of the nature and possibilities of natural theology, in what follows we shall set out a brief account of its leading themes, which will be expanded and extended in subsequent chapters.

"Nature" is an Indeterminate Concept

The concept of natural theology that became dominant in the twentieth century is that of proving the existence of God by an appeal to the natural world, without any appeal to divine revelation. Natural theology has come to be understood, to use William Alston's helpful definition, as "the enterprise of providing support for religious beliefs by starting from premises that neither are nor presuppose any religious beliefs."[11] The story of how this specific understanding of natural theology achieved dominance, marginalizing older and potentially more productive approaches, is itself of no small interest.[12] One of the major pressures leading to this development was the growing influence of the Enlightenment, which placed Christian theology under increasing pressure to offer a demonstration of its core beliefs on the basis of publicly accepted and universally accessible criteria – such as an appeal to nature and reason.

The "Age of Reason" tended to the view that the meaning of the term "nature" was self-evident. In part, the cultural triumph of the rationalist approach to natural theology in the eighteenth century rested on a general inherited consensus that "nature" designated a reasonably well-defined entity, capable of buttressing philosophical and theological reflection without being dependent on any preconceived or privileged religious ideas. The somewhat generic notions of "natural religion" or "religion of nature," which became significant around this time, are themselves grounded

---

[11] William P. Alston, *Perceiving God: The Epistemology of Religious Experience*, Ithaca, NY: Cornell University Press, 1991, p. 289.

[12] For an introduction, see Alister E. McGrath, "Towards the Restatement and Renewal of a Natural Theology: A Dialogue with the Classic English Tradition," in Alister E. McGrath (ed.), *The Order of Things: Explorations in Scientific Theology*, pp. 63–96, Oxford: Blackwell, 2006.

in the notion of a universal, objective natural realm, open to public scrutiny and interpretation.[13]

It is easy to understand the basis of such a widespread appeal to nature in the eighteenth century. On the one hand, Enlightenment writers looking for a secure universal foundation of knowledge, free of political manipulation or ecclesiastical influence, regarded nature as a potentially pure and unsullied source of natural wisdom.[14] On the other, Christian apologists anxious to meet increasing public skepticism about the reliability of the Bible as a source of divine revelation were able to shore up traditional beliefs concerning God through an appeal to nature.[15]

Relatively recent developments, however, have undermined the foundations of this older approach. Critical historical scholarship has suggested that the Enlightenment is more variegated and heterogeneous than an earlier generation of scholars believed,[16] making it problematic to speak of "an Enlightenment natural theology," as if this designated a single, well-defined entity. It is increasingly clear that the Enlightenment itself

---

[13] There is a large literature, represented by works such as Charles E. Raven, *Natural Religion and Christian Theology*, 2 vols, Cambridge, UK: Cambridge University Press, 1953; Peter A. Byrne, *Natural Religion and the Nature of Religion: The Legacy of Deism*, London: Routledge, 1989; Nicholas Roe, *The Politics of Nature: Wordsworth and Some Contemporaries*, New York: St. Martins Press, 1992; David T. Morgan, "Benjamin Franklin: Champion of Generic Religion," *Historian* 62 (2000): 723–9.

[14] See the points made by Richard S. Westfall, "The Scientific Revolution of the Seventeenth Century: A New World View," in John Torrance (ed.), *The Concept of Nature*, pp. 63–93, Oxford: Oxford University Press, 1992.

[15] The celebrated "Boyle Lectures," delivered over the period 1692–1732, are an excellent example of this approach. For Boyle's own views on natural theology, see Jan W. Wojcik, *Robert Boyle and the Limits of Reason*, Cambridge, UK: Cambridge University Press, 1997. Note also the older study of Harold Fisch, "The Scientist as Priest: A Note on Robert Boyle's Natural Theology," *Isis* 44 (1953): 252–65. These difficulties were initially hermeneutical, relating to problems in interpreting the text; as time progressed, the rise of critical historical and textual studies raised further concerns about the public defensibility of the Christian revelation. For an excellent study, see Henning Graf Reventloh, *The Authority of the Bible and the Rise of the Modern World*, London: SCM Press, 1984.

[16] See the analysis in James Schmidt, "What Enlightenment Project?" *Political Theory* 28 (2000): 734–57.

mandated a number of approaches to nature, even if these share some common themes.

Perhaps more significantly, the notion of "nature" proves to be rather more fluid than the Enlightenment appreciated. An extended engagement with the natural world leads to the insight that the terms "nature" and "the natural," far from referring to objective, autonomous entities, are conceptually malleable notions, patient of multiple interpretations – none of which is self-evident. Since World War II, there has been an increasing awareness that "nature" is essentially a constructed concept.[17] Concepts of nature and the natural – note the deliberate use of the plural – are themselves the outcome of a process of interpretation and evaluation, influenced by the social situation, vested interests, and agendas of those with power and status.[18] In the twentieth century, prevalent and influential ways of "seeing" nature have included:

Nature as a mindless force, causing inconvenience to humanity, and demanding to be tamed;

Nature as an open-air gymnasium, offering leisure and sports facilities to affluent individuals who want to demonstrate their sporting prowess;

Nature as a wild kingdom, encouraging scuba-diving, hiking, and hunting;

Nature as a supply depot – an aging and increasingly reluctant provider which produces (although with growing difficulty) minerals, water, food, and other services for humanity.[19]

These views of nature are not simply different; they are inconsistent with each other, their respective accentuations reflecting the different agendas of those who devised them in the first place. Nature, far from being a constant, robust, autonomous entity, is an intellectually plastic notion.

---

[17] For a detailed analysis of this point, see Alister E. McGrath, *A Scientific Theology: 1 – Nature*, London: T&T Clark, 2001, pp. 81–133.

[18] See Neil Evernden, *The Social Creation of Nature*, Baltimore, MD: Johns Hopkins University Press, 1992; Kate Soper, *What is Nature? Culture, Politics and the Non-Human*, Oxford: Blackwell, 1995.

[19] For these categories, I draw on Michael E. Soulé, "The Social Siege of Nature," in Michael E. Soulé and Gary Lease (eds), *Reinventing Nature: Responses to Postmodern Deconstruction*, pp. 137–70, Washington, DC: Island Press, 1995. This work includes excellent comments on the postmodern deconstruction of nature and its implications, not least for ecological concerns.

Definitions of nature may well tell us more about those who define it than what it is in itself.[20]

Natural Theology is an Empirical Discipline

One of the distinctive features of our approach to natural theology is the view that, while philosophical and theological reflection on the issues attending it are important, *empirical* questions cannot be avoided. For example, consider James Barr's excellent summary of traditional definitions of natural theology:

> Traditionally, "natural theology" has commonly meant something like this: that "by nature," that is, just by being human beings, men and women have a certain degree of knowledge of God and awareness of him, or at least a capacity for such awareness; and this knowledge or awareness exists anterior to the special revelation of God made through Jesus Christ, through the Church, through the Bible.[21]

This account provokes several fundamental and related questions about *nature* in general, and about *human nature* in particular. What does it mean "just" to be "human beings"? How can "knowledge of God" be calibrated? How can the "capacity" for an "awareness of God" be explored? And what are the implications for the reformulation of a natural theology?

These are questions about human psychology at least as much as they are questions of systematic theology or metaphysics. In this book, we shall take the psychological perspectives of this matter with the greatest seriousness, considering the processes by which human beings make sense of their environments. The influence of Enlightenment rationalism until recently has been such that natural theology has been understood primarily as an exercise in which human observers were able to read nature

---

[20] For some fascinating illustrations of this point, see the myriad of competing concepts explored in Hans Bak and Walter W. Holbling, *"Nature's Nation" Revisited: American Concepts of Nature from Wonder to Ecological Crisis*, Amsterdam: VU Press, 2003.

[21] Barr, *Biblical Faith and Natural Theology*, p. 1.

simply and objectively from a position of privilege. Yet the characteristic modernist notion that human observers are detached from nature has been called into question by the growing recognition in psychology that cognition is an embodied, situated activity of sense-making. Human beings are part of the natural order which they observe and interpret. Any notion of the "objectivity" of human interpretations of nature is undermined by the very nature of the psychological processes by which observation takes place. These considerations do not discredit the notion of natural theology itself; they do, however, cause severe difficulties for the particular approach to natural theology which emerged during the period of the Enlightenment.

It is to be recognized that the human observer is not a passive spectator but an active interpreter of the natural world. A deepening understanding of the psychology of human cognition is the occasion for a retrieval of Judeo-Christian accounts of our engagement with the world which recognize that humanity actively constructs a vision of reality.[22] This is consistent with a "critical realist" epistemology, which affirms both the existence of an extra-mental reality and the active, constructive role of the observer in representing and interpreting it.[23] While this could be argued to be consistent with a social constructivist position, which holds that human subjectivity imposes itself on what we mistakenly

---

[22] The notion has been explored in other manners, such as Philip Hefner's notion of humanity as the "created co-creator": Philip J. Hefner, *The Human Factor: Evolution, Culture, and Religion*, Minneapolis: Fortress Press, 1993; Gregory R. Peterson, "The Created Co-Creator: What It Is and Is Not," *Zygon* 39 (2004): 827–40. The idea can also be developed in a more literary manner, as in J. R. R. Tolkien's notion of the "subcreator," which views the artist in this view as an active participant in the creative process. Though artists may refract the light of truth that shines from the creator, they are nevertheless to be regarded as agents of that act of creation. See further Verlyn Flieger, *Splintered Light: Logos and Language in Tolkien's World*, rev. edn, Kent, OH: Kent State University, 2002, pp. 49–56. Hefner's notion of the "created co-creator" can, of course, also be developed in this direction: see Vitor Westhelle, "The Poet, the Practitioner, and the Beholder: Thoughts on the Created Co-Creator," *Zygon* 39 (2004): 747–54.

[23] This point was implicit in the famous debate between Karl Barth and Emil Brunner in 1934 over the validity and character of natural theology, to which we shall return later in this work: see pp. 158–64.

believe to be objective,[24] critical realism insists that human thought is constrained and informed by an engagement with an external reality. Where social constructivism holds that the vision of reality that humans construct reflects the outcome of human autonomy and creativity, rather than any "order of things" within nature itself, our approach insists that the human attempt to make sense of things is shaped by the way things actually are.

A Christian Natural Theology Concerns the Christian God

The quest for a viable Christian natural theology can be positioned against a continuing cultural interest in the transcendent. In a penetrating analysis of the failure of the Enlightenment to eliminate religion in the West, the Polish philosopher Leszek Kolakowski argues that the renewal of interest in the transcendent is indicative of the inner contradictions and vulnerabilities within Western culture. The "return of the sacred," he argues, is a telling sign of the failure of the *ersatz* Enlightenment "religion of humanity," in which a deficient "godlessness desperately attempts to replace the lost God with something else."[25] Natural theology is to be set within this general cultural context of continuing interest and yearning for the transcendent. There is a widespread concern to engage with the empirical world of everyday experience in such a way that it can point to the existence of the transcendent, disclose its character, or possibly lead into its presence.

For the Christian this quickly leads to a further thought: does a quest for the transcendent through nature lead to the God of Christianity – a trinitarian God, who became incarnate in Jesus Christ? It is no idle question. As we shall see, the British philosopher Iris Murdoch insisted upon the foundational role of the transcendent in any attempt to sustain

---

[24] For the issues, see Ian Hacking, *The Social Construction of What?* Cambridge, MA: Harvard University Press, 1999.

[25] Leszek Kolakowski, "Concern about God in an Apparently Godless Age," in *My Correct Views on Everything*, ed. Zbigniew Janowski, pp. 173–83, South Bend, IN: St. Augustine's Press, 2005; quote at p. 183. For a more rigorous exploration of this theme, see Charles Taylor, *A Secular Age*, Cambridge, MA: Belknap Press, 2007.

the notion of "the good" (pp. 291–2). Yet Murdoch regarded herself as an atheist. The quest for the transcendent does not necessarily entail belief in a god or plurality of gods.

Even those who do hold that the quest for the transcendent leads to belief in a single divinity would question whether this is necessarily to be identified with the God of Christianity. As we noted earlier, the Boyle lectures are widely regarded as the most significant public assertion of the "reasonableness" of Christianity in the early modern period. These lectures set out to demonstrate that there was a direct, publicly persuasive connection between nature and the Christian God in response to that age's growing emphasis upon rationalism and its increasing suspicion of ecclesiastical authority.[26]

Yet by the end of the eighteenth century, the lectures were widely regarded as discredited. In part, this was due to growing skepticism concerning their intellectual merits. "As the eighteenth century progressed, the 'reasonable' Christianity of the Boyle lecturers came to look increasingly flimsy and vulnerable."[27] Yet perhaps more seriously, this approach seemed to have an inbuilt tendency to lead to heterodox, rather than orthodox, forms of Christianity.[28]

Thus, while we would argue that a Christian natural theology has the potential to shed light on the cultural phenomenon of the desire to find the transcendent in nature, it seems that the quest for the transcendent in nature has not automatically led to the Christian God.

In contrast, the present study adopts a specifically Christian approach to natural theology from the outset, anchoring it in the Christ event. This is a book about natural *Christian* theology, which interprets natural theology as something that is both historically located in the life and

---

[26] Gilbert Burnet (ed.), *The Boyle Lectures (1692–1732): A Defence of Natural and Revealed Religion, Being an Abridgement of the Sermons Preached at the Lectures Founded by Robert Boyle*, 4 vols, Bristol: Thoemmes Press, 2000.

[27] Andrew Pyle, "Introduction," in *The Boyle Lectures (1692–1732)*, vol. 1, pp. vii–liii.

[28] For example, some of the most influential lecturers were Arians: Maurice Wiles, *Archetypal Heresy: Arianism Through the Ages*, Oxford: Oxford University Press, 1996, pp. 62–134. For a more general exploration of this point, see the important collection of studies in John Brooke and Ian McLean (eds), *Heterodoxy in Early Modern Science and Religion*, Oxford: Oxford University Press, 2006.

death of Jesus of Nazareth and theologically interpreted by the church. This theology places the general questions about nature and human nature in the specific context of the gospel of Jesus Christ. As already noted, its central claim is that the Christ event renders all theology "natural" because in it the natural order is redeemed. The basis of such a "natural Christian theology" is ultimately the doctrine of the incarnation.

A Christian natural theology is thus undertaken on the basis of a Christian vision of God and nature, which are in turn focused on the person of Christ. This approach to natural theology allows nature to be "seen" in the light of the Christian tradition. That tradition raises certain significant questions concerning both the observer, and what is being observed. What if nature is "fallen" – to note a concern we shall consider in more detail later – so that its capacity to disclose God is diminished or distorted? Or if human observers and interpreters of nature share its fallenness, entailing a double diminution or distortion of the glory of God? This point cannot be evaded by a selective reading of nature, which accentuates its beauty and orderedness, while disregarding its more ugly, chaotic aspects, particularly as seen in natural evil and suffering. A robust theological framework is thus essential if nature is to be engaged with coherently as an entirety, rather than adopting a highly eclectic, piecemeal approach to its interpretation.

A Natural Theology is Incarnational, Not Dualist

Many traditional approaches to natural theology presuppose an essentially dualist framework. An implicit assumption of ontological bipolarity underlies the affirmation that the transcendent can be accessed via the mundane, the eternal through the temporal, or the supernatural through the natural. As Thomas F. Torrance has pointed out, such dualist assumptions are deeply ingrained within the Western theological tradition, and can be argued to reflect the influence of speculative Hellenistic philosophy rather than its original Jewish intellectual context.[29] Yet a Christian natural theology does not necessarily presuppose any such dualism or set of bipolarities. Nature and supernature are not to be thought

---

[29] Thomas F. Torrance, *Theology in Reconciliation: Essays Towards Evangelical and Catholic Unity in East and West*, London: Chapman, 1975, pp. 27–8, 267–8.

of as two separate worlds, but as different expressions of the same reality.[30]

The Christian doctrine of the incarnation forces re-evaluation of such dichotomies, offering a new understanding of nature. As Greek patristic writers constantly emphasized, the pattern of creation, incarnation, and redemption was about the transformation of the entire category of the "natural," not merely about the redemption and renewal of human nature as one element, however important, of that domain.[31] The doctrine of the incarnation affirms the capacity of the natural to disclose the divine, both on account of its status as the *divine creation*, and as the object of *God's habitation*. This point was stressed by John of Damascus, in his controversy with those who held that material or physical objects could not be vehicles of divine disclosure or revelation.[32] God's decision to inhabit the material order in and through the incarnation affirms its God-bestowed – though not inevitable or automatic – capacity to reveal the divine.

Resonance, Not Proof: Natural Theology and Empirical Fit

As noted earlier, natural theology is widely understood to be "the enterprise of providing support for religious beliefs by starting from premises that neither are nor presuppose any religious beliefs" (William Alston).[33] Alston's definition clearly identifies the apologetic intention of traditional approaches to natural theology. As we noted earlier, the Boyle Lectures assumed that natural theology offered proofs for the existence of God.

---

[30] This thesis underlies the important work by Philip Yancey, *Rumors of Another World: What on Earth Are We Missing?* Grand Rapids, MI: Zondervan, 2003.

[31] H. E. W. Turner, *The Patristic Doctrine of Redemption: A Study of the Development of Doctrine During the First Five Centuries*, London: Mowbray, 1952.

[32] John of Damascus, *Contra imaginum calumniatores*, I, 16, in *Patristische Texte und Studien*, vol. 17, ed. P. Bonifatius Kotter OSB, Berlin/New York: de Gruyter, 1979, pp. 89–92.

[33] William P. Alston, *Perceiving God: The Epistemology of Religious Experience*, Ithaca, NY: Cornell University Press, 1991, p. 289.

Starting from nature, the existence of God is invoked as the only way of making sense of what is observed. For many of the early Boyle lecturers, the complexity and beauty of the physical world could only be explained on the basis of the existence of a creator God. For William Paley, author of the highly influential *Natural Theology* (1802),[34] the close observation of the biological world demanded a similar conclusion. Nature was to be compared to a watch, whose complex mechanism pointed to the existence of a divine watchmaker. While some of these writers saw their arguments as constituting "proofs" for God's existence, they are perhaps better seen as a retrospective validation of belief in God. This point underlies John Henry Newman's lapidary remark: "I believe in design because I believe in God; not in God because I see design."[35]

The approach to natural theology set out in this volume also has considerable apologetic potential. Nature is here interpreted as an "open secret" – a publicly accessible entity, whose true meaning is known only from the standpoint of the Christian faith.[36] This rests, however, not upon an attempt to "prove" the existence of God from observation of nature, but upon the capacity of the Christian worldview to comprehend what

---

[34] For the impact of this work on nineteenth-century British intellectual culture, including Charles Darwin, see Aileen Fyfe, "The Reception of William Paley's *Natural Theology* in the University of Cambridge," *British Journal for the History of Science* 30 (1997): 321–35. For the problems of Paley's approach, see Neal C. Gillespie, "Divine Design and the Industrial Revolution: William Paley's Abortive Reform of Natural Theology," *Isis* 81 (1990): 214–29.

[35] John Henry Newman, letter to William Robert Brownlow, April 13, 1870; in Charles Stephen Dessain and Thomas Gornall (eds), *The Letters and Diaries of John Henry Newman*, 31 vols, Oxford: Clarendon Press, 1963–2006, vol. 25, p. 97. For comment, see Noel Keith Roberts, "Newman on the Argument from Design," *New Blackfriars* 88 (2007): 56–66.

[36] We shall explore the critical idea of the "open secret" in greater detail in chapter 6. The image of the "open secret" is also found in Lesslie Newbigin's classic account of Christian mission as the declaration of an "open secret," which is "open" in that it is preached to all nations, yet "secret" in that it is manifest only to the eyes of faith: Lesslie Newbigin, *The Open Secret: Sketches for a Missionary Theology*, London: SPCK, 1978. For evaluations, see K. P. Aleaz, "The Gospel According to Lesslie Newbigin: An Evaluation," *Asia Journal of Theology* 13 (1999): 172–200; Wilbert R. Shenk, "Lesslie Newbigin's Contribution to Mission Theology," *International Bulletin of Missionary Research* 24/2 (2000): 59–64.

is observed, including the human capacity to make sense of things. The explanatory fecundity of Christianity is affirmed, in that it is seen to resonate with what is observed. "I believe in Christianity as I believe that the Sun has risen – not only because I see it, but because by it, I see everything else."[37] These concluding words of C. S. Lewis's paper "Is theology poetry?" set out the Christian view that belief in God illuminates the intellectual landscape, allowing things to be seen in their true perspective, so that the inner coherence of reality may be appreciated.

On this approach, apologetics is grounded in the resonance of worldview and observation, with the Christian way of seeing things being affirmed to offer a robust degree of empirical fit with what is actually observed – the "best explanation" of a complex and multifaceted phenomenon.[38] This basic approach can be seen in John Polkinghorne's discussion of the capacity of various worldviews to make sense of various aspects of reality, using four criteria of excellence: economy, scope, elegance, and fruitfulness. Polkinghorne here invokes theism as a more powerful explanatory tool than naturalism, and holds that a trinitarian theism is superior to a more generic theism in this respect.[39]

This approach is also found in the writings of Richard Dawkins, who argues that the best degree of empirical fit with observation is obtained, in the first place, through a Darwinian account of the evolution of species, and in the second, by the rejection of any notion of God, or of any concept of purpose within the natural order. "The universe we observe has precisely the properties we should expect if there is, at bottom, no design, no purpose, no evil and no good, nothing but blind pitiless indifference."[40]

---

[37] C. S. Lewis, "Is Theology Poetry?," in *Essay Collection and Other Short Pieces*, pp. 10–21, London: HarperCollins, 2000; quote at p. 21.

[38] For possible criteria for the "best explanation," see Peter Lipton, *Inference to the Best Explanation*, 2nd edn, London: Routledge, 2004.

[39] John C. Polkinghorne, "Physics and Metaphysics in a Trinitarian Perspective," *Theology and Science* 1 (2003): 33–49. The points are developed in greater detail in his *Science and the Trinity: The Christian Encounter with Reality*, New Haven, CT: Yale University Press, 2004. For more detailed reflections on the congruence of the Christian worldview with the phenomenon of "fine tuning," see Robin Collins, "A Scientific Argument for the Existence of God: The Fine-Tuning Design Argument," in Michael J. Murray (ed.), *Reason for the Hope Within*, pp. 47–75, Grand Rapids, MI: Eerdmans, 1999.

[40] Richard Dawkins, *River out of Eden: A Darwinian View of Life*, London: Phoenix, 1995, p. 133.

This is not about "proof," understood as a logically watertight demonstration, or the unambivalent closure of a scientific debate on the basis of an unassailable evidential basis.[41] Rather, it speaks of the "best explanation," as defined in terms of the convergence of theory and observation. Nature, as we have emphasized, is open to multiple interpretations. While each of those interpretations is underdetermined by the evidence,[42] it offers its own individual way of accounting for nature, which resonates to a greater or lesser extent with nature as experienced. The relevance of this to a reformulated natural theology will be clear. Where an earlier generation might have thought it could "prove" the existence of God by reflection on nature, this approach to natural theology holds that nature reinforces an existing belief in God through the resonance between observation and theory.

Yet natural theology does more than attempt to make intellectual sense of our experience of nature, as if it were limited to the enhancement of a rationalist account of reality. It enables a deepened appreciation of nature at the imaginative and aesthetic level, and also raises questions about how the "good life" can be undertaken within its bounds – matters to which we may now turn.

Beyond Sense-Making: The Good, the True, and the Beautiful

One of the weaknesses of approaches to natural theology to emerge from the Enlightenment is that they saw their task almost exclusively in terms of an enterprise of sense-making, having been obliged to operate within a rationalist straightjacket as a result of the intellectual agendas of the movement. There have, of course, been important challenges to this kind

---

[41] Both these ideas are, of course, highly problematic – consider, for example, Wittgenstein's insistence that true logical propositions are little more than tautologies, or Pierre Duhem's rebuttal of the notion of a "crucial experiment." See Yuri Balashov, "Duhem, Quine, and the Multiplicity of Scientific Tests," *Philosophy of Science* 61 (1994): 608–28; Leo K. C. Cheung, "Showing, Analysis and the Truth-Functionality of Logical Necessity in Wittgenstein's *Tractatus*," *Synthese* 139 (2004): 81–105.

[42] For the issue, see Larry Laudan and Jarrett Leplin, "Empirical Equivalence and Underdetermination," *Journal of Philosophy* 88 (1991): 449–72.

of aesthetic and imaginative deficit, most notably from within the Romantic movement, with its emphasis on the importance of feeling and imagination in any engagement with nature.[43] More recently, the waning of modernity has provided a congenial context for the liberation of natural theology, so that its deep intrinsic appeal to the human imagination may be realized. Natural theology is to be understood to include the totality of the human engagement with the natural world, embracing the human quest for truth, beauty, and goodness.

We invoke the so-called "Platonic triad" of truth, beauty, and goodness as a heuristic framework for natural theology. When properly understood, a renewed natural theology represents a distinctively Christian way of beholding, envisaging, and above all *appreciating* the natural order, capable of sustaining a broader engagement with the fundamental themes of human culture in general. While never losing sight of its moorings within the Christian theological tradition, natural theology can both inform and transform the human search for the transcendent, and provide a framework for understanding and advancing the age-old human quest for the good, the true, and the beautiful.

There is no doubt that, in the past, Christian theology was deeply involved in reflection on the good, the true, and the beautiful. By offering a richly textured account of the world, theology was able to inform and enrich the cultural context of earlier ages through the perception of the capacity of truth to illuminate both goodness and beauty.[44] Those connections – evident in the classic medieval notion of "a feeling for intelligible beauty" – have become strained, occasionally to the point of near-rupture, partly through the rise of the Enlightenment, though more particularly through certain trends within Protestantism that were unsympathetic to such broader cultural concerns. The approach to natural theology that we propose encourages the process of reconnection, offering new possibilities to theology within today's cultural dialogues.

An additional contemporary factor which acts as a stimulus for renewing and reconceptualizing natural theology must be noted. In the last few decades, the dialogue between the natural sciences and Christian theology

---

[43] Richard Eldridge, "Kant, Hölderlin, and the Experience of Longing," in *The Persistence of Romanticism: Essays in Philosophy and Literature*, pp. 31–51, Cambridge, UK: Cambridge University Press, 2001.

[44] See, for example, the important study of Umberto Eco, *Art and Beauty in the Middle Ages*, New Haven, CT: Yale University Press, 1986.

has accelerated, marking the end of the widespread, yet historically implausible, notion of the permanent warfare of science and theology.[45] This increasingly sophisticated and confident dialogue has given a new importance to natural theology as a potential conceptual meeting place for Christian theology and the natural sciences. Where some see boundaries as barriers, we see them as places of dialogue and exploration. Might the renewal of a Christian natural theology establish reliable and productive intellectual foundations for an enriched and deepened engagement between the natural sciences and Christian faith? If the approach presented in this book has merit, this would certainly seem to be the case.

Furthermore, the approach advocated in this book affirms that the empirical is a legitimate means of discovering and encountering the divine. The quest for truth through reflection on nature is to be recognized as an appropriate pathway towards encountering God. Though important questions remain about how it is to be interpreted, the approach to natural theology that we set out in this work affirms both the importance and the validity of an empirical engagement with nature.

Natural theology is thus too important a notion to be left to theologians, of whatever description. The debate over whether there is indeed a navigable channel between the natural and the transcendent, however these may be defined, capable of bearing traffic in both directions, reaches far beyond the boundaries of any single discipline. It is a matter that must involve theologians, philosophers, mathematicians, physicists, biologists, psychologists, artists, and the literary community. This volume cannot hope to provide an Arthurian round table for such a definitive discussion to take place; it can, at least, begin to map out its possible directions, and stimulate its development.

---

[45]   On which see Frank Miller Turner, "The Victorian Conflict between Science and Religion: A Professional Dimension," *Isis* 69 (1978): 356–76; David C. Lindberg and Ronald L. Numbers, "Beyond War and Peace: A Reappraisal of the Encounter between Christianity and Science," *Church History* 55 (1984): 338–54; Colin A. Russell, "The Conflict Metaphor and its Social Origins," *Science and Christian Faith* 1 (1989): 3–26.

PART I

The Human Quest for the Transcendent: The Context of Natural Theology

CHAPTER 2

The Persistence of the Transcendent

In spite of everything, we keep on talking about God. Even in seemingly godless ages, God lingers as a tantalizing presence, incapable of eradication by the most vicious of ideologies or technological mechanisms. As Leszek Kolakowski, the distinguished Polish philosopher and historian of Marxism, once commented, "God's unforgettableness means that He is present even in rejection."[1]

Kolakowski's point is well taken. Despite a formidable array of attempts to reduce, deconstruct, recategorize, or simply evade the notion of the transcendent,[2] it remains central to cultural and philosophical

---

[1] Leszek Kolakowski, "Concern about God in an Apparently Godless Age," in *My Correct Views on Everything*, ed. Zbigniew Janowski, pp. 173–83, South Bend, IN: St. Augustine's Press, 2005; quote at p. 183.

[2] See the important discussion of Paul D. Janz, *God, the Mind's Desire: Reference, Reason and Christian Thinking*, Cambridge, UK: Cambridge University Press, 2004, which analyzes a wide range of such criticisms. Janz's comments on Derrida are significant here:

> Derrida's approach is thus by far the most carefully consistent, sophisticated and intricate of all post-subject outlooks. Yet even he cannot in the end resist inserting a 'feel of meaning' – that is, the feel of aboutness, or of intentional reference (and as such a feel of purpose, obligation, responsibility) – into his post-structuralist enterprise in order to keep its purity from degenerating into mere bleakness.

reflection.[3] Indeed, the history of ideas suggests that the assertion of the hegemony of materialist approaches to reality invariably creates a backlash, generating a new interest in the domain of the transcendent.[4] The quest for the transcendent is so deeply embedded in the history of human thought that it needs more to be illustrated, rather than defended.[5]

Recent work in the cognitive science of religion has suggested that transcendent ideas or religious beliefs are "minimally counterintuitive concepts," which resonate with and are supported by "completely normal mental tools working in common natural and social contexts."[6] If this is so, it follows that religion and an interest in the transcendent will remain an integral part of human culture, in that they represent a "natural" outcome of human cognitive processes – in contrast with science, a correspondingly "unnatural" outcome, which requires constant defense and maintenance if it is to survive. This insight was anticipated by Nietzsche,

---

[3]　See the points made by Max Horkheimer in his interview with Helmut Gumnior: Max Horkheimer, *Die Sehnsucht nach dem ganz Anderen. Ein Interview mit Kommentar von Helmut Gumnior*, Hamburg: Furche-Verlag, 1971.

[4]　As noted and illustrated by J. W. Burrow, *The Crisis of Reason: European Thought, 1848–1914*, New Haven, CT: Yale University Press, 2000, pp. 56–67.

[5]　See Eugene Thomas Long's Presidential Address to the Metaphysical Society of America (1998), published as "Quest for Transcendence," *Review of Metaphysics* 52 (1998): 3–19. Illustrations of its persistence are easily provided – witness the appeal of the notion within children's literature: David Sandner, *The Fantastic Sublime: Romanticism and Transcendence in Nineteenth-Century Children's Fantasy Literature*, Westport, CT: Greenwood Press, 1996 (note especially the discussion of George MacDonald's *At the Back of the North Wind*, pp. 83–100).

[6]　Justin L. Barrett, *Why Would Anyone Believe in God?* Lanham, MD: AltaMira Press, 2004, pp. 21–30. Related arguments concerning the cognitive "naturalness" of transcendent beliefs are set out in Pascal Boyer, *The Naturalness of Religious Ideas: A Cognitive Theory of Religion*, Berkeley, CA: University of California Press, 1994. A further development of this approach is to be found in Robert N. McCauley, "The Naturalness of Religion and the Unnaturalness of Science," in F. Keil and R. Wilson (eds), *Explanation and Cognition*, pp. 61–85, Cambridge, MA: MIT Press, 2000. McCauley argues that, while religious belief is "natural," the natural sciences are sufficiently counterintuitive to be "unnatural." McCauley's analysis suggests that there is a significant parallel between systematic theology and science in respect of their "naturalness": natural *religion* may indeed be minimally counterintuitive; natural *theology*, in contrast, makes counterintuitive demands.

---

who pointed out that the metaphysical pressure to discover "God" never departs, but lingers within human culture and experience:

> How strong the metaphysical need is, and how hard nature makes it to bid it a final farewell can be seen from the fact that even when the free spirit has divested himself of everything metaphysical, the highest effects of art can easily set the metaphysical strings, which have long been silent or indeed snapped apart, vibrating in sympathy . . . He feels a profound stab in the heart and sighs for the man who will lead him back to his lost love, whether she be called religion or metaphysics.[7]

So what is "transcendence"? How may it be defined, or at least described? The term is used in at least three senses in recent literature.

1   *The idea of self-transcendence.* The term can be used to refer to mastering natural limitations through the use of technology or mental and physical strategies. For example, Thomas Nagel argues that transcendence designates an act of empathetic imagination which enables us to stand in another's position, and see things from an alternative standpoint.[8] If an objective view is to be achieved, Nagel suggests, human observers must be able to purge themselves of their idiosyncratic perceptions, often determined by their individual viewpoints, and rise above themselves to grasp a greater vision of reality. It is clear that transcendence here bears a somewhat reduced meaning, along the lines of: a capacity to transcend my personal viewpoints, thus allowing me to see things from a broader perspective.

2   *A realm beyond ordinary experience.* In its traditional sense, the word "transcendence" has ontological significance, referring to something that is held to exist beyond the realm of the mundane, yet which may be

---

[7]   Friedrich Wilhelm Nietzsche, *Human, All Too Human: A Book for Free Spirits*, Cambridge, UK: Cambridge University Press, 1986, p. 153. For this "metaphysical need," see Tyler T. Roberts, *Contesting Spirit: Nietzsche, Affirmation, Religion*, Princeton, NJ: Princeton University Press, 1998, pp. 49–53. Nietzsche's rejection of such a need may well reflect what Poellner terms the "heroic posture" of many Enlightenment and post-Enlightenment atheists: Peter Poellner, *Nietzsche and Metaphysics*, Oxford: Oxford University Press, 2000, p. 9: Nietzsche "cultivates the heroic posture of 'standing alone' "; cf. p. 181.

[8]   Thomas Nagel, *The View from Nowhere*, New York: Oxford University Press, 1986, 3, 11. The point is made, perhaps a little too playfully, in Thomas Nagel, "What is it Like to be a Bat?" *Philosophical Review* 83 (1974): 435–50.

encountered or experienced, even if only to a limited extent, within the ordinary world. This way of thinking about transcendence postulates a frontier beyond which human knowledge cannot penetrate, so that there is always a "beyond" that remains elusive. The noted physicist André Mercier (1913–99) expressed this basic idea as follows:

> Somehow reality always manages to resist man's final grasping. This resistance leads us to believe that reality in one sense always remains beyond the point of contact between itself and man. There seems to be a permanent "something" in reality which lies outside man's finite domination. Of this "something," we have only an idea.[9]

3 *Experiences which are interpreted to relate to a transcendent reality.* This third sense of the term is used psychologically to refer to experiences which are interpreted in transcendent terms. It is often used to describe a tantalizingly transient sensation that the individual has somehow entered the extraordinary – that the mundane has given way to something beyond it. William Wordsworth tried to capture this idea in the phrase "spots of time" – rare yet precious moments of profound feeling and imaginative strength, in which individuals grasp something of ultimate significance within their inner being.[10] It proves virtually impossible to express this experiential aspect of the transcendent in everyday language. Hans-Georg Gadamer suggested that transcendence is about "a kind of experience, for which a mere playing around with ideas cannot be substituted." It is, he suggested, something irreducible that is experienced as a "presence" (*Gegenwärtigkeit*) that does not permit a heightened precision of definition.[11]

Although this book engages with all three senses of "transcendence" as set out above, our particular concern in this book is with this third understanding of the idea. We shall argue throughout Part I that transcendence continues to be a meaningful concept in contemporary culture.

---

[9] André Mercier, *Thought and Being: An Inquiry into the Nature of Knowledge*, Basle: Verlag für Recht und Gesellschaft, 1959, p. 96.

[10] See the analysis in Thomas Weiskel, *The Romantic Sublime: Studies in the Structure and Psychology of Transcendence*, Baltimore, MD: Johns Hopkins University Press, 1986.

[11] Hans-Georg Gadamer and Jean Grondin, "Looking Back with Gadamer Over his Writings and Their Effective History," *Theory, Culture and Society* 23 (2006): 85–100.

It is a notion that is found in religious and secular literature alike, reflecting what seems to be a common human preoccupation.[12] Even though Western culture is often asserted to be "secular," there is widespread evidence of continuing interest in transcendent experiences, in which people form the impression that there is "something there"; that they were in contact with – to use Rudolf Otto's luminous phrase – "the wholly other"; with something boundless, limitless, and profoundly different, which was resistant to precise definition; which was not necessarily associated with any religious institutions or authorities; which they could not fully grasp, and which utterly surpassed the human capacity for verbal expression.[13]

However these experiences are to be interpreted, there is ample substantiation of their occurrence and perceived importance in contemporary culture. These experiences are not religious by definition; yet they have the potential to function as symbols, signposts, or pathways to recognizably religious commitments.[14] While not constituting proof in themselves of an ontologically distinct realm of "the transcendent," they nevertheless contribute significantly to the persistence of the notion of the transcendent, even in metaphysically impoverished times. The stability of the concept of the "transcendent" is thus partly due to its grounding in human experiences that appear to reinforce it.[15]

---

[12] See the illuminating studies of William A. Johnson, *The Search for Transcendence: A Theological Analysis of Nontheological Attempts to Define Transcendence*, New York: Harper & Row, 1974; Jerome A. Stone, *The Minimalist Vision of Transcendence: A Naturalist Philosophy of Religion*, Albany, NY: State University of New York Press, 1993; William C. Placher, *The Domestication of Transcendence: How Modern Thinking About God Went Wrong*, Louisville, KY: Westminster John Knox Press, 1996.

[13] For some recent studies, see Louis Roy, *Transcendent Experiences: Phenomenology and Critique*, University of Toronto Press, 2001 (and also his subsequent comments in "A Clarifying Note on *Transcendent Experiences*," *Toronto Journal of Theology* 20 (2004): 51–6); David Hay, *Something There: The Biology of the Human Spirit*, London: Darton, Longman and Todd, 2006.

[14] See Louis Dupré, *Religious Mystery and Rational Reflection*, Grand Rapids, MI: Eerdmans, 1998; John Haldane, "Philosophy, the Restless Heart, and the Meaning of Theism," *Ratio* 19 (2006): 421–40.

[15] See also Alister C. Hardy, *The Spiritual Nature of Man: A Study of Contemporary Religious Experience*, Oxford: Clarendon Press, 1980.

Natural Theology and the Transcendent

A Christian natural theology is the theological counterpart to the general cultural quest for the transcendent, offering both an explanation and conceptual positioning of the enterprise, while at the same time proposing an interpretative framework by which the human longing for the transcendent can, in the first place, be explained, and in the second, fulfilled. As we shall argue, such a natural theology resonates with this widespread perception that there is "something there," offering an explanation of both its origins and its transcendent significance.

It is widely thought that an intellectual framework similar to this underlies the celebrated "Areopagus address" of Paul to the Athenians (Acts 17: 22–31), generally regarded as one of the most significant encounters between the gospel and classical Greek culture described in early Christian literature.[16] Paul's argument, as recounted by Luke, is that a natural sense of divinity or transcendence that was known to the Greeks was fulfilled in the gospel of Jesus Christ. The Christian revelation both validates this human quest for the transcendent, while insisting its ultimate fulfillment can only take place through grace. That for which human nature yearns is intimated through nature, but not completely satisfied by it. For Thomas Aquinas, this was to be interpreted as the longing of the created soul for its creator and ultimate goal: "Every intellect naturally desires the divine substance."[17]

We suggest throughout this work that a Christian natural theology can be seen as a *specific instance* of a more general cultural phenomenon; at another level, however, it can be argued to provide the *conceptual foundation* of the more general phenomenon, creating conceptual space for it, and offering an explanation of its existence and form. Yet this is to run ahead of the argument. While it is entirely appropriate at this early

---

[16] See the analysis in Bertil Gärtner, *The Areopagus Speech and Natural Revelation*, Uppsala: Gleerup, 1955.

[17] Thomas Aquinas, *Summa contra Gentiles*, III, 57. The most famous exposition of this theme remains Henri de Lubac, *Surnaturel: études historiques*, Paris: Aubier, 1946. For an excellent commentary on this general principle, see Jean Borella, *Le sens du surnaturel*, Geneva: Editions ad Solem, 1996. Scholarly assertions of the "inevitability of religion" often reflect such considerations: see, for example, John Herman Randall, Jr., *The Meaning of Religion for Man*, New York: Harper Torchbooks, 1968, pp. 27–8.

stage to note that there is a clear connection between a properly defined Christian natural theology and the more general cultural interest in transcendent experiences, we must consider the concept of the "transcendent" in more detail before returning to this important issue. We shall consider three broad types of experiences often noted in such discussions – numinous, mystical, and epiphanic.[18]

Numinous experiences

Isidor Thorner argued that people who claim to have "religious" experiences believe three things:[19]

1 That their experience is extraordinary, quite distinct from everyday, normal experience.
2 That this experience is much more significant than such everyday experiences.
3 That these experiences refer or relate to something that cannot be located in the everyday empirical world.

We have already noted Rudolph Otto's concept of the "wholly other." For Otto, religious experience is an awareness of a *mysterium tremendum et fascinans*, which believers understand as a response to the transcendent. This transcendent object can thus be seen as the "foundational reality" of a faith tradition.[20]

Otto's concept of the "numinous" holds that such experiences are understood to be an awareness of a "wholly other" that is not itself located within the natural world, with which believers feel themselves to be in communion.[21] In contrast, mystical experiences – to which we

---

[18] For the problems encountered in defining and characterizing such experiences, see Bernard Spilka, Ralph W. Hood, Bruce Hunsberger, and Richard Gorsuch, *The Psychology of Religion: An Empirical Approach*, 3rd edn., New York: The Guilford Press, 2003, pp. 246–89.

[19] Isidor Thorner, "Prophetic and Mystic Experience: Comparison and Consequences," *Journal for the Scientific Study of Religion* 5 (1965): 82–96.

[20] Ralph W. Hood, "The Facilitation of Religious Experience," in R. W. Hood (ed.), *Handbook of Religious Experience*, pp. 569–97. Birmingham, AL: Religious Education Press, 1995.

[21] For a criticism of Otto's position, see Owen Ware, "Rudolf Otto's Ideal of the Holy: A Reappraisal," *Heythrop Journal* 48 (2007): 48–60.

now turn – do not relate to any one such perceptual object or "foundational reality"; instead, all objects are unified into a perception of unity or totality.[22]

Mystical experiences

In his landmark study *The Varieties of Religious Experience* (1902), William James drew extensively on a wide range of published works and personal testimonies, engaging with religious experience on its own terms, and taking accounts of such experiences at face value.[23] James argues that mystical experiences possess four leading characteristics:[24]

Ineffability: The experience "defies expression"; it cannot be described adequately in words. "Its quality must be directly experienced; it cannot be imparted or transferred to others."[25]

Noetic quality: Such an experience is seen to possess authority, giving insight and knowledge into deep truths, which are sustained over time. These "states of insight into depths of truth unplumbed by the discursive intellect" are understood to be "illuminations, revelations, full of significance and importance, all inarticulate though they remain."

Transiency: "Mystical states cannot be sustained for long." Usually they last from a few seconds to minutes and their quality cannot be accurately remembered, though the experience is recognized if it recurs. "When faded, their quality can but imperfectly be reproduced in memory."

Passivity: "Although the oncoming of mystical states may be facilitated by preliminary voluntary operations," once they have begun, the mystic feels out of control as if he or she "were grasped and held by a superior power."

---

[22] For a discussion of recent empirical study of mysticism, see Spilka et al., *The Psychology of Religion*, pp. 299–312.

[23] William James, *The Varieties of Religious Experience*, London: Longmans, Green & Co., 1902. For some helpful reflections on James's approach, see Nicholas Lash, *Easter in Ordinary: Reflections on Human Experience and the Knowledge of God*, Charlottesville, VA: University Press of Virginia, 1988, pp. 38–50.

[24] James, *The Varieties of Religious Experience*, pp. 380–1.

[25] This point is also emphasized by Rudolf Otto, who notes that such experiences are "inexpressible" or "ineffable": Rudolf Otto, *The Idea of the Holy*, London: Oxford University Press, 1977, p. 5.

While James notes that the second two characteristics are "less marked" than the others, he considers them to be integral to any phenomenology of religious experience.[26]

Epiphanic experiences

In his reflections on the human longing to transcend the mundane, the Oxford philosopher Stuart Hampshire pointed out that humanity was not totally in control of whatever it was that brought about such moments in which the world is seen in a completely new way. Such moments were, he argued, "epiphanic," lasting only a moment, yet disclosing something that seemed to possess immense significance.

> In the peculiar workings of their individual imaginations during these activities, men and women may arrive at a sense of transcendence, a kind of epiphany, in which they seem to themselves to have escaped for a time from the usual limits of possible experience, and to have alighted on a privileged moment that takes them outside their ordinary and confined routines.[27]

Hampshire's lucid description of such experiences emphasizes how they transfigure the natural world.[28] They are moments of detachment from time, of apparent atemporality, which seem charged with significance for human existence.

It is important to pause at this point, and notice the full implications of what Hampshire is saying. He is speaking of an immediate insight, prior to a subsequent intellectual process of analysis and reflection kicking into action. This "privileged moment" brings about a fleeting escape "from the usual limits of possible experience." As William James observed, these "privileged moments" carry an "enormous sense of inner authority and illumination," transfiguring the understanding of those who experience them, often evoking a deep sense "of being revelations of new depths of

---

[26] For some critical perspectives on James's account, see Spilka et al., *The Psychology of Religion*, pp. 247–8.

[27] Stuart Hampshire, *Innocence and Experience*, Cambridge, MA: Harvard University Press, 1989, pp. 131–2.

[28] See the important discussion of this notion in Arthur C. Danto, *The Transfiguration of the Commonplace: A Philosophy of Art*, Cambridge, MA: Harvard University Press, 1981, pp. 1–32. The allusions to the transfiguration of Christ (p. vii) may be noted here.

truth."[29] This is quite distinct from cognitive reflection on nature which is often protracted, involving extended reflection on what is permanently present to our senses. Any comprehensive attempt to engage with nature must take account of both these modes of engagement.[30]

In a recent study, James Pawelski examined various types of "epiphanic" experiences,[31] noting how they could take a variety of forms – such as religious (the transfiguration of Christ), philosophical (William James's reading of essays by the French philosopher Charles Renouvier), romantic (Romeo and Juliet's "love at first sight"), or aesthetic (Wordsworth's moment of aesthetic epiphany in his poem "Composed Upon Westminster Bridge, Sept. 3, 1802"). They carry with them a "sense of clarification, which seems to allow us to understand things in their true nature." Such epiphanies are like "bolts of lightning on a dark night that brilliantly illuminate everything in a single, instantaneous flash." He cites as an example of such a philosophical epiphany the process described by Plato in his *Symposium*, where one begins with the love of the beauty of a single body and moves to beauties of ever greater abstraction until "all of a sudden" one catches sight of the form of Beauty itself, leading to the birth of true virtue.

Pawelski notes that epiphanies often happen when they are least expected, and seem to be unconnected to the mundane reality that precedes them. (He stresses that "mundane" is to be interpreted neutrally, simply

---

[29] William James, *The Varieties of Religious Experience*, pp. 379–429.

[30] For an excellent exploration of Kant's concerns about transcendence as "posited fundamentally as an orientating or regulative device for the understanding," see Janz, *God, the Mind's Desire*. Janz's response to Kant's concerns deserves careful study, particularly his use of a "theology of the cross" as a foil to Kant's argument of the fundamental contamination of the category of the transcendent by human constructs and concepts, which conceal as much as reveal the glory of God. A somewhat less convincing engagement with the notion of transcendence from a critical realist perspective is to be found in Margaret Archer, Andrew Collier, and Douglas V. Porpora, *Transcendence: Critical Realism and God*, London: Routledge, 2004. It seems that the critical realist movement still has some way to go before it has quite mastered how to handle such theological notions within its framework. The markedly ambivalent response within the movement to Roy Bhaskar's notion of "meta-reality" is highly significant at this point (see pp. 50–3).

[31] James O. Pawelski, "Perception, Cognition, and Volition: The Radical and Integrated Individualism of William James," PhD Thesis, Pennsylvania State University, 1997.

as "everyday and ordinary," without any pejorative connotation which might imply it was "boring and sterile.") As with James's mystical experiences, epiphanies are also marked by a sense of atemporality and transiency. During such experiences, the subject usually has little sense of the passage of time, and after the epiphany is over, has difficulty judging how long it actually lasted. Epiphanies are momentary and transient, often leaving a sense "of loss and even of betrayal." These "momentary parts of the experiential flux" leave the subjects hoping that they are sustainable, only to discover that they are not.

The Triggers of Transcendent Experiences

So what triggers these sorts of experiences? A range of objects and events have been identified, including religious worship, contact with nature, and patterns of darkness and light. Wordsworth's poetry frequently alludes to epiphanies being triggered by aspects of nature, such as mountains. Proust's À la recherche du temps perdu frequently alludes to moments of encounter with the transcendent, triggered by mundane events and objects – not possessing significance in themselves, but nevertheless proving capable of stimulating rapturous experiences.[32] C. S. Lewis recalls experiencing a devastating sensation of desire in response to a seemingly insignificant occurrence – his brother bringing a biscuit tin containing plants into his childhood nursery.[33]

The relationship of the "transcendent" and "mundane" experiences has been the subject of much discussion, not least in relation to the reversion to the mundane after such a moment of apparent revelation. Rudolf Otto noted how such a "thrillingly vibrant and resonant" experience often faded away rapidly, leaving the soul to resume its "'profane', non-religious mood of everyday experience."[34] Or, to continue with C. S. Lewis's account of a childhood epiphanic experience of desire, "before I knew what I desired, the desire itself was gone, the whole glimpse withdrawn, the

---

[32] Bo Earle, "Involuntary Narration, Narrating Involition: Proust on Death, Repetition and Self-Becoming," *MLN* 117 (2002): 943–70. On the same phenomenon in Baudelaire, see Bo Earle, "'Tarrying with the Negative': Baudelaire, Mallarmé, and the Rhythm of Modernity," *MLN* 118 (2003): 1015–42.

[33] C. S. Lewis, *Surprised by Joy*, London: Collins, 1959, pp. 19–20.

[34] Otto, *Idea of the Holy*, p. 13.

world turned commonplace again, or only stirred by a longing for the longing that had just ceased."[35]

Many poets of the eighteenth and early nineteenth centuries gave thought to the implications of such moments of devastating insight, triggered off by an encounter with the natural order.[36] Wordsworth's attempts in *The Prelude* to articulate his "dim and undetermined sense" of "unknown modes of being" gave a conceptual framework to others seeking to articulate similar experiences, yet lacking the vocabulary to express them. Such moments seemed charged with significance, laden with insight about heaven and earth, God and humanity.[37] The sudden onset of a transformed view of reality, however fleeting, is a common theme in literature.[38] In recent years psychologists have begun to show a renewed interest in the phenomenon,[39]

---

[35] Lewis, *Surprised by Joy*, p. 20.

[36] See the extensive analysis in Shaun Irlam, *Elations: The Poetics of Enthusiasm in Eighteenth-Century Britain*, Stanford, CA: Stanford University Press, 1999, especially pp. 171–200; Ann Taves, *Fits, Trances, and Visions: Experiencing Religion and Explaining Experience from Wesley to James*, Princeton, NJ: Princeton University Press, 1999, especially pp. 261–307.

[37] For the basic questions, see the classic study of Earl Wassermann, "Nature Moralized: The Divine Analogy in the Eighteenth Century," *English Literary History* 20 (1953): 39–76.

[38] See especially the study of Martin Bidney, *Patterns of Epiphany: From Wordsworth to Tolstoy, Pater, and Barrett Browning*, Carbondale, IL: Southern Illinois University Press, 1997. More recently, the works of James Joyce illustrate this interest particularly well: Thomas Loe, "'The Dead' as Novella," *James Joyce Quarterly* 28 (1991): 485–97; Sandra Manoogian Pearce, "Edna O'Brien's 'Lantern Slides' and Joyce's 'The Dead': Shadows of a Bygone Era," *Studies in Short Fiction* 32 (1995): 437–50. Other twentieth-century examples are discussed in Morris Beja, *Epiphany in the Modern Novel*, London: Owen, 1971.

[39] This has been explored with reference to William James's notion of "religious experience," particularly by Pawelski and others. James tends to associate such "epiphanic experiences" primarily with religion; others, such as Mihaly Csikszentmihalyi, see it as having wider relevance. Csikszentmihalyi studied artists and others who were "creating meaning," many of which described an "ecstatic state" during the creative process – a feeling of being outside of what they were creating. See Mihaly Csikszentmihalyi, *Creativity: Flow and the Psychology of Discovery and Invention*, New York: Harper Collins, 1996. For comment, see William J. Gavin and James O. Pawelski, "James's 'Pure Experience' and Csikszentmihalyi's 'Flow': Existential Event or Methodological Postulate?" *Streams of William James* 6/2 (2004): 11–16.

not least because of a recognition that such experiences "allow individuals to forge connections to the larger universe and thereby provide meaning to their lives."[40]

These reflections raise some important and difficult questions. How, for example, do such transcendent experiences relate to the natural context within which they take place? They clearly cannot be dissociated from it; but how are they interconnected? Furthermore, the notion of epiphany does not necessarily imply that of theophany.[41] So how can epiphany, mystical experience, and a sense of the numinous be related, if at all, to a disclosure of the *divine*?[42] And in what way, if any, might they be stabilized, so that the transcendent might be known more fully? To run ahead of our discussion for a moment, it will be clear that these questions lead into the traditional Christian theological exploration of the relation of natural theology and the doctrine of the incarnation.

Such human experiences of transcendence are of fundamental importance to the phenomenon of religion, and are often regarded as essential to of any explanation of its universality.[43] In what follows, we shall explore this point in some detail, responding particularly to modernist attempts to eliminate any such transcendent referent from an understanding of religion, or to criticize religion as outmoded, precisely on account of such a referent.

---

[40] Christopher Peterson and Martin E. P. Seligman, *Character Strengths and Virtues: A Handbook and Classification*, Oxford: Oxford University Press, 2004, pp. 517–622. Note their comment: "the prototype of this strength category is spirituality, variously defined, but always referring to a belief in and commitment to the transcendent (nonmaterial) aspects of life."

[41] Bidney, *Patterns of Epiphany*, pp. 16–18.

[42] For the issue in the nineteenth century, see Ashton Nichols, *The Poetics of Epiphany: Nineteenth-Century Origins of the Modern Literary Moment*, Tuscaloosa, AL: University of Alabama Press, 1988, pp. 1–5.

[43] It should be stressed that this does not imply that every religion necessarily affirms a transcendent ground of its beliefs, or articulates its characteristic beliefs using this category. Most, of course, do – but not all. In part, this difficulty arises from the Western use of the term "religion" as a universal category, when it is best seen as a "fuzzy" category, with no clear center or well-defined perimeter. See, for example, Eleanor Rosch, "Principles of Categorization," in Eleanor Rosch and Barbara B. Lloyd (eds), *Cognition and Categorization*, pp. 27–48. Hillsdale, NJ: Lawrence Erlbaum, 1978.

The Transcendent and Religion

Religion is widely held to be associated with an experience of the transcendent.[44] This point can easily be obscured through a failure to consider the experiential dimensions of religion, often through the dominance of sociological models of religion which focus on its institutional aspects – such as beliefs and rituals. This has led, as David Wulff notes, to religion "becoming reified into a fixed system of ideas or ideological commitments."[45] Any account or description of religion would also have to include reference to religious experience, as well as to specific doctrines and practices, group affiliation, attitudes, and ethical actions.[46] Although the concept and potential objects of "religious experience" remain elusive to precise definition,[47] it is traditionally interpreted as an "experience of the transcendent."[48]

While significant problems of definition attend any attempt to generalize about religion,[49] it is now widely agreed that religion concerns and

---

[44] See, for example, John Hick, *An Interpretation of Religion: Human Responses to the Transcendent*, 2nd edn, Basingstoke: Palgrave Macmillan, 2004.

[45] David M. Wulff, *Psychology of Religion: Classic and Contemporary*, New York: Wiley, 1997, p. 46. See also the important comments in Peter C. Hill, "Giving Religion Away: What the Study of Religion Offers Psychology," *International Journal for the Psychology of Religion* 9 (1999): 229–49.

[46] See for instance the influential analysis in Rodney Stark and Charles Y. Glock, *American Piety: The Nature of Religious Commitment*, Berkeley, CA: University of California Press, 1968.

[47] Peter Antes, "What Do We Experience if We Have Religious Experience?" *Numen* 49 (2002): 336–42; Lieven Boeve and Laurence Paul Hemming, *Divinising Experience: Essays in the History of Religious Experience from Origen to Ricoeur*, Leuven: Peeters, 2004.

[48] See the extensive analysis in Lieven Boeve, Hans Geybels, and Stijn van den Bossche (eds), *Encountering Transcendence: Contributions to a Theology of Christian Religious Experience*, Leuven: Peeters, 2005.

[49] See Peter B. Clarke and Peter Byrne, *Religion Defined and Explained*, London: St Martin's Press, 1993, pp. 3–27. Such definitions, they note, "depend upon the particular purposes and prejudices of individual scholars." See also Philip E. Devine, "On the Definition of 'Religion'," *Faith and Philosophy* 3 (1986): 270–84; Peter A. Byrne, *Natural Religion and the Nature of Religion: The Legacy of Deism*, London: Routledge, 1989; Peter Harrison, *"Religion" and the Religions in the English Enlightenment*, Cambridge, UK: Cambridge University Press, 1990; John Redwood, *Reason, Ridicule*

engages the realm of the transcendent.[50] This recent judgment calls into question some influential, allegedly "objective" or "scientific," definitions of religion which emerged in the nineteenth century and the first half of the twentieth century. These were generally strongly reductionist or eliminative, aiming to collapse "the other" into "the same," typically arguing for the elimination of transcendent referents and an understanding of religion as elicited and shaped by social or psychological determinants.[51] Thus Emile Durkheim argued that religious belief arises from social experience and the public rituals that shape a community, and bind it together. Any notion of the transcendent is to be excluded from the scientific study of religion.[52] Such reductionist foreclosures have been subjected to severe criticism by scholars such as Mircea Eliade,[53] partly on account of their clear ideological prejudices, yet mainly on account of their manifest failure to deal with religion as an empirical phenomenon.

Yet these older accounts of religion, once lent intellectual and cultural plausibility by the modernist worldview, are now experiencing an erosion of plausibility directly related to the decline of modernism itself. The embargo imposed upon the "transcendent" has been lifted, not so much on account of a softening of this core prejudice of the Enlightenment, as on account of the general abandonment of this worldview as a whole. Although modernist writers tend to excoriate this renewed interest in the transcendent as a descent into irrationality, in reality it can be seen as a

and Religion: The Age of Enlightenment in England, 1660–1750, London: Thames and Hudson, 1996.

[50] See James E. Faulconer (ed.), Transcendence in Philosophy and Religion, Bloomington, IN: Indiana University Press, 2003.

[51] For discussion and analysis, see Samuel J. Preus, Explaining Religion: Criticism and Theory from Bodin to Freud, New Haven, CT: Yale University Press, 1987; Tomoko Masuzawa, In Search of Dreamtime: The Quest for the Origin of Religion, Chicago: University of Chicago Press, 1993; Daniel L. Pals, Seven Theories of Religion, New York: Oxford University Press, 1996; Andrew McKinnon, "Sociological Definitions, Language Games and the 'Essence' of Religion," Method and Theory in the Study of Religion 14 (2002): 61–83.

[52] Emile Durkheim, The Elementary Forms of Religious Life, New York: Free Press, 1995, pp. 420–1.

[53] Christian Wachtmann, Der Religionsbegriff bei Mircea Eliade, Frankfurt am Main/Berlin: Peter Lang, 1996.

correction of a previous overextension of reason's competency beyond its intended limits.[54]

This point has been stressed by Louis Dupré, in his careful and illuminating study *Passage to Modernity*, which remains a landmark in the scholarly analysis of the rise and fall of modernity.[55] In a later study, Dupré points out that "the principle of rationality that lies at the core of the Enlightenment project" represents a significant intensification of any prior notion of reason, or understanding of its limits.[56] Cultural aspirations outstripped epistemological resources. "The crisis of the Enlightenment" arose precisely because reason and its attendant concepts – such as "rationality" – were no longer construed on the Greek model of "an ordering principle inherent in reality" but as a human faculty that "submitted all reality to the structures of the mind." Having been elevated to such a position, it should not have been the cause for surprise that it proved incapable of delivering the rational and moral certainties that many had expected.

With the waning of modernity, the notion of the transcendent has returned to definitions of religion. In marked contrast to Durkheim's reductionist conception of religion, the term is now increasingly being accepted to designate "beliefs and practices with a transcendent referent," a trend which can be traced back to the mid-1980s.[57] Scholars of religion now prefer to speak of "aspects" or "dimensions" of religion, rather than offering inadequate and potentially unhelpful definitions of

---

[54] There is a huge literature. A useful point of entry is provided by Frederick C. Beiser, *The Fate of Reason: German Philosophy from Kant to Fichte*, Cambridge, MA: Harvard University Press, 1987, which documents some of the philosophical trends. Richard J. Bernstein, *Beyond Objectivism and Relativism: Science, Hermeneutics, and Praxis*, Philadelphia: University of Pennsylvania Press, 1991, notes the impact of the work of Thomas Kuhn and Paul Feyerabend on uncritical positivist readings of science (still encountered, of course, in the writings of Richard Dawkins).

[55] Louis K. Dupré, *Passage to Modernity: An Essay in the Hermeneutics of Nature and Culture*, New Haven, CT: Yale University Press, 1993.

[56] Louis K. Dupré, *The Enlightenment and the Intellectual Foundations of Modern Culture*, New Haven, CT: Yale University Press, 2004, pp. 12–17.

[57] Robert Towler, *The Need for Certainty: A Sociological Study of Conventional Religion*, London: Routledge & Kegan Paul, 1984, pp. 3–5.

religion. These are seen as a minimum list of the aspects which need to be considered in any attempt to gain a balanced view of any particular religion, or when offering a comparative perspective of the various religions.[58]

The decline of modernist antipathy to religion has made serious discussion of its place in human culture and intellectual life increasingly significant. A growing awareness of the importance of religion in relation to environmental issues – through, for example, the resacralization of nature – has created new interest in religious "readings" of nature.[59] The central point to be made is that religion seems to be a natural, inevitable aspect of human life and culture, despite modernist experiments in social engineering, aimed at its elimination in certain regions.[60] The ubiquity of religion from the earliest eras of the history of human civilization to the present is remarkable, pointing to, amongst other things, an enduring interest in the transcendent (in all its senses: see pp. 23–40), and its potential impact on human life and thought.[61] Not only has religion played a decisive role in creating human civilization; it is clear that it will continue to do so, despite the modernist attempt to unseat it.

The universality of religion, and especially the capacity of Christianity to establish "points of contact" with other religions, is of fundamental importance to any attempt to develop an authentically Christian natural

---

[58] See particularly Ninian Smart, *Choosing a Faith*, New York: Marion Boyars, 1995, pp. 16–21. See also his *Dimensions of the Sacred: An Anatomy of the World's Beliefs*, Berkeley, CA: University of California Press, 1996.

[59] See the survey article of Bron Taylor, "A Green Future for Religion?" *Futures* 36 (2004): 991–1008. A particularly good example of a work aiming to identify and develop such links is Rupert Sheldrake, *The Rebirth of Nature: The Greening of Science and God*, Rochester, VT: Park Street Press, 1994, pp. 182–203.

[60] For analysis and comment, see Alister E. McGrath, *The Twilight of Atheism: The Rise and Fall of Disbelief in the Modern World*, New York: Doubleday, 2004.

[61] There is a huge literature dealing with this issue, too vast to note here. Some representative works may be noted, including E. O. James, *The Ancient Gods: The History and Diffusion of Religion in the Ancient Near East and the Eastern Mediterranean*, London: Phoenix, 1999.

theology.[62] If the universality of religion reflects in part a corresponding transcultural, transhistorical human awareness of the transcendent, the empirical foundations are already in place for what is recognizably a natural theology. These foundations, it must be stressed, are empirical, based on observation, and are thus essentially *independent* of the Christian revelation. The Christian tradition, however, is capable of interpreting this transcendence in a specifically Christian manner. As we shall see later, this leads into a reformulated vision of the foundations and scope of a natural theology.

Yet we have only begun to explore the general human quest for the transcendent, which is not limited to human religious belief or activity. Even during the height of the modernist project, many continued to believe that an appeal to the transcendent was essential to human morality and self-fulfillment. In the chapter that follows, we shall analyze and explore the significance of this observation.

---

[62] A classic example, of considerable relevance to this discussion, is discussed in Xiaochao Wang, *Christianity and Imperial Culture: Chinese Christian Apologetics in the Seventeenth Century and Their Latin Patristic Equivalent*, Leiden: Brill, 1998. Similar comments apply to Paul's Areopagus address: Hans Conzelmann, "The Address of Paul on the Areopagus," in L. E. Keck and J. L. Martyn (eds), *Studies in Luke-Acts: Essays in Honor of Paul Schubert*, pp. 217–30. Nashville, TN: Abingdon Press, 1966.

CHAPTER 3

Thinking About the Transcendent: Three Recent Examples

In the previous chapter, we noted the continuing human awareness of the transcendent, and the persistent interest in exploring its potential implications.[1] Human beings seem to have a strong propensity to ask questions, to move beyond rather than merely ahead, seeking a vertical axis of transcendence as we press further along the horizontal axis of existence. Both the quest for the good life and the search for meaning seem to depend upon a recognition of a transcendent dimension to existence. Transcendent ideals, even if unrealizable, have the capacity to play a decisive role in human life,[2] especially in moral conduct, religious activism, and aesthetic appreciation.[3]

The idea of encountering the transcendent through nature played a highly significant role in earlier periods of thought, which persisted into

---

[1] Popular accounts of the domain of the transcendent sometimes conceived the notion in a naively realist way, evident in the eighth-century Annals of Ulster making reference to a "ship in the sky," anchored to the everyday world. Note the use of the image of the "anchor" in early Celtic works as a means of visualizing accessibility to various levels of reality: Miceal Ross, "Anchors in a Three-Decker World," *Folklore* 109 (1998): 63–76.

[2] As emphasized and illustrated by Dorothy Emmet, *The Role of the Unrealisable: A Study in Regulative Ideals*, New York: St. Martin's Press, 1994.

[3] Contemporary debates about the "sublime" had an important impact on William Blake's conception of art: see Steve Vine, "Blake's Material Sublime," *Studies in Romanticism* 41 (2002): 237–57.

the twentieth century despite the rise of a rationalist worldview which might have been expected to erode the notion.[4] An excellent example lies in the Romantic notion of the "sublime," understood as "a symbol of the mind's relation to a transcendent order," which articulates the capacity of a transcendent perspective to create habits of the mind adapted to the particularities and aspirations of the human situation.[5] For Johann Gottfried von Herder (1744–1803), the "sublime" represented an enlargement or expansion of the human spirit, linked with sensible objects, yet transcending them.[6] We see here the resituating of the category of "sublime" in the passions of the subject, rather than the qualities of the object, which was so characteristic of Romanticism.

"Transcendence" implies a reaching beyond natural limits, an awareness of something that lies beyond the boundaries of human experience. Such a theme pervades the writings of the Romantic poets, who

---

[4] For the eighteenth and nineteenth centuries, see the analysis in Conrad Cherry, *Nature and Religious Imagination: From Edwards to Bushnell*, Philadelphia: Fortress Press, 1980. For an account of contemporary notions of transcendence in twentieth-century writers, see Fergus Kerr, *Immortal Longings: Versions of Transcending Humanity*, London: SPCK, 1997. As Kerr wryly observes, his chosen secular authors – such as Martha Nussbaum, Luce Irigaray, Stanley Cavell, and Charles Taylor – have "much more interest in religion than fashionable philosophers are supposed to have in our supposedly post-religious age" (p. 123). Kerr's reading of Taylor, however, might profitably be set against that found in Stephen K. White, *Sustaining Affirmation: The Strengths of Weak Ontology in Political Theory*, Princeton, NJ: Princeton University Press, 2000, pp. 42–74.

[5] A point stressed by Thomas Weiskel, *The Romantic Sublime: Studies in the Structure and Psychology of Transcendence*, Baltimore, MD: Johns Hopkins University Press, 1986. For the concept in Samuel Taylor Coleridge, particularly in relation to Edmund Burke's more empirical notion of the sublime, see Raimonda Modiano, *Coleridge and the Concept of Nature*, Tallahassee, FL: Florida State University Press, 1985, pp. 101–37.

[6] Herder proposes a link between the "sublime" (*das Erhabne*) and the "beautiful," arguing that they represent the trunk and branches of the same tree: Johann Gottfried Herder, *Kalligone*, 3 vols, Leipzig: Hartknoch, 1800, vol. 2, pp. 39–41. On Herder's aesthetics, see Robert E. Norton, *Herder's Aesthetics and the European Enlightenment*, Ithaca, NY: Cornell University Press, 1991, pp. 155–202.

often spoke of standing on the "borderlands" of the transcendent.[7] Experience and language point beyond themselves, testifying that something lies on the far side of their frontiers, which can be experienced yet not grasped. Everyday language founders as it attempts to reach beyond the threshold of the empirical and observable. For William Wordsworth, human beings are "borderers," firmly based in the real world of human experience, yet reaching out in aspiration beyond its limits.[8]

An excellent example of this can be found in Book VI of Wordsworth's *Prelude*, which sees a physical journey across the Alps as a harbinger of a deeper journey and more significant destination.

> Imagination – here the Power so called
> Through sad incompetence of human speech,
> That awful Power rose from the mind's abyss
> Like an unfathered vapour that enwraps,
> At once, some lonely traveller. I was lost;
> Halted without an effort to break through;
> But to my conscious soul I now can say –
> "I recognise thy glory:" in such strength
> Of usurpation, when the light of sense
> Goes out, but with a flash that has revealed
> The invisible world, doth greatness make abode,
> There harbours; whether we be young or old,
> Our destiny, our being's heart and home,
> Is with infinitude, and only there.[9]

---

[7] See, for example, the excellent accounts in Peter Carafiol, *Transcendent Reason: James Marsh and the Forms of Romantic Thought*, Tallahassee, FL: University Presses of Florida, 1982; Robert M. Torrance, *Ideal and Spleen: The Crisis of Transcendent Vision in Romantic, Symbolist, and Modern Poetry*, New York: Garland Publishing, 1987.

[8] See the analysis of David S. Miall, "Wordsworth and *The Prelude*: The Problematics of Feeling," *Studies in Romanticism* 31 (1992): 233–53; Jonathan Wordsworth, *William Wordsworth: The Borders of Vision*, Oxford: Clarendon Press, 1984, passim.

[9] *Prelude* VI, ll. 592–605. For a discussion, see Richard J. Onorato, *The Character of the Poet: Wordsworth in the Prelude*, Princeton, NJ: Princeton University Press, 1971, pp. 156–7.

Wordsworth here speaks of a metaphorical journey of the imagination, directed towards an "infinitude" that is "our being's heart and home."[10] This realization follows immediately after the devastating flash of imaginative illumination that reveals "the invisible world," in a moment of epiphany that disappears before it has been fully appreciated or understood.[11]

Yet during the 1960s and 1970s, the concept of the transcendent was generally dismissed in academic circles as redundant and outmoded, resting on inadequate or outdated foundations.[12] As a result, discussion has been dominated by metaphysically modest concepts of the transcendent. As noted earlier (pp. 25–6), the notion is often defined in terms of self-transcendence, generally understood as the human capacity to transcend a specific situation.[13] Others have resisted what they regard as diminished conceptions of the transcendent, holding that the notion conveys a fundamental belief about the nature of the world, even the ultimate goal of humanity, framed in terms of ideals that are both independent of human agency and possess a capacity to illuminate, excite, and inspire human agency and action.[14] The vast theological project of the Jesuit writer Karl Rahner, begun in the 1930s, can be seen as an attempt to

---

[10]   For analysis, see David Ferris, "Where Three Paths Meet: History, Wordsworth, and the Simplon Pass," *Studies in Romanticism* 30 (1991): 391–438.

[11]   Robert Langbaum, "The Epiphanic Mode in Wordsworth and Modern Literature," *New Literary History* 14 (1983): 335–58.

[12]   An excellent example of a secularized notion of transcendence, reflecting the somewhat ephemeral philosophical and theological trends of the 1960s, may be found in Alistair Kee, *The Way of Transcendence: Christian Faith without Belief in God*, Harmondsworth: Pelican, 1971, especially pp. 221–3, 228–34. There are clear parallels with the pervasive criticism of classical metaphysics, also characteristic of this period: for an evaluation and response, see Alister E. McGrath, *A Scientific Theology: 3 – Theory*, London: T&T Clark, 2003, pp. 237–94.

[13]   This is the first of the three senses of "transcendence" we noted earlier: see p. 25.

[14]   This theme is developed in Václav Havel's speech "The Need for Transcendence in the Postmodern World," delivered at Independence Hall, Philadelphia, on 4 July, 1994 and published in *The Futurist* 29 (1995): 46–9. Havel was then President of the Czech Republic. For the important development of the concept in Heidegger, see Thomas A. F. Kelly, *Language and Transcendence: A Study in the Philosophy of Martin Heidegger and Karl-Otto Apel*, Berne: Peter Lang, 1994.

respond to the then prevailing secular loss of any sense of the transcendence of God. Whereas others met this challenge through adaptationist strategies, Rahner and his circle argued that the recovery of the sense of the transcendent could only be achieved through a reappropriation of the conceptual framework provided by the classical sources of Christian theology.[15]

More recently, however, an increasing sympathy towards the transcendent appears to have emerged within Western culture. Although the concept of the transcendent was clearly found problematic by academic philosophy during the 1960s and 1970s, it seems to be in the process of recovering much of its former allure. This is suggested particularly by the enduring popular perception of deeper levels of meaning within the universe than those that were allowed by the prevailing rationalist orthodoxy of that time.[16] Two examples may be noted of how the notion of transcendence remains embedded within popular culture, even during metaphysically attenuated times. J. R. R. Tolkien's *Lord of the Rings* owes its success partly to the seriousness with which it takes the human quest for meaning, and its implicit – and occasionally explicit – affirmation of "openness to the transcendent."[17] The more recent "Harry Potter phenomenon" has been widely interpreted as a symptom of a suppressed

---

[15] For an important study, see Russell R. Reno, *The Ordinary Transformed: Karl Rahner and the Christian Vision of Transcendence*, Grand Rapids, MI: Eerdmans, 1995. A more recent (re)interpretation of Rahner emphasizes his utility beyond the limits of modernity: Karen Kilby, *Karl Rahner: Theology and Philosophy*, London: Routledge, 2004.

[16] Alexei Panshin and Cory Panshin, *The World Beyond the Hill: Science Fiction and the Quest for Transcendence*, Los Angeles, CA: J. P. Tarcher, 1989. Individual studies of such authors repay careful study – see, for example, Edgar L. Chapman, "From Rebellious Rationalist to Mythmaker and Mystic: The Religious Quest of Philip José Farmer," in Robert Reilly (ed.), *The Transcendent Adventure: Studies of Religion in Science Fiction/Fantasy*, pp. 127–44, Westport, CT: Greenwood Press, 1985.

[17] As pointed out by Christopher Garbowski, *Recovery and Transcendence for the Contemporary Mythmaker: The Spiritual Dimension in the Works of J. R. R. Tolkien*, Lublin, Poland: Marie-Curie-Sklodowska University Press, 2000, pp. 16–18. While God is a "silent partner of dialogue" in the *Lord of the* Rings (p. 94), Garbowski suggests a much more overt concept of divinity in the *Silmarillion*.

longing for transcendence, and a reaction to the imaginative aridity of the modernism worldview.[18]

At a more academic level, there has been a growing recognition of the specific historical location of the factors that suppressed interest in the transcendent during the modern era;[19] the deconstruction of such modernist interests has opened the way to the reappropriation of the concept in the postmodern era. Analysts such as Dominique Janicaud have spoken of a "theological turn" in French phenomenology after Maurice Merleau-Ponty and Jean Paul Sartre, reflecting a cautious reaffirmation of a transcendent horizon to human thought.[20]

The quest for the transcendent, then, seems to remain integral to much reflection on human identity and action, even in superficially secular engagements with the world. Later in this work, we shall consider in more detail the all-important question of how the transcendent might be accessed from within the natural order. Before doing so, it is of interest to consider some twentieth-century secular evaluations of the notion of "the transcendent," which reinforce the perception that the concept is fundamental to the enterprise of being human. In what follows, we shall consider how three nonreligious writers regard the concept of the "transcendent" to be essential to the task of living a good life and achieving personal fulfillment. In each case, the concept of the transcendent emerges in response to significantly different agendas: Iris Murdoch's concern for a well-grounded ethic; Roy Bhaskar's reflections on social constructivism; and John Dewey's engagement with empiricism.

Iris Murdoch: The Transcendent and the Sublime

Although best known for her remarkable novels, Iris Murdoch (1919–99) was also a moral philosopher of substance, passionately concerned about what needed to be done if humanity was to break free from its selfishness,

---

[18]   See, for example, John Granger, *Looking for God in Harry Potter*, Wheaton, IL: SaltRiver, 2004.

[19]   For an excellent discussion of some of these factors, see Arthur Gibson, *Metaphysics and Transcendence*, London: Routledge, 2003, pp. 211–37.

[20]   For an analysis of this development and its implications, see James K. A. Smith, *Speech and Theology: Language and the Logic of Incarnation*, London: Routledge, 2002, pp. 16–63.

and act out the good life. Her famous formulation of the moral problem sets the scene admirably for our analysis:

> One of the main problems of moral philosophy might be formulated thus: are there any techniques for the purification and reorientation of an energy which is naturally selfish, in such a way that when moments of choice arrive we shall be sure of acting rightly?[21]

Murdoch's answer is complex, yet is ultimately possessed of a central theme: there must be a transcendent ideal, capable of capturing our minds and imaginations, captivating us with a vision of the good. Alluding to the Book of Common Prayer (1662), she sets out the connotations of the term "good": "the proper seriousness of the term refers us to a perfection which is perhaps never exemplified in the world we know ('There is no good in us') and which carries with it the idea of transcendence."[22]

Murdoch did not believe in God, as traditionally conceived; yet her disinclination to accept such a conventional notion did not prevent her from insisting on the critical role of the transcendent – above all, of "the Good" – in affecting and guiding the human moral quest.[23] It is as if something is intimating that this world is not of final significance, morally or metaphysically. We sense that our attempts to live the good life are ultimately judged by a standard that we have not ourselves created, but that is somehow built into the fabric of the world. It is our task, as reflective moral agents, to encounter this deep structure, and adjust our thinking and our acting accordingly.

Murdoch, writing from a Platonist perspective, sets out the issues in her characteristically robust manner:

> How do we know the very great are not the perfect? We see differences, we sense directions, and we know that the Good is still somewhere beyond. The self, the place where we live, is a place of illusion. Goodness is connected with the attempt to see the unself, to see and to respond to the real world in the light of a virtuous conscience. This is the non-metaphysical meaning of the idea of transcendence, to which philosophers have so constantly

[21] Iris Murdoch, *The Sovereignty of Good*, London: Routledge, 1970, p. 53.
[22] Iris Murdoch, *Existentialists and Mystics: Writings on Philosophy and Literature*, ed. Peter J. Conradi, London: Chatto & Windus, 1997, p. 376.
[23] Maria Antonaccio, "Imagining the Good: Iris Murdoch's Godless Theology," *Annual of the Society of Christian Ethics* 16 (1996): 223–42.

resorted in their explanations of goodness. "Good is a transcendent reality" means that virtue is the attempt to pierce the veil of selfish consciousness and join the world as it really is. It is an empirical fact about human nature that this attempt cannot be entirely successful.[24]

Despite her mild demythologization of the notion, the critical role of the notion of the "transcendent" in Murdoch's vision of the moral quest will be clear.

Murdoch was aware that the notion of transcendence is not without its difficulties, and that it was regarded with some disdain by Oxford philosophers during the 1960s and 1970s.[25] For many such writers, "any true transcendence" was a "consoling dream projected by human need on to an empty sky."[26] Writing in the face of relentless opposition to the notion, characteristic of that metaphysically impoverished period, Murdoch insisted that some such notion was required to make sense of human experience in general, and moral experience in particular. Human moral activity can be thought of as a pilgrimage towards "a distant moral goal, like a temple at the end of the pilgrimage," something that is "glimpsed but never reached."[27]

Where other voices of the era were insisting that morality was a matter of human invention,[28] Murdoch refused to concede the then fashionable insistence upon the distinction between fact and value.[29] Morality, she insists, is about seeing things as they really are. It is a form of realism, which ultimately depends upon the recognition that some ideal of perfection, ultimately lying beyond us, informs and challenges our moral reflections.

---

[24]   Murdoch, *The Sovereignty of Good*, p. 91. See also the more extended discussion in her *Metaphysics as a Guide to Morals*, London: Penguin, 1992.

[25]   For a useful introduction to the metaphysical austerities of the Oxford philosophical establishment of this time, see Peter J. Conradi, *Iris Murdoch: A Life*, London: HarperCollins, 2001, pp. 301–8.

[26]   Murdoch, *The Sovereignty of Good*, p. 57.

[27]   Murdoch, *Metaphysics*, p. 304.

[28]   See, for example, J. L. Mackie, *Ethics: Inventing Right and Wrong*, London: Penguin Books, 1977. For a discussion of such developments, see J. B. Schneewind, *The Invention of Autonomy: A History of Modern Moral Philosophy*, Cambridge, UK: Cambridge University Press, 1998.

[29]   On which see Alasdair MacIntyre, *After Virtue*, 2nd edn, Notre Dame, IN: University of Notre Dame Press, 1984, p. 56.

At the level of serious common sense and of an ordinary non-philosophical reflection about the nature of morals, it is perfectly obvious that goodness is connected with knowledge: not with impersonal quasi-scientific knowledge of the ordinary world, whatever that may be, but with a refined and honest perception of what is really the case, a patient and just discernment and exploration of what confronts one, which is the result not simply of opening one's eyes but of a certainly perfectly familiar kind of moral discipline.[30]

We can only choose within worlds that we can see – that we can visualize. To act as we should we must first see things as they are.

Murdoch is quite clear that the notion of the transcendent is not to be equated with God, even though there are important conceptual affinities and relationships to be discerned and explored.[31] Yet the notion of the transcendent remains fundamental. As Murdoch pointed out, we need to believe that, "as moral beings, we are immersed in a reality which transcends us and that moral progress consists in awareness of this reality and submission to its purposes."[32] The question of how that reality is "seen" thus becomes of decisive importance. How can one give visible, tangible expression to this authorizing, transcending, enabling ideal? How may one gain access to the realm of the transcendent, in order to live the good life?

And it is here that we encounter perhaps the Achilles heel of Murdoch's moral vision. Yet if there is a failure at this point, it is a profoundly enlightening failure, in that it points to the need to *know*, to *perceive* the Good before good can be done. For Murdoch, the ideal of "the Good" may lie beyond the limits of our volitional capacities;[33] yet

---

[30] Murdoch, *The Sovereignty of Good*, p. 37.

[31] For a useful assessment, see Stanley Hauerwas, "Murdochian Muddles: Can We Get Through Them if God Does Not Exist?" in Maria Antonaccio and William Schweiker (eds), *Iris Murdoch and the Search for Human Goodness*, pp. 190–208. Chicago: University of Chicago Press, 1996.

[32] Iris Murdoch, "Vision and Choice in Morality," *Proceedings of the Aristotelian* Society, Supplementary Volume 30 (1956): 32–58; quote at p. 56. For comment, see Lawrence Blum, "Iris Murdoch and the Domain of the Moral," *Philosophical Studies* 50 (1986): 343–67. On the general issue, see Michael DePaul, "Argument and Perception," *Journal of Philosophy* 85 (1988): 552–65.

[33] For a helpful discussion of "the Good" in this context, see Emmet, *The Role of the Unrealisable*, pp. 74–6.

it possesses the capacity to inspire us to *want* to attain it, and directs our efforts to do so. But how can we give substance to this ideal? It is one thing to be behaviorally unattainable; but what if it is also conceptually elusive, lacking in precision precisely because it is not susceptible to capture and interrogation? If "the Good" is to give direction to our moral longings – as opposed to merely exciting our longing to do good, while failing to inform us what this "good" might be – it must be in a form that we can "see" (to use an idiom that is characteristic of Murdoch's moral parlance). It needs to be made known and made accessible under the limiting conditions of human circumstances and history.

The importance of Murdoch's analysis of the role of the transcendent should be noted. For example, some liberal political visions rest on the assumption that there is no transcendent "good" which can inform or direct human reflections on "good" political systems, or "good" actions within their context.

Recent critiques of the philosophical foundations of liberalism have argued that, since it lacks any transcendent reference, it is unable to offer more by way of defense of the liberal political vision than the observation that it represents a particular set of practices with historic precedent in particular contexts, yet which have no intrinsic superiority over other forms of political organization.[34]

We shall return to such reflections later in this volume. Our attention now turns to our second witness to the significance of the transcendent: the philosopher Roy Bhaskar.

Roy Bhaskar: The Intimation of Meta-Reality

One of the most significant contributions in recent years to the philosophy of the sciences, both natural and social, has come from the philosopher Roy Bhaskar (born 1944), best known for his development of the

---

[34] See, for example, concerns expressed about the approaches of both Richard Rorty and John Rawls in J. Judd Owen, *Religion and the Demise of Liberal Rationalism: The Foundational Crisis of the Separation of Church and State*, Chicago: University of Chicago Press, 2001.

philosophy of "critical realism."[35] Bhaskar's "critical realism" – which is best understood as an amalgamation of the ideas of "critical naturalism" and "transcendental realism" – holds that there exists an objectively knowable, mind-independent reality, whilst acknowledging the activity of the human agent in the process of knowing. Bhaskar asserts the primacy of ontology over epistemology, emphasizing that the manner in which things may be known, and the extent of the ensuing knowledge, is influenced by how things are in themselves. Bhaskar's critical realism opened up important questions concerning the nature of reality, and the manner in which human reflective agents can represent and interpret what is observed.

More recently, however, Bhaskar has begun to speak openly of the importance of the transcendent for authentic human existence. Bhaskar's "spiritual turn" towards what he styled a "transcendental dialectical critical realism" was first set out in *From East to West*.[36] This was developed further in his concept of "meta-reality," which has been an integral part of his thought since 2002.[37] As he defines the notion, meta-reality denotes an attempt to embrace the totality of things, going beyond what is accessible to normal scientific analysis. For Bhaskar, this latter must be thought of as a "demi-reality," concerned primarily with social relationships and individual experience.[38] In order to transcend this limited conception of reality, a broader conception of "the real" is required. This, Bhaskar argues, is provided by the notion of "meta-reality."

---

[35] See Andrew Collier, *Critical Realism: An Introduction to Roy Bhaskar's Philosophy*, London: Verso, 1994. I make extensive, though not uncritical, use of this concept of critical realism throughout my scientific theology project: see especially Alister E. McGrath, *A Scientific Theology: 2 – Reality*, London: T&T Clark, 2002, pp. 195–244. For an assessment of my use of Bhaskar, see Brad Shipway, "The Theological Application of Bhaskar's Stratified Reality: The Scientific Theology of A. E. McGrath," *Journal of Critical Realism* 3 (2004): 191–203.

[36] Roy Bhaskar, *From East to West: Odyssey of a Soul*, New York: Routledge, 2000.

[37] For the controversy this has generated within critical realist circles, see Jamie Morgan, "What is Meta-Reality?" *Journal of Critical Realism* 1 (2003): 115–46.

[38] See, for example, Roy Bhaskar, *Meta-Reality: Creativity, Love and Freedom*, London: Sage Publications, 2002, p. vii; Roy Bhaskar, *Reflections on Meta-Reality: Transcendence, Emancipation and Everyday Life*, London: Sage Publications, 2002, p. xv.

The "meta" here connotes both the idea of transcendence, that is going to a level beyond or behind and between reality, while at the same time the "reality" in the title makes it clear that this level is still real, and so part of the very same totality that critical realism has been describing all along.[39]

Against modernity's program of the de-enchantment of nature, which involves the systematic elimination of any notion of transcendence, Bhaskar argues for its re-enchantment. By this, he does not mean the imposition of an arbitrary and improper transcendent viewpoint. Rather, reality *is* enchanted; "re-enchantment" designates the process of exposing and articulating this aspect of reality, against the modernist attempt to deny, eliminate, or marginalize it.[40] In one sense, Bhaskar's discovery of the "meta-real" is to be seen as a natural extension of his concept of the stratification of reality, in effect amounting to discerning a transcendent stratum as an integral element of any account of reality. Self-realization is thus transcendentally grounded.

Once more, it is important to stress that Bhaskar's notion of meta-reality does not make, and does not, in my view, necessarily require, reference to God. Bhaskar himself works within a categorical structure which he refers to as the "cosmic envelope," essentially independent of any particular theological commitments. Bhaskar's explicit turn, not merely to spirituality, but to an ontologically grounded realm of the spiritual, has raised concerns within some sections of the critical realist community, which are clearly uneasy at this development in his thinking.[41] It is, however, important to note that, where Karl Marx gave rise to a school of social analysis that excluded the transcendent as a distraction from worldly *praxis*, or simply as an irrelevance, Bhaskar, one of his more recent successors, appears to be reintroducing this same notion, convinced that, if it did not exist, we would be obliged to invent it.

---

[39] Bhaskar, *Reflections on Meta-Reality*, p. 175.

[40] Ibid., p. 243.

[41] For example, Jamie Morgan submits Bhaskar's claims to detailed philosophical probing, challenging his assumption that such strong ontological claims are necessary to ground an impulse to emancipation in human beings: Morgan, "What is Meta-Reality?," passim. These concerns about potential ontological inflation are set out more fully in Jamie Morgan, "Ontological Casuistry? Bhaskar's Meta-Reality, Fine Structure, and Human Disposition," *New Formations* 56 (2005): 133–46.

We conclude by considering a writer who is often thought to have had no time, or conceptual space, for the notion of the transcendent – the American pragmatist philosopher John Dewey.

John Dewey: The Curious Plausibility of the Transcendent

John Dewey (1859–1952) is seen as one of the most important American philosophers. He is widely credited, along with William James and Charles S. Peirce, with founding the pragmatist school of philosophy, often regarded as the first indigenous movement of philosophical thought to develop in the United States. For Dewey, knowledge is best understood in terms of an interaction of organism with environment, in which the agent actively intervenes to predict, form, and control future experience.[42]

Dewey's pragmatist philosophical credentials might suggest that he has no place for any concept of the "transcendent," let alone that he might choose to find a significant role for this allegedly outmoded notion in his conception of the identification and actualization of the good life. Jonathan Levin offers a fairly representative account of the mainstream assessment of pragmatism's dismissal of the transcendent. Pragmatists, he argues, "reject all explicitly supernatural trappings, while retaining and cultivating a naturalized, immanent idealism . . . [They] are never more 'spirited' than when insisting upon the wholly secular dimension of the pragmatist project."[43]

There can be no doubt of the hostility and suspicion directed towards the notion of transcendence within mainline pragmatism. For some, any engagement with an outmoded "metaphysics" was to be regarded as an unfortunate and unnecessary throwback to an earlier, now discredited, approach to philosophy. Others were anxious lest any interest in the

---

[42] For further discussion, see R. W. Sleeper, *The Necessity of Pragmatism: John Dewey's Conception of Philosophy*, New Haven, CT: Yale University Press, 1986.

[43] Jonathan Levin, *The Poetics of Transition: Emerson, Pragmatism, & American Literary Modernism*, Durham, NC: Duke University Press, 1999, pp. 5–6. Similar interpretations abound in popular and academic interpretations of the movement: see, for example, Louis Menand, *The Metaphysical Club: A Story of Ideas in America*, New York: Farrar, Straus, and Giroux, 2001.

notion of the transcendent might delay or defer engagement with more pressing matters.[44]

In his earlier works, before he had arrived at his mature pragmatic position, Dewey sought to encourage the philosophical assimilation of the ideas and methods of the natural sciences, particularly experimental psychology. Initially, Dewey appears to have believed that such an enterprise was possible through some form of idealism. Up to about 1890, Dewey clearly believed that there exists a transcendent reality in which we participate, providing us with a standpoint and a resource, permitting us to organize and comprehend human experience. Yet his reading of William James's *Principles of Psychology* (1891) appears to have changed his mind:[45] what is central is what human beings experience. Dewey now emphasized an empirical approach to life: only that which could be experienced, he argued, was open to scientific study.[46]

One important early consequence of this development was Dewey's reconception of the notion of truth.[47] In a series of essays published between 1906 and 1909, Dewey mounted a vigorous defense of the pragmatic theory of truth. Ideas are tools that are devised to cope with the world in which we find ourselves.[48] The traditional correspondence theory of truth, according to which a "true idea" is one which agrees with, or

---

[44] For exploration of its core themes and their developments, see Charles William Morris, *The Pragmatic Movement in American Philosophy*, New York: Braziller, 1970; David Jacobson, *Emerson's Pragmatic Vision: The Dance of the Eye*, University Park, PA: Pennsylvania State University Press, 1993; Ellen Kappy Suckiel, *The Pragmatic Philosophy of William James*, Notre Dame, IN: University of Notre Dame Press, 1982.

[45] For a discussion, see Thomas M. Alexander, *John Dewey's Theory of Art, Experience, and Nature: The Horizons of Feeling*, Albany, NY: State University of New York Press, 1987, pp. 15–55.

[46] See his important essays "The Postulate of Immediate Empiricism," *Journal of Philosophy* 2 (1905): 393–9; "Does Reality Possess Practical Character?" in *Essays Philosophical and Psychological in Honor of William James*, pp. 53–80, New York: Longmans, Green, and Co., 1908.

[47] For discussions, see H. S. Thayer, *The Logic of Pragmatism: An Examination of John Dewey's Logic*, New York: Humanities Press, 1952; Sleeper, *The Necessity of Pragmatism*.

[48] Menand, *Metaphysical Club*, pp. xi–xii. Note also his critique of those who wish to make ideas into ideologies (p. xii).

corresponds to, reality, merely begs the greater question of the precise nature of this alleged "agreement" or "correspondence." Dewey and James both insisted that an idea can be held to correspond to reality, and is therefore "true," if and only if it can be successfully deployed in human action in pursuit of human goals and interests – in other words, to use Dewey's characteristic vocabulary, if it leads to the resolution of a problematic situation:

> The pragmatic method is primarily a method of settling metaphysical disputes that otherwise might be interminable. Is the world one or many? – fated or free? – material or spiritual? – here are notions either of which may or may not hold good of the world; and disputes over such notions are unending. The pragmatic method in such cases is to try to interpret each notion by tracing its respective practical consequences. What difference would it practically make to any one if this notion rather than that notion were true? If no practical difference whatever can be traced, then the alternatives mean practically the same thing, and all dispute is idle. Whenever a dispute is serious, we ought to be able to show some practical difference that must follow from one side or the other's being right.[49]

Later, Dewey began to use the term "warranted assertibility" to describe the distinctive property of ideas that results from successful inquiry, believing that traditional terms such as "truth" had become tainted or rendered unusable through unhelpful conceptual accretions or associations.

In dealing with the question of how religious or mystical experience is to be interpreted, Dewey expressed hostility towards the introduction of supernatural interpretations. He suggested that these "have not grown from the experience itself," but have rather been developed independently of that experience.[50] Rather, Dewey argued that "the only reality is that

---

[49] William James, "What Pragmatism Means," in *Pragmatism: A New Name for Some Old Ways of Thinking*, pp. 17–32, New York: Longman Green and Co., 1907; quote at p. 18.

[50] See the analysis of Stanley Grean, "Elements of Transcendence in Dewey's Naturalistic Humanism," *Journal of the American Academy of Religion* 52 (1984): 263–88, especially pp. 272–4.

of ordinary experience,"[51] rejecting the notion of the "supernatural" as a category lying beyond the realm of this ordinary experience. Dewey's approach is "to examine the actual state of experience and to isolate the factors necessary for an intelligible interpretation of that experience."[52] But in fact it seems that Dewey conceded some notion that could be interpreted as the "transcendent" in order to make sense of human experience.

It has been a commonplace to argue that Dewey's naturalism limits his vision of reality to the everyday world. Dewey, it is argued, does not appeal to some hypothetical "transcendentally ideal experience," a notion which he is widely held to deprecate.[53] Yet Dewey's account of experience is more nuanced than such interpretations allow. Experience is not, for Dewey, a static entity or substance. Rather, it is a structured process, in which "new powers and aspects of nature are revealed by our activities which explore, discover and determine possibilities of the world and the human situation."[54] The transcendent may not be "given" in nature, as some kind of fixed, constitutive essence. Yet the notion may *emerge* through goal-directed human activity. Nature, for Dewey, has potentialities which are actualized under certain conditions. It is this insight that underlies his belief in a group of universal values to which all people can have access simply by virtue of their humanity, leading him to argue that, at some fundamental level, one could have faith that, more often than not, they will find their way to those universals.[55] Though not "given," they "emerge," being brought to explicit realization through the process of engagement with nature.

---

[51] The view of John R. Shook, *Dewey's Empirical Theory of Knowledge and Reality*, Nashville, TN: Vanderbilt University Press, 2000, pp. 210–11. For some representative contributions to this debate, see William Ernest Hocking, "Dewey's Concepts of Experience and Nature," *Philosophical Review* 49 (1940): 228–44; Morris R. Cohen, "Some Difficulties in Dewey's Naturalistic Metaphysics," *Philosophical Review* 49 (1940): 196–220.

[52] Raymond D. Boisvert, *Dewey's Metaphysics*, New York: Fordham University Press, 1988, p. 158.

[53] E.g., see James Gouinlock, *John Dewey's Philosophy of Value*, New York: Humanities Press, 1972, especially p. 273.

[54] Alexander, *John Dewey's Theory of Art, Experience, and Nature*, p. 96.

[55] This consideration underlies Dewey's defense of democracy: see the analysis in David Fott, *John Dewey: America's Philosopher of Democracy*, Lanham, MD: Rowman and Littlefield, 1998.

This point becomes particularly clear in Dewey's analysis of consciousness, but is equally applicable to his discussion of transcendence. Dewey insists that the only way to "avoid a sharp separation between the mind which is the center of the processes of experiencing and the natural world" is to "acknowledge that all modes of experiencing are ways in which some genuine traits of nature come to manifest realization."[56]

A recognition of this point has led to significant revisionist accounts of Dewey's notion of the transcendent, and the manner in which it is implicated in his pragmatic synthesis. *Can human experience or thought reach beyond itself?* To put it simply, it seems that "Dewey's desire to promote 'ordinary experience,' 'concrete human experience,' and 'common experience' could not be fulfilled without a conception of a transcendent ideal,"[57] albeit emergent. Dewey's pragmatic instincts, it seems, could not be sustained without the capacity of humanity to self-transcend its situation.

The subtle role of what corresponds to the "transcendent" in Dewey's account of human existence is best seen from his discussion of the struggle for the good.[58] Although pragmatic concerns abound in this discussion, what appears to represent an appeal to the "transcendent" is used as a tool to encourage and enable humanity to outrun the seen and touched. Although such ideals feature in his earlier writings, they recur later, contextualized yet not abandoned.

Perhaps the clearest instance of this is in his later work *A Common Faith*, originally given as the Terry Lectures at Yale University during the academic year 1933–4.[59] Although these are often regarded as somewhat minimalist in their theological affirmations, they can be understood as representing a succinct, focused exploration of the significance of the pursuit of what other might call the "transcendent" (Dewey was cautious about being too explicitly religious here) in the quest for human goodness and fulfillment.[60] Once more, we find the notion of transcendent as a tool for human self-actualization, acting as a stimulus to advancement at every level. Although generally secular in his outlook, Dewey can nevertheless

---

[56] John Dewey, *Experience and Nature*, 2nd edn, New York: Dover, 1958, p. 24.
[57] Victor Kestenbaum, *The Grace and Severity of the Ideal: John Dewey and the Transcendent*. Chicago: University of Chicago Press, 2002, p. 26.
[58] Ibid, pp. 28–53.
[59] John Dewey, *A Common Faith*, New Haven, CT: Yale University Press, 1934.
[60] Kestenbaum, *The Grace and Severity of the Ideal*, pp. 175–99.

be argued to have integrated the transcendent into his worldview. The concept emerges as a result of goal-directed activity, and plays an important role in sustaining that activity, and making sense of it.

The three thinkers considered in the present chapter can each, in different ways, be seen as indicating how the notion of the transcendent remains significant for human reflection on issues of identity, agency, and value. This naturally leads us on to consider how human beings seek to access the transcendent. If it potentially plays such a significant role in human reflection and enablement, how can it be encountered? In what follows, we shall consider some strategies and practices that have been devised in order to grasp more fully the transcendence that many believe to lie behind, within, or beyond human experience.

CHAPTER 4

Accessing the Transcendent: Strategies and Practices

In the previous two chapters, we considered the persistence of the notion of the transcendent, observing in Chapter 3 that a concern with the transcendent emerges in unexpected cultural and intellectual locations. It is generally experienced and conceptualized as fleeting and elusive yet desirable and of profound importance. Transcendent experiences are felt to be desirable as experiences in their own right, but there is also a sense that such experiences bring with them insights that may help us answer the big questions of life – insights that disclose ultimate meaning, impart personal significance, inform and enable morality. For some, such experiences are to be interpreted in terms of a "higher being"; for others, in terms of a "higher state of being."[1] Yet, as we have seen, despite these wide variations in interpretation, a concern for the "transcendent" often nestles deep within philosophies that are, at least on the face of it, thoroughly secular in their outlook.

The inherent desirability of the transcendent has led many to want more than sporadic, unpredictable, and partial access to its presumed benefits. Over many human generations and across many and varied human cultures specific practices have developed based on the belief that it is possible to encounter the transcendent from within the ordinary circumstances of natural existence. Four major approaches will be noted:

---

[1] Eugene d'Aquili and Andrew B. Newberg, *The Mystical Mind: Probing the Biology of Religious Experience*, Minneapolis: Fortress Press, 1999, p. 1.

1 *Ascending from nature* to the transcendent. Here, nature is seen primarily as a "base camp" for reaching a peak that soars above it.
2 *Seeing through nature* to the transcendent. This approach treats nature
   as a gateway or pointer towards the transcendent that lies beyond it.
3 *Withdrawing from nature* into the human interior. This approach
   prioritizes the inner psychological world as the place of encounter with
   the transcendent.
4 *Discerning in nature* that which is transcendent. Unlike the other three
   approaches, this does not rest on a dualistic view of nature and the
   transcendent, nor on the imagery of movement away from nature to
   something "better." Nature is seen as holding *within it* the capacity
   to disclose or be transfigured by the transcendent.[2]

These four categories are illustrative rather than exhaustive. Nor are they
mutually exclusive, in that there is clearly potential for traffic between them.
The boundaries between the approaches are porous and somewhat fuzzy;
they are offered primarily as a convenient means of organizing a vast body
of material, rather than as a rigid or prescriptive account of the possibilities.
Nevertheless, it is helpful to distinguish – not necessarily to adjudicate –
between them in order to appreciate their distinct emphases and approaches.

We begin by considering the idea of ascending from nature to experience the transcendent.

Ascending to the Transcendent from Nature

The first approach likens the quest for the transcendent to climbing a
mountain or ladder.[3] At first sight, the notion of an ascent towards the

---

[2] On this, see especially Paul S. Fiddes, "'Where Shall Wisdom Be Found?' Job 28
as a Riddle for Ancient and Modern Readers," in John Barton and David Reimer
(eds), *After the Exile: Essays in Honor of Rex Mason*, pp. 171–90, Macon, GA:
Mercer University Press, 1996.
[3] For this theme in Christian theology, see John Haldane, "Admiring the High
Mountains: The Aesthetics of Environment," *Environmental Values* 3 (1994): 97–
106. For the appeal of the "ascent of mountains" to New Age mysticism, see Julius
Evola, *Meditations on the Peaks: Mountain Climbing as Metaphor for the Spiritual
Quest*, Rochester, VT: Inner Traditions, 1998, pp. 1–8. For the Christian application
of the image of the ascent of a spiritual ladder, see Christopher B. Kaiser, "Climbing
Jacob's Ladder: John Calvin and the Early Church on our Eucharistic Ascent to
Heaven," *Scottish Journal of Theology* 56 (2003): 247–67.

transcendent seems to betray a curiously physical conception of the notion. It is, so to speak, "up there," and thus requires human observers and seekers to ascend, in order to encounter it.[4] For some, the biblical emphasis upon the importance of mountains in relation to divine revelation – for example, the giving of the Mosaic Law on Sinai, or Jesus of Nazareth's resorting to mountains when wishing to be alone – would seem to resonate with this notion.[5] Was not the fabled Tower of Babel intended to be a human construction, erected to enable humanity to encounter the divine under terms of its own choosing?[6]

This understanding of encountering the transcendent is also found in the writings of the *Merkabah* mystics. Based on the visions of the prophet Ezekiel,[7] this type of Jewish mysticism emphasized the utter transcendence of God, thus heightening the problem of mediation. How could humanity know this God? Or see the face of God, when it appeared to be inaccessible?[8] The answer provided to this question by the *Merkabah* mystics took its cues from the chariot (Hebrew: *merkabah*) mentioned in the prophecy of Ezekiel, which was seen as a means of transporting individuals nearer to the presence of God. Through appropriate techniques, the mystic is enabled to journey higher and higher, passing through heaven

---

[4]   As seen in the mountain gods of ancient China and elsewhere: see, for example, Terry F. Kleeman, "Mountain Deities in China: The Domestication of the Mountain God and the Subjugation of the Margins," *Journal of the American Oriental Society* 114 (1994): 226–38.

[5]   Leland Ryken, James C. Wilhoit, and Tremper Longman III (eds), *Dictionary of Biblical Imagery*, Downers Grove, IL: InterVarsity Press, 1998, pp. 572–4.

[6]   This is certainly how Karl Barth interpreted this biblical image, and his use of the image as a paradigm of the human situation merits close study: Karl Barth, "Die Gerechtigkeit Gottes," in *Das Wort Gottes und die Theologie*, pp. 5–17, Munich: Kaiser Verlag, 1925. For the use made of the "Tower of Babel" in medieval English reflections on the nature of human culture, see Robert M. Luiza, "The Tower of Babel: *The Wanderer* and the Ruins of History," *Studies in the Literary Imagination* 36 (2003): 1–35.

[7]   David J. Halperin, *The Faces of the Chariot: Early Jewish Responses to Ezekiel's Vision*, Tübingen: Mohr, 1988.

[8]   For this theme in the Old Testament, see Samuel E. Balantine, *The Hidden God: The Hiding Face of God in the Old Testament*, Oxford: Oxford University Press, 1983.

after heaven and glory after glory, until eventually drawing near to – but never reaching – the divine throne.[9]

A related approach is found in various apocalyptic writings, taking the form of visions of the end-times in which the visionary is transported, typically in a dream, to a place at which he is able to see the vast panorama of world history from a privileged viewpoint.[10] The seer remains located in the present, yet is given a "god's-eye" view of history, permitting his own situation to be seen in its context, as well as showing its outcome. Typically, but not invariably, the message is one of hope: today's oppression of God's people will give way to liberation.

Yet not all understood the concept of "ascent" in such a literal sense.[11] The metaphor of ascent merely uses the notion of physical ascent in a heuristic manner, to indicate primarily the need to move beyond one's present situation – as in the metaphysical poet Henry Vaughan's frequent use of mountain imagery to denote the human longing for "the world beyond."[12] The notion of "ascent" implies improvement, perhaps reflecting an essentially neo-Platonic anthropology which encourages us to think of "higher" motives within human nature. A "ladder of ascent" may be constructed, conceived either as a theoretical framework or a specific praxis or technique, enabling practitioners to transcend their present situation.

The biblical image of the "ladder of Jacob" (Genesis 28: 10–22) is often incorporated into such discussions of an ascent towards God, and

---

[9] Timo Eskola, *Messiah and the Throne: Jewish Merkabah Mysticism and the Early Christian Exaltation Discourse*, Tübingen: Mohr, 2001; Vita Daphna Arbel, *Beholders of Divine Secrets: Mysticism and Myth in the Hekhalot and Merkavah Literature*, Albany, NY: State University of New York Press, 2003.

[10] For reflections on the sociological location and distinctive ideas of such movements, see Klaus Koch, *The Rediscovery of Apocalyptic*, Napierville, IL: Alec R. Allenson, 1972, pp. 28–33; Christopher Rowland, *The Open Heaven: A Study of Apocalyptic in Judaism and early Christianity*, London: SPCK, 1982; Adela Y. Collins, *Cosmology and Eschatology in Jewish and Christian Apocalypticism*, Leiden: E. J. Brill, 1996; John J. Collins, *Apocalypticism in the Dead Sea Scrolls*, London: Routledge, 1997.

[11] The *sursum corda* of the Christian Eucharist is an exhortation to the congregation to partake in its raising to heaven by Christ; see Alexander Schmemann, *The World as Sacrament*, London: Darton, Longman & Todd, 1966, pp. 43–4.

[12] Robert Ellrodt, *Seven Metaphysical Poets: A Structural Study of the Unchanging Self*, Oxford: Oxford University Press, 2000, pp. 228–30.

the beholding of the divine glory.[13] Although the Genesis narrative clearly states that Jacob saw God's face, it does not offer any description of God, or the "house of God" which Jacob encountered. Yet the text proved an important stimulus to the imagery and ideas of Jewish mysticism, evident in "The Ladder of Jacob," a Jewish pseudepigraphon now only preserved in Slavonic, believed to date from the first century.[14]

In her careful study of the motif of ascent in Western literature, Martha Nussbaum has suggested that three families of "ladders of ascent" can be identified: Platonic, Christian, and Romantic.[15] Nussbaum herself is critical of these "techniques of transcendence," primarily because she believes that they "climb so high above real life" that they devalue the ordinary, and divert attention from the phenomena of daily life. This concern being acknowledged, however, the motif of ascent remains extremely significant as both a cultural and literary tool. In what follows, we shall consider representatives of each of Nussbaum's families of ladders.

The first is the Platonic. Plato's *Symposium* includes a remarkable speech by Diotima, which explores how a fundamentally erotic notion of love may be transfigured into something more sublime. The passionate human erotic longing for another begins by focusing on the beauty of a human body. Then, by a complex process of abstraction, the lover is invited to

---

[13]   The image plays a major role in Anders Nygren's classic analysis of some of the central theological themes of Western Christendom: Anders Nygren, *Agape and Eros: A Study of the Christian Idea of Love*, Philadelphia: Westminster Press, 1953, pp. 621–37. For the medieval development of the image, including Luther, see David C. Steinmetz, "Luther and the Ascent of Jacob's Ladder," *Church History* 55 (1986): 179–92.

[14]   James L. Kugel, "The Ladder of Jacob," *Harvard Theological Review* 88 (1995): 209–27. For its theological distinctives, see Andrei A. Orlov, "The Face as the Heavenly Counterpart of the Visionary in the Slavonic *Ladder of Jacob*," in Craig A. Evans (ed.), *Of Scribes and Sages: Early Jewish Interpretation and Transmission of Scripture*, pp. 37–76, London: T&T Clark, 2004.

[15]   Martha C. Nussbaum, *Upheavals of Thought: The Intelligence of Emotions*, Cambridge, UK: Cambridge University Press, 2001, p. 14. For her detailed analysis of each "family," see pp. 457–714. Nussbaum's approach should be contextualized, if its significance is to be fully appreciated: see especially the judicious analysis in Ronald L. Hall, *The Human Embrace: The Love of Philosophy and the Philosophy of Love: Kierkegaard, Cavell, Nussbaum*, University Park, PA: Pennsylvania State University Press, 2000, pp. 173–256, especially pp. 207–15.

---

turn from the erotic contemplation of the human body to a more elevated contemplation of the "good" and the "beautiful," which the human body imperfectly reflects.[16]

Erotic desire mingles a high love of beauty with what are arguably the more base matters of human relationships, such as jealousy, grief, and betrayal. Surely, Diotima suggests, it must be possible to abstract what is good and beautiful from human love, and leave its negative aspects behind? More than that: cannot the ultimate human longing for goodness and beauty be dissociated from the particularities of time and space, in order to allow the mind to rise upwards, towards the contemplation of what is eternally good and beautiful, rather than its imperfect and transitory earthly manifestations? Plato thus argues for the need to rise upwards, moving from the human experience of love towards its true perfection in the eternal world of forms.

The second of Nussbaum's family of "ladders" is Christian.[17] This invitation to ascend from the mundane to the transcendent is developed in different ways by Augustine of Hippo and Dante, each of whom reworks the Platonic notion of love to reflect a more specifically Christian vision of God and human destiny. Yet the principle remains the same: the need to rise upwards. Stanley Fish, discerning the same theological trajectory in Milton's *Paradise Lost*, comments:

> The arc of the narrative describes a Platonic ascent, which culminates (for the reader who is able to move with it) in the simultaneous apprehension of the absolute form of the Good and the Beautiful, "without shape or colour, intangible, visible only to reason, the soul's pilot."[18]

---

[16] Nussbaum, *Upheavals of Thought*, pp. 486–500. On the development of such themes in Dante, see her "Beatrice's Dante: Loving the Individual?" *Apeiron* 26 (1993): 161–78.

[17] Nussbaum, *Upheavals of Thought*, pp. 527–90. While Nussbaum focuses here on Augustine and Dante, her analysis would, I think, have been sharpened by including Bonaventura's *Itinerarium mentis ad Deum*.

[18] Stanley E. Fish, *Surprised by Sin: The Reader in* Paradise Lost, 2nd edn, London: Macmillan, 1997, p. 90, citing Plato's *Phaedrus*, 247c. Fish's discussion is amplified by studies such as A. J. Smith, *The Metaphysics of Love: Studies in Renaissance Love Poetry from Dante to Milton*, Cambridge, UK: Cambridge University Press, 1985, pp. 94–102, 114–45.

We can see here a clear line of continuity with this great theme of human wisdom. Although Milton clearly wishes to distance himself from the neo-Platonism of writings such as Pietro Bembo's *The Courtier*,[19] his engagement with the idea demonstrates both its abiding influence, and the capacity of the Christian tradition (here in its Reformed form) to reconceptualize and redirect its imagery.

So what can hinder such an ascent? What binds the soul to this base world, preventing it from rising upwards? One influential answer which may be noted, yet need not necessarily be endorsed, is offered by writers as divergent as Augustine of Hippo and John Updike.[20] On this view, humanity is addicted to sensory experience and the desire for possession, and is unable to break free from their lure. Humanity may discern its true goal, but lacks the capability to burst the bonds of its present situation. The issue for Augustine is that of grace – the divine supplementation of human capacities to discern and to act. If we cannot escape from our addiction to this sensory world, how can we attain the transcendent, unless we are assisted to do so? Might the transcendent that lures us to itself also provide the necessary enablement to achieve that goal?

The third family of "ladders of ascent" identified by Nussbaum does not rest on specifically Christian theological foundations, even though they may be interpreted in the light of such a framework.[21] This approach is found in Romanticism, which can be seen as attempting to bridge the gap between the natural and the transcendent. "Romantic imagination was a mediation between the worldly and otherworldly whose definitive act was the simulation of transcendental release."[22] As examples of such approaches, Nussbaum cites the "leap of desire" found in the writings of Emily Brontë, and the "theme of ascent" in the works of Gustav Mahler. This approach could easily be extended far beyond Nussbaum's

---

[19]   Clay Daniel, "Milton's Neo-Platonic Angel?" *Studies in English Literature* 44 (2004): 173–88.

[20]   Richard Eldridge, "Plights of Embodied Soul: Dramas of Sin and Salvation in Augustine and Updike," in *The Persistence of Romanticism: Essays in Philosophy and Literature*, pp. 205–28, Cambridge, UK: Cambridge University Press, 2001.

[21]   Nussbaum, *Upheavals of Thought*, pp. 591–678.

[22]   Alan Liu, "Local Transcendence: Cultural Criticism, Postmodernism, and the Romanticism of Detail," *Representations* 32 (1990): 75–113; quote at p. 76.

chosen representatives – for example, to include the "consolation literature" which became so significant a feature of American culture in the period following the Civil War.[23] Nussbaum's analysis here is an example of the continuing interest on the part of the academy in the transcendent, though coupled with an ambivalence towards specifically Christian construals of the notion.

The "ladder" approach to the transcendent is particularly well adapted for expressing the idea of self-transcendence – the desire to surpass our present situation, to rise above ourselves and go beyond our present limitations and horizons, whether this is articulated in humanist terms (as essentially a process of human growth), or in more Christian terms as dying to one's old self, and rising to a new way of life, through divine grace.

Seeing the Transcendent Through Nature

A second approach treats nature as a window, through which the transcendent may be viewed. It holds that nature is potentially transparent to the transcendent, allowing its radiance to irradiate the natural, tempered as appropriate by its defining characteristics.[24] It is a theme that is encountered throughout cultural history, whether religious or secular. The phrase "transparency to the transcendent" occurs, in various forms, in the writings of Karlfried Graf Durckheim (1896–1988), but has become particularly associated with the influential interpretation of mythology of Joseph Campbell (1904–87).[25] For Campbell, "transcendence" was the key

---

[23]   Ann Douglas, "Heaven Our Home: Consolation Literature in the Northern United States, 1830–1880," in Philippe Ariès and David E. Stannard (eds), *Death in America*, pp. 49–68, Philadelphia: University of Pennsylvania Press, 1975.
[24]   E.g., see Karlfried Graf Durckheim, *The Way of Transformation: Daily Life as Spiritual Exercise*, London: Allen & Unwin, 1988.
[25]   On which see David L. Miller, "The Flight of the Wild Gander: The Postmodern Meaning of 'Meaning'," in Daniel C. Noel (ed.), *Paths to the Power of Myth: Joseph Campbell and the Study of Religion*, pp. 108–17, New York: Crossroad, 1990; William D. Dinges, "Joseph Campbell and the Contemporary American Spiritual Milieu," in Lawrence Madden (ed.), *The Joseph Campbell Phenomenon*, pp. 9–40, Washington, DC: Pastoral, 1992.

to any correct understanding of mythology.[26] Although unknown and unknowable,[27] the transcendent could be known in various adapted and accommodated forms, which he referred to as "masks."

Campbell held that myths allowed "an opening of the sense of religious awe to some sphere of secular experience," thus enabling individuals within the secular world to gain a sense of wonder normally only associated with religious experience.[28] These myths – again, when rightly interpreted – were "transparent to transcendence."[29] Although insisting that the transcendent lay "beyond definition, categories, names and forms," being incapable of being represented fully, Campbell suggests that it could nevertheless be known through its "masks" – that is, through particular mythical narratives and images.[30] These "masks," according to Campbell, arise from human consciousness requiring some kind of symbolic interfaces with transcendence. Campbell, following Karlfried Graf Durkheim, insisted that mythic symbols and metaphors could become "opaque." This, he argues, tends to happen when the sign is confused with the thing that is signified, so that its transparency to the transcendent is compromised precisely on account of the sign's ceasing to act as a sign.

A similar theme can be found within Christian writings, particularly those of the English metaphysical poet George Herbert (1593–1633). The idea of "transparency to the transcendent" is here often represented

---

[26] Joseph Campbell, *The Hero's Journey: Joseph Campbell on His Life and Work*, Shaftesbury: Element, 1999, p. 162.

[27] Joseph Campbell, *The Power of Myth*, New York: Doubleday, 1988, p. 49.

[28] Joseph Campbell, *The Flight of the Wild Gander: Explorations in the Mythological Dimension*, New York: Viking Press, 1969, p. 193. For related ideas in J. R. R. Tolkien, see Verlyn Flieger, *Splintered Light: Logos and Language in Tolkien's World*, rev. edn, Kent, OH: Kent State University, 2002, pp. 67–72.

[29] Campbell, *The Hero's Journey*, p. 40.

[30] Campbell, *The Flight of the Wild Gander*, p. 196. Note that Campbell often uses the term "God" to refer to the transcendent in general, while reserving the phrase "masks of God" to denote its manifestations or disclosures in history. For the background to this notion, see Robert C. Neville, *Behind the Masks of God: An Essay Toward Comparative Theology*, Albany, NY: State University of New York Press, 1991. Neville argues that the limitations of such "masks" must be recognized, in that "divine reality is never exhausted in a finite collection of symbols or theological assertions" (pp. 168–9).

using the image of a window. In the poem "The Windows," Herbert ponders the question of how a preacher can be "a window, through thy grace" for the transcendent truths of faith. How can such a frail creature, made of "brittle crazie glasse," reflect the glory of God? For Herbert, the answer lies in divine grace, through which humanity "can become a window through which the glory of God shines,"[31] its limitations and shortcomings transcended.

Yet Herbert's most celebrated reflections on the transparency of the natural to the transcendent is to be found in his poem *The Elixir*.[32]

> A man that looks on glass,
> On it may stay his eye,
> Or, if he pleaseth, through it pass,
> And then the heav'n espy.

Herbert's imagery here develops a familiar Pauline image, as expressed in the language of the King James Bible – that of "seeing through a glass, darkly," knowing things only in part (1 Corinthians 13: 12). *The Elixir* subtly transposes this image, allowing it to illuminate the human attempt to view the transcendent.

In a similar way, in her essay "The Love of God and Affliction" Simone Weil speaks of nature becoming transparent to God as a window allows light access to a darkened room: "This obedience of things in relation to God is what the transparency of a window pane is in relation to light."[33] Yet she declines to limit the transcendent to the visible, often employing metaphors that imply that it is also tangible: "We must feel the reality

---

[31] T. R. Barnes, *English Verse: Voice and Movement*, Cambridge, UK: Cambridge University Press, 1967, pp. 73–4. See also Reuben Arthur Brower, *The Fields of Light: An Experiment in Critical Reading*, Oxford: Oxford University Press, 1951, pp. 44–5.

[32] For some helpful reflections on Herbert's theology, unfortunately making little reference to this theologically profound poem, see Elizabeth Clarke, *Theory and Theology in George Herbert's Poetry: "Divinitie and Poesy Met,"* Oxford: Clarendon Press, 1997. For the imagery of Christ as the philosopher's stone, see the important study of Stanton J. Linden, *Darke Hierogliphicks: Alchemy in English Literature from Chaucer to the Restoration*, Lexington, KY: University of Kentucky Press, 1996, pp. 190–2.

[33] Simone Weil, *On Science, Necessity and the Love of God*, London: Oxford University Press, 1968, p. 199.

and presence of God through all external things, without exception, as clearly as our hand feels the substance of paper through the penholder and the nib."[34] Weil's point is that one must develop an "apprenticeship" which enables us to cultivate habits of thought and ways of "reading" the book of nature which enable us to sense the transcendent through it, even though this may be obscure or unclear.[35]

Withdrawing from Nature to Find the Transcendent Within Oneself

The natural world offers a richness of visual and auditory stimulation. For some, this offers an invitation to reflect on what is seen and heard, as a means of deepening one's engagement with nature, and leading to an experience of the transcendent. For others, however, these sights and sounds overwhelm other more subtle "signals of transcendence."[36] It is by withdrawing from the distractions of worldly stimulation that one may concentrate on more subtle signals from within.[37]

This felt need to withdraw from the excessive stimulation of the natural realm underlies the discipline of "desert spirituality."[38] This approach holds that entering into the wilderness involves a stripping bare from internal and external distractions, freeing the individual to listen to the "voice within."[39] Withdrawal into the desert, silence, fasting – all these disciplines are means by which individuals can set distractions to one side, and, in theistic terms, come like Elijah to a place where they can hear the

---

[34] Simone Weil, *Waiting for God*, New York: Harper & Row, 1951, p. 44.

[35] Weil, *On Science, Necessity and the Love of God*, p. 180: "As one has to learn to read, or to practice a trade, so one must learn to feel in all things, first and almost solely, the obedience of the universe to God."

[36] Peter Berger, *A Rumor of Angels: Modern Society and the Rediscovery of the Supernatural*, Garden City, NY: Doubleday, 1969.

[37] This is a leading theme in the spirituality of Thomas Merton. See especially his essay "Notes for a Philosophy of Solitude," in *Disputed Questions*, New York: Farrar, Straus and Cudahy, 1960, pp. 177–207.

[38] See, for example, Belden C. Lane, *The Solace of Fierce Landscapes: Exploring Desert and Mountain Spirituality*, New York: Oxford University Press, 1998.

[39] Thomas Merton, *The Inner Experience: Notes on Contemplation*, San Francisco: HarperSanFrancisco, 2003, pp. 6–18.

"still, small voice" (1 Kings 19: 11–12).[40] The absence of sensory stimulation allows us to disregard and detach ourselves from the external, and focus on the internal pointers to transcendence – such as John Calvin's "sense of divinity," which he holds to be innate to human experience.[41] Yet it must also be noted that many spiritual writers suggest that some of the "voices" that may be heard are ones that need to be challenged, in that they might turn out to be one's own "personal demons," rather than the voice of God. The process of spiritual growth involves identifying and confronting these forces. This point is often explored with reference to the Gospel accounts of Jesus of Nazareth's temptation in the wilderness, in which these themes play a prominent role.[42]

So how is this "voice within" to be understood? William James pointed to the sixteenth-century Spanish spiritual writer Teresa of Avila (1515–82) as the "expert of experts" in describing the sensed revelation of new depths of truth.[43] Teresa spoke of the "ascent of the soul" in four stages, the first of which involves the disengagement of the person from external stimuli in order to develop a deepened internal awareness of the landscape of faith. Her image of the "interior castle of the soul" expresses the idea of an inner quest for the transcendent. In other religious traditions, especially Buddhism, substantially the same technique is developed, but directed towards alternative understandings of reality.[44] Meditation is seen

---

[40] The growing appreciation of the "spiritual disciplines" has been one of the most noticeable features of recent Protestant spirituality: see Richard J. Foster, Celebration of Discipline: The Path to Spiritual Growth, London: Hodder and Stoughton, 1989; Dallas Willard, "Spiritual Disciplines, Spiritual Formation, and Restoration of the Soul," Journal of Psychology and Theology 26 (1998): 101–9.

[41] Calvin identified two sources of a natural knowledge of God: the external ordering of the world, and the internal sensus divinitatis. See Paul Helm, "John Calvin, the Sensus Divinitatis and the Noetic Effects of Sin," International Journal of Philosophy of Religion 43 (1998): 87–107.

[42] See David L. Wee, "The Temptation of Christ and the Motif of Divine Duplicity in the Corpus Christi Cycle Drama," Modern Philology 72 (1974): 1–16.

[43] David M. Wulff, Psychology of Religion: Classic and Contemporary, 2nd edn, New York: Wiley, 1997, p. 488.

[44] See the collection of essays in Rita M. Gross and Terry C. Muck, Christians Talk About Buddhist Meditation, Buddhists Talk About Christian Prayer, London: Continuum, 2003.

as a means of breaking free from the illusions of the world, and discovering the depths of the inner being.[45]

This approach to experiencing the transcendent involves the development of practices aimed at facilitating the tuning into this inner landscape. Since human being are embodied selves, it is to be expected that such techniques should have demonstrable psychophysiological effects. Religious traditions have developed a range of techniques for the "deliberate facilitation of religious experience" – such as fasting, meditation, and other forms of spiritual discipline.[46] Since mystical experiences involve changes in brain chemistry,[47] there has been considerable interest recently in whether it might be possible to trigger such experiences by pharmacological means. Might there be ways of bringing about a more direct facilitation of these physiological changes as primary ways into this deep inner terrain where the transcendent is thought to be found, and which is removed from the natural external world?

This is not a new question. It is well known that many religious traditions have used a variety of naturally occurring substances – such as mescaline – in their rituals to achieve a heightened "spiritual" experience.[48] This has raised the question of whether psychedelic drugs, natural or synthetic, can facilitate or produce the kind of experience that many would describe as "religious" or "transcendent."[49] The growing availability of such substances has led to increased interest in drug-induced

---

[45] These approaches have often been interpreted or given a sense of intellectual direction using C. G. Jung's ideas of the "collective unconsciousness" and the "archetypes." On the basis of his analysis of the dreams and fantasies of his patients, Jung concluded that they could not be explained on the basis of their past experiences. They were, he argued, best understood as "primordial images," not arising from past experience, but from the human psyche. Archetypes were to be understood as "a kind of readiness to produce over and over again the same or similar mythical ideas": Wulff, *Psychology of Religion*, pp. 426–31.

[46] Wulff, *Psychology of Religion*, pp. 69–95.

[47] Studies of Zen meditation, for example, have indicated that there is at least a gross relationship between the brain wave patterns observed during meditation and the degree of "spiritual advancement" of the subject. Bernard Spilka, Ralph W. Hood, Bruce Hunsberger, and Richard Gorsuch, *The Psychology of Religion: An Empirical Approach*, 3rd edn, New York: The Guilford Press, 2003, pp. 257–69.

[48] For a list of such substances, see Wulff, *Psychology of Religion*, p. 91.

[49] Spilka et al., *The Psychology of Religion*, pp. 283–8.

experiences and experiences that many would regard as "transcendent" or "religious."[50] Some have argued that drug-induced experiences cannot be distinguished phenomenologically from allegedly "religious" or "transcendent" experiences. The term "entheogen" has been increasingly used to refer to such substances since about 1975, conveying the idea of bringing out the inner divine.

According to Samuel Taylor Coleridge, his poem *Kubla Khan* (1798) was the outcome of a period of sustained clarity resulting from opium-induced sleep. Its exploration of the relation of the human imagination to the "mystical" and "spiritual" has often been noted.[51] In May 1953, Aldous Huxley took mescaline under controlled conditions, in order to study its impact on his experience. Where terms like "the beatific vision" had previously meant nothing to him, he commented that "for the first time I understood, not on the verbal level, not by inchoate hints or at a distance, but precisely and completely what those prodigious syllables referred to." He found himself experiencing a "sacramental vision of reality,"[52] in which things were seen with a curious intensification. This has led some to suggest that such psychedelic drugs might be expected to be capable of triggering intense mystical or revelatory experiences, especially where the subjects are religious, and the context is conducive.[53]

One of the most widely discussed experiments in this field was carried out by Walter Pahnke (1931–71). After gaining degrees in theology and medicine from Harvard University, Pahnke undertook a study of drug-induced mystical experiences as part of his doctoral research. On Good Friday 1962, Pahnke conducted an experiment with 20 students from Andover-Newton Theological Seminary in which half were given 30 mg of psilocybin and half 200 mg of an active placebo in the context of a religious service. Pahnke's intention was to discover whether a psychedelic drug could engender a genuine religious experience. Nine out of ten of the students who received psilocybin reported religious or mystical experiences while only one of ten in the placebo group reported the

---

[50]   Andrew Weil, *The Natural Mind: An Investigation of Drugs and the Higher Consciousness*, rev. edn, Boston: Houghton Mifflin, 1986.

[51]   Robert F. Fleissner, *Sources, Meaning, and Influences of Coleridge's Kubla Khan: Xanadu Re-Routed: A Study in the Ways of Romantic Variety*, Lewiston, NY: Edwin Mellen, 2000.

[52]   Aldous Huxley, *The Doors of Perception*, London: Chatto & Windus, 1954.

[53]   Wulff, *Psychology of Religion*, p. 92.

same.[54] Pahnke concluded that such drugs were capable of triggering mystical experiences, under appropriate circumstances. In drawing this conclusion, Pahnke used an empirical measure of mysticism which had been developed earlier by W. T. Stace.[55] The debate over the implications of such studies continues.[56]

Discerning the Transcendent in Nature

The fourth approach to the question of how to gain access to the transcendent involves not so much a looking beyond or turning away from nature but engagement with nature through a process of discernment – that is, of adopting a certain way of looking at things, of "seeing" things as they really and actually are, which allows the observer to see the transcendent signified by, or indicated within, the natural order. There is no suggestion here of a distinct transcendent realm above, beyond, or even within the natural; rather, the natural is understood at least to disclose, and perhaps even to *become* the transcendent, *when rightly interpreted*. Without a particular hermeneutical framework, the natural remains as it was. There is no epiphany, no transfiguration, without discernment.

This general approach can easily be aligned with recent discussions of the nature of scientific observation. The traditional empiricist view held that observation was an essentially passive process in which information was received by, or imprinted on, the mind. Observation was thus regarded as a veridical process. This view has been successfully challenged, partly through the recognition of the active nature of the process of observation. William James's 1878 essay "Remarks on Spencer's Definition of Mind as Correspondence," which insisted upon the active nature of observation, emphasizes this point. According to James,

---

[54]   For a critical assessment of the experiment, see Wulff, *Psychology of Religion*, pp. 188–93.

[55]   The categories include (1) sense of unity, (2) transcendence of time and space, (3) sense of sacredness, (4) sense of objective reality, (5) deeply felt positive mood, (6) ineffability, (7) paradoxicality, and (8) transiency. See Spilka et al., *The Psychology of Religion*, pp. 320–3.

[56]   See Huston Smith, *Cleansing the Doors of Perception: The Religious Significance of Entheogenic Plants and Substances*, New York: Putnam, 2000.

The knower is an actor, and co-efficient of the truth on one side, whilst on the other he registers the truth which he helps to create. Mental interests, hypotheses, postulates, so far as they are bases for human action – action which to a great extent transforms the world – help to *make* the truth which they declare.[57]

This insight, it should be noted, does not pose a challenge to the notion that there exists a world, independent of the observer. It is to acknowledge that the knower is involved in the process of knowing, and that this involvement must somehow be expressed within a realist perspective on the world.[58]

Developing such insights, N. R. Hanson and others emphasized the importance of theoretical commitments, whether consciously articulated or not, in shaping how nature was observed. Nature is not merely *seen*; it is *seen as something*. The process of observation, he insisted, was theory-laden.[59] The essential point here is that observational terms often have theoretical notions embedded within them.[60] This does not call the reality of the external world into question, nor need it lead to unconstrained or

---

[57] William James, *Essays in Radical Empiricism*, Cambridge, MA: Harvard University Press, 1976, p. 21.

[58] These principles underlie most forms of modern critical realism – see, for example, Alister E. McGrath, *A Scientific Theology: 2 – Reality*, London: T&T Clark, 2002, pp. 195–244. For an alternative perspective, see Paul L. Allen, *Ernan McMullin and Critical Realism in the Science–Theology Dialogue*, Aldershot: Ashgate, 2006, pp. 13–47.

[59] N. R. Hanson, *Patterns of Discovery: An Inquiry into the Conceptual Foundations of Science*, Cambridge, UK: Cambridge University Press, 1958. For further discussion, see R. E. Grandy (ed.), *Theories and Observation in Science*, Englewood Cliffs, NJ: Prentice-Hall, 1973. The arguments of John Dewey are also of interest here: Christopher B. Kulp, *The End of Epistemology: Dewey and His Current Allies on the Spectator Theory of Knowledge*, Westport, CT: Greenwood Press, 1992, especially pp. 21–69.

[60] Hanson illustrates this by noting Galileo's use of the term "crater" to describe the "holes and discontinuities" he observed in the lunar surface through his telescope. This introduced a theoretical element into his observations: "To speak of a concavity as a crater is to commit oneself to its origin, to say that its creation was quick, violent, explosive," Hanson, *Patterns of Discovery*, p. 56.

arbitrary interpretation of nature.[61] Yet it does point to the importance of appreciating how nature may be actively "seen" in significantly different manners by different observers, who bring different conceptual frameworks to the active, constructive process of observation.[62]

The importance of this point is clear. The observer who is precommitted to seeing the world as devoid of any transcendent dimension will "see" nature in a manner that differs significantly from another observer, contemplating that same world, who "sees" it as being richly signed with vestiges and images of the divine.[63] Christian natural theology could perhaps be understood as the outcome of reading nature in the light of the trinitarian God. Bonaventure suggests that the many features of nature should be seen as "shadows, echoes and pictures" of God its creator, which "are set before us in order that we might know God."[64]

A slightly different, though related, approach is found in the *Spiritual Canticles* of John of the Cross. God is here portrayed as one who, having created the world, then passes through it, leaving a fragrance or imprint behind in doing so. For John, the process of discernment does not primarily concern a static presence of God within the world, but takes the form of discerning the trail of God's active and personal movement through the world, leaving signs and marks that can be identified and appreciated by those with insight.

---

[61] See Shelby D. Hunt, "A Realist Theory of Empirical Testing Resolving the Theory-Ladenness/Objectivity Debate," *Philosophy of the Social Sciences* 24 (1994): 133–58; William F. Brewer and Bruce L. Lambert, "The Theory-Ladenness of Observation and the Theory-Ladenness of the Rest of the Scientific Process," *Philosophy of Science* 68 (2001): S176–86.

[62] This does not, of course, imply that such theoretical frameworks are permanent fixtures. Perceived accumulated tensions between theory and experiences are the most significant factor in bringing about theory change in both science and religion. For the classic presentation of this point, see Thomas S. Kuhn, *The Structure of Scientific Revolutions*, 2nd edn, Chicago: University of Chicago Press, 1970.

[63] Compare the very different readings of nature found in Richard Dawkins, *Unweaving the Rainbow: Science, Delusion and the Appetite for Wonder*, London: Penguin, 1998, and Thomas Aquinas's *Summa contra Gentiles*. On the latter, see especially Norman Kretzmann, *The Metaphysics of Creation: Aquinas's Natural Theology in Summa Contra Gentiles II*, Oxford: Clarendon Press, 1999.

[64] Bonaventure, *Itinerarium Mentis in Deum*, 2.

O forests and woods,
Planted by the hand of my beloved!
O meadow of greenness,
Embellished with flowers,
Has he passed by you?
Pouring out a thousand graces,
He passed by these groves in haste,
And, having looked at them
With only his countenance,
Clothed them with beauty.[65]

In seeking God, the poet aims to contemplate God's footprints (*vestigia*) and other signs of God's wayfaring within the creation. God cannot be seen face to face; nevertheless, God's fragrance can be sensed, and the trail discerned after God has passed through the world. God creates, inhabits, and traverses the natural order.

The basic principle of discerning the divine in nature is also a feature of the parables of Jesus of Nazareth, which we shall explore more thoroughly later in this work. Yet here the notion of active seeing is also sharply emphasized: though the natural world is open to public gaze, its proper interpretation is hidden. The "mystery of the kingdom," though presented in a publicly accessible form, remains opaque to those lacking the capacity to discern it. A further biblical example is the account of the calling of Samuel (1 Samuel 3), in which the disclosure of the divine call takes place within the natural order, and is initially mistaken for part of that natural realm. The issue is that of *discernment* – the "seeing" (or "hearing") of the divine presence and activity within and under the natural, not over and above it. We shall return to consider both these important examples later in this work (pp. 118–26, 174–7).[66]

---

[65] *Cántico espirituel* 3–4, in John of the Cross, *Obras completas*, Burgos: Editorial Monte Carmelo, 2000, pp. 694–5.

[66] This approach to the transcendent is often linked with the notion of "transignification" – a change in the perceived significance of an entity, rather than a change in the entity itself. Although this idea can be found in secular cultural debates, it is particularly associated with Christian discussions about the meaning of the eucharistic bread and wine: do these change their identity, their inner nature – and hence their signification? For a classic analysis, see Joseph Ratzinger, "Das Problem der Transubstantiation und der Frage nach dem Sinne der Eucharistie," *Theologische Quartalschrift* 147 (1967): 129–58. See also John H. McKenna, "Eucharistic Presence: An Invitation to Dialogue," *Theological Studies* 60 (1999): 294–332.

All the examples noted thus far have to do with discerning God, as creator, in nature. It is of no small importance to note that such an approach appears to resonate particularly well with a Christian view of reality. However, it is equally important to note that this approach is also adopted by those who do not insist on equating the transcendent and the divine. Percy Bysshe Shelley, for example, in rejecting any Christian notion of God, nevertheless held that some nameless transcendent power could be discerned within nature. In his "Hymn to Intellectual Beauty," for example, Shelley posits an intuited higher "power," which saturates nature with its presence and beauty.[67]

> The awful shadow of some unseen Power
> Floats though unseen among us, – visiting
> This various world with as inconstant wing
> As summer winds that creep from flower to flower.

Nature thus elicits the knowledge of "some unseen power," whose shadow can be discerned within its order and structures.[68]

One important consequence of this approach to accessing the transcendent (by discerning it within the natural order) is its dissolving of the distinction, widely believed to originate in its present form during the Middle Ages, between the "natural" and "supernatural."[69] A rejection of any valid theological distinction between "nature" and "supernature" is a leading feature of the approach to natural theology associated with Thomas F. Torrance. In his discussion of the "transformation of natural

---

[67] For this theme in Romantic writings of this period, see especially Martin Priestman, *Romantic Atheism: Poetry and Freethought, 1780–1830*, Cambridge, UK: Cambridge University Press, 1999, pp. 219–52.

[68] Many other examples of such secular notions of transcendence could be mentioned – such as those encountered in early New England transcendentalism: Paul F. Boller, *American Transcendentalism, 1830–1860: An Intellectual Inquiry*, New York: Putnam, 1974, pp. 64–98. During his agnostic period (1859–75), Ruskin retained his belief that the transcendent could be known through an aesthetic appreciation of nature: George P. Landow, *The Aesthetic and Critical Theories of John Ruskin*, Princeton, NJ: Princeton University Press, 1971.

[69] For historical and theological comment, see Spencer Pearce, "Nature and Supernature in the Dialogues of Girolamo Fracastoro," *Sixteenth Century Journal* 27 (1996): 111–32; John Milbank, *The Suspended Middle: Henri de Lubac and the Debate Concerning the Supernatural*, London: SCM Press, 2005.

theology," which formed part of the 1978 Richards Lectures, given at the University of Virginia at Charlottesville, Torrance pointed out the implications of the characteristic insight of Athanasius of Alexandria that knowledge of God and knowledge of the world share the same ultimate foundations in the rationality of God the creator. There is no need to invoke a distinction between "natural" and "supernatural" knowledge, in that these are both integrated within Athanasius's understanding of God and the world, which finds its focus in the doctrine of the incarnation. Natural theology, when rightly understood, is to be embedded within an "integrated theological understanding of creation and redemption."[70]

For some, the process of discerning God within nature is to be grounded in the philosophy of panentheism. This posits a divinity which, while interpenetrating every part of nature, is nevertheless fully distinct from the natural. For the panentheist, God is present in all things, while nevertheless extending beyond the realm of nature.[71] The term – if not the idea – appears to have been introduced to English language theology by William Inge, sometime Dean of St Paul's Cathedral, London. In his 1906 Paddock Lectures, delivered at the General Theological Seminary, New York, Inge spoke of new possibilities for natural theology, based on an appeal to an awareness of the presence of the divine within the natural order.[72] Its most significant development is generally regarded to lie in the "process philosophy" of Alfred North Whitehead (1861–1947), as set out in *Process and Reality* (1929).[73] This philosophy is characterized by its

---

[70] Published as Thomas F. Torrance, *The Ground and Grammar of Theology*, Charlottesville, VA: The University of Virginia Press, 1980, pp. 77–8.

[71] The best manifesto for such an approach is currently Philip Clayton and A. R. Peacocke (eds), *In Whom We Live and Move and Have Our Being: Panentheistic Reflections on God's Presence in a Scientific World*, Grand Rapids, MI: Eerdmans, 2004. For its Orthodox expression, see John O'Donnell, "The Trinitarian Panentheism of Sergej Bulgakov," *Gregorianum* 76 (1995): 31–45. This is not to be confused with pantheism, which denies the theistic view that God transcends the world; if one is to speak of "pantheistic transcendence," this must be located within the natural world itself: see Michael P. Levine, *Pantheism: A Non-Theistic Concept of Deity*, London: Routledge, 1994, pp. 97–117.

[72] William R. Inge, *Personal Idealism and Mysticism*, 2nd edn, London: Longmans, Green, 1913, p. 69.

[73] Alfred North Whitehead, *Process and Reality: An Essay in Cosmology*, New York, Macmillan, 1929.

view of God inhabiting the "process"[74] as one who is able to influence its development from within.

In this chapter, we have described four attitudes towards how the transcendent may be known in relationship with nature. While none of them are specifically Christian, it will be clear that two of them have a particular resonance with fundamental themes of the Christian tradition. The idea of "seeing the transcendent through nature" is given theological weight and legitimation, especially by the doctrine of creation; that of "discerning the transcendent in nature" by the doctrine of the incarnation. Both approaches require a degree of engagement with nature, on the one hand, and a "discerning eye" – a capacity to interpret or approach nature in a certain way – on the other. We shall develop this point further later in this book.

From what has been said, it is clear that the human interest in encountering or experiencing the transcendent requires a certain kind of perceptiveness. So how do human beings perceive the world? The perception of the transcendent takes place within this world, on the basis of the parameters of natural human faculties. In the final chapter of this descriptive account of human attempts to experience the transcendent, we therefore turn to consider the psychology of human perception.

---

[74] For an explanation of this term, see Nicholas Rescher, *Process Metaphysics: An Introduction to Process Philosophy*. Albany, NY: State University of New York Press, 1996, pp. 38–42, and *Process Philosophy: A Survey of Basic Issues*, Pittsburgh, PA: University of Pittsburgh Press, 2000, pp. 22–58. Whitehead's development of a philosophy of organism reflects his basic concern to develop continuity between the biological, physical, and psychological sciences. On this approach, any distinctive characteristic of human beings – such as consciousness – had to be present, at least in an incipient form, at lower levels within the process, in order that it could emerge when an appropriate level of complexity of organization had developed. Whitehead thus regarded God as an essential element within the process, to ensure its stability and explain the law-like regularities in the wider process of becoming. While this approach to God's presence within the world does not entail the negation of God's transcendence, it requires at least some degree of redefinition. Such redefinition may be found in Charles Hartshorne, *The Divine Relativity: A Social Conception of God*, New Haven, CT: Yale University Press, 1948, p. 20, which speaks of God as "the self-surpassing surpasser of all." For comment, see Daniel A. Dombrowski, *Analytic Theism, Hartshorne, and the Concept of God*, Albany, NY: State University of New York Press, 1996.

CHAPTER 5

Discernment and the Psychology of Perception*

Discerning the transcendent within nature involves engagement *with* nature. This is also true, to an extent, of an approach to nature that sees it as a sign or pointer to the transcendent. But the relationship between human beings and nature is complex. Humans inhabit the natural world, are dependent on it and subject to its laws. They are also observers of the natural world, uniquely capable of both what might be called "quasi-objective" thought about nature and "reflexive" thought about themselves as part of nature. More than any other species humans can act strategically on the natural world, using their knowledge of nature to enable "transcendence" of some of the limitations it would otherwise impose upon them. Perhaps uniquely among animals, human beings are aware of their own mortality and the inevitability of death – that despite their technological sophistication they will eventually succumb to natural processes. The inevitability of death signals something else. Human beings are not simply located within the natural order; they are *part of it*.[1]

---

* Note that this chapter was written by Joanna Collicutt, lecturer in the psychology of religion at Heythrop College, London University.

[1] Antonio R. Damasio, *Descartes' Error: Emotion, Reason, and the Human Brain*, New York: Putnam, 1994, p. 118: "The mind is embodied, in the full sense of the term, not just embrained." For a critical response see, e.g., Shaun Gallagher, *How the Body Shapes the Mind*, Oxford: Clarendon Press, 2005, pp. 133–6.

Human beings are embodied, and human minds are embrained.[2] Without brain function there can be no mental life, as least as we commonly understand it. Our awareness of our inner and outer worlds is dependent on adequate function of our brains, specifically the cerebral cortex and upper portions of the brainstem.[3] Neither science, nor our own experience, provides any support for the existence of disembodied human minds in this world.[4] The neurologists Jeffrey Saver and John Rabin argue that *all* human experience – including religious experience – is "brain-based," regarding this "as an unexceptional claim."[5]

To recognize that all human experience – including transcendent, religious, and aesthetic experience – is brain-based, is not to embrace a reductionist position in which higher human consciousness is somehow explained away as a series of events in the cerebral cortex.[6] It is not to adjudicate on either side of the rather sterile debate about whether mind

---

[2]   See, e.g., Francisco J. Varela, Evan Thompson, and Eleanor Rosch, *The Embodied Mind: Cognitive Science and Human Experience*, Cambridge, MA: MIT Press, 1991; George Lakoff and Mark Johnson, *Philosophy in the Flesh: The Embodied Mind and its Challenge to Western Thought*, New York: Basic Books, 1999, p. 536: "Real human reason is embodied, mostly imaginative and metaphorical, largely unconscious and emotionally engaged."

[3]   J. Adams, D. Graham, and B. Jennet, "The Neuropathology of the Vegetative State after an Acute Brain Insult," *Brain* 123 (2000): 1327–38.

[4]   Disembodied nonhuman minds may be another matter. There is a tendency for people to believe in supernatural agents such as ghosts, spirits, and ancestors. See Justin L. Barrett, *Why Would Anyone Believe in God?* Lanham, MD: AltaMira Press, 2004, pp. 21–30.

[5]   J. Saver and J. Rabin. "The Neural Substrates of Religious Experience," *Journal of Neuropsychiatry & Clinical Neuroscience* 9 (1997): 498–510; quote at p. 498. For a more detailed discussion, see Warren S. Brown, Nancey C. Murphy, and H. Newton Malony (eds), *Whatever Happened to the Soul? Scientific and Theological Portraits of Human Nature*, Minneapolis: Fortress Press, 1998. Some have registered concern at this point, suggesting that this represents a new form of Cartesianism, replacing the old dialectic of "mind–body" with that of "brain–body": e.g., Max R. Bennett and Peter M. S. Hacker, *Philosophical Foundations of Neuroscience*, Oxford: Blackwell, 2003, p. 114.

[6]   A point stressed in many of the contributions to Rafael E. Núñez and Walter J. Freeman (eds), *Reclaiming Cognition: The Primacy of Action, Intention and Emotion*, Bowling Green, OH: Imprint Academic, 1999.

---

activity causes brain activity or vice versa.[7] Neither is it to rule out the reality of the transcendent (however this is construed). It is merely to assert that for human beings in this world the transcendent is accessed, and the spiritual life expressed exclusively through the medium of our material bodies. Just as we are mortal so are we material beings. Dallas Willard, a contemporary philosopher with interests in Christian spirituality, puts it this way:

> Spirituality in human beings is not an extra or "superior" mode of existence. It's not a hidden stream of separate reality, a separate life running in parallel with our bodily existence. . . . It is, rather, a relationship of our *embodied selves* to God that has the natural and irrepressible effect of making us alive to the Kingdom of God here and now in the *material world*.[8]

This understanding leads to the important insight that human discernment of the transcendent within the natural world takes place within the parameters of naturally endowed human perceptual abilities: psychological processes underpinned by a living material substance – the human brain. Human beings remain located within the natural world, even when experiencing and reflecting on what might be termed "the spiritual" or "the transcendent." Functional cognitive and perceptual systems are a necessary – though of course not *sufficient* – condition for seeing the natural world in a particular way (and in fact are also necessary for experiences of leaving this world behind).[9] Furthermore, these natural

---

[7] For an interesting discussion of the issues here see Margaret Boden, "Consciousness and Human Identity: An Interdisciplinary Perspective," in J. Cornwell (ed.), *Consciousness and Human Identity*, pp. 1–20. Oxford: Oxford University Press, 1998.

[8] Dallas Willard, *The Spirit of the Discipline: Understanding how God Changes Lives*, London: Hodder & Stoughton, 1988, p. 31 (my emphasis).

[9] Biblical accounts are interesting in this respect. Note the very clear locating in physical place and real time of the visionary experiences described in Isaiah 6: 1, Ezekiel 8: 1, Daniel 10: 4–5, Acts 10: 9, and Revelation 1: 9–10. Of course the grounding in a specific time and place may reflect literary convention at least as much as it reflects a psychological or spiritual phenomenon. The times and places chosen by a biblical writer may have a particular significance. For instance, the location of John's vision on Patmos and Ezekiel's vision in Babylon may communicate an assurance of God's presence in a place of exile: Christopher Rowland, *The Open Heaven:*

faculties not only indicate the setting conditions for the human engagement with nature. They may also act as pointers to, or bear the imprint of, something that lies beyond.

It follows from what has been said that any attempt to understand how human beings respond to the natural world – even where this response may be described as "spiritual" – requires a consideration of cognitive neuroscience. This chapter therefore gives a basic account of current understandings of human perception informed by the disciplines of cognitive psychology, developmental psychology, neuropsychology, and neurology.

The emergence of the modern concept of "perception" is a fascinating subject in its own right, demonstrating a growing concern to inject evidence-based approaches to the process of human understanding, in the face of rival rationalist theories.[10] The very earliest experimental psychologists drew a distinction between "sensation" – the taking in of data by the individual senses (for instance sensing heat against one's skin) – and "perception" – the combining and making sense of those data (perceiving that one's hand is resting on a hot-plate).[11] This model has been superseded by contemporary cognitive psychology, which has shown the situation to be far more complex, with the simple conceptual distinction between sensation and perception now being recognized as unsustainable. Nevertheless, the basic notion of perception being a "making sense"

A Study of Apocalyptic in Judaism and Early Christianity, London: SPCK, 1982, p. 59. Yet this literary convention, the choice of physical place and time to signify deeper truths, is completely consistent with an understanding of spiritual experience – including journeys and ascents to other worlds where the body feels as if it has been left behind – that is grounded in this world. Paul's discussion of a bodily "thorn" in juxtaposition with his account of a heavenly ascent is particularly enlightening in this respect (2 Corinthians 12: 7). The medieval "other-world" literature, particularly Dante's *Commedia*, is also significant: Alison Morgan, *Dante and the Medieval Other World*, Cambridge, UK: Cambridge University Press, 1990.

[10] For the earlier period, see John W. Yolton, *Perception and Reality: A History from Descartes to Kant*, Ithaca, NY: Cornell University Press, 1996. A more general survey may be found in D. W. Hamlyn, *Sensation and Perception: A History of the Philosophy of Perception*, London: Routledge & Kegan Paul, 1961.

[11] Hermann von Helmholtz, *Handbuch der physiologischen Optik*, Leipzig: Voss, 1867. For a translation and bibliography, see James P. C. Southall, *Helmholtz's treatise on physiological optics*. 3 vols. Bristol: Thoemmes, 2000.

---

of sensory input remains helpful, and forms the basis of the account which follows.

Perception is Brain-Based

Human beings deal with sensory information coming from the outside world and from our own inner organs. These sensory organs are highly specialized, and respond to light waves, sound waves, physical touch, pressure, vibration, movement, and characteristics of the chemical composition of the environment. Each of these sensory organs operates through its own specific processes, such as the chemical reactions in the cells of the retina in the eye or the mechanical vibration of the small bones in the middle ear. Yet all are connected to nerve cells that operate through a single type of process – the transmission of electrical impulses, via a number of relay stations in the brain, to a final destination also in the brain. The construction (or perhaps reconstruction[12]) of meaning from raw sensory information is a largely unconscious process underpinned by activity in both relay stations and final destinations in the brain, and it is this brain-based process of perception that corresponds to our subjective experience of the world. We experience painful or erotic touch, taste anchovies, see a rose, hear a baby cry, know we have just tripped and are about to fall, through the activity of our brains.

The phenomena of *cortical blindness* and *visual agnosia* illustrate this well, and will now be discussed in some detail. Visual experience occurs when light falls on the receptor cells in the retina at the back of the eye causing chemical changes in these cells, which in turn lead to electrical impulses passing along nerve cells in the visual pathways that terminate in the *visual cortex* of the brain. The brain is divided into two essentially symmetrical cerebral hemispheres, and the visual cortex of each hemisphere is a relatively large area towards the rear in the *occipital lobes*. It is highly complex in organization. The arrangement of the cells in the visual cortex is like a series of maps of the *visual fields*[13] of the eyes.

---

[12]   For the theme of experience as reconstruction in the philosophy of John Dewey, see Thomas M. Alexander, *John Dewey's Theory of Art, Experience, and Nature: The Horizons of Feeling*, Albany, NY: State University of New York Press, 1987, p. 96.

[13]   The visual field of each eye is the area in the environment from which the retina can receive light rays at any one moment, its "view."

Each map plots out the visual field in terms of specific physical features of varying complexity such as orientation, color, and movement.

The pathways coming from each eye cross over each other at quite an early point in their journey to the visual cortex in such a way that each half of the visual cortex receives information from half the visual field of both eyes, rather than from all the visual field of one eye. The visual cortex in the left cerebral hemisphere receives information from the right visual field and vice versa.

It is obvious that if the eyes are damaged visual impairment or blindness will result. What should be clear from the above account is that blindness can also arise from damage to the *pathways* that lead from the eye to the visual cortex, even if the eye is intact and responding to light input normally, because the visual cortex is receiving either no input or degraded input from the visual pathway. This is the sort of visual impairment that can, sadly, be a feature of some forms of multiple sclerosis.

Even if the eyes themselves and most of the visual pathways are intact, visual impairment can still occur if the visual cortex (the destination) itself is damaged. This can happen when its blood supply is cut off, for instance as the result of a stroke. This results in the phenomenon of *visual field loss*, where only parts of the visual field can be seen accurately, if at all.[14] In extreme cases the entire visual cortex on both sides of the brain can be damaged with resultant cortical blindness. In these cases the eyes and visual pathways are completely intact, and information is received and transmitted by the sense organs and visual pathways entirely normally. But the visual cortex cannot register this information. The person cannot see.

Visual agnosia is a more subtle and even more interesting phenomenon, and for our purposes it is perhaps more instructive. It can occur when a different part of the cerebral cortex, further forward in the *temporal lobes*, but connected to the visual cortex, is damaged. In cases of visual

---

[14]   For instance, if the blood supply to the visual cortex of the right side of the brain has been compromised loss or abnormality of vision in the left visual field will occur. The individual will not be able to see the left side of space when staring straight ahead, and must learn to compensate by turning his or her head. (This is a fairly common scenario. The two cerebral hemispheres have largely independent blood supplies. This is why there is often also paralysis or weakness on only one side of the body after a stroke.)

agnosia the individual can see objects but cannot identify them. That is, because the eyes, the visual pathways, and visual cortex are intact, the person can process the physical characteristics of the environment adequately. What goes wrong is the linking of these physical characteristics with stored knowledge of *meaning*. A person of normal intelligence who has this problem, when confronted with an apple typically would be unable to name it but might say, "It's round, it has a smooth shiny surface, it's green, it has something hard and brown sticking out of the top – do you use it for combing your hair?"

These examples of cortical blindness and visual agnosia illustrate a number of points. First, intact brain function is essential to normal perception. Secondly, the process of perception is highly complex and involves multiple components. Thirdly, this process involves coherent and connected representations of physical information gathered by the sense organs. Fourthly, it also involves representations that are based on memory for meaning, function, and significance. Fifthly, while these multiple processes and representations work seamlessly together in normal perception, and thus give the impression that perception is a simple and unitary process, the fact that they can become dissociated from each other, for instance in the case of visual agnosia, shows that what is crucial to perception is the linking of incoming sensory input to an existing understanding of the world. People with visual agnosia can "see" – but they cannot make sense of what they see. To use the words of Isaiah 6: 9, they literally "see without perceiving." We shall develop this point in relation to the parables of Jesus of Nazareth in Chapter 6.

Perception Involves Dynamic Mental Structures

Perception involves the making of representations. In psychology, these are often referred to as *schemas* (or *schemata*). It is helpful to think of these as mental maps of the world, sets of rules or scripts for negotiating the world, or more typological-based systems (or schemes) for classifying the world. Schemas are invoked in psychological accounts of many aspects of mental functioning, especially that involving conceptual thought. Our present discussion concentrates upon *perceptual* schemas, but also includes some examples of conceptual schemas.

In the adult, perception is essentially a fitting of sensory input into schemas of varying complexity that represent the individual's environment in terms of its spatial layout, the identity of objects, and the relationship between them.[15] Thus the process of perception is rather like a multiple-choice examination. To identify an object the question to be answered is essentially of the sort, "Does it fit a, b, c, or none of the above?" rather than the more open, "What is it?" There is a good reason for perception to proceed in this way. It is the same as the reason why multiple-choice examination questions were developed. It is economical in terms of effort and time.

Schemas help make the world understandable because they make it more predictable and manageable. They organize a potentially overwhelming amount of sensory information into bite-size chunks. Schemas have to be sufficiently flexible to be applicable to a wide range of sensory input. Their effectiveness depends on sensory input being reasonably regular and amenable to organization. The process of fitting sensory input into perceptual schemas does, nevertheless, involve some degree of distortion. Schemas facilitate the processing of information but also have the potential not just to oversimplify but to introduce systematic bias. This is especially the case where existing schemas cannot begin to do justice to the sensory information on which they are operating – where the answer to the multiple-choice question is "None of the above." A nice example of this, involving higher order conceptual schemas, can be found in John 1: 19–23, where the priests and Levites run through a number of hypotheses about the identity of John the Baptist before being told

---

[15] While these schemas are clearly constrained to some degree by the organization of the brain, it is important to understand that they may not necessarily be identified with single brain centers. A schema may actually correspond to the synchronized activity of a number of specific nerve cells in widely distributed parts of the brain. For instance, the schematic representation of an apple is likely to include, among other things, the habitual actions that are associated with it, not just its visual features. There is no "apple center" in the brain (just as there is no "God spot": see, e.g., Mario Beauregard and Vincent Paquette, "Neural Correlates of a Mystical Experience in Carmelite Nuns," *Neuroscience Letters* 405 (2006): 186–90). This is why an individual with visual agnosia, who cannot say and genuinely does not know what the function of an apple might be when questioned directly, may nevertheless pick one up and eat it perfectly appropriately in the context of a meal. The action parts of the apple schema have remained intact because the corresponding parts of the brain have escaped damage.

explicitly "None of the above" (the Messiah, Elijah, or the prophet). This response calls forth more questioning and perplexity, itself typical of the human response to the challenge posed by sensory information that "doesn't fit."[16]

So where do perceptual schemas come from? The development of perceptual and conceptual schemas in the young child is a question that has exercised psychologists for many years. As William James put it in 1890, the newborn child is faced with an environment which is potentially nothing but a "blooming, buzzing confusion." Are there essentially universal pre-existent mental structures waiting to come into play from birth and through childhood to help a child make sense of this environment, or do they develop as a result of the child's experience in the world? A wealth of experiments carried out over the last century indicates that both of these are true to some extent. For instance, children enter the world with surprisingly good abilities to locate objects.[17] They also seem to be preprogrammed to develop perceptually in certain directions, and "from an early age to form categories and

---

[16] A similar pattern, again at the conceptual rather than the perceptual level, can be seen in the development of Christology in the early church. Historical analysis of this process suggests that the first Christians may be thought of as developing "tacit Christologies," initially through attempting to make their experience of Jesus of Nazareth conform to existing models, absorbed from the two sources that the early church knew best: Judaism and the Hellenistic paganism of the eastern Mediterranean region. For reflections on this process, see Alister E. McGrath, "Assimilation in the Development of Doctrine: The Theological Significance of Jean Piaget," in Alister E. McGrath (ed.), *The Order of Things: Explorations in Scientific Theology*, pp. 169–82. Oxford: Blackwell Publishing, 2006. For an excellent recent survey of the issues contested within early Judean Jewish Christianity, see Larry W. Hurtado, *Lord Jesus Christ: Devotion to Jesus in Earliest Christianity*, Grand Rapids, MI: Eerdmans, 2003, pp. 155–216; Friedrich Prinz, "Die Kirche und die pagane Kulturtradition. Formen der Abwehr, Adaption und Anverwandlung," *Historische Zeitschrift* 276 (2002): 281–303. For an eventual revision of the categories or schemas used to characterize Jesus of Nazareth, see Rowan Williams, "Does it Make Sense to Speak of Pre-Nicene Orthodoxy?" in Rowan Williams (ed.), *The Making of Orthodoxy*, pp. 1–23, Cambridge, UK: Cambridge University Press, 1989.

[17] T. G. R. Bower, *Development in Infancy*, 2nd edn, San Francisco: W. H. Freeman, 1982.

use those categories to organise and make sense of the world around them."[18]

The cognitive structures that humans use to represent the physical world are not random or infinitely variable. For instance even quite young babies appear to be well attuned to statistical correlations between features of the environment, and also to conditional probabilities linking the occurrence of events.[19] As David Hume pointed out, this is the basis of the more developed abstract concept of causality, and it thus appears that human beings come into the world "prepared" to infer causal relationships.[20] However, it appears that it is the experience of *action* in the world of both physical objects and social relationships that enables these mental maps to be fully articulated.[21] For instance, the influential Swiss developmental psychologist Jean Piaget (1896–1980) and subsequent investigators have shown that the concept that an object is a "thing" itself involves an amalgamation of the concept of place and of movement, arrived at through close observation of the behavior of objects.[22]

Thus the process of developing perceptual schemas seems to be one of active construction of representations of the physical world, but

---

[18] Lisa M. Oakes and David H. Rakison, "Issues in the Early Developments of Concepts and Categories," in L. M. Oakes and D. H. Rakison (eds), *Early Category Development: Making Sense of the Blooming, Buzzing Confusion*, pp. 1–20, Oxford: Oxford University Press, 2003; quote at p. 20.

[19] See, e.g., J. Saffran, R. Aslin, and E. Newport, "Statistical Learning by 8-Month-Old Infants," *Science* 274 (1996): 1926–8; R. Aslin, J. Saffran, and E. Newport, "Computation of Conditional Probability Statistics by 8-Month-Old Infants," *Psychological Science 9* (1998): 321–4. For an accessible and comprehensive discussion see A. Gopnik, A. Meltzoff, and P. Kuhl, *The Scientist in the Crib: What Early Learning Tells us About the Mind*, New York, Harper Collins, 2001.

[20] For an exhaustive discussion, see Fred Wilson, *Hume's Defence of Causal Inference*, Toronto: University of Toronto Press, 1997.

[21] See Lev S. Vygotsky, *Mind in Society: The Development of Higher Psychological Processes*, Cambridge, MA: Harvard University Press, 1978; Margaret C. Donaldson, *Children's Minds*, London: Fontana Press, 1987.

[22] Jean Piaget, *The Construction of Reality in the Child*, London: Routledge & Kegan Paul, 1955; T. G. R. Bower and J. Patterson, "The Separation of Place, Movement and Time in the World of the Infant," *Journal of Experimental Child Psychology* 15 (1973): 161–8.

---

many of the constructions arrived at themselves seem to be largely invariant. Children acquire basic concepts of color, number, identity, and so forth in a particular developmental order with small variation between cultures. The elaboration and verbal expression of these basic physical concepts may, however, be highly influenced by culture.[23] While some schemas, or components of schemas, are largely "culture-free," others, especially those incorporating verbal classification systems, are culture-dependent.[24]

The account of perception that we have given thus far is of a dialectic process in which sensory input is made sense of in terms of pre-existing perceptual schemas, which have themselves developed as part of the process of acting on sensory input. The perceiver both acts on the world and is acted upon by the world. Processing is both top-down and bottom-up. The perceiver organizes data, but the organizational system employed is itself influenced by the type of data it is required to handle, and has some invariant features or predispositions built into it, presumably as the outcome of natural selection.

The two sides of this process have been referred to as "assimilation of" and "accommodation to" the world by Piaget.[25] For Piaget, there exists a process of "reflecting abstraction" through which human beings interact with their environment. Human beings are not born with such structures, nor do they absorb them passively from their environment: they construct them through a process of interaction (which Piaget terms

---

[23] Jean Piaget, "Intellectual Evolution from Adolescence to Adulthood," *Human Development* 15 (1972): 1–12; P. M. Greenfield and C. P. Childs, "Understanding Sibling Concepts: A Developmental Study of Kin Terms in Zinacantan," in P. Dasen (ed.), *Piagetian Psychology: Cross-Cultural Contributions*, pp. 335–58, New York: Gardner Press, 1977; Angeline S. Lillard, "Ethnopsychologies: Cultural Variations in Theory of Mind," *Psychological Bulletin* 123 (1998): 2–32; Michael Tomasello, *The Cultural Origins of Human Cognition*, Cambridge, MA: Harvard University Press, 2000.
[24] The perception of color is particularly salutary in this respect. For a helpful discussion see Varela et al., *The Embodied Mind*, pp. 157–71.
[25] Jean Piaget, *The Origins of Intelligence in the Child*, London: Routledge & Kegan Paul, 1952. Piaget thus uses the term "accommodation" in a sense which is quite distinct from that found in much theological writing: see the comments at note 75. This clearly has the potential to create considerable confusion for psychologically uninformed theologians.

"equilibration"),[26] in which equilibrium is achieved between assimilation and accommodation. Assimilation may be defined as the "act of incorporating objects or aspects of objects into learned activities," where accommodation is "the modification of an activity or ability in the face of environmental demands."[27] Generally these two processes balance each other, but accommodation to the world begins to dominate when the perceiver encounters phenomena that do not readily fit into existing schemas. This sort of situation involves cognitive challenge and possibly stress, but the outcome may often be a reorganization or development of schemas so that they are more differentiated, complex, and in keeping with the sensory phenomena.[28] Thus there is a cycle of assimilation–challenge–accommodation–assimilation–challenge–accommodation underpinning the process of perception and its development.[29]

Mental representations of the world must underpin behavior that is effective – that is, behavior that has good survival value. For instance, being able to interpret sensory data as indicating that a hard object is rapidly moving towards you enables you to move out of the way and avoid death or injury. To this extent perception is data driven and realistic – it has real consequences for the perceiver. But the mental representation itself may not necessarily be a literal veridical reproduction of the way the

---

[26] Jean Piaget, "Problems of Equilibration," in M. H. Appel and L. S. Goldberg (eds), *Topics in Cognitive Development*, vol. 1, pp. 3–14, New York: Plenum, 1977.
[27] As defined by Guy R. Lefrançois, *Theories of Human Learning*, 3rd edn, Pacific Grove, CA: Brooks/Cole Publishers, 1995, pp. 329–30.
[28] See Ronnie Janoff-Bulamn, *Shattered Assumptions*, New York: Free Press, 1992; R. Tedsechi and L. Calhoun, *Trauma and Transformation*, Thousand Oaks, CA: Sage, 1995, for accounts of how this process may occur in the adult in response to adversity and trauma.
[29] Note how this account of perception is strikingly similar to Kuhnian accounts of the scientific endeavor, and Hegel's dialectical account of historical development: see, e.g., Michael Rosen, *Hegel's Dialectic and its Criticism*, Cambridge, UK: Cambridge University Press, 1982; Paul Hoyningen-Huene, *Reconstructing Scientific Revolutions: Thomas S. Kuhn's Philosophy of Science*, Chicago: University of Chicago Press, 1993. It is a model that has also been applied to personality development by Erik Erikson and to the emergence of existential questioning and spirituality by Kenneth Pargament: see Erik H. Erikson, *Identity and the Life Cycle*, New York: W. W. Norton, 1980; Kenneth I. Pargament, *The Psychology of Religion and Coping: Theory, Research, Practice*, New York: Guilford Press, 1997.

world is – it is a working model constructed from a particular physical and functional perspective, and must therefore be considered critically.[30]

Scientific theories of perception and perceptual development vary considerably in detail, but in general terms most conform to the account we have given in this section. They are consistent with a "critical realist" position, to which we shall return later in this work. Perhaps most importantly, however, the account of perception that we have offered has important implications for a Christian understanding of the nature of revelation. From what has been said, it will be clear that revelation does not bypass schemas. Any account of revelation needs to give due weight to the manner in which human beings create and use conceptual schemes. This is an issue which is of general importance, but is of particular interest in connection with the Barth–Brunner debate over natural theology in 1934, to be considered later (pp. 158–64).

Before considering this aspect of the matter further, we shall consider the notion of "objective perception," which has played such a significant role in classical approaches to natural theology.[31]

Perception is Egocentric and Enactive

It is essential to appreciate that there is no such thing as objective human perception. Perception always takes place from the point of view of the perceiver. The world is therefore represented from the perspective of a location in physical space and time, a location in the social and cultural group, and in terms of personal agendas and goals.[32]

---

[30] See, for example, the important collection of studies brought together in Alva Noèe (ed.), *Is the Visual World a Grand Illusion?* Thorverton, UK: Imprint Academic, 2002.

[31] See the analysis of the rise and fall of the classic English tradition of natural theology in Alister E. McGrath, *The Order of Things: Explorations in Scientific Theology*, Oxford: Blackwell Publishing, 2006, pp. 63–96.

[32] See especially Mark Johnson, *The Body in the Mind: The Bodily Basis of Meaning, Imagination, and Reason*, Chicago: University of Chicago Press, 1987; Patricia S. Churchland, *Neurophilosophy: Toward a Unified Science of the Mind-Brain*, Cambridge, MA: MIT Press, 1986. For an evaluation of the importance of Johnson's approach for an understanding of the human imagination, especially in literary contexts, see David S. Miall, "Mark Johnson, Metaphor, and Feeling," *Journal of Literary Semantics* 26 (1997): 191–210.

The perception of space illustrates this well. Most adult human beings can be educated to represent space on paper in terms of Euclidean geometry – drawing and interpreting maps defined, for instance, by Cartesian coordinates.[33] But there is no evidence from the natural behavior of human beings that their cognitive and perceptual systems naturally treat space in this way. For instance, many well-educated and intelligent people have persistent difficulty with map-reading and never use maps at all. The use of landmarks is the more natural and generally preferred strategy for getting from A to B. Road maps tend to be used prior to a journey specifically to generate a list of landmarks (perhaps stated in terms of road numbers and exits that are signposted to particular towns) and the distances traveled between them. These are what guide the journey, and it is in fact in these sorts of terms that space is represented by the perceptual system.[34]

In this respect, as J. F. Stein has noted, behavior is analogous to brain function.

> It is the location of whole objects with respect to the observer, rather than their absolute position in real space, which appears to be defined in the posterior parietal lobe of the cerebral cortex; how to reach objects rather than how different parts of space are filled.[35]

The basic question that is asked in spatial perception is not "What is the absolute location of x?" but rather something like, "Where is x in relation to me, taking into account the fact that I may be moving

---

[33] In an earlier section we discussed the arrangement of nerve cells in the visual cortex, which form a series of "maps" corresponding to the visual field. This is not a representation of *space* but of information from one sensory modality.

[34] An excellent illustration is provided by the London Underground map, designed by Henry C. Beck in 1933, which bears no relationship to "real" or "objective" geography, but is a triumph of human-friendly design over literal cartography, through its clear indication of landmarks (stations), action prompts (intersections), and simplified directions. See further Ken Garland, *Mr Beck's Underground Map*, Harrow Weald: Capital Transport, 1994.

[35] John F. Stein, "Space and the Parietal Association Areas," in J. Paillard (ed.), *Brain and Space*, pp. 185–222, Oxford: Oxford University Press, 1992; quote at p. 212.

about?"[36] Achieving an answer requires the coordination of information coming in through the eyes, through the ears, and from sense receptors in the skin and the muscles to form a dynamic multimodal representation of the perceiver in relation to the object. This relation, rather than being defined in terms of static distances between points, appears rather to be represented in terms of movement and action patterns. As Michael Arbib has pointed out, concepts such as distance with respect to a fixed absolute frame of reference are *secondary* and *abstracted* inferences.

> We move in a world where the position and orientation of objects can be described in Euclidean terms. But we do not receive signals corresponding to some co-ordinate system for this Euclidean space. . . . The task of perception is *not to reconstruct* a Euclidean model of the surroundings. Perception is *action-oriented*, combining current stimuli and stored knowledge to determine a course of action appropriate to the task at hand.[37]

So the representation of space in human perception is highly egocentric[38] and "enactive." There is evidence that there are separate cognitive-perceptual

---

[36] For one possible model, see Pietro Morasso and Vittorio Sanguineti, "Self-Organizing Body Schema for Motor Planning," *Journal of Motor Behaviour* 27 (1995): 52–66; Vittorio Sanguineti and Pietro Morasso, "How the Brain Discovers the Existence of External Allocentric Space," *Neurocomputing* 12 (1996): 289–310.

[37] Michael Arbib, "Interaction of Multiple Representations of Space in the Brain," in J. Paillard (ed.), *Brain and Space*, pp. 379–403, Oxford: Oxford University Press, 1991; quote at p. 380.

[38] The same applies to social space. Young children and many adults can be profoundly egocentric in their relationships with other people. Yet for skilled negotiation of human relationships an ability to see things from the point of view of others is essential. This ability to infer the mental states, beliefs, intentions, and desires of others by observing their behavior is commonly referred to as having a developed "theory of mind." It is underpinned by activity in widespread areas of the brain, particularly the frontal lobes. Just as humans build up schematic representations of the physical world throughout childhood, they also continue to build up schematic representations of the social and existential world and their place in it throughout their lives. See Andrea D. Rowe, Peter R. Bullock, Charles E. Polkey, and Robin G. Morris, "'Theory of Mind' Impairments and their Relationship to Executive Functioning Following Frontal Lobe Excisions," *Brain* 124 (2001): 600–16; D. Stuss and V. Anderson, "The Frontal Lobes and Theory of Mind: Developmental Concepts from Adult Focal Lesion Research," *Brain and Cognition* 55 (2004): 69–83.

representations of the "personal space" occupied by the body, the "peripersonal space" that is within reaching distance, and the "extrapersonal" space beyond this. Anyone who has observed the self-examination, repeated careful attempts at reaching, and environmental exploration carried out by young infants will have an insight into how these particular representations or schemas may develop.

Yet, as we have already noted, human beings (or some human beings) are also able to achieve "allocentric" representations of space, which to some extent free them from their own perspective and enable them to take a bird's-eye view – an idea which, for some, could be expressed in terms of "self-transcendence." Thus one advantage of using a map is that it opens up a range of options, can tell us if there is an alternative way to get from A to B if we run into problems on our usual route. Allocentric representation of space requires the ability to carry out mental rotations, a skill that is beyond young children, and may depend on the activity of two symmetrical small structures deep in the brain, the hippocampi, that continue to develop through childhood. This type of representation of space is perhaps better thought of as a characteristic of abstract thinking rather than of our direct interaction with the world. The bird's-eye views that are achieved are not egocentric but neither is any one of them objective in an absolute sense. A bird's-eye view is not a God's-eye view. Alternative and multiple perspectives are nevertheless still perspectives.

We now turn to the perception of objects. This is also egocentric to the extent that objects tend to be represented in terms of their utility for the individual as much as in terms of their physical characteristics. Thus infants as young as 10 months incorporate a concept of rolling into their representation of spherical shape and drinking in their representation of cup shapes.[39] The form and function of objects appear to be inextricably linked in the human mind. Indeed this is evident in the play of children who often, to the annoyance of their parents, tend to use toys and other objects for things other than their "proper" function – turning a rocking horse upside down to make a boat, sweeping the floor with a doll's hair, using a palm cross as a sword, using up-ended books to make a tunnel for toy cars, and so on. This type of play reflects the active exploration of the multiple potential uses of objects which come to be understood as things that can cut, roll, stab, tickle, clean, give shelter, bear weight,

---

[39]   Piaget, *The Construction of Reality in the Child*, pp. 86–96.

or extend one's reach. In later life invention and improvisation will draw on this stored perceptual knowledge that is laid down in childhood.

Thus the question involved in the perception of objects is just as much "Can it do d, e, or f for me . . . ?" and "Do I respond to it by doing x, y, or z . . . ?" as it is "Does it fit a, b, or c . . . ?" This approach to the world of objects can also be seen in many human approaches to the transcendent. As we saw in Chapter 3, transcendent experiences are sought out and valued precisely because of their functional significance, their capacity to advance human agendas of intellectual enlightenment, physical, or psychological well-being. The positive relationship between spiritual practices, such as meditation, and health is well attested.[40] Indeed, certain techniques which originated in religious or spiritual settings have been transported and applied in modified form in mainstream healthcare. One example is "mindfulness" training, an aspect of Buddhist *dharma*, that is used to help patients with various health conditions literally to transcend them.[41]

Transcendent experiences are also valued for their capacity to "allow individuals to forge connections to the larger universe and thereby provide meaning to their lives,"[42] something that is understood by humanistic and positive psychologists as contributing to a higher goal of "making the lives of all people more productive and fulfilling."[43]

This rather functional approach to transcendent experience and aspiration can also be seen in conceptions and descriptions of the divine in terms of what God can do for human beings. Examples abound throughout the Bible, and include "savior" (Isaiah 45: 21, Luke 1: 47), "redeemer" (Psalm 19: 14), "helper" (Hebrews 13: 6). These sorts of concepts certainly do not exhaust the possible ways of talking and thinking about God, but they do illustrate that one salient theme in the human

---

[40] T. Seeman, L. Dubin, and M. Seeman, "Religiosity/Spirituality and Health: A Critical Review of the Evidence for Biological Pathways," *American Psychologist* 58 (2003): 53–63.

[41] J. Kabat-Zinn, "Mindfulness-Based Interventions in Context: Past, Present, and Future," *Clinical Psychology: Science and Practice* 10 (2003): 144–56.

[42] Christopher Petersen and Martin E. P. Seligman, *Character Strengths and Virtues: Handbook and Classification*, New York: Oxford University Press, 2004, p. 519.

[43] Martin Seligman, "Positive Psychology, Positive Prevention, and Positive Therapy," in C. Snyder and S. Lopez (eds), *Handbook of Positive Psychology*, pp. 3–9, New York: Oxford University Press, 2002; quote at p. 4.

experience of the divine is the *function of God* in relation to human agendas. This is perhaps best illustrated by Psalm 23: 1–4, where God's action in relation to the psalmist is fitted, very beautifully, into the pre-existing category of "shepherding."

Of course, theologians may object that God is neither a functional object in general, nor our shepherd in particular. But the point is that the psychological processes that operate in the perception of objects are also evident in the human experience of God. God is experienced from a particular perspective – often a perspective of need and limitation requiring functional assistance; the response required of the perceiver is inherent in the act of perception;[44] and the presence of the divine is made sense of in terms of pre-existing schemas. So, for instance, I need help; I look for a helper on whom I can rely; the experience I have is of being helped; I make sense of the experience in terms of what I already know about helpers (see Psalm 121).

A second possible theological objection to the idea of "God as functional object" is that, whereas human beings act on objects, God is the actor in the divine–human relationship.[45] In fact, a Christian theological case can be made for the situation being more balanced and reciprocal. On this understanding, while God is the ultimate initiator of action, humans act in response; God speaks and humans reply. Yet for humans to respond *appropriately* they must perceive God appropriately, must see that God is relevant to their own concerns. In the "primeval swamp," a man who sees a stick as a potential tool for fighting off wild beasts will live, whereas a man who sees it just as a stick will die. Without in any way suggesting that God is simply an object, the Christian faith holds that an appropriate response to God makes the difference between life and death (see, for example, John 1: 10–13). God acts; but if human beings

---

[44] This discussion of the response required on the part of the perceiver can be extended to include the theological idea of "faith." In this sense of the term, "faith" refers to both the means by which we see, and the response required by what we see. For a classic, though dense, account of these issues, see Ray L. Hart, *Unfinished Man and the Imagination: Toward an Ontology and a Rhetoric of Revelation*, New York: Herder & Herder, 1968.

[45] A point made by Emil Brunner and other theologians influenced by Martin Buber's "dialogical personalism." See, e.g., Roman Rössler, *Person und Glaube: Der Personalismus der Gottesbeziehung bei Emil Brunner*, Munich: Kaiser Verlag, 1965; Egon Brinkschmidt, *Martin Buber und Karl Barth: Theologie zwischen Dialogik und Dialektik*, Neukirchen-Vluyn: Neukirchener Verlag, 2000.

are to benefit from those actions and live they must first *identify* God, and realize that a response is required.

Perception Pays Attention to Significance

In the previous section we argued that there is no such thing as "objective" human perception because the perceiver operates from a given perspective. We now go on to suggest that there is also no such thing as comprehensive human perception, or human omniscience. This is because human beings, like all living creatures, have limited capacities. Humans are only able to process those aspects of their environment that come into the receptive fields of their sensory organs, either because of the location or response characteristics of these organs.

For instance, the human visual field is limited compared to those of herbivores and birds, whose eyes are further apart on the sides of their heads. Similarly, the range of sound wave frequencies that a human being can detect is limited when compared to dogs or bats. This is a simple matter of natural selection. Species evolve to fit the demands of their environment and lifestyle. In the human the largely overlapping visual fields of the two eyes enable stereoscopic vision and effective depth perception. The cost of this is a relative narrowing of the total visual field (approximately 110 degrees in comparison to 200 degrees for a hare and 360 degrees for many species of fish). Human beings do not have the developed sonar system of the bat because they are active in the daylight hours and can find their way about using visual information. Sensory information is taken in on a species-specific "need to know" basis and this is because living creatures cannot know or perceive everything. In evolution one particular "design solution" precludes others,[46] and adaptation to specific environments precludes adaptation to others. To quote Alexander Pope:

> Why has not man a microscopic eye?
> For this plain reason: man is not a fly.[47]

---

[46] We use this phrase advisedly, and do not interpret it in the terms associated with the "intelligent design" movement. For a criticism of this movement, see Robert T. Pennock, *Intelligent Design Creationism and its Critics: Philosophical, Theological, and Scientific Perspectives*, Cambridge, MA: MIT Press, 2001.

[47] Alexander Pope, *Essay on Man*, Epistle 1, l. 39.

Yet humans have developed microscopes because their highly developed intellectual capacities have enabled them to transcend their biological limitations to a significant extent. Human beings are unique in having reached an understanding of the fact that there is more to the universe than that which can be perceived directly through the sense organs, and in having developed technologies that exploit this fact. Nevertheless, just as Euclidean and other sophisticated geometries give only an illusion of objectivity in the perception of space (pp. 93–4), the technologically extended perceptual abilities of humans give a sense of omniscience that is also illusory.

Human beings know that there is more to the world than meets the eye. To return to the Pauline metaphor we considered in Chapter 4, through technology we may catch a glimpse "through a glass darkly" of some of the realities that lie beyond the eye's reach – for example, delighting in images transmitted from the surface of Mars, or the inside of the brain. Yet much more continues to elude us, and technology cannot by its very nature allow us to perceive "face to face."[48]

Moreover, human beings are limited in another, and more important, respect than the *type* of stimuli to which their sense organs can respond. They are limited in the *amount* of information that they can process. While the human brain has the capacity to *store* vast quantities of information, it can only work actively with small amounts of information at any one time, and is thus also limited in its speed of processing.

Attention is integral to perception. We orientate ourselves in a certain direction because our attention has been attracted. We notice only some features of the environment through selective attention. We sustain concentration on one thing to the exclusion of all else through focused attention, or balance competing attentional demands through divided attention. Indeed, the human perceptual representation of space, considered on page 94, is best thought of as a map with *attentional* rather than geographical coordinates, within which movement trajectories are plotted. The part of the brain concerned with spatial perception also plays a key role in attention.[49]

The psychologists Nakamura and Csikszentmihalyi summarize the egocentric, enactive, and attention-dominated character of human perception as follows:

---

[48]   1 Corinthians 13: 12.

[49]   Michael I. Posner and Steven E. Petersen, "The Attentional System of the Human Brain," *Annual Review of Neuroscience* 13 (1990): 25–42.

It is the *subjectively perceived* opportunities for action that determine experience. That is, there is no objectively defined body of information and set of challenges within the stream of the person's experience, but rather the information that is selectively attended to and the opportunities for action that are perceived. Likewise, it is not meaningful to speak about a person's skills and attentional capacities in objective terms; what enters into lived experience are those capacities for action and those attentional resources and biases . . . that are engaged by this presently encountered environment.[50]

The notion of "attentional bias," introduced in this passage, refers to the fact that, while some things in the environment capture attention because of their physical salience (e.g., a loud noise), others are attended to because of human agendas and interests, including short-term motivational states such as hunger and thirst. That is, the perceptual system not only asks questions about the identity and location of things in the environment but, through the operation of attention, also asks questions about their significance. Asking the question "Is it significant?" represents one major way through which input from the environment is prioritized by the system to make best use of its limited capacity.

How is this significance determined? First, it relates to the physical survival of the individual. The silent approach of an adder will hold attention more readily than a noisy radio on a family picnic. A quietly crying baby will wake a mother who sleeps through a loud thunderstorm. Secondly, it relates to the psychological survival of individuals, the maintenance and development of their personal identity (and the survival of their culture if they are deeply embedded in it). Perhaps the best simple demonstration of this is the "cocktail party effect," a phenomenon that has been well known to psychologists for many years. In an environment where multiple conversations are taking place, and it is difficult to hear anything, people can reliably detect their own name spoken at low volume in another part of the room. One's name is, of course, a key identity marker.

Some attentional biases relating to physical survival may be "hard wired" into the system and be invariant across a species. For example, humans and other primates are biologically predisposed to pay attention to faces. This is evident from the earliest hours of life in human infants who gaze

---

[50] Jeanne Nakamura and Mihaly Csikszentmihalyi, "The Concept of Flow," in C. Snyder and S. Lopez (eds), *Handbook of Positive Psychology*, pp. 89–105, New York: Oxford University Press, 2002; quote at p. 91.

at face-like configurations in preference to random patterns of similar complexity.[51] As they grow older a differential interest in the face of the mother or primary care giver emerges, though more recent evidence suggests that the mother's face can be distinguished from others on the basis of gross characteristics even in newborn infants. There is obvious survival value in paying attention to socially significant stimuli in general, and in being able to identify the specific person who is most likely to give help and nurture. Adult human beings are excellent at discriminating between familiar and unfamiliar faces even after one exposure, if not always so good at putting a name to a face. They are much less skilled at identifying random patterns. This basic human ability is taken for granted in the well-established identification parade procedure so often used as a source of police evidence.

There is a very specific brain base for this perceptual ability located in the temporal lobe of the right cerebral hemisphere. People who have sustained damage to this brain area develop a distressing problem known as *prosopagnosia* – the inability to recognize familiar faces.[52]

The excellent ability to attend to, perceive, and recognize human faces is a characteristic of all human beings because it serves an agenda that is central to all human beings – physical survival as part of a social group. But there is also room for specific personal agendas in the perceptual process, which can be refined to meet the goals of the individual. People can develop similar perceptual skills in relation to visual stimuli other than human faces, presumably by paying close attention to them. There are cases of farmers with prosopagnosia who have also lost the ability to recognize individual cows in their herds, and of birdwatchers suffering from the same condition who are no longer able to identify bird species.[53] It appears that these specialized skills are underpinned by an area of the brain adjacent to, but not identical with, that responsible for the processing of human faces.[54] The close analogy between the processes of identifying

---

[51] Robert L. Fantz, "The Origin of Form Perception," *Scientific American* 203 (1961): 66–72.

[52] A famous account of this condition is given by the writer Oliver Sacks in his book of neuropsychological case studies, *The Man Who Mistook His Wife for a Hat*, London: Pan, 1986, pp. 7–21.

[53] B. Bornstein, H. Sroka, and H. Munitz, "Prosopagnosia with Animal Face Agnosia," *Cortex* 5 (1969): 164–9.

[54] J. McNeil and E. Warrington, "Prosopagnosia: A Face-Specific Disorder," *Quarterly Journal of Experimental Psychology* 46 (1993): 1–10.

humans and herd animals is developed and exploited in John 10, an excellent example of the natural theology of the Gospels, which we will explore more fully later (Chapter 6).

In summary, just as some schemas or mental structures are universal to the human species and many more arise in response to cultural or personal context, some attention-grabbing aspects of the environment may be significant for the whole species, while many more are only significant to a particular individual or culture. It is important to note that the attentional and perceptual processes relating to an object's significance are equally brain-based whether the origin of that significance is "biological" or "cultural." Whether the wiring involved is hard or flexible, it is still wiring. It is also very important to understand that the process we have been describing is *not* an initial "neutral" survey of the environment followed by filtering to prioritize only what is significant. The environment is viewed *from the beginning*, as it were, through "significance spectacles." While conceptually distinct, the processes of perception and attention are psychologically integral.

Perception Can Be Modulated by Motivation and Affect

Where sensory input is significant for the physical survival of the individual, it is often tagged in some way so that it becomes compelling. Sex, pain, and emotions such as fear are all examples of this sort of affective tagging, as it were turning on the heat, bringing an issue immediately to the center of consciousness, enabling and energizing appropriate action.

Advertisers are well aware of this phenomenon, and freely exploit the compelling nature of sexual images in attracting attention. Pain is not generally thought of as an emotion, but it does have an affective component, which is instructive for our present discussion.[55] Pain signals injury. Injury must not be ignored but attended to, and it should be prioritized. Pain captures our attention. When we experience even mild

---

[55] Just as there are specific receptors, pathways, and brain areas dealing with visual information, so there are corresponding receptors, pathways, and brain areas that are associated with pain. For example, adequate function of the frontal lobes of the cerebral cortex appears to be necessary for the "hurting" (affective) but not for the "sensing" (perceptual) component of pain.

pain it is hard to concentrate on anything else. Pain is sometimes described as "nagging" precisely because it has the capacity to intrude into consciousness.

One interesting feature of pain is that, despite its compelling nature, the subjective experience of pain can be completely eradicated for a time if even more significant considerations have come into play. People who have sustained injuries in the course of fleeing for their lives or rescuing others from danger often report that it was only after the event that they realized that they had been running on a broken ankle or clinging to burning wreckage. Perception is affected by the action demands of situations.

Emotions such as fear also modulate the process of perception. The human perceptual system is universally attuned to certain features of the environment, such as rapidly approaching objects, sudden loss of physical support, screams, blood, and injury, so that they automatically elicit fear. There is also a tendency for many people to develop fears of snakes, insects, heights, wide or enclosed spaces. In fact, given the right conditions, human beings can learn to be afraid of almost anything, and the learning of fear is characteristically rapid.[56]

The types of emotional features to which the perceptual system is attuned vary from person to person. They depend to a large extent on the previous experience of dangerous situations, especially situations which have been associated with a high degree of physiological arousal. In extreme situations people can become not only attuned to certain specific reminders of a dangerous situation, but also *hypervigilant*, attending to

---

[56] Feelings of fear, changes in heart rate and respiration, freezing or running away can all begin before an object is fully processed perceptually. It seems that a "quick and dirty" analysis of the physical features of a stimulus early in the chain of perceptual processing can activate the parts of the brain concerned with emotion, specifically the amygdalae, two symmetrical almond-shaped structures deep in the brain. In this way behavior is energized by fear so that one can be running away before one is fully aware of what one is running from, for instance only realizing later that the object in question was a garden hose and not a snake. Rapid responses have survival value in this context. This sort of reaction, based on rudimentary feature detection, bypasses the higher order and more leisurely and constructional perceptual processes that are taking place at the same time, underpinned by activity in other brain areas, and thus saves valuable milliseconds. See, e.g., Joseph E. LeDoux, *The Emotional Brain: The Mysterious Underpinnings of Emotional Life*, New York: Simon & Schuster, 1996.

these features at the expense of all others in any and every situation. Hypervigilance is quite a common consequence of psychological trauma, and seems to develop because the conceptual schemas about the way the world is have become dominated by threat. This can be interpreted as an overaccommodation to the traumatic experience. For example, a person who has been knocked down by a white van may become much more aware of white vans in his or her environment and start to flinch at the approach of any light-colored vehicle.

This phenomenon can be subtle, preconscious, and paradoxical so that the distressing and potentially overwhelming stimuli are actively filtered out of consciousness rather than attended to. It can also affect the perception of what appear to be neutral stimuli.[57]

Traumatic events such as road accidents and sexual assault are at the extremely unpleasant end of the emotional spectrum. But they illustrate a point that holds good at lower levels of emotional arousal, in less extreme situations, and where the emotions involved are more pleasant (as in infant face recognition): there is a strong "top-down" component to perception, with higher order beliefs and emotional state modulating the processing of sensory information. This phenomenon is most evident when the sensory information is novel or ambiguous, open to multiple interpretations. That is why, when one is anxious, it is often more reassuring to sleep with the lights on. It is also the reason underlying the development of "projective tests" early in the history of psychiatry and psychoanalysis. The most famous projective test is the Rorschach collection of inkblots. These stimuli are so ambiguous that they were thought to be particularly suitable for detecting the patient's underlying agendas and conflicts because these would be "projected" onto the inkblots as part of the perceptual process. The history of the use of these tests is highly controversial,[58] but the basic idea behind the Rorschach is valid, and of greater relevance to our wider theme because ambiguous and novel sensory conditions are often associated with religious or spiritual perceptual experiences.

---

[57] See, e.g., K. Cassiday, R. McNally, and S. Zeitlin, "Cognitive Processing of Trauma Cues in Rape Victims with Post-Traumatic Stress Disorder," *Cognitive Therapy and Research* 16 (1992): 283–95.

[58] See, for example, Jim Wood, Teresa Nezworski, and O. Lilienfeld Scott, *What's Wrong with the Rorschach?: Science Confronts the Controversial Inkblot Test*, San Francisco, CA: Jossey-Bass, 2003.

Human Perception and Natural Theology

So what are the implications of this analysis of the natural human processes underlying an encounter with the natural world for any understanding of natural theology? In what follows, we shall note some obvious applications, while postponing some specific items to appropriate points later in this study.

The understanding of human perception that we have explored in this work does not sit well with the idea of systematic theology as an allocentric, static representation of truth, which believers are meant to accept passively. The egocentric nature of human perception suggests that if God is to enter our categories, God needs to encounter us dynamically in a place in which we will see God from our perspective. Yet although this approach exists in an uneasy relationship with neo-scholastic approaches to theology, it fits in well with those approaches to theology which emphasize the provisionality of its formulations, and its openness to correction and development. Critical realism, for example, stresses the reality of the external world, while insisting on human activity in the constructing of mental representations of this reality.[59] Theology will always be a work in progress.

Equally, revelation is not something that can be "pinned down" and codified exhaustively. Karl Barth's expression of the dynamic nature of divine action in self-disclosure makes this point well: it is, he suggested, like a bird in flight, having no "stationary point."[60] Yet although we cannot hope to capture this divine revelation in its totality, we can grasp it with sufficient clarity to enable us to live, act, and think on its basis – including exploring its relevance for natural theology.

The cognitive neuroscience of perception presents a clear picture of human beings as creatures who exist in relation to the natural world, are

---

[59] On this point, see Alister E. McGrath, *A Scientific Theology: 2 – Reality*, London: T&T Clark, 2002, pp. 195–226. It is a point familiar to readers of William James, who stressed that the *knower* is also an *actor*, in that "he registers the truth which he helps to create." In that the human mind interacts with its perceptions of the external world, it must follow, he argues, that human observers "help to *make* the truth which they declare." William James, *Essays in Radical Empiricism*, Cambridge, MA: Harvard University Press, 1976, p. 21.

[60] Karl Barth, *Römerbrief*, 8th edn, Zurich: Zollikon, 947, pp. 5–6, 72–4. For a more complete account of the social dynamics of revelation, see Alister E. McGrath, *A Scientific Theology: 3 – Theory*, T&T Clark, 2003, pp. 138–93.

shaped by it, but also shape it according to their own agenda. Humans are not detached observers of nature, considering it at their leisure as, for instance, a piece of indirect evidence for divine existence and action. They are in fact *participants in* nature. Humans are also finite beings of limited capacity, and view the natural world from a limited perspective. They are active constructors of their own perceptual realities, not passive recipients of information. But the process of construction is influenced by real events in, and real properties of, the natural world. Some aspects of perception are biologically determined and are invariant, others are individually and culturally influenced and are flexible. Much of perception involves emotions, values, and agendas. All perception is brain-based.

So does the brain somehow *invent* the notion of God? Some writers have argued that the "almost irresistible natural tendency" to explain natural phenomena as the "results of deliberate actions by thinking, feeling, supernatural agents" demonstrates that God is to be considered as an imaginary construction of the human mind.[61] Yet it is important to point out that a recognition of the "naturalness" of religious concepts can easily be accommodated within a theistic perspective,[62] and lead on to the development of a natural theology which is informed by the insights of the cognitive sciences.

The core issue is whether a recognition of the role of neuroscience in the human process of perception and cognition demands that we reduce the concept of revelation or the cognate notion of the "knowledge of God" to purely natural categories – a conclusion which certainly has been drawn by some within the field of cognitive science.[63] Perhaps the most familiar statement of such views is to be found with Francis Crick, who famously stated this view as follows:

---

[61] Todd Tremlin, *Minds and Gods: The Cognitive Foundations of Religion*, New York: Oxford University Press, 2006.

[62] See, for example, Justin L. Barrett, "The Naturalness of Religious Concepts: An Emerging Cognitive Science of Religion," in P. Antes, A. Geertz and R. R. Warne (eds), *New Approaches to the Study of Religion. Volume 2: Textual, Comparative, Sociological, and Cognitive Approaches*, pp. 401–18, Berlin: de Gruyter, 2004. More generally, see Barrett's *Why Would Anyone Believe in God?*

[63] For works in the field which take such views, see Benjamin Libet, Anthony Freeman, and Keith Sutherland (eds), *The Volitional Brain: Towards a Neuroscience of Free Will*, Thorverton, UK: Imprint Academic, 1999; Michael S. Gazzaniga, *The Mind's Past*, Berkeley, CA: University of California Press, 1998, and *The Cognitive Neurosciences*, 3rd edn, Cambridge, MA: MIT Press, 2004.

"You", your joys and your sorrows, your memories and your ambitions, your sense of personal identity and free-will, are in fact no more than the behaviour of a vast assembly of nerve cells and their associated molecules. As Lewis Carroll's Alice might have phrased it: "You're nothing but a pack of neurons!"[64]

Those who draw such conclusions have their critics within the discipline of the cognitive sciences,[65] who argue that a recognition of the embodiment of the human mind does not lead to an intellectually reductionist outlook, and is perfectly capable of accommodating historical, cultural, and historical factors.[66] There is no doubt that such approaches pose a fundamental challenge to philosophies such as Cartesianism and Kantianism that assume one can study human thought in isolation from its physical processes. Yet their implications for religious thought are much more nuanced.

However revelation is to be understood,[67] it involves human cognition and perception, which recognize it for what it actually is.[68] Revelation

---

[64] Francis H. C. Crick, *The Astonishing Hypothesis: The Scientific Search for the Soul*, London: Simon & Schuster, 1994, p. 3. For a seriously flawed attempt to explore this issue further, see John W. Bowker, *The Sacred Neuron: Extraordinary New Discoveries Linking Science and Religion*, London: I. B. Tauris, 2005. For an assessment, see Alister E. McGrath, "Spirituality and Well-Being: Some Recent Discussions," *Brain* 129 (2006): 278–82.

[65] We have already noted Varela et al., *The Embodied Mind*. See further especially Walter J. Freeman, *Societies of Brains: A Study in the Neuroscience of Love and Hate*, Hillsdale, NJ: Lawrence Erlbaum Associates, 1995, and *How Brains Make Up Their Minds*, New York: Columbia University Press, 2000. See also Nancey Murphy's defense of "nonreductive physicalism" at this point in *Bodies and Souls, or Spirited Bodies?* Cambridge, UK: Cambridge University Press, 2006, 83–5.

[66] See for example, Lakoff and Johnson, *Philosophy in the Flesh*. Note especially their engagement with ethical issues (pp. 291–2), which they argue to be illuminated, not undermined, by their approach.

[67] For some possibilities, see Avery R. Dulles, *Models of Revelation*, Maryknoll, NY: Orbis Books, 1992.

[68] Although this theme is of importance throughout the history of Christian theology, it plays a particularly significant role in the theology of Karl Barth. Yet the idea also plays an important role for writers as diverse as Martin Heidegger and Jacques Derrida: see, e.g., the discussion in Oliver Davies, "Soundings: Towards a Theological Poetics of Silence," in Oliver Davies and Denys Turner (eds), *Silence and the Word: Negative Theology and Incarnation*, pp. 201–22. Cambridge, UK: Cambridge University Press, 2002.

takes place within history, culture, and the natural order, and does not bypass its categories. Christianity long ago turned its back decisively against Gnostic interpretations of revelation and salvation, which conceived such processes in purely spiritual terms, disregarding their physical aspects. Revelation may involve the interpretation of historical events,[69] the hearing of the word of God,[70] the reading of Scripture,[71] experience of the presence of God,[72] or reflection on the natural world – the fundamental theme of this work. As John of Damascus stressed in the eighth century, revelation does not circumvent the natural, material world; the incarnation represents an extension and confirmation, not a contradiction, of earlier modes of revelation.[73] Yet that process of interpretation and appropriation also includes human perception, which simply cannot be eliminated for the sake of theological convenience.[74]

The human process of perception cannot be overlooked or marginalized in any account of the theological interpretation of nature. This has important implications for our understanding of the way in which God's

---

[69] A theme particularly associated with (though by no means limited to) Wolfhart Pannenberg: see Wolfhart Pannenberg, "Redemptive Event and History," in *Basic Questions in Theology*, pp. 15–80, London: SCM Press, 1970. For reaction, see Lothar Steiger, "Offenbarungsgeschichte und theologische Vernunft," *Zeitschrift für Theologie und Kirche* 59 (1962): 88–113.

[70] On which see particularly Nicholas Wolterstorff, *Divine Discourse: Philosophical Reflections on the Claim that God Speaks*, Cambridge, UK: Cambridge University Press, 1995.

[71] N. T. Wright, "'Word of God' and Scripture in the Apostolic Church," in *Scripture and the Authority of God*, pp. 35–44, London: SPCK, 2005.

[72] For discussions, see Caroline Franks Davis, *The Evidential Force of Religious Experience*, Oxford: Clarendon Press, 1989; William P. Alston, *Perceiving God: The Epistemology of Religious Experience*, Ithaca, NY: Cornell University Press, 1991.

[73] This point is made particularly clearly in his *Contra imaginum calumniatores* I, 16; in *Patristische Texte und Studien* vol. 17, ed. P. Bonifatius Kotter OSB., Berlin/ New York: de Gruyter, 1979, 89.1–4; 92.90–1. Note especially the point that to read Scripture is to engage with a natural entity (ink, paper, and so forth), which has the capacity to point beyond itself.

[74] In Chapter 6 we shall consider Jesus of Nazareth's "parables of the kingdom," and note how these involve the active interpretation of natural objects and events in certain ways. Interpretation of the parables is an *active* process, involving the engagement of the mind and imagination in the construction of alternative meanings for stories and events.

self-revelation may take place, both in the context of nature and through nature to humans, which strongly suggests that God would appear to the human perceptual system in a manner that allows it to detect, identify, and make sense of God's presence.[75] Since perception involves both accommodation to, and assimilation of, the environment, the relationship between human beings and the natural world cannot be considered to be wholly passive or exclusively active. At least some degree of reciprocity must be acknowledged.[76] Despite Karl Barth's often-stated concerns about the "reduction" of theology to anthropology, a concern to understand how revelation happens does not involve the "reduction" of theology to psychology – or to anything else, for that matter.

God's self-revelation does not happen in a vacuum – the revelation is to people who apprehend God through faith, itself a sort of "enactive perception." The notion of *communication between* God and humanity may thus be a better description of what is really going on than the notion of *revelation* of God *to* humanity.[77] This observation is not without relevance to the 1934 debate between Karl Barth and Emil Brunner over natural theology, to be discussed in detail in Chapter 7, in which the issue of human activity in the process of discerning and appropriating salvation becomes important. The analysis just presented suggests that Emil Brunner might be a more congenial dialogue partner for theology and cognitive neuropsychology than Karl Barth, as is evident from his willingness to engage in questions of the human involvement in revelation. In contrast, Karl Barth seems to hold that revelation bypasses human conceptual schemas altogether, although this conclusion appears to result from a

---

[75] This idea is often expressed in the theological notion of "accommodation" (which is not to be confused with Piaget's concept bearing the same name). The essential point being made by the theological notion is that God's self-revelation is adapted to the realities of human capacities to discern it. Accommodation is here understood as a God-initiated process of adaptation in revelation, rather than as a human response to revelation. See Stephen D. Benin, *The Footprints of God: Divine Accommodation in Jewish and Christian Thought*, Albany: State University of New York, 1993.

[76] This mirrors aspects of the biblical account of the relationship between human beings and God as reciprocal and cooperative. God reveals himself, but this revelation is apprehended through faith (John 1: 9–12; Romans 1: 17).

[77] See especially Emil Brunner, *Wahrheit als Begegnung*, Zürich: Zwingli-Verlag, 1963, which stresses the divine–human encounter in terms that acknowledge human perception and response.

fundamental disinclination to engage with empirical questions, rather than a detailed consideration of the issues that these raise.[78]

Conclusion to Part I

In this chapter, we have explored how human beings, who are located in this world, seek to make sense of it. In that humanity stands within the natural order, even when observing it, such concerns clearly form part of any renewed and reconceived natural theology. Nothing that has been stated in this analysis can be held to invalidate the notion of natural theology. It nevertheless alerts us to the fact that many classical approaches to this style of theology – such as that encountered in the celebrated Boyle Lectures of the eighteenth century – can no longer be regarded as viable or defensible. Whatever theological objections may be raised concerning such approaches to natural theology, it is clearly important to appreciate that they ultimately rest on deeply problematic understandings of how humanity interacts with nature – and above all, how nature is *seen*.

In bringing the first part of this work to a close, we may reiterate the continuing interest in the concept of "transcendence," and the variety of ways in which this is understood. Throughout this part of this volume, we have been concerned to describe human experiences attributed to the transcendent, and note some aspects of the debate about how they are to be interpreted. This description has not been informed or shaped by specifically Christian beliefs or agendas, even though we have occasionally reflected on the implications of such observations for Christian theology.

---

[78] A similar belief may be encountered in apocalyptic movements: see Rowland, *The Open Heaven*, p. 14, which notes that their "belief that God's will can be discerned by means of a mode of revelation which unfolds directly the hidden things of God," or that "truths which are beyond man's capacity to deduce from his circumstances are revealed directly by means of the manifestations of the divine counsels" (p. 17). The issue here is not the actuality of divine revelation, but the belief that such revelation circumvents the human reflective process which recognizes revelation as such. For Barth's general lack of interest in the natural sciences, see Harold P. Nebelsick, "Karl Barth's Understanding of Science," in John Thompson (ed.), *Theology Beyond Christendom: Essays on the Centenary of the Birth of Karl Barth*, pp. 165–214, Allison Park, PA: Pickwick Publications, 1986.

Yet the time has now come to move from a general description to a specifically Christian analysis, moving away from a generalized notion of "the transcendent" to "God" – and more specifically still, to "the God and Father of our Lord Jesus Christ" (1 Peter 1: 3). How can an authentically *Christian* natural theology be developed? This is the subject of the second part of our analysis. We shall begin our analysis from first principles. And for Christian theology, the ultimate foundation of its ideas is ultimately Jesus of Nazareth – to whom we may now turn.

PART II

The Foundations of Natural Theology: Ground-Clearing and Rediscovery

CHAPTER 6

The Open Secret:
The Ambiguity of Nature

The core of any natural theology has to do with the issue of discernment, the ability to perceive "heaven in ordinarie" (George Herbert). Above all, it is a question of *seeing*. Yet all humans inhabit and observe the same reality. It is not as if one set of humans is presently inhabiting and experiencing a "natural" world, and another a "supernatural" world, as if this was some kind of parallel universe. In this sense we may agree with Ronald Gregor Smith's comment, made at the height of the 1960s euphoria over desacralization and secularization: "the world at which the theologian looks and the world at which the secularist looks are one and the same."[1] Yet important though this insight may be, Smith's terse statement does not do justice to one of the most fundamental issues relating to natural theology. It fails to acknowledge that there is a critical distinction between *looking at* and *seeing*. For, as we discussed in Chapter 5, "seeing" involves the linking of incoming sensory information to an existing understanding of the world, an understanding that has been shaped by the agenda of the viewer, situated as he or she is at a particular vantage point.

If natural theology is about seeing – looking at the natural world and discerning or perceiving the divine – it is perhaps surprising that recent

---

[1] Ronald Gregor Smith, *The Free Man: Studies in Christian Anthropology*, London: Collins, 1969, p. 45.

discussions of natural theology have not taken the opportunity to engage with the teaching of Jesus of Nazareth, where the question of the right way of "seeing" nature has a place of decisive importance. Indeed, one might go further, and suggest that the last century has seen a tendency within Christian theology to marginalize Jesus of Nazareth as a theological voice.[2] Too often, Jesus is seen as the object of theological speculation and construction, rather than as an authoritative voice in the theological task itself. It is clear that the teaching of Jesus of Nazareth strongly endorses the notion that nature has the capacity to disclose the divine. When talking about the divine, Jesus often makes an extensive appeal to various aspects of the natural world, thus rendering his message both powerful and accessible.

Yet at the same time, and almost equally strongly, we find in the teaching of Jesus the idea that human beings are only capable of perceiving the divine in or through nature under certain conditions (though tantalizingly little is said about what these conditions are). Nature is not merely neutral;[3] it is ambiguous. It may be silent or may even actively conceal the divine. "Truly, you are a God who hides yourself" (Isaiah 45: 15).[4] Jesus of Nazareth's approach to nature, which forms the starting point of the present work, holds that nature is fundamentally ambiguous, capable of disclosing the kingdom of God – but, as we shall see, equally capable of concealing it.

---

[2]   The importance of this question for Latin American liberation theology during the 1970s and 1980s should be noted: see David Batstone, *From Conquest to Struggle: Jesus of Nazareth in Latin America*, Albany, NY: State University of New York Press, 1991.

[3]   It is widely agreed that nature can be "read" in theist, atheist, or agnostic ways: see, e.g., Alister E. McGrath, *Dawkins' God: Genes, Memes and the Meaning of Life*, Oxford: Blackwell, 2004. Yet this does not contradict the principle of the fundamental ambiguity of nature – namely, that nature itself cannot be said to mandate or authorize any specific reading.

[4]   This text plays an important role in Martin Luther's "theology of the cross," with its leading theme of a "hidden God." See Hellmut Bandt, *Luthers Lehre vom Verborgenen Gott: Eine Untersuchung zu dem offenbarungsgeschichtlichen Ansatz seiner Theologie*, Berlin: Evangelische Verlagsanstalt, 1958; Alister E. McGrath, *Luther's Theology of the Cross: Martin Luther's Theological Breakthrough*, Oxford: Blackwell, 1985.

The Mystery of the Kingdom: Jesus of Nazareth and the Natural Realm

One of the most distinctive features of the teaching of Jesus of Nazareth is his use of parables.[5] Much scholarly attention has been devoted to issues of undoubted interest and potential importance concerning the parables of Jesus – such as his use of the parabolic genre in relation to that of contemporary Judaism,[6] the differences in presentation of parables between the synoptic Gospels and their implications for questions concerning their dating and literary priority,[7] the hermeneutical use of the parables,[8] and their relationship to the Jewish wisdom tradition.[9] Yet

---

[5]   For recent discussions, see Robert H. Stein, "The Genre of the Parables," in Richard N. Longecker (ed.), *The Challenge of Jesus' Parables*, pp. 30–50, Grand Rapids, MI: Eerdmans, 2000. For a classic account, see C. H. Dodd, *The Parables of the Kingdom*, New York: Charles Scribner's Sons, 1961. John Dominic Crossan suggests that three genres of parables may be discerned, corresponding to the three "modes of the kingdom's temporality": parables of advent, reversal, and action. John Dominic Crossan, *In Parables: The Challenge of the Historical Jesus*, New York: Harper & Row, 1973. Note especially Crossan's comment (p. xv): "The term 'historical Jesus' really means the language of Jesus, and especially the parables themselves." For the contrast between how Jesus and the Pharisees used parables, see Jacob Neusner, *The Rabbinic Traditions About the Pharisees Before 70*, 3 vols, Leiden: E. J. Brill, 1971.

[6]   For example, Birger Gerhardsson, "The Narrative Meshalim in the Synoptic Gospels: A Comparison with the Narrative Meshalim in the Old Testament," *New Testament Studies* 34 (1988): 339–63; David Stern, *Parables in Midrash: Narrative and Exegesis in Rabbinic Literature*, Cambridge, MA: Harvard University Press, 1991, pp. 188–206; Craig A. Evans, "Parables in Early Judaism," in Richard N. Longecker (ed.), *The Challenge of Jesus' Parables*, pp. 51–75, Grand Rapids, MI: Eerdmans, 2000.

[7]   For example, certain parables are held to illuminate the nature of the hypothetical source "Q": see John S. Kloppenborg, *The Formation of Q: Trajectories in Ancient Wisdom Collections*, Philadelphia: Fortress Press, 1987.

[8]   Teresa Okure, " 'I Will Open My Mouth in Parables' (Matt 13:35): A Case for a Gospel-Based Biblical Hermeneutic," *New Testament Studies* 46 (2000): 445–63.

[9]   Marie Noonan Sabin, *Reopening the Word: Reading Mark as Theology in the Context of Early Judaism*, Oxford: Oxford University Press, 2002, pp. 171–203.

one aspect of the parables has not received anything like the attention it deserves – the simple, seemingly uncontestable fact that Jesus, as presented in the Gospels,[10] and received by the church, appeals to the world of nature as a means of disclosing the kingdom of God. For John Dominic Crossan, the parables were the key to encountering and experiencing the "kingdom of God" – the arrival of which, he insists, is to be spoken of in terms of "transcendence."[11] So is there a "natural theology" to be found within the teaching of Jesus?[12]

It is clear that Jesus used nature as a means of teaching about the kingdom of God. The world of nature that we find in the Gospels is that of rural first-century Palestine. It is a world where agrarian concerns – such as the growth of seeds, the fruitfulness of trees, imminent changes in the weather, and the well-being of animals – were ever-present. As in all human societies, concerns about human relationships – such as family dynamics, business ethics, and social status – are also very evident. The parables of Jesus are framed in terms of these basic elements, which would have made them universally accessible to Jesus's original audience, at least at first sight.[13]

---

[10] Even the more skeptical New Testament scholarship holds that the parabolic form is to be regarded as a distinctive element of the ministry of Jesus.

[11] John Dominic Crossan, *The Dark Interval: Towards a Theology of Story*, Sonoma, CA: Eagle, 1988), p. 100. See also his *Finding is the First Act: Trove Fairytales and Jesus' Treasure Parable*, Philadelphia: Fortress Press, 1979.

[12] For this suggestion, regrettably not developed in any detail, see Charles E. Raven, *Natural Religion and Christian Theology*, 2 vols, Cambridge, UK: Cambridge University Press, 1953, vol. 1, pp. 31–2. In order to address this question without introducing anachronism we need to make clear the minimum criteria by which a "natural theology" may be identified. These are simply that there is evidence of a systematic approach to thinking about the divine using concepts derived from nature which does not appeal to privileged sources of knowledge – or, to put this another way, "the enterprise of providing support for religious beliefs by starting from premises that neither are nor presuppose any religious beliefs," following William P. Alston, *Perceiving God: The Epistemology of Religious Experience*, Ithaca, NY: Cornell University Press, 1991, p. 289.

[13] Bernard Brandon Scott, *Hear Then the Parable: A Commentary on the Parables of Jesus*, Minneapolis: Fortress Press, 1989. Scott identifies the basic elements as "family, village, and city"; "masters and servants"; and "home and farm." Other ways of categorizing the parables are also possible. The need to read the parables against this specific cultural milieu has been stressed by Kenneth Bailey: see Kenneth

Though there are allusions to the Hebrew Scriptures in several of Jesus's parables,[14] their recognition is not necessary for making sense of the parable. Rabbinic parables were often used to clarify or explain biblical texts.[15] Here, a knowledge of the texts in question, not to mention some awareness of the debates over their interpretation, is demanded by the parable. In marked contrast, Jesus's parables are essentially self-contained.[16] Where rabbinic parables are used as an aid to biblical exegesis, Jesus makes an appeal directly to nature without explicitly invoking biblical passages as intermediaries.[17]

As this point is of such importance to our suggestion that Jesus may rightly be regarded as making use of a developed "natural theology," understood as an interpretative framework by which nature may be "seen" in a way that connects with the transcendent, this must be pursued further. The critical point is that, as recorded in the synoptic tradition, the

---

E. Bailey, *Poet and Peasant: A Literary-Cultural Approach to the Parables in Luke*, Grand Rapids: Eerdmans, 1976. Bailey's failure to clarify the ideological boundaries of his proposed "oriental exegesis" should be noted: see particularly Vernon K. Robbins, *Jesus the Teacher: A Socio-Rhetorical Interpretation of Mark*, revised edn, Philadelphia: Fortress Press, 1992, p. xxxviii.

[14] Such as the use of imagery from Ezekiel 34: 11–16 in the Parable of the Lost Sheep (Luke 15: 3–7). On the interpretation of this and related parables, see Stephen C. Barton, "Parables on God's Love and Forgiveness (Luke 15: 1–32)," in Richard N. Longenecker (ed.), *The Challenge of Jesus' Parables*, pp. 199–216, Grand Rapids, MI: Eerdmans, 2000.

[15] Daniel Boyarin, *Intertextuality and the Reading of Midrash*, Bloomington, IN: Indiana University Press, 1990, pp. 80–3.

[16] Parables are sometimes presented in the synoptic Gospels as answers to specific questions, often concerning personal ethics. For the new scholarly interest in the parables in relation to Christian ethics, see William C. Spohn, "Jesus and Christian Ethics," *Theological Studies* 56 (1995): 92–107.

[17] It is nevertheless clear that many parables have biblical allusions. For example, it is impossible to read any of the parables relating to vineyards without being reminded of the rich tradition of interpretation based on the Isaianic identification of Israel as God's vineyard. The parable of the "wicked tenants" illustrates this point particularly well: see Richard I. Dillon, "Towards a Tradition-History of the Parables of the True Israel (Mt 21.33–22.14)," *Biblical Research* 47 (1966): 1–42. For an excellent analysis of this specific parable, see Klyne B. Snodgrass, *The Parable of the Wicked Tenants: An Inquiry into Parable Interpretation*, Tübingen: Mohr, 1983. A recognition of this implied textual background thus leads to a deepened appreciation of the parable. Yet it is not essential to the point being made, or the accessibility of the parable itself.

---

parables of Jesus are not subordinate to a broader agenda of the interpretation of the biblical tradition of Israel.[18] This would immediately cause
the parables to be a "closed text, not an open one,"[19] precisely because
a parable, when *subordinated* to a biblical text, is actually *limited* by that
text. Although the parable may be invoked to aid interpretation of the
biblical passage, the biblical passage determines – or at least restricts –
the interpretation of that parable.

Jesus's parables are open. An appeal is made to an aspect of the natural
order, where the interpretation is generally left indefinite and imprecise.
The audience is forced to make its own interpretation, for none is imposed
upon it. Where contemporary rabbinic parables tended to close down
interpretative possibilities, Jesus's parables are invitational, calling their
hearers to reflect. As Marcus Borg points out:

> The appeal is not to the will – not "Do this" – but rather, "Consider seeing
> it this way." As invitational forms of speech, the parables do not invoke
> external authority . . . Rather, their authority rests in themselves – that is, in
> their ability to involve and affect the imagination.[20]

It has often been pointed out that the parables do not make significant
intellectual demands of their audience, thus making them accessible to
many.[21] The hearers of the parables would have found their subject matter
immediately intelligible, in that it connected up effortlessly with their
everyday experience of family life, farming, and personal relationships.
Yet the fact that the parables do not demand much in the way of prior
knowledge or education is counterbalanced by the demand on the hearers

---

[18] The sole possible exception seems to be the Lucan parable of the Good Samaritan
(Luke 10: 25–37), which could be seen as an interpretation of Leviticus 19: 18,
clarifying the identity of one's neighbors. For a careful analysis, see Gerhard Sellin,
"Lukas als Gleichniszähler: Die Erzählung vom barmherzigen Samariter (Lk. 10: 25–
37)," *Zeitschrift für Neutestamentliche Wissenschaft* 65 (1974): 166–89. However,
it can equally be seen as a response to a generalized question.

[19] Boyarin, *Intertextuality and the Reading of Midrash*, p. 82.

[20] Marcus J. Borg, *Meeting Jesus Again for the First Time: The Historical Jesus
and the Heart of Contemporary Faith*, San Francisco: Harper, 1994, p. 74.

[21] Arland J. Hultgren, *The Parables of Jesus: A Commentary*, Grand Rapids, MI:
Eerdmans, 2000, pp. 8–10, contrasting Jesus's parables with those of Plato and Aristotle in this respect.

to make their own interpretation, one that does not rely on received wisdom but is instead their own immediate and authentic response.

For while the *imagery* of the parables is readily grasped, their *meaning* is often veiled, as if it were shrouded in mystery. An appeal to the familiar, the accessible, and the readily understood does not *automatically* become a gateway to deeper truths. For this reason, John Dominic Crossan characterized the life and preaching of Jesus of Nazareth as "the Message of an Open Secret."[22] To grasp the meaning of the parables, they have to be approached and interpreted from a certain angle. It is only if rightly interpreted by the human observer – only if intentionally "seen in this way" – that any given aspect of nature has the capacity to illuminate the ideas and values of the kingdom of God.

It is not so much that these parables are intrinsically "dark sayings"; most are vividly alive, rich in narrative depth, and capable of being grasped immediately by the imagination. Nor are the parables essentially obscure, unapproachable, or couched in portentous language that makes them inaccessible to the crowd. The problem is determining their meaning. The imagery of the parables may be accessible; their significance remains a mystery, save for those "in the know."

The fourth chapter of Mark's Gospel, containing three parables concerning seeds,[23] is a particularly illuminating text in this respect.[24] On

---

[22] John Dominic Crossan, *The Historical Jesus: The Life of a Mediterranean Jewish Peasant*, San Francisco: HarperSanFrancisco, 1991, p. 349. Elsewhere, Crossan argued that it was difficult to sustain Paul Ricoeur's notion of the "surplus of meaning" of parables, symbols, and metaphors. Might they instead be characterized by "void of meaning" at their core? John Dominic Crossan, *Cliffs of Fall: Paradox and Polyvalency in the Parables of Jesus*, New York: Seabury, 1980, pp. 9–10.

[23] The parable of the sower (4: 3–8, 14–20), the parable of the seed growing secretly (4: 26–9), and the parable of the mustard seed (4: 30–2). See Hultgren, *The Parables of Jesus*, pp. 181–202, 385–403. On the last, see especially Alberto Casalengo, "La parabola del franello di senape (Mc 4.30–32)," *Rivista biblica* 26 (1978): 139–61.

[24] This point is fundamental to the way in which parables are presented, used, and interpreted in the Gospel of Mark, where the theme of "mystery" or "secret" becomes of major importance in relation to discerning both the identity of Jesus of Nazareth, and the nature of his teaching concerning the coming kingdom of God. Aloysius M. Ambrozic, *The Hidden Kingdom: A Redactional-Critical Study of the References to the Kingdom of God in Mark's Gospel*, Washington, DC: Catholic

hearing Jesus tell the parable of the sown seed,[25] the disciples ask for some clarification. Jesus's response is enigmatic, not so much in that he conceals things from his audience, but in that he identifies the incapacity of those "outside" (*hoi exo*) to understand what the parables mean.[26] "To you has been given the secret [*mysterion*] of the kingdom of God, but for those outside, everything is in parables" (Mark 4: 11). To those who are outside, the parables are baffling, seemingly hardening their lack of perception, in order that "they may indeed look, but not perceive, and may indeed listen, but not understand" (Mark 4: 12).[27]

There is, of course, a further aspect of the parables that should be mentioned at this point – the eschatological tension between the "now" and the "not yet" of the kingdom of God. The resurrection of Christ can be seen as inaugurating a new era, characterized by a "new creation." This Pauline idea establishes a tension between nature as an empirical reality, and as a future hope.[28] We shall return to consider this point more fully in our discussion of the significance of the economy of salvation for a Christian natural theology.

In part, it is the *form* of parables that may represent a stumbling block to the hearer.[29] They are marked by paradox and incongruity – as in the case of the tiny mustard seed that grows into an enormous shrub. Their open-ended character or ambiguity means that more than one interpretation is possible, so that the responsibility of discerning the correct

Biblical Association of America, 1972; Christopher M. Tuckett, *The Messianic Secret*, Philadelphia: Fortress Press, 1983, and especially Heikki Räisänen, *The "Messianic Secret" in Mark*, Edinburgh: T&T Clark, 1990.

[25] This can be understood as a "parable about parables": see, for instance, Jeremy Duff and Joanna Collicutt McGrath, *Meeting Jesus: Human Responses to a Yearning God*, London: SPCK, 2006, pp. 26–32.

[26] James G. Williams, *Gospel Against Parable: Mark's Language of Mystery*, Sheffield: Almond, 1985, pp. 41–154.

[27] This section (Mark 4: 10–12) is found only in Mark's account of this parable, and includes a free citation of Isaiah 6: 9–10. For a detailed analysis of the pericope, see Ambrozic, *The Hidden Kingdom*, pp. 46–106. The Greek *hina* ("so that" or "in order that") is clearly intentional, not consequential.

[28] Moyer V. Hubbard, *New Creation in Paul's Letters and Thought*, Cambridge, UK: Cambridge University Press, 2002.

[29] Note Crossan's comment that parables are "stories that shatter the deep structure of our accepted world": Crossan, *The Dark Interval*, p. 100.

meaning actually lies with the hearer. The hearer must therefore be able to engage with this paradox, incongruity, and ambiguity, not be repelled by it.[30]

But the substantial content of the parables is also important, for in them the safe and familiar natural world is often presented in ways that are dangerous and novel. The hearer is invited to see the natural world in a different way. The natural world, seen in a particular way, is presented as evidence for the character of the kingdom of God, or the attributes of the divine. The statement that believers need not worry about what to wear because the flowers of the Galilean hillside are beautiful (Matthew 6: 28) is ridiculous unless nature is seen in a particular light. This saying of Jesus is of particular interest because in it he uses his own and his listener's *aesthetic* response to an aspect of the natural world to engender a sense of security in God.[31] The "argument" of the parable is that God can be trusted to provide for us, not because of promises in the Hebrew Scriptures, nor on account of our personal experience of God's provision, but because of God's generous, even extravagant, provision for the natural order. The human capacity to discern the beauty of nature is here transposed into a theological affirmation of the care of God for humanity. There are surely here some strong assumptions about the significance of nature and the capacity of human beings to discern it.

It is, of course, possible that Jesus's extensive appeal to nature in his "parables of the kingdom" is nothing more than an opportunistic

---

[30] The parables of Jesus demand engagement on the part of their hearers. Considered psychologically, they use familiar building blocks, which put the audience at ease. Yet they are combined in ways that challenge and subvert existing schemas, by showing their inadequacy to do justice to Jesus himself, or to the kingdom of God. (The old wineskins cannot contain the new wine that is the phenomenon of Jesus.) New or more nuanced schemas are needed if the word, for which the parable is a vehicle, is to take root and flourish in the psyche of the hearer. See also Keith J. Holyoak and Paul Thagard, *Mental Leaps: Analogy in Creative Thought*, Cambridge, MA: MIT Press, 1995, pp. 1–38.

[31] It should be noted that Jesus's agenda is never to *prove* the existence of God – a theme that has dominated Enlightenment understandings of the goals of natural theology. Like all his contemporaries, Jesus took the existence of God for granted. His "natural theology" uses the natural world as a way of exploring the character of God as he meets with the men and women God created.

approach governed by the exigencies of the situation.[32] In making use of what lay to hand – which is determined by contingencies of physical and social geography, the happenstances of history, the weather, and the rhythms of the seasons – Jesus was perhaps doing no more than any skilled teacher who is perfectly attuned to the mindset of his or her audience. Yet for this approach to be viable the teacher must at the very least believe that what lies to hand is reasonably suitable to illustrate the point he or she wishes to make, and that the connection between the illustration and the point will be received by the audience.

Is there a deeper rationale for this appeal to nature? Do the parables of Jesus of Nazareth both presuppose and express some kind of homology or correspondence between the natural and the divine? This question cannot be answered with any degree of confidence. But what is clear is that, for whatever reason, Jesus's preaching of the kingdom of God rests upon the capacity of nature, when properly interpreted, to disclose the things of God. There does not appear to be a theological system here – more of an extempore coda on a series of fluid natural themes, undergirded by a theology which only becomes manifest to those "in the know."

The parables emphasize what happens *naturally*. Seeds grow. Yeast spreads throughout dough. Sheep get lost. The same principle applies to humanity. Fathers naturally care for their children, and want to give them good things. A discerning merchant naturally wants to have the best pearl. The character of this natural behavior may be good, neutral, or bad. The point is that Jesus is able to use an appeal to natural behavior to communicate the coming of the kingdom. He does not endorse such behavior; he simply uses it as a gateway.

An example will clarify this point. In an important passage dealing with prayer in Matthew's Gospel, Jesus makes the following statement: "If you then, who are evil [*poneros*], know how to give good gifts to your children, how much more will your Father in heaven give good things to those who ask him!" (Matthew 7: 11).[33] We do not have here a concept

---

[32] It will be clear that the absence of a clear understanding of the process by which parables were transmitted and the Gospels redacted means that such questions can never be answered with any degree of certainty: see, e.g., Mark S. Goodacre, *The Synoptic Problem: A Way Through the Maze*, London: Sheffield Academic Press, 2001.

[33] For discussion of the passage, see Anna Wierzbicka, *What Did Jesus Mean?: Explaining the Sermon on the Mount and the Parables in Simple and Universal Human Concepts*, Oxford: Oxford University Press, 2001, pp. 186–91.

of analogy that affirms that human beings are good, and thus possess some inherent capacity to mirror or model the only one who is truly good, namely God. Instead, we find a direct statement that the "evil," often seemingly selfish, fallen, and thoroughly natural behavior of people has the capacity, when rightly interpreted, to reflect the nature of God. This statement of Jesus causes considerable difficulty for those wishing to deny any capacity of the natural to mirror the divine. Perhaps more significantly, it also elevates the status of empirical – not idealized! – human behavior as a means of modeling God.[34]

The parables of Jesus thus make it clear that the empirical world – the ordinary, unsanitized, everyday domain of human experience – can function as a channel for the good news of the kingdom of God, when appropriately interpreted. That belief lies at the heart of a Christian natural theology. Yet the correct interpretation of nature is not self-evident. Nature is a "mystery," something that needs to be disclosed. It is an "open secret," a publicly accessible entity with a hidden inner meaning. Nature can indeed tell us about God – but only if it is seen in a certain light, which is not self-evident.

This idea of a "hidden meaning" or "covert interpretation" of nature is to be contrasted with the belief that nature is capable of being interpreted in a single way, valid for all times, places, and cultures. This belief in a universal "natural philosophy," available to all people at all times through rational reflection on the natural order, was characteristic of the Enlightenment, and has had a deep impact upon Western thought, particularly understandings of "natural theology."

---

[34] A second example is provided by one of the most difficult of the parables – the parable of the unjust steward, found only in Luke's Gospel (Luke 16:1–8.) Many interpreters of this parable have been puzzled by its apparent endorsement of self-serving behavior. Jesus's argument seems to take the following form: it is natural, when confronted with an imminent catastrophe, to take immediate steps to safeguard one's future. As the coming of the kingdom of God is also imminent, should one not take equally urgent action to prepare oneself for the new situation that will result after this watershed? For comment, see Dennis J. Ireland, *Stewardship and the Kingdom of God: An Historical, Exegetical, and Contextual Study of the Parable of the Unjust Steward in Luke 16:1–13*, Leiden: Brill, 1992; H. J. B. Combrink, "A Social-Scientific Perspective on the Parable of the 'Unjust' Steward (Lk 16:1–8a)," *Neotestamentica* 30 (1996): 281–306; Hultgren, *The Parables of Jesus*, pp. 146–57; Duff and Collicutt McGrath, *Meeting Jesus*, pp. 97–114.

In view of the enormous influence of the Enlightenment on the shaping of natural theology in the modern period, we shall explore this in some detail in the following chapter, noting some significant difficulties attending the family of natural theologies to emerge from this complex and variegated movement. In particular, we shall note how the polyvalence of nature creates significant difficulties for those approaches to natural theology that assume it possesses a public significance which can be identified by an "objective observer."

Yet the problem is still more complex than this, in that "nature" is not merely open to many conflicting interpretations; it is a *stratified* notion, possessing a number of interconnected levels, each of which plays a role in determining how it is to be interpreted.[35] In the following section, we shall explore the importance of this point, with particular reference to the use of nature found in the "I am" sayings of the Fourth Gospel.

The Levels of Nature: The Johannine "I am" Sayings

The concept of the "stratification" of the natural world holds that the study of nature suggests that it is experienced and encountered not only from a number of perspectives, but also at a number of levels. Three such levels may be noted for the purposes of this section.[36]

1   The level of the observable world of star-studded night skies, plants and animals, landscapes and sunsets, which have inspired the vision of artists as much as the attention of theologians. This has been the traditional domain of natural theology in the classic sense of the term, as seen, for example, in the Boyle Lectures of the eighteenth century, or Paley's landmark work *Natural Theology* (1802).
2   The level of human interaction with this world. Humanity, as part of the natural order, possesses a capacity to observe and interpret which, as we have seen, also entails action. This aspect of nature itself

---

[35]   Alister E. McGrath, "Stratification: Levels of Reality and the Limits of Reductionism," in *The Order of Things: Explorations in Scientific Theology*, pp. 97–116, Oxford: Blackwell Publishing, 2006.

[36]   Alister E. McGrath, *A Scientific Theology: 1 – Nature*, Edinburgh: T&T Clark, 2001, pp. 249–57.

requires observation and interpretation, and is in its turn an integral part of any natural theology. As we noted earlier, modernist approaches to natural theology tended to exclude the status of the observer from their reflections, implicitly assuming an objectivity of judgment that did not actually exist in practice. Perception, as we stressed earlier, is now accepted to be an egocentric and enactive process, integrally bound up with determining a course of action appropriate to the situation.

3 The level of human culture and society, in which ideas and values are modulated, developed, and transmitted in a way that goes beyond the individual observer and reflector. As used in anthropology, the term "culture" is generally taken to refer to something real, to be found outside the minds of individuals, and objectified in the form of a collection of objects, symbols, techniques, values, beliefs, practices, and institutions that the individuals of a culture share[37] – such as "the set of values and symbols passed on from generation to generation."[38] The approach of Clifford Geertz is often referred to as "symbolic anthropology," on account of its emphasis upon the role of symbols in shaping culture.[39] As Geertz himself summarized his method:

> Believing, with Max Weber, that man is an animal suspended in webs of significance he himself has spun, I take cultures to be those webs, and the analysis of it to be therefore not an experimental science in search of law but an interpretive one in search of meaning.[40]

---

[37] Johannes Fabian, *Moments of Freedom: Anthropology and Popular Culture*, Charlottesville, VA: University Press of Virginia, 1998, pp. x–xi.

[38] Ted C. Lewellen, *The Anthropology of Globalization: Cultural Anthropology Enters the 21st Century*, Westport, CT: Bergin & Garvey, 2002, p. 2. For an overview of the notion, including criticism of modernist homogenization and reification of culture, see Nigel Rapport and Joanna Overing, *Social and Cultural Anthropology: The Key Concepts*, London: Routledge, 2000, pp. 92–102.

[39] For reflections and criticism, see Richard Parker, "From Symbolism to Interpretation: Reflections on the Work of Clifford Geertz," *Anthropology and Humanism Quarterly* 10 (1985): 62–7; Bradd Shore, *Culture in Mind: Cognition, Culture, and the Problem of Meaning*, Oxford: Oxford University Press, 1998, pp. 32–5.

[40] Clifford Geertz, *The Interpretation of Cultures: Selected Essays*, London: Fontana, 1973, p. 5. For a sustained criticism of this approach, see Dan Sperber, *Rethinking Symbolism*, Cambridge, UK: Cambridge University Press, 1975.

Sociologically, it is important to appreciate that attitudes to and under-standings of nature are often "socially constructed."[41] A "social construc-tion" (or "social construct") is a concept or practice which may appear to be natural and obvious to those who accept it, but which is in reality the creation of a particular society. As we shall see, the "I am" sayings are clearly shaped by socially constructed associations between certain aspects of nature and the beliefs, values, and cultus of ancient Israel. The basis of such "social constructs" thus lies primarily – though not necessarily exclusively – in a negotiated social network of meanings, rather than in any essential feature of the aspect of nature in question.

Each of the three levels can legitimately be regarded as "natural," even though it represents a different stratum of nature. These different levels may require different modes of investigation – some physical, some biolog-ical, some psychological, some anthropological, and some sociological – yet all are nevertheless to be seen as constituting "the natural." One of the reasons why the kind of critical realism developed by Roy Bhaskar is so attractive is its capacity to recognize these different levels of reality, and explore them as individual yet potentially interactive domains of a greater whole.[42]

Once this point is recognized, its implications for natural theology will be obvious – namely, that level (1) is not viewed directly, but through a prism or interpretative framework which emerges at levels (2) and (3), as discussed in Chapter 5 (pp. 86–92). Nature itself is "seen" in ways that, though provisional and in principle open to revision, are shaped by history and culture. An aspect of nature is thus "seen" and interpreted through a lens which is a cultural or social artifact – but must sill be regarded as being "natural," despite having been constructed. Indeed, in

---

[41] See the seminal early study of Peter L. Berger and Thomas Luckmann, *The Social Construction of Reality: A Treatise in the Sociology of Knowledge*, Harmonds-worth, UK: Penguin Books, 1971. More recently, see Karin Knorr-Cetina, *Epistemic Cultures: How the Sciences Make Knowledge*, Cambridge, MA: Harvard University Press, 1999.

[42] These boundaries are often somewhat fuzzy and blurred. For an introduction to Bhaskar's approach, see Andrew Collier, *Critical Realism: An Introduction to Roy Bhaskar's Philosophy*, London: Verso, 1994. I explored its theological potential elsewhere: Alister E. McGrath, *A Scientific Theology: 2 – Reality*, London: T&T Clark, 2002, pp. 195–244. For critical comment, see Brad Shipway, "The Theological Application of Bhaskar's Stratified Reality: The Scientific Theology of A. E. McGrath," *Journal of Critical Realism* 3 (2004): 191–203.

one sense, culture is a system of symbols, the outcome of a process of endowing persons, things, and events with meanings. In much the same way, a cultural group can be considered to be a group of persons who share such a set of meanings.

Earlier in this chapter, we explored how the synoptic Gospels record that Jesus of Nazareth used "parables of creation" to teach about the Kingdom of God. Here, nature is clearly understood to have the capacity, when rightly interpreted, to disclose the good news. The Fourth Gospel also understands nature to possess such a capacity, although this is developed in a significantly different direction. In it we find natural symbols, already possessing certain cultural and religious meanings, developed in new and significant ways, which presuppose, build upon, and ultimately transcend their original meaning.

One of the most distinctive features of the Fourth Gospel is the group of sayings based on the Greek phase *egō eimi* – "I am."[43] Although this striking phrase is found elsewhere in the Gospel witness to Christ – for example, in the Gospel of Mark[44] – it plays a characteristic and decisive role in the Johannine witness to the identity and significance of Jesus of Nazareth. Understandably, scholarly interest has focused on the Christological significance of these sayings. The result has been that their implications for natural theology have been relatively neglected. This is unfortunate for, as with the parables of the synoptic Gospels, the "I am" sayings make an appeal to the world of nature.

Each saying appears to have a common structure, linking the explicit phrase *egō eimi* with an "image-term" (e.g., a vine, or light) and an adjective with the article repeated, or a genitive phrase implying uniqueness.[45] The background to these sayings is complex, and is increasingly being recognized as resting on the imagery, phraseology, and theological

---

[43]   For what follows, see Eduard Schweizer, *Ego eimi: Die religionsgeschichtliche Herkunft und theologische Bedeutung der johanneischen Bildreden, zugleich ein Beitrag zur Quellenfrage des vierten Evangeliums*, 2nd edn, Göttingen: Vandenhoeck & Ruprecht, 1965, pp. 64–197; David Mark Ball, *"I Am" in John's Gospel: Literary Function, Background and Theological Implications*, Sheffield: Sheffield Academic Press, 1996; and especially Catrin Williams, *I Am He: The Interpretation of "Anî Hû" in Jewish and Early Christian Literature*, Tübingen: Mohr Siebeck, 2000, pp. 255–303.

[44]   Williams, *I Am He*, pp. 214–54.

[45]   Schweizer, *Ego eimi*, p. 33.

motifs of Isaiah 40–55.[46] This section of the Book of Isaiah is redolent with themes of interconnection, weaving together such motifs as the restoration of Zion, the renewal of nature, the coming of a new era, and the vindication of God. The "I am" sayings, taken collectively, establish a link between this network of associations and expectations and the identity of Christ as the one who fulfills them.[47] The sayings involve an appeal, not only *directly* to nature itself, but to existing *interpretations* and *associations* of nature, already rooted in Israel's past history and future hopes.[48] The sayings do not appeal simply to natural objects or aspects of nature as such, but to these things as they have been assimilated and interpreted within the tradition of Israel. Part of the function of this tradition is to transmit and embody a way of thinking about, and hence *seeing*, nature that can be understood as a "web of significance" (Clifford Geertz, quoting Max Weber). The "I am" sayings can thus be seen as fitting within a matrix that was in part socially constructed, reflecting assumptions and aspirations that were deeply embedded within the history of Israel.

At one level, these saying are responses to elements of nature – such as water, or a vine. Yet the sayings are not based on simple, unmediated observation of nature, but on an inherited way of "seeing" it. A tradition of interpretation of these images emerged within Israel, evident in the

---

[46]   This recognition has been somewhat belated. F. W. Young, "A Study of the Relation of Isaiah to the Fourth Gospel," *Zeitschrift für die Neutestamentliche Wissenschaft* 46 (1955): 215–33, makes no reference to the "I am" sayings at all, despite their obvious Isaianic associations. For the best study of this relationship, see Williams, *I Am He*, pp. 15–54; 255–303. Note that this section of the Book of Isaiah is often referred to as "Second Isaiah." It may be noted that there are seven occurrences of the phrase *ani hu* in the Hebrew Bible, and two of the emphatic variation *anoki anoki hu* (Isaiah 43:25, 51:12). The Fourth Gospel has seven absolute "I am" sayings, with the seventh repeated twice (18: 5, 6, 8).

[47]   Andreas Obermann, *Die christologische Erfüllung der Schrift im Johannesevangelium: eine Untersuchung zur johanneischen Hermeneutik anhand der Schriftzitate*, Tübingen: Mohr, 1996, pp. 228–9. The use of this form of phrase does not necessarily imply that Jesus was claiming to be God, *tout court*; rather, it could be taken to mean that "Jesus is the bearer of the divine name": James F. McGrath, *John's Apologetic Christology: Legitimation and Development in Johannine Christology*, Cambridge, UK: Cambridge University Press, 2001, pp. 104–6.

[48]   Ball, *"I Am" in John's Gospel*, pp. 205–48.

texts gathered together as Isaiah 40–55 – and this inherited interpretation thence became, for the inculcated listener, part of the "natural" images themselves.

The case of Jesus being the "true vine" illustrates this point well. A vine is clearly an image drawn from the world of nature, which serves as a vehicle for the greater truth it articulates. Yet it is an image with existing associations, inherited from the history of Israel.[49] Sayings such as "I am the true vine" are not to be seen as "fulfillments" of a single Old Testament prophecy, but rather as taking "the picture of Israel as the vine of Yahweh" and proceeding to apply this "entire impression" to the person of Jesus.[50] A natural entity or process, already possessing associations with Israel's God, is thus refocused on the person of Jesus of Nazareth, leading to transference of both the image and its associations.

These sayings relate to our account of human perception (pp. 86–92), and demonstrate that in John's Gospel divine revelation involves the inhabitation of human psychological and cultural categories. Consider the saying "I am the good shepherd" (John 10: 11, 14). First, to make sense of this, it needs to be interpreted within a specific schema – in this case, the tradition of conceiving and speaking of Yahweh as the one who shepherds Israel. To discern or perceive the implications of this statement for the identity of Jesus in relation to this God, it has to be received within this specific schema – rather than one which interprets shepherding purely at the level of human agency, whether negatively as an image of human control or oppression, or positively as an image of care.

Second, it offers an account of the significance of Jesus that is affectively tagged, has implications for action, and relates to a human agenda of need. The saying does not offer a precise theological topography – as, for example, in a formalized doctrine of the incarnation, or of the two natures. These can be seen as legitimate secondary abstract inferences from the saying; they are not, however, its primary focus. The primary question is the utility of this statement for the perceiver. As we noted earlier, the issue is the human perspective of need and limitation which requires functional assistance. If Jesus is indeed our good shepherd, who does not

---

[49] See the use of this image in Isaiah 5: 1–7, 27: 2–6; Jeremiah 2: 21; Ezekiel 17: 1–10, 19: 10–14; and Psalm 80: 8–19. For an exhaustive account of these associations, see Rainer Borig, *Der wahre Weinstock: Untersuchungen zu Jo 15, 1–10*, Munich: Kösel Verlag, 1967, pp. 79–93.
[50] Ball, *"I Am" in John's Gospel*, pp. 247–8.

abandon us in the face of danger (to which the listener is alerted by the affect-laden image of ravening wolves in John 10: 12), how does this affect the way in which we live and behave? The response required of the perceiver is inherent in the act of perception. It is a response of trust and following (see also John 14: 5–6).[51]

Finally, and arguably, the saying can be understood to be embodied. That is, the use of the "I am" formula can be understood to imply something more than an analogical relation between Jesus and the good shepherd. There is a feeling of a substantial or material connection, and this has considerable importance for a Christian natural theology. The "I am" sayings can be read as having ontological implications, not merely for the relation of Father and Son,[52] but for the relation of God and the world. They suggest that in some sense, nature is "instressed" with a capacity to reveal the divine. While needing to be seen in a certain way, the natural world has an intrinsic ability to disclose the things of God. The parables of Jesus allow us to see God *through* nature; the "I am" sayings suggest we are to find God *within* nature. While some might argue that there is an essentially arbitrary connection between these sayings and what they represent, a case can certainly be made for suggesting that it rests on something deeper, embedded within the order of things.

While, as we have seen, the "I am" sayings are concerned with function, these sayings also concern identity and being. We continue with the example of the good shepherd. At first sight, this might seem analogous to earlier traditional statements concerning God as a shepherd – as at Ezekiel 34: 15 and Psalm 23: 1. Yet these Hebrew texts are expressed in terms of divine action: for example, in Psalm 23: 1, "the Lord shepherds me."[53] The reference here is thus to God's actions or functions. The emphasis in John 10: 14, on the other hand, is primarily an assertion of identity: Jesus *is* the good shepherd.

So does the "I am" linguistic form itself carry with it any ontological implications? It is important to appreciate that the "I am" sayings are set

---

[51] On this phenomenon, see John Bowlby, *Attachment and Loss, Volume I: Attachment*, London, Hogarth Press, 1969; M. Ainsworth, M. Biehar, E. Waters, and S. Wall, *Patterns of Attachment: A Psychological Study of the Strange Situation*, Hillsdale, NJ: Erlbaum, 1978.

[52] See, for example, Christian Cebulj, *Ich bin es: Studien zur Identitätsbildung im Johannesevangelium*, Stuttgart: Verlag Katholisches Bibelwerk, 2000.

[53] See the Douai–Reims translation: "The Lord ruleth me."

within the context of a theological framework which affirms, as one of its central motifs, that "the Word became flesh, and dwelt among us" (John 1: 14). This certainly suggests that an ontological interpretation of the sayings may be intended.

And if this is the case, it follows that insights about God may not merely be accessible *through* nature; in some way, they may be embedded *within* nature. The "I am" sayings can be seen as expressing the idea that God is known in nature – provided nature is seen in a certain way, using a certain set of assumptions. If the "I am" sayings are indeed to be linked with the doctrine of the incarnation, we can speak of nature being emblazoned or "instressed" with the nature and mark of God. The doctrine of creation enables us to see nature in such a way that it can act as a signpost which points to God; the doctrine of the incarnation enables us to see nature in a way that discloses God within itself.

To explore this point in more detail, we may consider the natural theology of the Jesuit poet Gerard Manley Hopkins (1844–89), noted for his emphasis on seeing God in nature.[54]

Gerard Manley Hopkins on "Seeing" Nature

Natural theology has to do with the issue of discerning God in nature. It is about *seeing* things as they really are. In the third volume of his *Modern Painters* (1856), John Ruskin (1819–1900) declared that "the greatest thing a human soul ever does in this world is to see something, and tell what it saw in a plain way . . . To see clearly is poetry, prophecy, and religion – all in one."[55] For Ruskin, the act of "seeing" nature correctly was essential if the higher work of imaginative penetration and reconfiguration of nature to teach greater truths was to take place. Everything depended on this act of discernment and representation. Yet this raises the all-important question: is this act of discernment itself the "natural"

---

[54] This point is admirably brought out in R. K. R. Thornton, *All My Eyes See: The Visual World of Gerard Manley Hopkins*, Sunderland: Ceolfrith Press, 1975. This work was published to accompany an exhibition at the Sunderland Arts Centre Exhibition celebrating Hopkins' poetry.

[55] John Ruskin, *Works*, 39 vols, ed. E. T. Cook and A. Wedderburn, London: Allen, 1903–12, vol. 5, p. 333. See further the material presented in Susan P. Casteras (ed.), *John Ruskin and the Victorian Eye*, New York: Harry N. Abrams, 1993.

outcome of an engagement with the world – or does it have to be acquired, developed, informed, and calibrated on the basis of something else?

Hopkins insists that we must cultivate the habit of seeing nature correctly, in that this alone holds the key to its appreciation. Yet the predominant trend within the Western theological tradition has tended to assume that our engagement with nature is cerebral and cognitive – the discernment of order and patterns, leading to an orderly, rational deduction of the existence of a creator God. Hopkins invites us to see nature in another way. In this, he was influenced by Ruskin, who encouraged a move away from rational analysis to the development of "seeing" as an instrument of aesthetic discernment.[56]

In his early nature journals, written while he was in his twenties, Hopkins seems to develop a quasi-mystical mode of seeing, capable of discerning previously hidden depths and significance within the natural world.[57] Even the most seemingly ordinary things – a star in the night sky, a bird in flight – are to be seen in a new, theological light; they are marked – or, to use Hopkins' distinctive vocabulary, they are "instressed" – by God's creative act. Hopkins followed Ruskin in cultivating the "instrument

---

[56] The influence of William Pater should also be noted, especially his emphasis on the need to "escape from abstract theory to intuition, to the exercise of sight and touch." William Pater, *Renaissance: Studies in Art and Poetry*, ed. Donald L. Hill, Berkeley, CA: University of California Press, 1980, p. 147. Pater's emphasis on the primacy of sensation has often been noted: see, for example, Graham Hough, *The Last Romantics*, New York: Barnes & Noble, 1961, pp. 134–74; F. C. McGrath, *The Sensible Spirit: Walter Pater and the Modernist Paradigm*, Tampa, FL: University Presses of Florida, 1986, pp. 54–72. For the friendship between Pater and Hopkins, see David J. Delaura, *Hebrew and Hellene in Victorian England: Newman, Arnold, and Pater*, Austin, TX: University of Texas Press, 1969, p. 339.

[57] See the comments of Leo Truchlar, *Über Literatur und andere Künste: 12 Versuche*, Vienna: Böhlau, 2000, pp. 51–70, especially pp. 62–3. Hopkins' emphasis on "seeing" nature has strong echoes in the environmental theology of Joseph Sittler, especially his *Essays on Nature and Grace*, Philadelphia: Fortress, 1972: see Nathan A. Scott, "The Poetry and Theology of Earth: Reflections on the Testimony of Joseph Sittler and Gerard Manley Hopkins," *Journal of Religion* 54 (1974): 102–18. As Paul Santmire remarks, Sittler's emphasis on "seeing" rather than "hearing" must be set within the Reformation debates over these matters: H. Paul Santmire, "A Reformation Theology of Nature Transfigured: Joseph Sittler's Invitation to See as Well as to Hear," *Theology Today* 61 (2005): 509–27.

of sight" in engaging the natural world, though he did not always "see" nature quite as Ruskin saw it.[58]

There are echoes of this theme throughout Hopkins' poetry, which regularly discloses his concern with the individuality of creatures and objects, the utterly unique self carried by each of them, reflecting some fractional part of God's all-inclusive perfection. For Hopkins, any given thing has a distinct place within nature as a whole, is created by God, and possesses an "inscape" – that is, an essence or identity embodied in the thing and "dealt out" by it for others to witness, and thereby apprehend God in and through it.[59] Hopkins develops the notion of "inscape" to mean far more than a positive aesthetic sensory impression, occasioned by the sight of nature: it is essentially an *in*sight, made possible by divine grace, into ultimate spiritual reality, the way things really are – not so much seeing nature as pointing to God, but seeing every individual aspect and element of the natural order, as it were, from God's side.[60] Hopkins, it might be argued, sets out to awaken us to see each individual thing's inscape, which bears the stamp of the divine.[61]

This insight is famously and dramatically set out in the first two bold sentences of "God's Grandeur," which in themselves are enough to demonstrate Hopkins' conviction that, in some way, God's glory is radiated through the natural order.

> The world is charged with the grandeur of God.
> It will flame out, like shining from shook foil.[62]

---

[58] Tom Zaniello, "Alpine Art and Science: Hopkins' Swiss Adventure," *Hopkins Quarterly* 27 (2000): 3–15.

[59] Hopkins' distinct concept of "inscape" can be thought of as the expression of the inner core of individuality, or the distinctive character given to (or dealt to) an aspect of nature by its creator. There are obvious parallels with the Scotist notion of *heacceitas*, although they are not identical notions: see Christopher Devlin, "The Image and Word," *The Month* 3 (1950): 199–201.

[60] A point made particularly by W. H. Gardner, "A Note on Hopkins and Duns Scotus," *Scrutiny* 5 (1936): 61–70.

[61] This is stressed by Rebecca Melora Corinne Boggs, "Poetic Genesis, the Self and Nature's Things in Hopkins," *Studies in English Literature* 37 (1997): 831–55.

[62] The poem was written in 1877. Other poems that explore this theme, although in significantly different ways, were also written around this time: "The Windhover" (1877), "Hurrahing in Harvest" (1877), "As Kingfishers Catch Fire" (1877), and "Binsey Poplars" (1879).

Even though nature is fallen,[63] humanity can still discover God within it. Humanity may have brutalized nature – hints of the devastating environmental impact of the Industrial Revolution can be found throughout the poem – but divine grandeur still radiates from its wreckage, with the potential to recharge itself. Other poets of this era – such as Matthew Arnold – may lament the loss of any sense of divine presence; Hopkins can be said to re-enact the immanence of divine presence within nature through forging ways of "seeing" that nature in such a way that its divine significance may be appreciated. Nature may be "seared with trade; bleared, smeared with toil," wearing "man's smudge." Yet it has not lost its capacity to disclose the transcendent reality of God.[64]

Or has it? On a closer reading of the poem, Hopkins seems to be saying that nature itself is inarticulate, and has to await interpretation through human agency. Nature does not itself proclaim the divine glory; yet such glory may be discerned within it. The "shook foil" is not the same as a "shaking foil," in that it implies that the active agency of disclosure lies outside nature, not within it. By whom is nature "shook," so that the glory of God might shine forth?

The final lines of "God's Grandeur" certainly point to the divine renewal of the nature that humanity has disfigured. Yet they also hint of something else – namely, God's enabling of humanity to find the divine presence and nature, even within the smudged beauty of the world:

> Because the Holy Ghost over the bent
> World broods with warm breast and with ah! bright wings.

We are here confronted with the possibility that the act of "seeing" God's glory may not lie within humanity's own grasp. It is an insight of grace, of revelation. Can we really speak of nature having a capacity to reveal the divine glory, when we are incapable of discerning it without divine assistance? Might nature actually be mute and silent? If nature is itself

---

[63] Terry Eagleton, "Nature and the Fall in Hopkins: A Reading of 'God's Grandeur'," *Essays in Criticism* 23 (1973): 68–75; Michael Lackey, "'God's Grandeur': Gerard Manley Hopkins' Reply to the Speculative Atheist," *Victorian Poetry* 39 (2001): 83–90.

[64] Millar reads "God's Grandeur" as an attempt on Hopkins' part to persuade himself of the presence of God, where others around him had abandoned any such idea: J. Hillis Millar, *The Disappearance of God: Five Nineteenth-Century Writers*, Cambridge, MA: Harvard University Press, 1963, p. 359.

inactive and passive, what is the mechanism of the disclosure of glory? Is glory *disclosed*, or is it *discerned*?

This issue is explored most fully in the poem "Ribblesdale," written in 1883, during Hopkins' period as a master at Stonyhurst College in Lancashire (September 1882–February 1884). As this poem is not well known, it is here reproduced in full.

> Earth, sweet Earth, sweet landscape, with leavés throng
> And louchéd low grass, heaven that dost appeal
> To, with no tongue to plead, no heart to feel;
> That canst but only be, but dost that long –
> Thou canst but be, but that thou well dost; strong
> Thy plea with him who dealt, nay does now deal,
> Thy lovely dale down thus and thus bids reel
> Thy river, and o'er gives all to rack or wrong.
>
> And what is Earth's eye, tongue, or heart else, where
> Else, but in dear and dogged man? – Ah, the heir
> To his own selfbent so bound, so tied to his turn,
> To thriftless reave both our rich round world bare
> And none reck of world after, this bids wear
> Earth brows of such care, care and dear concern.

We see here the structure of the Italian (or Petrarchan) sonnet which is characteristic of Hopkins' poetry at this point: an opening octave, setting the question; a concluding sestet, answering it.[65] The same structure shapes "God's Grandeur."[66] The basic question is this: "earth, sweet earth" cannot speak for itself. It has "no tongue to plead, no heart to feel." So how can it be known? The answer is that it must find its voice through its only surrogate, "in dear and dogged man."[67] Nature can only exist; it has no mind to interpret, and no tongue to communicate that interpretation.

---

[65] For documentation and analysis of this point, see Lesley Higgins, " 'To Prove Him With Hard Questions': Answerability in Hopkins' Writings," *Victorian Poetry* 37 (2001): 37–68.

[66] Other poems showing this Petrarchan sonnet structure include "The Lantern Out of Doors," "Peace," "Hurrahing the Harvest," "Felix Randall" and "No Worst, There is None."

[67] Hopkins added a note at this point, explaining that he intended this as a reference to Romans 8: 19, "For the creation waits with eager longing for the revealing of the children of God."

This point is made more explicitly in one of Hopkins' sermons. After citing Psalm 19: 1 – "The heavens declare the glory of God" – Hopkins comments:

> They glorify God, *but they do not know it.* The birds sing to him, the thunder speaks of his terror, the lion is like his strength, the sea is like his greatness, the honey is like his sweetness; they are something like him, they make him known, they tell of him, they give him glory, but they do not know they do, they do not know him, they never can . . . But man can know God, *can mean to give him glory.* This then was why he was made, to give God glory and to mean to give it.[68]

Nature does not "know" that it is praising and glorifying God, even though it has been created to do so, and is doing so. Humanity, however, while possessing that same creation mandate to glorify and praise, knows that it is doing so, and intends to do so.

Nature, then, does not possess the capacity to interpret itself to humanity. Far from being a self-interpreting, autonomous entity, capable of determining the conditions under which it will be interrogated and the parameters of its subsequent intellectual molding and positioning, its fate lies in the minds of human beings. Yet Hopkins has another point to make, again reinforcing skepticism over any "correct" interpretation of nature. Introducing a note of what seems close to hermeneutical despondency, Hopkins notes that this interpreter of nature is "selfbent" – so wedded to the everyday realities and tasks of life within the world, that any transcendent dimension to nature is lost through humanity's self-absorption, which blinds it to the voice and actions of "him who dealt, nay does now deal."

For Hopkins, nature is inarticulate, mute, silent, without a voice. It has "no tongue to plead, no heart to feel." It is the human translator and interpreter who must be and act as "Earth's eye, tongue, or heart." Might Hopkins have Jesus of Nazareth in mind here, particularly his interpretation of nature? Hopkins is quite clear: nature cannot interpret itself. There is no *right* interpretation of nature forced upon us and authenticated by nature itself. Nature may give, but not command. Humanity must make and proclaim those judgments – and be held accountable for them. But to whom is humanity accountable? Nature itself cannot be

---

[68] *Sermons and Devotional Writings of Gerard Manley Hopkins*, ed. Christopher Devlin. London: Oxford University Press, 1959, p. 239.

our judge, although it may most certainly provide us with the evidence on which a judgment may be made.

Hopkins thus brings us to the point at which any twenty-first-century natural theology must begin: the explicit recognition that nature itself is conceptually and hermeneutically inarticulate. It is for us to interpret nature, knowing that those interpretations are of our own creation. Yet this does not mean that all such interpretations are of equal validity, nor that the quest for the "best explanation" or "most authentic account" of nature is meaningless, or lies beyond our grasp. Hopkins' argument merely confirms that there is no self-evidently "natural" interpretation of nature. Nature is something of a mystery, an enigma which defies neat interpretations. Such a realization may close off one avenue of inquiry, but it does not close down the inquiry itself.

This way of thinking resonates strongly both with the synoptic Gospels' account of the preaching of Jesus of Nazareth concerning the manifestation of the kingdom of God, and the traditional Christian theological perspective which insists that we ultimately need to be told about the nature and purposes of God. We can get so far "on our own steam" – to use a characteristic turn of phrase due to C. S. Lewis – but then stall, needing further help. The insight that nature has the capacity to disclose God is only given from the standpoint of knowing that God, and the attending realization that the Christian vision of God entails that the created order has a God-given potential to tell of its creator.

A Christian natural theology rests on the premise that, although nature may be publicly observable, the key to its proper interpretation is not given within the natural order itself. The key to the "mystery" of the true significance of nature is mediated through the Christian tradition. Those who are "outside" – to use the language of Mark 4 – will never "see" the true meaning of the open secret of nature. The Christian notion of a self-disclosing God is neither a necessary nor sufficient condition for nature to be able to point to that God, nor for it to be denied that function. Yet when the specific content – as opposed to the mere act – of divine self-disclosure is considered, a conceptual framework emerges which has the potential to allow nature to be "read" in this highly significant manner.

This approach stands in contrast to the Enlightenment approach to the interpretation of nature, which held that this publicly accessible reality could be understood in a clear, distinct, and objective manner. We shall evaluate this approach in some detail in the following chapter.

CHAPTER 7

A Dead End? Enlightenment Approaches to Natural Theology

In the previous chapter, we explored how the parables of Jesus of Nazareth affirm that nature, when rightly interpreted, has the capacity to disclose God. This is clearly an insight of critical importance for natural theology, in that it seems to suggest that nature holds the key to a knowledge of God. Yet, as we have seen, the parables of Jesus of Nazareth also suggest that even though the natural world is publicly accessible, its true meaning may lie hidden. The poems of Gerard Manley Hopkins take this further, suggesting that nature is silent and voiceless, requiring a human interpreter to speak on its behalf. So how, then, can nature be said to "speak"? Or to "disclose" the presence and nature of God?

In the present chapter, we shall explore a particularly influential alternative answer to this question, which has had a definitive impact on the shaping of modern approaches to natural theology. A family of natural theologies emerged during this period, shaped by the Enlightenment assumption that nature could be interpreted unproblematically, through judicious use of unaided human reason, to disclose reliable knowledge of God. There is no "secret" or "hidden" meaning of nature, in that the human mind is capable of uncovering its true, public meaning.

The term "Enlightenment" is widely used to refer to the great intellectual and cultural movement, originating in the eighteenth century, that went on to sweep across much of Europe and North America.[1] It is often

---

[1] The English term "Enlightenment" came into general circulation in the late nineteenth century to refer to the movements previously known as *les lumières* and *die Aufklärung*.

seen as having shaped the modern world, especially through its confidence in the power of human reason, its commitment to individual freedom of expression against ecclesiastical or royal tyranny, and its assumption that these values would improve the human condition everywhere. The movement is often considered to have inspired and justified the fundamental nineteenth- and twentieth-century achievements of industrialization, liberalism, and democracy.[2] Western theology has been deeply shaped by the ideas of the Enlightenment – both its positive emphasis upon the competency of reason and the possibility of objectivity of judgment, and its negative critiques of the coherence of the concept of supernatural revelation, and the capacity of Scripture to disclose truths that allegedly lie beyond reason.

The Enlightenment and its Natural Theologies: Historical Reflections

A note of caution, however, needs to be injected at this point. The continued use of the singular term "Enlightenment" is becoming increasingly problematic, in that recent scholarship has suggested that this great movement in Western thought is better conceived as a "family of Enlightenments," sharing a common commitment to a core of ideas and values, yet demonstrating diversity at other points.[3] The idea that the Enlightenment was characterized by a definite set of ideas has proved very difficult to sustain historically; it is better conceived as "an attitude of mind, rather

---

[2]   For a careful and informed assessment of the historical evidence for such bold claims, see John Robertson, *The Case for the Enlightenment: Scotland and Naples 1680–1760*, Cambridge, UK: Cambridge University Press, 2005, pp. 1–50.

[3]   See especially James Schmidt (ed.), *What is Enlightenment: Eighteenth-Century Answers and Twentieth-Century Questions* (Philosophical Traditions, 7), Berkeley, CA: University of California Press, 1996, pp. 1–44; Maiken Umbach, *Federalism and Enlightenment in Germany, 1740–1806*, London: Hambledon, 2000, pp. 25–78. For the argument that the Enlightenment possessed a fundamental unity, see especially Jonathan I. Israel, *Radical Enlightenment: Philosophy and the Making of Modernity 1650–1750*, Oxford: Oxford University Press, 2001, and *Enlightenment Contested: Philosophy, Modernity, and the Emancipation of Man 1670–1752*, Oxford: Oxford University Press, 2006.

than a coherent set of beliefs."[4] This historical observation suggests that it is necessary to speak of a "family of Enlightenment natural theologies," given both the intellectual and social diversity of the movement itself, and especially the diverse attitudes to "nature" it developed. There is no single controlling narrative of an "Enlightenment natural theology," even though a number of themes and concerns can be discerned as significant catalysts to the development and shaping of such theologies.

It is widely accepted that part of the "attitude of mind" that shaped the Enlightenment was an appeal to the universalities of *reason* and *nature* as objective grounds of judgment, especially in the face of ecclesiastical appeals to epistemic – and hence social – privilege. This, as we noted earlier, represented a move away from the classical Greek model of reason as "an ordering principle inherent in reality," and its replacement with an epistemologically inflated notion of a human faculty that "submitted all reality to the structures of the mind."[5]

The appeal to *nature* as a universal ground of judgment can be argued to be, at least in some respects, an accident of history, shaped by events and circumstances of bygone ages. Classic Greek thinkers, anxious over the intellectual limitations of opinion, mere conventions, or subjective prejudices in the realm of moral judgments, sought to find a reliable, universal ground for secure knowledge. In their quest for what we might now call "the objective," they found that some such notion already lay to hand – the idea of "nature." If they had chosen some other term, the history of Western philosophy and theology might well have been rather different.[6]

For these thinkers, nature was to be contrasted with what humans had constructed – not simply in terms of the contrast between natural

---

[4]   Thomas Munck, *The Enlightenment: A Comparative Social History, 1721–1794*, London: Arnold, 2000, p. 7. See also James Schmidt, "What Enlightenment Project?" *Political Theory* 28 (2000): 734–57.

[5]   Louis K. Dupré, *The Enlightenment and the Intellectual Foundations of Modern Culture*, New Haven, CT: Yale University Press, 2004, pp. 12–17.

[6]   As pointed out by Arthur O. Lovejoy and George Boas, *Primitivism and Related Ideas in Antiquity*, New York: Octagon Books, 1973, p. 110. For a more recent account of the development of this category in Greek philosophy, see Gerard Naddaf, *The Greek Concept of Nature*, Albany, NY: State University of New York Press, 2005, pp. 11–35.

phenomena and human fabrications – such as trees versus houses, oceans versus cities – but between *ideas* which resonated with the way things actually were, rather than representing human inventions.[7] For instance, the late fifth-century thinker Antiphon the Sophist argued that a contrast could and should be drawn between "nature" and "laws": the former is something given, in itself stable and immutable; whereas the latter are either arbitrary constructions or self-serving conventions established by humanity.[8]

"Nature," both for some classical Greek writers and their successors in the Enlightenment, thus came to designate what was believed to be an objective reality, a secure ground of judgment which transcended human conventions, and was not dependent upon the consensus or influence of any community for its legitimation.[9] It was not difficult to see how the notion of a "natural theology" conveyed the idea of secure and reliable knowledge of the divine, divested of any distortions or accretions arising from social or ecclesiastical vested interests.[10]

While the Enlightenment can be characterized in a number of ways, there are good reasons for suggesting that it is most helpfully understood

---

[7] For detailed discussion of the relationship between *physis* and *techne* in Aristotle, see Fred D. Miller, *Nature, Justice and Rights in Aristotle's Politics*, Oxford: Clarendon Press, 1995; Helen S. Lang, *The Order of Nature in Aristotle's Physics: Place and the Elements*, Cambridge, UK: Cambridge University Press, 1998. The modification of Aristotle's definition by Philoponus of Alexandria, allowing it to incorporate Christian elements, should be noted here: E. M. Macierowski and R. F. Hassing, "John Philoponus on Aristotle's Definition of Nature: A Translation from the Greek with Introduction and Notes," *Ancient Philosophy* 8 (1988): 73–100.

[8] Geoffrey E. R. Lloyd, "Greek Antiquity: The Invention of Nature," in John Torrance (ed.), *The Concept of Nature*, pp. 1–24, Oxford: Oxford University Press, 1992. Note especially pp. 10–12.

[9] Richard Rorty sees this quest for objectivity as an attempt to evade the parochialism of happenstance, of "being confined within the horizons of the group into which one happens to be born": Richard Rorty, *Objectivity, Relativism and Truth. Philosophical Papers*, Cambridge, UK: Cambridge University Press, 1991, pp. 21–34.

[10] There is an inexact but illuminating parallel here with the emergence of the concept of *physis* in Ionian science in the fifth century BC, partly as a means of re-directing philosophical discourse away from mythological cosmogonies towards a study of "nature as an all-inclusive system ordered by immanent law." See Naddaf, *Greek Concept of Nature*, pp. 15–16.

as a quest for reliable and valid knowledge.[11] Its driving vision was expressed in John Locke's celebrated words: "I know there is truth opposite to falsehood, that it may be found if people will, and is worth the seeking, and is not only the most valuable, but the pleasantest thing in the world."[12]

So how is this truth to be identified? What objective ground of judgment might be proposed, lying beyond the contingencies and corruptions of politics, religion, and power? This concern lay at the heart of the Enlightenment quest for a public, invariant, and reliable foundation of knowledge. A primary motivation for this search for objectivity was growing pessimism about the capacity of religion or prevailing cultural norms to provide a secure, universal basis for knowledge. Growing suspicion of both the intellectual foundations and ethical consequences of religious belief led many to establish truth on the basis of an appeal to pure human reason, untainted by the foibles of outdated traditions, arbitrary prejudice, or cultural and historical location.[13] Reason was held to transcend all human boundaries, offering the only secure foundation for valid human beliefs and values.

A confidence in the autonomy of human reason lies at the heart of the Enlightenment.[14] "Reason" here designates a capacity to analyze and understand, that Enlightenment writers believed to be universal for all humanity, irrespective of their cultural or historical location. A number of factors gave particular credibility to this belief, especially the epoch-making discoveries of Isaac Newton (1642–1727) regarding the relationship of the orbits of the planets and gravitational force. Newton's discovery of the laws of motion had a profound and lasting impact that spread far beyond the sphere of physics, in that they suggested that nature and everything in it was governed by underlying "laws," so that the natural world could be explored and understood by observation and reason. This was held to imply that there were rational, universally valid

---

[11]   This view is defended with reference to scientific enterprise by John M. Ziman, *Reliable Knowledge: An Exploration of the Grounds for Belief in Science*, Cambridge, UK: Cambridge University Press, 1978.

[12]   *The Works of John Locke*, 10 vols, London: Thomas Tegg, 1823, vol. 8, p. 447.

[13]   Mark O. Webb, "Natural Theology and the Concept of Perfection in Descartes, Spinoza and Leibniz," *Religious Studies* 25 (1989): 459–75.

[14]   Frederick C. Beiser, *The Sovereignty of Reason: The Defense of Rationality in the Early English Enlightenment*, Princeton, NJ: Princeton University Press, 1996.

answers to the fundamental questions asked by an enquiring mind, which could be established without recourse to divine revelation. Indeed, it could be argued that the idea of "the transcendent" was potentially subversive of the Enlightenment mindset, which focused mainly on the power of human intelligence to grasp and explain the natural world, and to discover natural causes of phenomena which had previously been considered supernatural.

In such an intellectual environment, the church's public defense of the existence of God on the basis of an appeal to tradition or the Bible became increasingly problematic. The emergence of the fledgling discipline of "biblical criticism" eroded confidence in the reliability of the text of Scripture, while the growing influence of "doctrinal criticism" challenged its traditional interpretations, and the rise of rationalism called the need for divine revelation into question.[15] One apologetic strategy was to attempt to devise arguments for the Christian faith based purely upon reason; the other was to make an appeal to the "universal and publick manuscript, that lies expansed unto the eyes of all"[16] – namely, nature itself.[17]

The primary motivation for undertaking natural theology within English Christianity during the late seventeenth and eighteenth centuries was thus in no small part due to apologetic concerns.[18] The church itself did not reject divine revelation – the idea that God's self and will are made known to humanity. Rather, it realized that it needed to defend the existence of such a God to an intellectual culture which was inclined to be skeptical about this notion. The church, realizing that it was increasingly difficult to base a dialogue with English academic thought upon the Bible, sought an alternative common ground for its apologetic discourse – and

---

[15] Hans Waldenfels and Leo Scheffczyk, *Die Offenbarung von der Reformation bis zur Gegenwart*, Freiburg: Herder, 1977.

[16] This phrase is due to Sir Thomas Browne, *Religio Medici*, II.xiv–xviii.

[17] This growing skepticism concerning the "supernatural" or "transcendent" resulted in the emergence of revisionist readings of the Bible. The origins of the "Quest for the Historical Jesus" lie partly in the Enlightenment's suspicion of any account of Jesus which rested on or incorporated miracles or any form of supernatural intervention. See William J. Abraham, *Divine Revelation and the Limits of Historical Criticism*, Oxford: Oxford University Press, 1982.

[18] For comment, see Alister E. McGrath, "Towards the Restatement and Renewal of a Natural Theology: A Dialogue with the Classic English Tradition," in *The Order of Things: Explorations in Scientific Theology*, pp. 63–96, Oxford: Blackwell Publishing, 2006.

found it in the realm of nature.[19] Natural theology thus rapidly became an apologetic tool of no small importance.

By the early eighteenth century, the concept of "natural theology" was firmly established within English religious culture as a means of demonstrating God's existence without recourse to any religious beliefs or presuppositions.[20] This represented an adaptation of the concept to the realities of the English religious situation, primarily in response to the agenda of the Enlightenment. The abiding influence of the Enlightenment's agenda upon Western theology until relatively recently led to this situation-specific understanding of "natural theology" being assumed to be normative. In fact, it is only one possibility – and one heavily shaped by modernist assumptions, now increasingly being called into question.

As we shall argue in the following section, one of the more challenging insights disclosed through an extended engagement with the natural world is that "nature" and "the natural," far from being objective, autonomous entities, are conceptually malleable notions, patient of multiple interpretations. The influence of power, vested interests, ideological agendas, and social pressures on allegedly "natural" concepts such as goodness, truth, and beauty can be seen in the early eighteenth-century English debate over "natural" qualities, such as beauty, in art and literature.

Following the Enlightenment belief in a universal and objective natural order, many were drawn to appeal to nature as the ground of aesthetic and moral judgments. In the case of England, many leading cultural figures

---

[19] For the dangers attending such an appeal to nature, see Peter A. Byrne, *Natural Religion and the Religion of Nature: The Legacy of Deism*, London: Routledge, 1989.

[20] For the background, see John Gascoigne, "From Bentley to the Victorians: The Rise and Fall of British Newtonian Natural Theology," *Science in Context* 2 (1988): 219–56; John Hedley Brooke, *Science and Religion: Some Historical Perspectives*, Cambridge, UK: Cambridge University Press, 1991. Alternative designations existed, including "physical theology" and "physicotheology." These terms are especially associated with the Boyle Lectures of the early eighteenth century: see Ernest Lee Tuveson, *The Imagination as a Means of Grace; Locke and the Aesthetics of Romanticism*, Berkeley, CA: University of California Press, 1960, pp. 57–8. As used, for example, by Cotton Mather in his 1715 work *The Christian Philosopher*, the term "physicotheology" means something like a "theology that seeks to prove the existence and attributes of God from the evidence of purpose and design in the universe." See Cotton Mather, *The Christian Philosopher*, ed. Winton U. Solberg, Urbana, IL: University of Illinois Press, 1994, p. xliii.

– such as Joseph Addison, Henry Fielding, William Hogarth, Joshua Reynolds and Anthony Ashley-Cooper, third Earl of Shaftesbury – held different views on these allegedly "natural" values, reflecting their differing sociological location as much as their different artistic analyses.[21] To define nature is thus not simply to respond to some objective aspect of the world, which must be normative for our thinking. It is also, perhaps predominantly, to *impose* such a meaning upon it, choosing to view it in a certain way, which may reflect the agendas of those wishing to define it.

In Chapter 5 (pp. 80–110), we noted how contemporary scientific understandings of human cognition and perception erode the idea of an "objective" or "detached" view of the environment, central to Enlightenment views about both nature and natural theology. The late twentieth century has also seen the case for such an objective natural theology weakened further through a growing general cultural appreciation that the term "nature" does not designate an objective, autonomous reality, but essentially designates the ways in which human observers choose to see, interpret, and inhabit the natural world. There are many concepts of nature, in that nature itself is essentially tractable and indeterminate, highly susceptible to conceptual manipulation by the human mind. In view of the importance of this observation for the concept of natural theology, we must consider it in more detail.

The Multiple Translations and Interpretations of the "Book of Nature"

Central to the argument of this book is the belief that there exists a distinctively *Christian* way of "seeing" nature – and hence of thinking and acting within it. As both the parables of Jesus of Nazareth and the "I am" sayings indicate (pp. 126–33), nature has to be approached and understood in a particular way if it is to yield insights into the kingdom of God. A Christian natural theology is about seeing nature in a specific manner, which allows the observer to discern in what is seen the truth, beauty, and goodness of a trinitarian God who is already known; and

---

[21]   See the debates in works such as John Barrell, *The Political Theory of Painting from Reynolds to Hazlitt: The Body of the Public*, New Haven, CT: Yale University Press, 1986, and *Painting and the Politics of Culture: New Essays on British Art, 1700–1850*, Oxford: Clarendon Press, 1992.

which allows nature to function as a pathway towards this same God for secular culture as a whole. The "meaning" of nature is not something that is self-evident, but something that requires to be discerned. The Christian vision of reality includes an understanding of nature, specific to the Christian faith, which provides an intellectual foundation for the discipline traditionally known as "natural theology," while at the same time demanding and enabling its reconception.

The force of this point becomes clear when it is set alongside the conceptual indeterminacy of nature. If nature is open to multiple readings and interpretations, none of which can ultimately be justified with reference to the natural order itself, the traditional approach to natural theology becomes even more implausible. We shall explore this point in what follows, drawing initially on some insights from the Jewish Marxist philosopher Simone Weil (1909–43), who developed a strong interest in Christian ideas late in her life.[22]

The image of "reading" is for Weil a metaphor for the human encounter with reality, through which meaning is discerned within the world.[23] In her "Essay on the Notion of Reading," she explored the factors that shape our "reading" of the natural world, leading us to interpret and inhabit it in different ways. Like a text, nature is "read" or "interpreted" in a wide variety of manners. Similarly, scientific theories can be "read" or "interpreted" in markedly divergent manners: some thus interpret Darwin's theory of natural selection as entailing atheism, where others see it as strongly supportive of belief in theism.[24] Yet while nature is patient of such multiple readings, it neither demands them, nor legitimates them. Nature does not provide its own authorized interpretation. The implications of this point for natural theology are best appreciated by considering how the apparent plausibility of early modern approaches to natural theology has been severely eroded by the recognition of the active role of the reader and interpreter of nature.

---

[22] Francine du Plessis Gray, *Simone Weil*, New York: Viking, 2001, pp. 103–25, 215–30.

[23] See the careful analysis in Diogenes Allen and Eric O. Springsted, *Spirit, Nature, and Community: Issues in the Thought of Simone Weil*, Albany, NY: State University of New York Press, 1994, pp. 53–76.

[24] See the radically different approaches in Richard Dawkins, *River Out of Eden: A Darwinian View of Life*, London: Phoenix, 1995; and Arthur R. Peacocke, *Paths from Science Towards God: The End of All Our Exploring*, Oxford: Oneworld, 2001.

The exegetical optimism of early modern "readings" of nature can be seen from Robert Boyle's 1674 tract *The Excellency of Theology Compared with Natural Theology*. In this work, Boyle noted that "as the two great books, of nature and of scripture, have the same author, so the study of the latter does not at all hinder an inquisitive man's delight in the study of the former."[25] At times Boyle referred to the world as "God's epistle written to mankind." This metaphor of the "two books" with the one divine author was of considerable importance in holding together Christian theology and piety and the emerging interest and knowledge of the natural world in the seventeenth and early eighteenth centuries.[26] Boyle's fundamental assumption, typical of his age, was that the "reading" of the "book of nature" was straightforward and unproblematic.

Yet this textual metaphor raises as many questions as it answers. In the first place, texts require to be translated. Is the "book of nature" written in a language that humanity is unable to understand? Does it possess a rationality to which humanity can gain access? The theological tension here is clear. The heavens may indeed declare the glory of God (Psalm 19: 1); but God's thoughts are higher than our thoughts – and hence seemingly inaccessible (Isaiah 55: 9).

The successes of the natural sciences in explaining and predicting events in the natural world led many to the conclusion that the "book of nature" was written in the language of mathematics[27] – a language to which at least some human minds were adapted. The "unreasonable effectiveness of mathematics" requires explanation,[28] not least on account of the apparently perplexing fact that mathematics, supposedly the free creation of the human mind, possesses a remarkable capacity to describe

---

[25] *The Works of the Honourable Robert Boyle*, ed. Thomas Birch, 2nd edn, 6 vols, London: Rivingtons, 1772, vol. 4, pp. 1–66. For Boyle's views on how nature was to be defined, see J. E. McGuire, "Boyle's Conception of Nature," *Journal of the History of Ideas* 33 (1972): 523–42.

[26] See, e.g., Frank E. Manuel, *The Religion of Isaac Newton*, Oxford: Clarendon Press, 1974, p. 31; Arthur R. Peacocke, *Creation and the World of Science*, Oxford: Oxford University Press, 1979, pp. 1–7.

[27] See especially Joella G. Yoder, *Unrolling Time: Christiaan Huygens and the Mathematization of Nature*, Cambridge, UK: Cambridge University Press, 1988.

[28] For this famous phrase, see Eugene Wigner, "The Unreasonable Effectiveness of Mathematics," *Communications on Pure and Applied Mathematics* 13 (1960): 1–14.

the behavior of the universe. As Roger Penrose and others have pointed out, mathematically based physical theories – including Newtonian dynamics, Maxwellian electrodynamics, special and general relativity, thermodynamics and quantum electrodynamics – have a "superb" ability to "mirror nature."[29] Mathematics offers a puzzling degree of correlation with the natural world, which can be accounted for, at least to some extent, either by a Platonic notion of "recollection" or a Christian doctrine of creation, which postulates a direct collection of the mind of God with the rationalities of the created order and the human mind, as created in the image of God.[30]

If the universe is indeed written in the "language of mathematics," as both Kepler and Galileo believed to be the case, it can perhaps be held to be capable of translation by human beings. Yet texts, once translated, require interpretation. And both translation and interpretation are active, and to some extent interconnected, mental processes. In using the textual analogue of the "book of nature," the difficulties encountered in making sense of the natural order are brought into sharp focus, not least through the helpful comparison with the issues of textual translation and interpretation. The complexity of recent biblical hermeneutical debates makes it clear that identifying a specific text as authoritative, and subsequently being able to translate it into the thought-world of its reader, is only a prelude to the greater task of interpretation. To give an obvious example: the great English translation of the Bible known variously as the "Authorized Version" or the "King James Version" (1611) was a landmark in English biblical translation.[31] Yet it most emphatically did not resolve the intractable hermeneutical debates within English-language Christianity between Roman Catholics, Anglicans, and Puritans.

---

[29] Roger Penrose, "The Modern Physicist's View of Nature," in John Torrance (ed.), *The Concept of Nature*, pp. 117–66, Oxford: Oxford University Press, 1992. For a more extensive exploration of the issues, see Roger Penrose, *The Road to Reality: A Complete Guide to the Laws of the Universe*, London: Jonathan Cape, 2004.

[30] Alister E. McGrath, *A Scientific Theology: 1 – Nature*. Edinburgh: T&T Clark, 2001, pp. 209–14.

[31] See David Daiches, *The King James Version of the Bible*, Chicago: University of Chicago Press, 1941; Ward Allen, *Translating for King James: Notes made by a Translator of King James' Bible*, Nashville, TN: Vanderbilt University Press, 1969; Alister McGrath, *In the Beginning: The Story of the King James Bible*, New York: Doubleday, 2001.

Any text, it must be pointed out, is subject to substantially the same questions.[32] Who, for example, has the right to interpret a text – a spiritual or cultural elite, or anyone who can read? In the case of the Christian Bible, this issue was central to the controversy occasioned by John Wycliffe in the fourteenth century.[33] There is a fundamental issue of power here. As Kantik Ghosh points out, Wycliffe treats Scripture above all as an "ideologically empowering concept."[34] Those who resisted Wycliffe's demands for the democratization of biblical interpretation have offered a traditionalist theological defense of their elitist conception of the right to interpret the Bible;[35] nevertheless, the motivation of issues of power and the consolidation of the *status quo* can hardly be overlooked.

These questions have been of importance at a series of critical junctures in the history of the church – such as the European Reformations of the sixteenth century, the Oxford Movement of the nineteenth century, or the rise of feminism in the late twentieth century. In every case, the question of how the Bible is to be interpreted proved to be critically important, with the interpretations offered closely attuned to the agendas and objectives of the movements themselves.[36] Indeed, it can be argued that the history of the Christian church can be construed as the history of biblical

---

[32]   See the comprehensive survey of issues presented in D. C. Greetham, *Theories of the Text*, Oxford: Oxford University Press, 1999. Of particular importance are his comments on the ontology of the text (pp. 26–63) and the issue of intentionality (pp. 157–205).

[33]   For Wycliffe and his followers the translation of the Bible was also an aspect of this democratization of biblical interpretation: see Kantik Ghosh, *The Wycliffite Heresy: Authority and the Interpretation of Texts*, Cambridge, UK: Cambridge University Press, 2002, pp. 86–111.

[34]   Ibid., p. 22. There is an interesting parallel here with John Ruskin, whose insistence on the right of people to view and appreciate art without a prior knowledge of art theory earned him the sobriquet "the Luther of the arts."

[35]   Ibid., pp. 67–85.

[36]   On the Reformation, see particularly Alister E. McGrath, *The Intellectual Origins of the European Reformation*, 2nd edn, Oxford: Blackwell, 2003. On the Oxford Movement, see Balthasar Fischer, "Eine Predigt Johann Henry Newmans aus dem Jahre 1840 zur Frage des christlichen Psalmenverständnisses," in Ernst Haag (ed.), *Freude an der Weisung des Herrn: Beiträge zur Theologie der Psalmen*, pp. 69–79, Stuttgart: Katholisches Bibelwerk, 1986; Jeffrey W. Barbeau, "Newman and the Interpretation of Inspired Scripture," *Theological Studies* 63 (2002): 53–68. On feminism, see the helpful introduction of Elisabeth Schüssler Fiorenza, *Wisdom Ways: Introducing*

interpretation.[37] The Bible did not disclose how it was to be interpreted, opening up a multiplicity of possibilities.[38]

Such issues are of importance in every area of textual engagement. For instance, Homer's *Odyssey* exhibits the problem particularly clearly.[39] Nathaniel Hawthorne's important and influential novel *The Scarlet Letter* (1850) is a playful exploration of the multiple interpretations that can be offered of signs, when no specific interpretation was intended by their sender; indeed, where there is arguably no meaning intended at all.[40] *The Scarlet Letter* shows how given signs can be interpreted in quite different manners, dependent upon the worldview of the interpreter, so that one person might interpret a natural phenomenon such as a meteor through an Enlightenment prism, another through a Puritan prism. The meaning intended by a sign's originator may not be that imposed upon it (or arguably discerned within it) by its interpreters.[41] The poetry of Gerard Manley Hopkins raises the same issues, not least in relation to his late poem "Epithalamion."[42] But which interpretation is right? Which can be considered as being *intended*? Which is authorized, and which the pure invention of the reader?

While the dynamics of the changing patterns of received interpretations of texts are as yet not fully understood, it is clear that the historical

---

Feminist Biblical Interpretation, Maryknoll, NY: Orbis Books, 2001. For the often neglected historical aspects of this question, see Marla J. Selvidge, *Notorious Voices: Feminist Biblical Interpretation, 1550–1920*, New York: Continuum, 1996.

[37] This is the famous thesis of Gerhard Ebeling, *Kirchengeschichte als Geschichte der Auslegung der Heiligen Schrift*, Tübingen: Mohr, 1947.

[38] For the implications of this point for the shaping of Protestantism, see Alister E. McGrath, *Christianity's Dangerous Idea: The Protestant Revolution*, San Francisco: HarperOne, 2007.

[39] A point brought out by Marylin A. Katz, *Penelope's Renown: Meaning and Indeterminacy in the Odyssey*, Princeton, NJ: Princeton University Press, 1991.

[40] Richard Hull, "Sent Meaning vs. Attached Meaning: Two Interpretations of Interpretation in *The Scarlet Letter*," *American Transcendental Quarterly* 14 (2000): 143–58.

[41] For the general point at issue, see Kevin Hart, *The Trespass of the Sign*, Cambridge, UK: Cambridge University Press, 1989.

[42] Simon Humphries, "'All by Turn and Turn About': The Indeterminacy of Hopkins' 'Epithalamion'," *Victorian Poetry* 38 (2000): 343–63; Michael M. Kaylor, "'Beautiful Dripping Fragments': A Whitmanesque Reading of Hopkins' 'Epithalamion'," *Victorian Poetry* 40 (2002): 157–87.

stability of a given interpretation cannot be taken to imply that this interpretation is intellectually defensible or permanent. The predominant eighteenth-century tendency to read the "Book of Nature" as a witness to the character of God was in fact little more than that age's consensus on the matter – capable of sustaining a traditional "natural theology" only for as long as that consensus lasted. Throughout this period, nature was "seen" as God's creation, with no rival reading of nature being taken with any degree of seriousness. This process of interpretation can be understood at both the psychological and sociological level, reflecting the tendency of both the human mind and social groups to construct and impose interpretative frameworks on experience. The remarkable success of William Paley's *Natural Theology* and the *Bridgewater Treatises* perpetuated the notion that nature was self-evidently to be interpreted in this way.[43] Yet an historical contingency, resting primarily on cultural memories, was here being mistaken for intellectual necessity.

The question of how intellectual historians can account for the "changing certainties" of interpretive communities remains open. For reasons that are not entirely understood, certain ways of interpreting texts gain the ascendancy, and claim to represent the current orthodoxy – only to be displaced by others, in what often seems to represent a Kuhnian paradigm shift, as much as a reasoned, reflective change of viewpoint. Stanley Fish, drawing somewhat selectively on Ludwig Wittgenstein's notion of certainty, seems to suggest that critics read texts in certain ways, holding that these ways are certainly correct, until other critics persuade them that these texts can be read in better ways.[44] Yet this represents the critic as a passive agent, depending on other (active?) critics to bring about a paradigm shift.[45]

---

[43] See the analysis of Aileen Fyfe, "The Reception of William Paley's *Natural Theology* in the University of Cambridge," *British Journal for the History of Science* 30 (1997): 321–35.

[44] Stanley E. Fish, *Is There a Text in this Class?: The Authority of Interpretive Communities*, Cambridge, MA: Harvard University Press, 1980. For an evaluation of this approach, see Michael Fischer, *Does Deconstruction Make Any Difference? Poststructuralism and the Defense of Poetry in Modern Criticism*, Bloomington, IN: Indiana University Press, 1985, pp. 44–51.

[45] See the excellent – but inconclusive – analysis of Reed Way Dasenbrock, "Accounting for the Changing Certaities of Interpretative Communities," *MLN* 101 (1986): 1022–41.

The natural and logical outcome of such skepticism about the "intended" or "correct" interpretation of nature is found in postmodernity's increasingly aggressive examination of the role of vested interests and questions of power in relation to interpretation. One of the most significant aspects of the postmodern deconstruction of literary criticism is the demonstration of the severe difficulties attending any notion of a "definitive interpretation" or a "correct reading" of a given text. Jacques Derrida introduced the idea of "dissemination" to denote the idea that every reading of a text enables new meanings, by placing a text into a new context.[46] As that context is open, it can never absolutely determine one interpretation, nor even a clearly defined group of interpretations. For these reasons, a text can never be completely exhausted; there will always be something more or something else that can be said about it. This point is often summarized in Derrida's slogan *il n'y a pas de hors-texte*, carrying with it the idea that there is no extratextual reality which can be invoked to determine whether a text has been read "correctly."[47] Postmodernity generally takes the view that the meaning of texts is incoherent, indeterminate, or something that is to be decided by the reader. For postmodern writers, there is no "meaning *in* the text"; the meaning is constructed, supplied or imposed by the active reader.[48]

On the basis of this approach, the hermeneutical uncertainties that are encountered in interpreting any text are now accepted to apply equally to an attempt to interpret the "book of nature." If nature can be conceived as analogous to a text, the hermeneutical significance of this analogy cannot be evaded – not least in that Derridean deconstruction, applied to the "book of nature," leads to the assertion that there is no reality external to this text, which is therefore open to a wide variety of cultural readings. There is no means of assessing such readings, as this would involve the imposition of a metanarrative, limiting the freedom of the

---

[46] Jacques Derrida, *La dissemination*, Paris: Editions du Seuil, 1972.

[47] In fact, this represents a truncated, and hence distorted, account of Derrida's point. The text ought to be expanded to read: "*Il n'y a que du texte, il n'y a que du hors-texte, au total d'une 'préface incessante'.*" See Derrida, *Dissemination*, p. 50. For a reflection, see Patrick Ffrench, " 'Tel Quel' and Surrealism: A Re-evaluation. Has the Avant-Garde Become a Theory?" *The Romantic Review* 88 (1997): 189–96.

[48] For a well-informed critical evaluation of this trend in biblical interpretation, see Kevin J. Vanhoozer, *Is there a Meaning in this Text?: The Bible, the Reader, and the Morality of Literary Knowledge*, Grand Rapids, MI: Zondervan, 1998.

reader of the text. The indeterminacy associated with the act of reading applies to nature as much as to the Bible, or any other text. The identity and intentions of the author are not of significance, and a variety of constructions – including the Christian reading of the "book of nature" as God's creation – may be placed upon the reading of this textual analogue. Nature now seems indeterminate, open to multiple, idiosyncratic interpretation.

Nevertheless, these conclusions must be treated with caution. While there is a proper place for a critique of the Enlightenment's unrealistic aspirations to total objectivity of judgment, postmodernity must be seen as representing an ultimately indefensible alternative. A critical attitude to the Enlightenment on this specific issue does not lead to the problematic conclusion that no degree of objectivity is possible at all, so that all beliefs or interpretations can be held to be of equal merit.[49] The proper response to the Enlightenment's unrealistic aspirations to objectivity is not to abandon any attempt at critical evaluation of interpretative possibilities, but to encourage a realistic and cautious attempt to determine which of the various interpretations of nature may be regarded as the "best explanation," as judged by criteria such as parsimony, elegance, or explanatory power.

The importance of this analysis for the approaches to natural theology which arose during the "Age of Reason" will be clear. The Enlightenment assumption that nature could be read in a single, definitive manner is now recognized to be a historical contingency, resting on covert intellectual assumptions that prevailed within English culture during the early eighteenth century. Far from being a necessary or self-evidently correct way of interpreting nature, binding on every rational person, Enlightenment "readings" of the natural world – such as that associated with William Paley – had to be seen as one of a number of possibilities, which happened to have gained the ascendancy at that time. In this light, the case for a tradition-specific manner of interpreting nature – such as a Christian theology of nature, grounded in the notion of the "economy of salvation" – becomes increasingly persuasive. We shall consider this matter further in the following chapter.

---

[49] For an exploration of such points, see Christopher Norris, *Against Relativism: Philosophy of Science, Deconstruction and Critical Theory*, Oxford: Blackwell, 1997, pp. 1–65.

The Flawed Psychological Assumptions of the Enlightenment

Any natural theology rests on implicit psychological and anthropological assumptions, which are often ignored or assumed to be inconsequential for its outcome.[50] The approaches to natural theology characteristic of the eighteenth century treated human beings as detached, objective observers of nature, seeking to offer an explanation and theoretical representation of what they observe. It seemed an entirely "natural" approach, as judged from the standpoint of the Cartesian and Kantian traditions of the Enlightenment. It rests implicitly on the Cartesian distinction between res cognitans and res extensa, which is typically expressed in the idea of an observing subject reflecting on an external object. Humanity observes nature, and reflects on how it is best to be understood.

Prior to Immanuel Kant, there appears to have been a general assumption within the Enlightenment that God could be considered as an entity within nature, or detached from it, and that the scientific study of nature might provide evidence for (or perhaps merely consistent with) God's existence and attributes. As we saw in an earlier section, this was a fundamental assumption of the original Boyle Lectures. The traditional approach to natural theology was also grounded on the assumption – once more, characteristic of the Boyle Lectures – that humans already are, or could become, nonparticipatory observers of nature. These assumptions led to the human observer being regarded as a subject, and God being demoted to an object, by the rise of natural science in the seventeenth and eighteenth centuries.[51] This represents a decline from an earlier understanding of natural theology, which held that God cannot be objectified in this way.[52]

---

[50] See Nicholas Lash, *Easter in Ordinary: Reflections on Human Experience and the Knowledge of God*, Charlottesville: University Press of Virginia, 1988, pp. 89–90.

[51] The relation of subject and object was of major importance in theological debates of this era. One of the most important surveys of the issue is found in James Brown's 1953 Croall lectures at Edinburgh University: see James Brown, *Subject and Object in Modern Theology*, London: SCM Press, 1955.

[52] See Hans Urs von Balthasar, *Presence and Thought: An Essay on the Religious Philosophy of Gregory of Nyssa*, San Francisco: Ignatius Press, 1995.

Both Hume and Kant began to see the flaws in this Enlightenment scheme, through which a meaningful place for God was retained within natural philosophy. Hume's natural philosophy effectively eliminated God from any description of nature, achieving an elegant and parsimonious account of observations that might otherwise have been taken as pointing towards God's existence, or regarded as confirmation of selected divine attributes.[53] Kant argued that God was not a knowable object or phenomenon, but a transcendent reality only accessible by faith.[54] Kant's approach thus erects a theologically impervious barrier between nature and God, preventing human enquiries into nature from reaching any meaningful conclusions concerning God.[55]

Yet the types of natural theology to emerge from the Enlightenment are ultimately not consistent with the contemporary recognition that human cognition is an embodied, situated activity. As we emphasized earlier (see pp. 80–4), human beings are part of the natural order, and their reflections on the significance of that order take place within nature, not above it. While the Christian tradition has always posited a rigorous theological distinction between humanity and the remainder of the natural world,[56]

---

[53]   Wesley C. Salmon, "Religion and Science: A New Look at Hume's *Dialogues*," *Philosophical Studies* 33 (1978): 143–76. While William Paley seemed able to overlook such awkard considerations in formulating his natural theology, his more recent successors have had to be considerably more cautious in their approach.

[54]   What can be known of nature is constrained by *a priori* human ideas and categories, which are capable of assimilating *phenomena*, but not the whole transcendental reality (*noumena*) that lies behind or alongside them. For the implications of this distinction for Kant's account of religion, see Claus Dierksmeier, *Das Noumenon Religion: eine Untersuchung zur Stellung der Religion im System der praktischen Philosophie Kants*, Berlin: de Gruyter, 1998.

[55]   A point perhaps best seen in his reflections on the ontological argument: Otto Samuel, "Der ontologische Gottesbeweis bei Karl Barth, Immanuel Kant und Anselm von Canterbury," *Theologische Blätter* 14 (1935): 141–53.

[56]   The notion of the "image of God" has been of especial importance in clarifying the relationship between God, humanity, and the remainder of creation. Humanity, though located within the created order, is distinguished from it by bearing the image of God. For the development of this theological motif in the early Alexandrian tradition, see Peter Schwanz, *Imago Dei als christologisch-anthropologisches Problem in der Geschichte der Alten Kirche von Paulus bis Clemens von Alexandrien*, Halle: Niemeyer, 1970.

---

this does not alter the fact that our process of reflection on that world takes place within the context of our being agents within it. Martin Heidegger's notion of "being-in-the-world" articulates the insight that the condition of our creating disengaged representations of reality is that we should already be engaged in coping with that world, dealing with it as an experienced reality.[57] Similarly, Maurice Merleau-Ponty stressed that perception and representation take place within the context of an embodied agent purposefully engaging with the world. Merleau-Ponty is critical of the approaches of Descartes and Kant, who he believes to have failed to appreciate that "the perceiving mind is an incarnated mind." This leads him to reject those "doctrines which treat perception as a simple result of the action of external things on our body."[58] This acknowledgement that humanity exists as part of the natural world is a significant contextual factor in any account of revelation. A proper understanding of how the human mind works is essential if we are to understand the potential errors that may arise in encountering and explaining the natural order.

The Barth–Brunner Controversy (1934) and Human Perception

Given these points, it is perhaps surprising that the Enlightenment model of perception continues to have influence over discussions of natural theology. This is especially clear from one of the most significant debates of the twentieth century to focus on this topic – the 1934 exchange of views between Emil Brunner and Karl Barth. This landmark debate did not involve the Christian theological constituency as a whole, but was limited to two Swiss Protestant theologians, each already associated with the "dialectical" approach to theology, which emphasized the infinite separation

---

[57] See the analysis in Søren Overgaard, *Husserl and Heidegger on Being in the World*, Dordrecht: Kluwer, 2004. A similar insight is found in the writings of John Dewey: see Thomas M. Alexander, *John Dewey's Theory of Art, Experience, and Nature: The Horizons of Feeling*, Albany, NY: State University of New York Press, 1987, pp. 119–82.

[58] Maurice Merleau-Ponty, *The Primacy of Perception and Other Essays on Phenomenological Psychology, the Philosophy of Art, History and Politics*, ed. James M. Edie, trans. William Cobb, Evanston, IL: Northwestern Univ. Press, 1964, p. 3.

of – and hence "dialectic" between – divinity and humanity.[59] Both Barth and Brunner had severe misgivings about existing approaches to natural theology. Yet where Barth believed that it lay beyond redemption, Brunner believed that it was capable of renewal.

In 1934, Brunner published "Nature and Grace: A Conversation with Karl Barth", in which he argued that "the task of our theological generation is to find a way back to a legitimate natural theology."[60] It is important to note that Brunner explicitly excludes any notion of natural theology as "a self-sufficient rational system of natural knowledge of God."[61] For Brunner, the key to a renewed natural theology lay in the doctrine of creation, specifically the idea that human beings are created in the *imago Dei*, the "image of God." Human nature is constituted in such a way that there is an analogue with the being of God. Despite the sinfulness of human nature, the ability to discern God in nature remains. Sinful human beings remain able to recognize God in nature and in the events of history, and to be aware of their guilt before God. There is thus a "point of contact" (*Anknüpfungspunkt*) for divine revelation within human nature.

Brunner here argued that human nature is constituted in such a way that there is a ready-made point of contact for divine revelation. Revelation thus addresses itself to a human nature which already has some idea of what that revelation is about. For example, consider the gospel command to "repent of sin." Brunner argues that this makes little sense, unless human beings already have some idea of what "sin" is. The gospel demand to repent is thus addressed to an audience which already has at least something of an idea of what "sin" and "repentance" might mean. Revelation brings with it a fuller understanding of what sin means – but in doing so, it builds upon an existing human awareness of sin.

Karl Barth reacted with anger to this suggestion. His published reply to Brunner – which brought their long-standing friendship to an abrupt end – has one of the shortest titles in the history of religious publishing:

---

[59] For their interaction in this debate, see John W. Hart, *Karl Barth vs. Emil Brunner: The Formation and Dissolution of a Theological Alliance, 1916–1936*, New York: Peter Lang, 2001, pp. 149–76.

[60] Emil Brunner, "Natur und Gnade: Zum Gespräch mit Karl Barth," in *Ein offenes Wort. Vorträge und Aufsätze 1917–1934*, ed. Rudolf Wehrli, pp. 333–66, Zürich: Theologischer Verlag, 1981, pp. 374–5: "Es ist die Aufgabe unserer theologischen Generation, sich zur rechten theologia naturalis zurückzufinden."

[61] Ibid., p. 374.

Nein! ("No!"). Barth was determined to rebut Brunner's positive evaluation of natural theology. It seemed to imply that God needed help to become known, or that human beings somehow cooperated with God in the act of revelation. He insisted that there was no point of contact needed other than that which the Holy Spirit established. For Barth, there was no "point of contact" inherent within human nature. Any such "point of contact" was itself evoked by the Word of God, rather than something which was a permanent endowed feature of human nature.

The Barth–Brunner debate took place in 1934, the year in which Adolf Hitler gained power in Germany. Underlying Brunner's appeal to nature is an idea, which can be traced back to Luther, known as "the orders of creation." According to Luther, God providentially established certain "orders" within creation, in order to prevent it collapsing into chaos. Those orders included the family, the church, and the state. (The close alliance between the church and the state in German Lutheran thought can be seen as reflecting this idea.) Nineteenth-century German liberal Protestantism had absorbed this idea, and developed a theology which allowed German culture, including a positive assessment of the state, to become of major importance theologically. Part of Barth's concern was that Brunner, perhaps unwittingly, has laid a theological foundation for allowing the state to become a model for God.

It was inevitable that this controversy should become enmeshed with the political situation in Germany at the time.[62] The publication of the Barth–Brunner correspondence has allowed clarification of both the content and the stridency of Barth's opposition to Brunner's natural theology, which Barth saw as having unacceptable implications for both ecclesiology and church politics as Nazism rose to cultural dominance. This came to be linked particularly with the differences between Barth and Brunner over the "Oxford Group" of Frank Buchman, which was actively courting Nazi officials at that time.[63]

Barth took the view that Brunner's natural theology, if applied in the contemporary German context, would endorse, and lend theological

---

[62] As noted by James Barr, *Biblical Faith and Natural Theology*, Oxford: Clarendon Press, 1993, pp. 111–17. Barr's views require some modification in the light of the publication of the Barth–Brunner correspondence, which allow a better appreciation of the precise political issue involved.

[63] See the critically important material presented in Hart, *Karl Barth vs. Emil Brunner*, pp. 177–200.

credibility to, the position of the pro-Nazi "German Christians." Barth was not here suggesting that the *cause* of his disagreement with Brunner was political. Nevertheless, these considerations make it clear that the political circumstances of that critical period made the issue of natural theology particularly important, with Brunner's position being alleged to lend weight to the German Christians, rather than the Confessing Church.

The correspondence between Karl Barth and Emil Brunner makes it clear that Barth and Brunner had already exchanged views on some matters of relevance to natural theology – such as the notions of the image of God in humanity, the point of contact, and the relation of nature and grace – in their earlier correspondence.[64] These tensions thus did not come into being in 1934, but can be traced back to the beginning of their relationship. This was not a "new" controversy, but a public manifestation of tensions and differences that had been building up for some time in private.

All of these observations serve as important reminders that natural theology has implications for a broader range of issues than simply making sense of the world. Yet our concern at this point focuses on the important role played by Enlightenment assumptions about perception within this controversy. One of Brunner's most fundamental criticisms of Barth is that he allows no conceptual space for the active involvement of humanity in the process of the interpretation of nature. It is a familiar criticism, responding to Barth's often-expressed concern that theology might become beholden to anthropology or psychology.[65] Yet does Barth's concern legitimate the evasion of any attempt to understand the human perceptual processes which are involved in the identification and interpretation of revelation?

---

[64] For the best study of this relationship in the period leading up to, and immediately after, the 1934 controversy on natural theology, see Hart, *Karl Barth vs. Emil Brunner*. Hart traces back the tensions in their relationship back to 1918, by which time Brunner had already expressed concern about the "one-sidedness" of Barth's conception of revelation (pp. 16–17).

[65] Daniel J. Price, *Karl Barth's Anthropology in Light of Modern Thought*, Grand Rapids, MI: Eerdmans, 2002 offers a positive account of Barth's engagement with anthropology which places him much closer to Brunner than most Barth scholars would allow. Price seems to interpret Barth through the prism of Emil Brunner, especially Brunner's landmark article "The New Barth: Observations on Karl Barth's Doctrine of Man," *Scottish Journal of Theology* 4 (1951): 123–35.

Barth's notion of "revealedness" may appear theologically pellucid; it is, regrettably, psychologically opaque, offering little in the way of clarification of how human beings arrive at the epistemologically decisive insight that *this* event or *this* person is indeed to be accepted as divine self-revelation, where others are not.

The fundamental point is, as we shall see, that both Barth and Brunner understood perception as an essentially passive process which can be redirected and shaped in an inscrutable manner by divine grace. While Barth appears to have reversed the Enlightenment's judgment that God was a passive object and humanity an active subject,[66] so that humanity is now to be seen as the object of God's action, Barth continued to operate with a psychology of perception that was characteristic of the Enlightenment. There seems to be no recognition that an understanding of the process of perception is relevant to the theologically critical judgments as to what is divine revelation, and what is not.

Both Barth and Brunner depend upon implicit perceptual judgments in developing their approaches to natural theology. How do we discern revelation? How can one person interpret an event as God's self-revelation, and another as something natural, with no divine connection or referent? How does Christian theology relate to the empirical world? Brunner, for his part, argues that a distinctive aspect of human identity was *Wortmächtigkeit* ("a capacity for words").[67] This capacity for words means that humanity, and humanity alone, has the capacity to receive the Word of God.[68] Despite the Fall, humanity has never lost its distinctive capacity

---

[66] For comment, see Alister E. McGrath, "Karl Barth als Aufklärer? Der Zusammenhang seiner Lehre vom Werke Christi mit der Erwählungslehre," *Kerygma und Dogma* 30 (1984): 273–83. Although this article relates especially to Barth's soteriology, the points apply equally to his epistemology.

[67] Brunner, "Natur und Gnade," p. 348. Some – such as John Baillie – have suggested that Barth appears to have misread this anthropological capacity as *Offenbarungsmächtigkeit* – "a capacity for revelation" – which is clearly not what Brunner intended. Nevertheless, Barth's interpretation is entirely understandable, given Brunner's statements concerning the "permanent capacity for revelation" (*dauernde Offenbarungsmächtigkeit*) of the created order. For an interesting debate over this issue, see Trevor Hart, "A Capacity for Ambiguity? The Barth–Brunner Debate revisited," *Tyndale Bulletin* 44 (1993): 289–305; Stephen Andrews, "The Ambiguity of Capacity: A Rejoinder to Trevor Hart," *Tyndale Bulletin* 45 (1994): 169–79.

[68] Brunner, "Natur und Gnade," p. 348.

for words, which is the precondition of any capacity to hear and respond to the Word of God. Yet this formal human capacity for words does not imply a material capacity to recognize and respond to divine revelation. Anyone can hear God's word; the question, however, is *how we hear it in a particular way*. The point that Brunner is trying to make is that, if revelation is not *recognized as* revelation, it cannot *be* revelation. "The Word of God itself creates the human capability [*Fähigkeit*] to believe the Word of God, and thus the capability to hear it in such a way that is only possible as a believer."[69] This, for Brunner, is a matter of divine grace, not natural human achievement. Yet it is clear that this human "capability to hear [the Word of God] in such a way" requires clarification, in that it involves the process of perception.

A similar point is made by Barth, who offers a trinitarian account of revelation based on the notions of revealer, revelation, and revealedness.[70] This significant distinction between *Offenbarung* and *Offenbarkeit* points to the capacity of people to "look at" an event, yet for only some to "see" it as divine revelation. Barth's important analysis of the relationship of trinitarian foundations of the doctrine of the Word of God emphasizes that revelation needs to be *perceived as* revelation before it can *be* revelation. Yet this act of perception is passed over, apparently being assumed to require no comment or analysis.

Despite their significant differences, Barth and Brunner seem united in their belief that revelation involves an act of *perception* – the recognition of something for what it really is, when that reality, though publicly accessible, possesses a deeper meaning that is veiled or hidden. Both Barth and Brunner hold that this perception is a human act that lies beyond unaided human endeavor, and must therefore be understood as resting on an act of divine grace. Of the two writers, it is clear that it is Brunner who is more open to reflecting on the nature of perception, and its implications for his account of revelation in general, and natural theology in particular.

---

[69] Ibid., p. 349.

[70] See the classic study of Eberhard Jüngel, *Gottes Sein ist im Werden: Verantwortliche Rede vom Sein Gottes bei Karl Barth: eine Paraphrase*, Tübingen: Mohr, 1965. For concerns that Barth's doctrine of the Trinity is fundamentally modalist at this juncture, see the discussion in Dennis W. Jowers, "The Reproach of Modalism: A Difficulty for Karl Barth's Doctrine of the Trinity," *Scottish Journal of Theology* 36 (2003): 231–46.

Yet this recognition of the importance of the activity of perception is not accompanied, in either case, with any concern to explore how human perception takes place empirically,[71] despite the potential of such an engagement for clarifying how misunderstandings of revelation can arise. Barth in particular tends to treat the human mind as a bystander, rather than active participant, in the process of revelation through the reception and transmission of the word. Yet humanity clearly brings *something* to the encounter with the divine, suggesting that a dialogue with psychology would be theologically productive.[72] The result of Barth's denial of natural theology is that a breach is opened between human experience and the Christian faith, which gives the impression that "Christian faith is an irrelevant superstructure over human reality."[73]

A "revealed" or dogmatic theology which sets itself against what is known of the process of natural perception, or ignores it altogether (as with Barth), does not offer a satisfactory model for a dialogue between an incarnated God and humanity. While Emil Brunner recognizes the importance of such a dialogue, he offers such a psychologically naive account of perception that his analysis of the divine–human interaction in revelation must be judged to be unworkable. For, as we have already emphasized, any theology of revelation always articulates an implicit anthropology and psychology, whether or not theologians choose to make this explicit.[74] For this reason, we believe that theology must enter into dialogue with what is known of human perception, and ensure that a psychologically informed approach to natural theology is developed.

It is, however, appropriate to end this chapter by summarizing some of the major concerns raised against the family of natural theologies which emerged from the Enlightenment.

---

[71] Barth's response to this expression of concern would be to stress the need for a *theological* account of humanity, rather than to become dependent upon an understanding of human nature that does not derive from the Christian revelation. For a not entirely successful attempt to involve Barth in a somewhat forced dialogue with object relations psychology (represented by R. D. W. Fairbairn), see Price, *Karl Barth's Anthropology in Light of Modern Thought*.

[72] See the exploration of this point in Lash, *Easter in Ordinary*, pp. 105–30.

[73] Barr, *Biblical Faith and Natural Theology*, p. 50.

[74] For a welcome discussion of this point, see Lash, *Easter in Ordinary*, pp. 89–90: "our theology is always correlative to our anthropology. The correlations may, and indeed should, be mutual."

Enlightenment Styles of Natural Theology:
Concluding Criticisms

As we have noted, many theologians and philosophers sympathetic to the Enlightenment appear to have believed that there existed a self-authenticating, objective, and universal means of engaging with the world of nature, which either was in itself, or could function as the basis of, a generalized natural theology. Such a belief lay behind the great enterprise of "natural theology" in the modernist sense of the term, particularly during the eighteenth century.

Yet it is now recognized that there are a number of difficulties facing such an approach, the cumulative force of which is sufficient to suggest that a new paradigm is required for Christian natural theology, capable of accommodating the merits of the older model, whilst repositioning it conceptually and correcting its shortcomings. The basic problem is that the Enlightenment treated perception as a simple act of reading off the one meaning of nature from an objective viewpoint obtained by rational means, to yield an "allocentric" (see p. 95) representation of reality that was free from dogma. Yet this account of the process is open to criticism at three points, as follows.

1   The Enlightenment account of perception is not "natural," in that it fails to appreciate that rationality is something that is acquired through training – as, for example, in the creation of "maps" (p. 84). Furthermore, rationality is highly culturally located, not, as the Enlightenment mistakenly assumed on *a priori* grounds, independent of culture and history.

The Enlightenment's failure to recognize that perception involves the acquisition of certain interpretative habits is of importance at two levels. In the first place, a distinction must be drawn between "natural" and "unnatural" ways of interpreting the world.[75] Certain interpretations of the world can be defined as "natural," either in the sense of being intuitive, obvious, familiar, or "noncultural" (Pascal Boyer). It is increasingly argued that religious interpretation of natural phenomena belong in this

---

[75]   See the important essay by Robert N. McCauley, "The Naturalness of Religion and the Unnaturalness of Science," in F. Keil and R. Wilson (eds), *Explanation and Cognition*, pp. 61–85, Cambridge, MA: MIT Press, 2000.

category.[76] In contrast, certain other ways of interpreting nature – including the natural sciences – must be regarded as "unnatural," in that they demand certain assumptions and procedures which are counterintuitive and unfamiliar, and therefore need to be taught to individuals.[77] Whereas some Enlightenment writers appear to have believed that the scientific method was "natural," many argue that the method has to be learned or acquired, and reinforced socially through institutions.

Secondly, there is an illuminating parallel, which we noted earlier (pp. 147–55), with the familiar metaphor of "reading" the book of nature. The capacity to interpret a text is an acquired skill. The naive reader might adopt a reading strategy appropriate for a quite distinct literary genre, misreading fiction as history. The importance of the issue is especially evident in complex works, such as the paradoxical novels of Iris Murdoch, which are open to multiple, competing readings.[78] Do readers need to possess certain core competencies before reading a new text?[79] Some would argue that the reader must be *prepared* for the task of reading, already possessing a certain familiarity with how texts work, and being alert to signals within the text as to how it is to be read.[80]

So how is the reader of the "book of nature" to be prepared for that encounter, when there are no directly analogous texts by which such preparation may take place? It is an important question, not easily answered. Yet its significance is easily appreciated by reflecting on conventions of

---

[76] Pascal Boyer, *The Naturalness of Religious Ideas: A Cognitive Theory of Religion*, Berkeley, CA: University of California Press, 1994.

[77] Lewis Wolpert, *The Unnatural Nature of Science*, London: Faber and Faber, 1992.

[78] Compare the different readings of *The Unicorn* offered by A. S. Byatt, Guy Backus, and Elizabeth Dipple, analyzed by Barbara Stevens Heusel, *Iris Murdoch's Paradoxical Novels: Thirty Years of Critical Reception*, Rochester, NY: Camden House, 2001.

[79] As argued by Jonathan D. Culler, *Structuralist Poetics: Structuralism, Linguistics and the Study of Literature*, London: Routledge, 2002. This could be correlated with Noam Chomsky's account of language, which draws a sharp distinction between competence and performance, correlating the former with the deep structure, and the latter with the surface structure, of a text. See Noam Chomsky, *Aspects of the Theory of Syntax*, Cambridge, MA: MIT Press, 1965.

[80] The same issue arises in interpreting and evaluating art: as Kendall Walton has argued, the competency to discern the category of art to which a work belongs is essential to its interpretation. Kendall Walton, "Categories of Art," *Philosophical Review* 79 (1970): 334–67.

literary interpretation – for example, those of the medieval period. In a lucid analysis of how certain texts were read during the medieval period, Robert Sturges highlights the importance of "the two competing semiologies of the Middle Ages." The first of these is Augustinian (although Sturges regards it as more fundamentally neo-Platonic than Christian), which seeks to avoid indeterminacy in language and to safeguard its access to higher truths through the fundamental assumption that language possessed a transcendental reference. The second, which Sturges finds exemplified in a literary context by the rhetorical treatises of Matthew of Vendôme (abbot of Saint Denis from 1254–87) and Geoffrey of Vinsauf (fl. circa 1200), "began to suggest that new literary works could legitimately be created with an emphasis on their own surface beauty and the aesthetic pleasure they could give, rather than on any spiritual truths to be discovered through symbolic deep reading."[81] These two habits of reading, each with their own inner logic and understandings of signs, inevitably lead to radically different interpretation of texts. The same issues emerge in reading the text of nature.

2   "Nature" needs to be defined and translated, recognizing that it is a constructed notion. Both the subject matter and the phenomenon of nature are determined by individual and group agendas and culture. What we know of human psychological cognitive processes underlying perception is borne out of the multiple interpretations of nature we see in history and culture, reflecting the emergence of different schemas. Indeed, the way in which the human mind functions is consistent with and analogous to the way in which culture functions – for example, in imposing order on phenomena.

The point here is that "rationality" is itself shaped by cultural and historical factors, embedded in traditions. Richard Rorty draws on the authority of both John Dewey and Michel Foucault in asserting that "rationality is what history and society make it."[82] If rationality is a

---

[81]   Robert S. Sturges, *Medieval Interpretation: Models of Reading in Literary Narrative, 1100–1500*, Carbondale, IL: Southern Illinois University Press, 1991, p. 12.

[82]   Richard Rorty, *The Consequences of Pragmatism*, Minneapolis, MN: University of Minneapolis Press, 1982, p. 204. Rorty's account of both Dewey and Foucault requires nuancing at this point, as noted by James D. Marshall, "On What We May Hope: Rorty on Dewey and Foucault," *Studies in Philosophy and Education* 13 (1994): 307–23, especially pp. 312–13.

socially constructed notion, reflecting a society's norms and values at a given historical point, and prone to erosion and evolution over time, a natural theology based upon it can do little more than reflect, however critically, the way in which a given society chose to view nature at that moment in history. Such a natural theology would thus be shaped by the contingencies of history and culture, rather than resting on the alleged universality of "necessary truths of reason."

This is the point that emerges from the metahistorical analysis of Alasdair MacIntyre, who argued that "the legacy of the Enlightenment has been the provision of an ideal of rational justification which it has proved impossible to attain."[83] If reason is capable of delivering unambivalent, objective judgments, why did so many questions remain open and disputed, even within the Enlightenment itself? For MacIntyre, the only conclusion that can be drawn from this signal rationalist failure is that the notion of a universal rationality is an aspiration, an ideal, rather than an actually existing entity, capable of being realized. Instead, he argued, we must bow to the evidence of history, and accept that there are competing tradition-mediated rationalities, which cannot be totally detached from the traditions which mediate them. They may have pretensions to universality; nevertheless, the historical record discloses that they are actually specific to traditions.[84]

3 Attempts to construct a "natural" theology must therefore be recognized to be just as culturally bound as the "revealed" or "dogmatic" theology that they attempt to evade or displace. Natural theology is rather more dogmatic, and dogmatic theology rather more natural, than many appear to have realized. There is an important parallel here with the famous "Quest for the Historical Jesus," which mistakenly assumed, in the first place, that history could be reconstructed and interpreted unambiguously (note the parallel with the process of interpreting nature), and in the second, that a metaphysically minimalist Christology was to be regarded as more authentic than more complex and developed alternatives.[85] The "historical Jesus" proved to be rather less empirical than his

---

[83] Alasdair MacIntyre, *Whose Justice? Which Rationality?* Notre Dame, IN: University of Notre Dame Press, 1988, p. 6.

[84] Ibid., p. 334.

[85] A point made repeatedly by Martin Kähler, *Der sogenannte historische Jesus und der geschichtliche, biblische Christus*, Munich: Kaiser Verlag, 1953, pp. 40–5.

advocates appreciated, just as the "Christ of faith" turned out to have a more substantial empirical foundation than rationalist critics allowed.[86]

It therefore follows that attempts to interpret nature are culturally shaped. Nature is patient of a vast variety of interpretations – including, but not limited to, Christian, Jewish, Islamic, panentheist, pantheist, atheist, and agnostic readings – while demanding none of them. The endless argument over whether the natural sciences entail atheism, various forms of theism, or simply agnosticism illustrates this point.[87] The argument lies beyond resolution, primarily on account of the conceptual malleability of nature itself. Might nature have to be recognized as a text whose meaning is indeterminate, if it has any meaning at all? None of the multiplicity of interpretative frameworks that are brought to bear upon nature can be regarded as being authorized or legitimated by nature itself. There is no universal metacriterion which determines which of these multiple readings is to be preferred.

This reinforces our criticism of those who propose a sharp distinction between the "natural" and the "dogmatic," in that this appears to presuppose that the former category avoids the interpretative schemas that are so characteristic of the latter. The observation of nature is theory-laden, reflecting the ideological precommitments, conscious or otherwise, of the observer.[88] To use a familiar theological counterpart, the notion of the presuppositionless interpretation of nature is just as problematic as that of the presuppositionless interpretation of the Bible.[89] Nature may be interpreted on the basis of the (dogmatic) assumption that reality is

---

[86] See the discussions in Paula Fredrikson, *From Jesus to Christ: The Origins of the New Testament Images of Jesus*, New Haven, CT: Yale University Press, 1988; N. T. Wright, *The New Testament and the People of God*, Minneapolis, MN: Fortress, 1992.

[87] For representative contributions, see Richard Dawkins, *Unweaving the Rainbow: Science, Delusion and the Appetite for Wonder*, London: Penguin, 1998; Mary Midgley, *Evolution as a Religion: Strange Hopes and Stranger Fears*, 2nd edn, London: Routledge, 2002; Alister E. McGrath, *Dawkins' God: Genes, Memes and the Meaning of Life*, Oxford: Blackwell Publishing, 2004.

[88] A point often emphasized by Norwood Hanson: see, e.g., N. R. Hanson, *Patterns of Discovery: An Inquiry into the Conceptual Foundations of Science*, Cambridge, UK: Cambridge University Press, 1958.

[89] Rudolf Bultmann, "Is Exegesis without Presuppositions Possible?" in Kurt Mueller-Vollmer (ed.), *The Hermeneutics Reader: Texts of the German Tradition from the Enlightenment to the Present*, pp. 241–8, Oxford: Blackwell, 1986.

limited to what may be observed; it may also be interpreted in the light of the very different set of beliefs associated with the Christian tradition, which offer a quite distinct interpretation of what is observed.

Yet these three concerns, important though they are, do not require the abandonment of natural theology; they point instead to its need for renewal and reinvigoration. While it seems inevitable that the quest for any universal, self-evidently "right" or "objective" interpretation of nature will have to be recognized as unsustainable in the light of the problematic history of the enterprise, this merely points to the need to consider tradition-mediated rationalities instead. In other words, a specific interpretation of nature is adopted, which is believed to be (but cannot be *proved* to be) the best account possible in terms of criteria of explanatory excellence – such as the degree of empirical fit, conceptual elegance, and fecundity. Such an approach will be both internally coherent and grounded in reality,[90] recognizing that it represents a tradition, while claiming that this tradition offers the best explanation of what may be observed in nature, culture, and human experience – including the existence of rival traditions.[91]

Natural theology, as this notion has come to be (mis)understood in the twentieth century, is thus a child of the Enlightenment: its distinctive features and assumptions have been shaped to a significant extent by the cultural and intellectual circumstances of that time. This, however, is only one of a number of ways of conceiving the nature and approach of a "natural theology." The approach has, of late, languished in the face of increasing criticism on theological, philosophical, and scientific grounds, and a general sense that it has run out of intellectual steam.[92] A new approach – or the renewal and refurbishment of an older one – is needed. We therefore turn to consider the Christian notion of a "self-disclosing God," and its implications for a natural theology.

---

[90] For the importance of these two criteria, see Alister E. McGrath, *A Scientific Theology: 2 – Reality*, London: T&T Clark, 2002, pp. 38–54.

[91] See the extended discussion in McGrath, *A Scientific Theology: 2 – Reality*, pp. 55–120.

[92] For comments on the discontentment with natural theology in the English-language world, see Richard Swinburne, "Natural Theology, its 'Dwindling Probabilities' and 'Lack of Rapport'," *Faith and Philosophy* 21 (2004): 533–46.

CHAPTER 8

A Christian Approach to Natural Theology

In the previous chapter, we examined the failure of the generalized forms of natural theology that were so characteristic of the Enlightenment. In their place, we wish to reaffirm the importance of reconceiving natural theology as an enterprise which derives its legitimization and mandate from within the Christian tradition, rather than from some allegedly "universal" general principles. The dynamic mental structures which Christians use to interpret experience arise partly from adaptation to the specific notions of the Christian tradition, which include distinct and often counterintuitive notions about the nature of God, and God's involvement in the world. This naturally leads us to explore what form of engagement with the natural order is mandated by the specific ideas of the Christian tradition.

The approach to natural theology developed in this work holds that the matrix of interconnecting ideas that make up the web of Christian doctrine provides an intellectual framework that makes the enterprise of natural theology possible. However, this type of natural theology is not to be understood as an autonomous discipline, capable of discovering God under terms and conditions of its own choosing. Rather, it is a theologically grounded discipline, deriving both its intellectual justification and its explanatory success from the Christian tradition.

On "Seeing" Glory: The Prologue to John's Gospel

In the first part of this work, we noted how the human quest for the transcendent is to be seen as a general cultural phenomenon, not necessarily linked with any specifically religious tradition or agenda. Yet it is clear that this general quest is given a definite form and direction by the specifics of the Christian tradition. Christian faith makes possible a particular way of "seeing" the world, which allows it to be perceived as a created reflection of divine glory and wisdom. Both the parables of Jesus of Nazareth and contemporary understandings of cognition and perception emphasize that "seeing" is not the same as "perceiving."[1]

The importance of "seeing" correctly is clearly stated in the prologue to John's Gospel (John 1: 1–18), which needs to be read carefully and in its totality with this specific agenda in mind.

In the beginning was the Word, and the Word was with God, and the Word was God. He was in the beginning with God. All things came into being through him, and without him not one thing came into being. What has come into being in him was life, and the life was the light of all people. The light shines in the darkness, and the darkness did not overcome it.

There was a man sent from God, whose name was John. He came as a witness to testify to the light, so that all might believe through him. He himself was not the light, but he came to testify to the light. The true light, which enlightens everyone, was coming into the world. He was in the world, and the world came into being through him; yet the world did not know him. He came to what was his own, and his own people did not accept him. But to all who received him, who believed in his name, he gave power to become children of God, who were born, not of blood or of the will of the flesh or of the will of man, but of God.

And the Word became flesh and lived among us, and we have seen his glory, the glory as of a father's only son, full of grace and truth. (John testified to him and cried out, "This was he of whom I said, 'He who comes after me ranks ahead of me because he was before me.'") From his fullness we have all received, grace upon grace. The law indeed was given through Moses; grace and truth came through Jesus Christ. No one has ever seen

---

[1] Note also that Paul speaks of the human capacity to "see" the "invisible things of God" in or through the created order (Romans 1: 20). Yet one may see such things without perceiving their full significance, or discerning the "big picture" to which they point.

God. It is God the only Son, who is close to the Father's heart, who has made him known.

This prologue sets out the intellectual foundations of an incarnational approach to natural theology. It opens by laying out a doctrine of creation, in which supreme emphasis is placed on the logos – the word, which brought all things into existence. There is no notion here of "natural theology" as an antecedent conceptual system. Instead, we find the idea of the illumination of an otherwise shadowy, opaque, and ambiguous creation through the same "Word" that originally created it, and subsequently entered into it as the "Word become flesh." The prologue continues by declaring that the one who has made God known also enlightens our minds so that we may see him reflected in the creation. He "came to what was his own," inhabiting both the physical space and cultural categories of the people of Israel, in order that they might perceive his true significance.

The divine light of the *logos* allows us to "see" the created order in the proper way, so that human limitations in discerning the divine might be overcome. Yet Christ, as the Word incarnate, does more than illuminate and interpret the created order. He is the one who enters into that order, thus transforming its capacity to point to God. And there is more: Christ himself discloses the nature and glory of the hitherto invisible God in a human person. The disclosure of the glory of God thus comes through nature, not above nature. The enfleshed Word of God makes God known to humanity in and through the natural order. This theologically dense and profound passage does more than provide a link between the doctrine of creation and a natural theology; it provides a framework linking creation, incarnation, and revelation.

"We have seen his glory." The Word enters into history and nature, and is able to witness – to make itself seen and known – in and through historical and natural forms. The essentially invisible and unapproachable God chooses to enter the created order in a visible and approachable manner. The formless Word enters into the forms of the natural order, in order that humanity may discern the invisible God through the visible things of creation – and supremely, through the Word become flesh. By entering nature, the Word assumed natural forms – and hence became accessible to natural processes of perception. Although there is a clear distinction between the way in which the Word is understood to be present and known in creation and in Jesus Christ, there is also an essential continuity between them which must not be understated.

This theological framework allows us to explore how the imperceivable God became accessible to human perception, both in the natural world and in Jesus Christ. Revelation takes place in and through nature and history, not beyond them. When seen in the right way – when *illuminated*, to use the language of John's prologue – nature and history have the capacity to disclose God. The natural realm can serve as a conduit, however limited, to the divine – once its capacity to do so is perceived.

In view of the importance of this statement, we shall consider a neglected biblical exemplar, which brings out the point at issue with particular clarity – the call of Samuel (1 Samuel 3: 3–10). Karl Barth's critique of natural theology has often itself been criticized for resting on a less than adequate engagement with the Bible.[2] It is perhaps ironic that this passage has played such a small role in many discussions of natural theology, possibly because its significance is so easily overlooked. Yet it serves as a highly appropriate prelude to any account of how a Christian natural theology may be constructed.

A Biblical Example: The Call of Samuel

The biblical account of the call of Samuel in the temple at Shiloh opens by noting that the "word of the LORD was rare" in those days, before relating how Samuel heard and responded to the call of the Lord.

> Samuel was lying down in the temple of the LORD, where the ark of God was. Then the LORD called, "Samuel! Samuel!" and he said, "Here I am!" and ran to Eli, and said, "Here I am, for you called me." But he said, "I did not call; lie down again." So he went and lay down. The LORD called again, "Samuel!" Samuel got up and went to Eli, and said, "Here I am, for you called me." But he said, "I did not call, my son; lie down again." Now Samuel did not yet know the LORD, and the word of the LORD had not yet been revealed to him. The LORD called Samuel again, a third time. And he got up and went to Eli, and said, "Here I am, for you called me." Then Eli perceived that the LORD was calling the boy. Therefore Eli said to Samuel, "Go, lie down; and if he calls you, you shall say, 'Speak, LORD, for your servant is listening.'" So Samuel went and lay down in his place. Now the LORD came and stood there, calling as

---

[2] For example, see James Barr, *Biblical Faith and Natural Theology*, Oxford: Clarendon Press, 1993.

before, "Samuel! Samuel!" And Samuel said, "Speak, for your servant is listening"

(1 Samuel 3: 3–10)

The central core of the narrative is that Samuel hears his name being spoken four times during the night. On the first three occasions, he believes that Eli is calling him, and runs to find him. On the fourth occasion, Samuel correctly interprets the calling of his name as coming from God, following Eli's suggestion to interpret the event in this manner.

Most scholarly accounts of this passage fail to see that the central issue is *discernment*.[3] An event within nature is viewed in a new manner, and seen to possess a new significance. Walter Moberly rightly identifies this central concern, and summarizes its significance as follows: "God then speaks to Samuel. But His speaking instantly poses the central issue of the story, that is discernment. For when God speaks, Samuel does not recognize the voice as God's voice."[4] So what are the implications of this?

Moberly notes two important characteristics of the depiction of Samuel's experience. First, Samuel hears the voice of God *as a human voice*. There is nothing intrinsic to the experience that labels it as either supernatural or specifically divine. Secondly, he mistakes the voice for that of a familiar adult whom he knows to be within calling distance. This second characteristic – the interpretation of the novel in terms of the familiar, and in terms that make sense in the light of the experience and worldview of the perceiver – is a dominant feature of human perception, as we noted earlier (pp. 90–1). Moberly points out that the call of God may not be recognizable as such, in that it is mediated in and through the natural realm. In this case, "the voice of God, while not being reducible to that which is human, may be inseparably linked with the human." The voice of God sounds like the voice of Eli.

---

[3] See, for example, Murray Newman, "The Prophetic Call of Samuel," in B. W. Anderson and W. J. Harrelson (eds), *Israel's Prophetic Heritage: Essays in Honor of James Muilenburg*, pp. 86–97, London: SCM Press, 1962. The interesting thesis of Robert K. Gnuse, *The Dream Theophany of Samuel: Its Structure in Relation to Ancient Near Eastern Dreams and its Theological Significance*, Lanham, MD: University Press of America, 1984, should also be noted, although the absence of the specific word "dream" makes his thesis problematic.

[4] R. W. L. Moberly, "To Hear the Master's Voice: Revelation and Spiritual Discernment in the Call of Samuel," *Scottish Journal of Theology* 48 (1995): 443–68; quote at pp. 458–9.

Initially, Samuel interprets the voice as a natural phenomenon. To use the psychological categories introduced earlier (pp. 86–92), the schema that he brings to bear in interpreting the voice is that of nature as a self-contained, closed entity. He interprets the voice as an aspect of the natural order. His third meeting with Eli, however, offers him an alternative schema, which allows him to interpret events within nature as having the capacity to disclose the transcendent.

On the first three occasions, Samuel assumes that the natural sound he has heard has a natural referent, and behaves accordingly. Why? The text offers an explanation: because "Samuel did not yet know the LORD; the word of the LORD had not yet been revealed to him" (1 Samuel 3: 7). The turning point of the narrative takes place when Eli offers an alternative interpretative framework. Confronted with the evident failure of the most obvious schema, Samuel is invited to consider an alternative explanation of his experience (1 Samuel 3: 9). Eli can here be seen as a representative of the tradition of Israel, which offers an alternative way of interpreting nature – in this case, as a gateway to the transcendent. God is made known through the natural order.

The biblical account of the call of Samuel clearly sheds light on the process of spiritual discernment which allows the transcendent to be found in and through the natural. It illustrates a general pattern in which humans, when confronted with the divine, have no alternative but to make sense of their experience in terms of categories with which they are already familiar. Samuel "hears" what he subsequently realizes to be the voice of God; yet he does not recognize it as such at the time. It is initially *heard* – but it is not *heard as* God's call.[5]

Eli can be seen here as acting as a catalyst for a change in schemas. The narrative of the call is as much about the recognition of the presence of God as it is about responding to the divine call. Eli offers Samuel an alternative way of "seeing" the world, which mandates the idea that a natural event may be a means of divine disclosure. Moberly interprets the text as representing "on the one hand, the divine accommodating Himself to the human" and "on the other hand, the human growth in perceiving the divine through already familiar categories."[6] He suggests

---

[5] Notice the parallel with Hanson's point about the theory-laden nature of observation, expressed in terms of "seeing as," discussed earlier: pp. 74–5.

[6] Moberly, "To Hear the Master's Voice," p. 461.

that Eli functions as a preliminary cognitive model for God for the young and inexperienced Samuel, who "did not yet know the LORD," that enables him to grow beyond it into a more mature understanding of God.

Thus far, our analysis points to an assimilative account of the call of Samuel, to use Piaget's categories. On this view, Samuel initially has difficulty in interpreting the significance of the voice he hears during the night. Eli is able to provide an alternative framework for making sense of this experience, setting it in the context of the history of Israel and the cultic importance of its temple. Samuel's experience is thus assimilated into Israel's understanding of the nature of God. Yet it is important to note that Samuel's experience has the potential to *change* the tradition of Israel. This accommodative dimension is evident in that the experience identifies Samuel, rather than Eli, as God's anointed one. Samuel's experience thus resonates with, while still changing, the traditions of Israel.[7]

The Christian Tradition as a Framework for Natural Theology

It is clearly beyond the scope of this book to present even a synopsis of the Christian faith, let alone a defense of some of its core ideas (such as the doctrines of the incarnation and Trinity), or an exploration of the variant positions that are encountered within its ample girth.[8] For the specific purposes of this undertaking, these must be assumed, or at least be allowed to shape our discussion. There is an entirely proper debate to be had concerning the fundamentals of Christian belief; our concern, however, has to do with the difference that these make to the way in

---

[7] A similar observation may be made concerning the resurrection of Jesus of Nazareth: see Joanna Collicutt McGrath, "Post-traumatic Growth and the Origins of Early Christianity," *Mental Health, Religion and Culture* 9 (2006): 291–306.

[8] For typical discussions, see Alister E. McGrath, *Christian Theology: An Introduction*, 4th edn, Oxford: Blackwell, 2007; Colin E. Gunton, *The Christian Faith: An Introduction to Christian Doctrine*, Oxford: Blackwell, 2002; David Willis, *Clues to the Nicene Creed: A Brief Outline of the Faith*, Grand Rapids, MI: Eerdmans, 2005.

which nature is perceived. Christian theology offers a way of beholding the world, a framework for enabling it to be understood, appreciated, and inhabited in a certain way.[9]

In what follows, we shall consider some of the leading themes of the Christian tradition, and explore how they bear upon the question of how nature is perceived from the standpoint of faith. These serve both to undergird a Christian approach to natural theology, and to distinguish it from its Deist alternatives.[10] The main themes that will be examined in this chapter are:

1   The idea of a transcendent God who chooses to self-disclose in history and nature.
2   The belief that there is an analogous relationship between God and nature, grounded in the created character of the natural order.
3   The principle that humanity is created in the image of God, and thus endowed with some capacity to discern traces of God within or through nature.
4   The concept of the "economy of salvation," which situates reflection on nature within a framework based on its "fall" and future restoration.
5   The doctrine of the incarnation, which holds that God entered into the natural order in Christ, in order to transform and redeem it. It should be noted here that, while the first three, and possibly the fourth, of these ideas are common to the Judeo-Christian tradition, this final belief is distinctively Christian.[11]

These themes illustrate, but do not exhaust, the distinctively Christian framework through which the natural world is seen. In what follows, we shall consider each of these themes individually.

---

[9]   For further discussion, see Alister E. McGrath, *A Scientific Theology: 3 – Theory*, London: T&T Clark, 2003, pp. 3–76.

[10]   On the importance of this point, see Alister E. McGrath, *A Scientific Theology: 1 – Nature*, Edinburgh: T&T Clark, 2001, pp. 181–9.

[11]   The title of Jacob Neusner's important book on this theme is perhaps a little misleading, in that Neusner understands the term "incarnation" in a reduced sense to mean "the representation of God in human terms": see Jacob Neusner, *The Incarnation of God: The Character of Divinity in Formative Judaism*, Philadelphia: Fortress Press, 1988.

Natural Theology and a Self-Disclosing God

We begin our discussion by considering Christianity's distinctive idea of a *transcendent God who chooses to self-disclose.* It is essential to appreciate that the concept of a transcendent God does not in itself entail divine self-disclosure.[12] Indeed, many classical conceptions of a transcendent divinity – such as that associated with Aristotle – preclude the notion of divine revelation almost as a matter of definition. Yet the Christian understanding of God is one who wills to self-disclose name and nature. It is this God who must be correlated with the enterprise of natural theology. As we noted in the prologue to John's Gospel (pp. 172–4), the Word comes to us, entering into the world in order to make God known, and reveal God's glory.

This central Christian theme must therefore be considered against the background of philosophical and theological wrestling with the question of how a transcendent God may be known.[13] The critical issue is that of mediation. Ancient Israel held that certain figures played a role in the mediation of guidance and knowledge to the community, such as Moses and the prophets. During the era of Second Temple Judaism, the question of mediation between God and Israel became particularly significant, with various heavenly or angelic figures being postulated as potential agents of divine revelation.[14] While the evidence suggests that

---

[12]   For some of the tensions between early Christianity and the classic tradition arising from the latter's notion of God, see Ekkehard Mühlenberg, *Die Unendlichkeit Gottes bei Gregor von Nyssa: Gregors Kritik am Gottesbegriff der klassischen Metaphysik*, Göttingen: Vandenhoeck & Ruprecht, 1966.

[13]   The development of the religious thought of Simone Weil is particularly illuminating here, in view of her early view that the only possible mediator between the transcendent and the world is the human mind. Her move towards a concept of Christ as mediator is partly due to the epistemic aporia of this earlier approach: see Eric O. Springsted, *Christus Mediator: Platonic Mediation in the Thought of Simone Weil*, Chico, CA: Scholars Press, 1983.

[14]   See the analysis in Michael Mach, *Entwicklungsstudien des jüdischen Engelglaubens in vorrabbinischer Zeit*, Tübingen: J. C. B. Mohr, 1992. For some possible connections with issues in Pauline Christology, see Andrew Chester, "Jewish Messianic Expectations and Mediatorial Figures and Pauline Christology," in Martin Hengel and Ulrich Heckel (eds), *Paulus und das antike Judentum*, pp. 17–89, Tübingen: J. C. B. Mohr, 1991.

such mediatorial figures were not themselves regarded as divine within contemporary Judaism,[15] the emergence of such additional revelatory pathways serves to emphasize the importance of the question of how a transcendent God may be known.[16] The issue regularly resurfaces in Jewish reflections on the questions, as is clear from the writings of the medieval writer Maimomides,[17] or more recently in the works of Franz Rosenzweig.[18]

Yet the actuality of divine revelation does not, in itself and of itself, mandate a natural theology. Nor does the notion of divine transcendence entail the notion that nature discloses God; indeed, it may even exclude this possibility altogether. Within a polytheistic or henotheistic worldview,[19] for example, it is perfectly possible to suggest that the "true God" was not involved in creation, which was entrusted to some subordinate divine

[15] The best study of this remains Larry W. Hurtado, *Lord Jesus Christ: Devotion to Jesus in Earliest Christianity*, Grand Rapids, MI: Eerdmans, 2003, pp. 32–53. For the view that such mediatorial figures were regarded as divine, see Margaret Barker, *The Great Angel: A Study of Israel's Second God*, London: SPCK, 1992.

[16] The contrast between Christianity and Second Temple Judaism is quite marked at this point. Even at the height of Christian speculation about the role of angels, they were never given a mediatorial role in respect of either revelation or salvation: David Keck, *Angels and Angelology in the Middle Ages*, Oxford: Oxford University Press, 1998, pp. 28–46. The question of such mediation is of importance within the Jewish mystical tradition: see, e.g., Rebecca Macy Lesses, *Ritual Practices to Gain Power: Angels, Incantations, and Revelation in Early Jewish Mysticism*, Harrisburg, PA: Trinity Press International, 1998; Nathaniel Deutsch, *Guardians of the Gate: Angelic Vice-Regency in Late Antiquity*, Leiden: Brill, 1999.

[17] Kenneth Seeskin, *Searching for a Distant God: The Legacy of Maimonides*, New York: Oxford University Press, 2000, pp. 43–65. For similar themes in contemporary Jewish mysticism, see Ephraim Kanarfogel, *Peering Through the Lattices: Mystical, Magical and Pietistic Dimensions in the Tosafist Period*, Detroit: Wayne State University Press, 2000.

[18] Norbert M. Samuelson, *Revelation and the God of Israel*, Cambridge, UK: Cambridge University Press, 2002, pp. 43–65.

[19] The term "henotheism" was introduced by Friedrich Max Müller (1823–1900) to denote a theology or worldview which accepted the existence of many gods, yet insisted that only one was to be worshiped and obeyed. For the notion in ancient Israel, see Mark Smith, *The Early History of God: Yahweh and the Other Deities in Ancient Israel*, Grand Rapids, MI: Eerdmans, 2002.

agency. A natural theology would thus disclose something of the nature of this lesser deity, rather than the "true" or "ultimate" God.

A further possibility must also be noted. A transcendent God might chose to self-disclose in an exclusive manner, which implied that nature was incapable of disclosing anything reliable about God, and might mislead the faithful into making idolatrous or blasphemous judgments. The issue is thus whether such a God can be said to authorize and enable nature to reflect something of God's nature and character. To appreciate the importance of this point, we shall explore the place of natural theology within Islam, a monotheistic religious belief system which, like Christianity, has a strong doctrine of divine revelation,[20] but understands both what is disclosed and the manner of its disclosure in a very different fashion to that associated with Christianity.

As has often been pointed out, there is no direct equivalent to the Christian notion of "natural theology" within Islam. In general, Islam recognizes no true knowledge of God outside the Qu'ran, thus raising serious difficulties for any notion of natural theology. The term *kalam* is often used to designate the general area of philosophical inquiry which might be taken to include natural theology;[21] yet this does not necessarily entail the notion that knowledge of God may be had through nature. The question has led to some serious disputes within Islam,[22] with the result that shifting patterns of Qu'ranic interpretation make generalizations in this area problematic.

In his careful study of the development of *kalam*, Richard Frank argues that the traditional Ash'arite view of *kalam* is that it is a "rational metaphysics" or a "universal religious science" which "proves the basic articles of Muslim religious belief" without actually making a formal appeal to

---

[20] See, for example, the analysis in William C. Chittick, *The Self-Disclosure of God: Principles of Ibn al-'Arabi's Cosmology*, Albany, NY: State University of New York Press, 1998.

[21] For a useful contextualization, see Sachiko Murata and William C. Chittick, *The Vision of Islam*, St Paul, MN: Paragon House, 1994, pp. 242–6. *Kalam* literally means "speech" or "word," and is often used to translate the Greek term *logos*.

[22] This question lies beyond the scope of the present work. However, an understanding of many of the issues may be gained from George Makdisi, *Ibn 'Aqil: Religion and Culture in Classical Islam*, Edinburgh: Edinburgh University Press, 1997.

any specific religious beliefs as such.[23] *Kalam* is here clearly understood as representing some kind of natural theology, suggesting a resonance between this approach and the type of Christian natural theology we have sought to critique in this volume – namely defending religious beliefs on the basis of "premises that neither are nor presuppose any religious beliefs."[24]

Yet *kalam* is not regarded with much enthusiasm by many within modern Islam. Other Muslim theologians, classic and contemporary, have been severely critical of it, most notably Al-Ghazali, who regarded natural philosophy and theology as posing a significant threat to Islamic orthodoxy.[25] As Franks points out, this reflects serious tensions within Islam over the status of nature, and its capacity to disclose God, or inform human speculation concerning the divine nature. Since about 1500, the view of Al-Ghazali has gained the ascendancy, with important implications for Islamic attitudes towards the enterprise of seeking the transcendent within nature. Whereas Western Christian theology embraced natural theology in the modern period, Islam moved with equally great enthusiasm to reject it.

The "golden era" of Islamic engagement with issues of natural theology and philosophy is generally regarded as falling between the ninth and fifteenth centuries.[26] During this era, something approaching a notion of "natural theology" may be discerned, although the parallels are often more remote and indirect than some have appreciated. Yet developments within Islam after that period led to a growing tendency to emphasize the Qu'ran as the sole source of knowledge of God, firmly relegating any notion of natural theology to the murky realms of heterodoxy. The

---

[23]   Richard M. Frank, *Al-Ghazali and the Ash'arite School*, Durham, NC: Duke University Press, 1994, pp. 5, 9. For a critique of Frank's analysis, see Ahmad Dallal, "Ghazali and the Perils of Interpretation: Review Essay of *Al-Ghazali and the Ash'arite School*, by Richard M. Frank," *Journal of the American Oriental Society* 122 (2002): 773–87.

[24]   The definition offered by William P. Alston, *Perceiving God: The Epistemology of Religious Experience*. Ithaca, NY: Cornell University Press, 1991, p. 289, discussed earlier in this volume.

[25]   Frank, *Al-Ghazali and the Ash'arite School*, pp. 16–17.

[26]   Edward Grant, *The Foundations of Modern Science in the Middle Ages: Their Religious, Institutional and Intellectual Contexts*, Cambridge, UK: Cambridge University Press, 1996, pp. 176–86.

concern raised by Islamic writers can be summarized thus: if either nature or human reason is understood to possess any capacity to disclose God, the unique revelational status of the Qu'ran will be compromised.[27]

The contrast with the mainstream of Judeo-Christian theology at this point is both impressive and decisive. Both Old and New Testaments mandate an engagement with the natural order. This is particularly evident within the Wisdom literature, for which there is no Qu'ranic equivalent.[28] God is declared to have created the world "in wisdom" (Proverbs 3: 19); traces of that wisdom may be discerned by the spiritually enlightened human mind. The fundamental assumption here is that certain patterns may be discerned by the "wise" within their experience of the world. While this assumption is widespread within the literature of the Ancient Near East, the Old Testament wisdom literature generally links the theme of a natural knowledge of God with the divine activity of creation and the preservation of Israel. Nevertheless, the means of knowing something of the divine wisdom from the creation undermines any exclusive appeal to a written document as a means of knowing God.[29]

Similar ideas are found in the New Testament. The most obvious example of an appeal to nature as a means of grounding the proclamation of the Christian gospel is found in Luke's account of Paul's Areopagus address (Acts 17: 16–34). This passage has been subjected to intense scrutiny, partly on account of its historical relationship to classical Greek wisdom, and partly because of its obvious importance for Christian natural theology.[30] Here, Paul appeals to an inchoate "sense of divinity" and an awareness of the ordering of the world, present in each individual,

---

[27] Substantially the same concern, of course, was expressed in a Christian context by Karl Barth.

[28] It may, of course, be noted that some scholars suggest that the Wisdom literature sits uneasily alongside the works of the Law: see, e.g., Franz-Josef Steiert, *Die Weisheit Israels – ein Fremdkörper im Alten Testament? Eine Untersuchung zum Buch der Sprüche auf dem Hintergrund der ägyptischen Weisheitslehren*, Freiburg im Breisgau: Herder, 1990.

[29] See the discussion of key passages in Barr, *Biblical Faith and Natural Theology.*

[30] For two classic analyses, see Bertil Gärtner, *The Areopagus Speech and Natural Revelation*, Uppsala: Gleerup, 1955; Heinz Kulling, *Geoffenbartes Geheimnis: Eine Auslegung von Apostelgeschichte 17, 16–34*, Zurich: Theologischer Verlag, 1993.

as an apologetic device, serving as a "point of contact" for the gospel proclamation.[31]

The Judeo-Christian tradition holds that nature possesses a derivative capacity to disclose something of God's wisdom, without undermining or displacing divine revelation itself. The contrast with Islam is therefore instructive and illuminating, in that it demonstrates that there is no *necessary* connection between the idea of a "revealing God" and "natural theology." Such a connection exists only if the substance of that revelation mandates an expectation that the natural realm can disclose something of God, and offers some guidance as to the character, focus, and scope of such knowledge. To use an image due to Michael Polanyi, we could say that the natural order, when viewed through the prism of the Christian tradition, ceases to be a noise and becomes a tune.[32]

This theme is prominent in the writings of Emil Brunner, and, as noted earlier (p. 159), played no small part in his 1934 controversy with Karl Barth over the legitimacy and limits of natural theology. Brunner argues that, since God "leaves the imprint of his nature [*der Stempel seines Wesens*] upon what he does," it follows that it is a fundamentally Christian belief that "the creation of the world is at the same time a revelation, a self-communication of God."[33] While sin diminishes the human capacity to recognize and respond to such a self-communication of God, there is no biblical warrant for suggesting that sin destroys the "perceptibility of God in his works." Basing his argument on Romans 1, Brunner insists "that God did not leave himself without witness [*unbezeugt*] to the heathen." Only someone "who stands within the revelation in Christ" can therefore be said to possess a "true natural knowledge of God."

---

[31] Paul's use of rhetorical devices must also be noted at this point: see, e.g., W. S. Kurz, "Hellenistic Rhetoric in the Christological Proofs of Luke-Acts," *Catholic Biblical Quarterly* 42 (1980): 171–95. However, these merely amplify the understanding of revelation implicit within Paul's address, and do not seek to ground the gospel proclamation elsewhere.

[32] Michael Polanyi, "Science and Reality," *British Journal for the Philosophy of Science*, 18 (1967): 177–96, especially p. 191. For comment, see Thomas F. Torrance, *Reality and Scientific Theology*, Edinburgh: Scottish Academic Press, 1985, p. 55.

[33] Emil Brunner, "Natur und Gnade: Zum Gespräch mit Karl Barth," in Rudolf Wehrli (ed.), *Ein offenes Wort. Vorträge und Aufsätze 1917–1934*, pp. 333–66, Zürich: Theologischer Verlag, 1981, p. 343.

Brunner's argument, when fully developed, endorses our conclusion that nature can only be fully and properly known from within the Christian tradition.

Yet the argument needs to be taken further than this. As we shall consider later in this chapter, the distinctively Christian understanding of divine self-revelation focuses on the incarnation, which discloses a God who chooses to inhabit the natural world, and is made known in a historical and personal form (the obvious divergence from Judaism and Islam in this respect being particularly striking). For the Christian, nature can be seen as both the medium of God's self-disclosure and inhabitation. God chooses to self-disclose by entering the order of God's own creating.

We shall consider the implications of the doctrine of the incarnation for a Christian natural theology towards the end of this chapter. For the moment, however, we must turn to consider an important aspect of the Christian doctrine of creation – the idea of an analogy or correspondence between God and the created order.

Natural Theology and an Analogy Between God and the Creation

While the idea that the world can be said to be "created" is character-istic of many religions,[34] and could thus be said (though not without significant qualification) to be part of a "generalized" conception of the nature and activity of God, Christianity develops such ideas in its own distinctive manner, especially in the postbiblical period. To determine what specific concept of creation is *characteristic* of Christianity demands a careful exposition of its leading themes;[35] to determine what is *distinctive* of Christianity entails a rigorous comparison with other religions and worldviews, not necessarily religious, including atheism, deism, Islam,

---

[34] David Adams Leeming, *A Dictionary of Creation Myths*, New York: Oxford University Press, 1995.

[35] One of the best recent analyses of the doctrine is Colin E. Gunton, *The Triune Creator: A Historical and Systematic Study*, Edinburgh: Edinburgh University Press, 1998. For my own analysis of the notion and its rich implications, particularly for natural theology, see McGrath, *A Scientific Theology: 1 – Nature*, pp. 81–133.

and Judaism.[36] The Christian understanding of creation is not an isolated conceptual entity, which can be studied and analyzed independently of other aspects of Christian theology. Christian doctrine is perhaps best thought of as a complex web, a system of interrelated, interdependent and interactive ideas, rather than a collection of isolated notions, each hermetically sealed within its own watertight compartment.

In the first place, the doctrine of creation is about more than the assertion of a temporal beginning to all things.[37] Questions of origination are intertangled with deeper concerns about purpose, relationship, and integrity. The doctrine of creation has at least as much to do with why there is anything at all as it has to do with the question of the unfolding of life in the universe.[38] In the case of Israel, creation was more about establishing points of orientation and connection for the people of God than mere historical belief about the origins of humanity.[39]

In the second place, the Christian account of creation is set within the context of the economy of salvation. There is thus a presumption of interconnectedness between creation, redemption, and consummation, which places a theological interdiction against seeing creation as an isolated action or event, complete in itself. In particular, the Christian conception of creation is linked to that of incarnation. Creation and redemption are affirmed to be the work of the same divine *Logos*, embedded in

---

[36] There is a huge literature, bearing witness to a rich variety, synchronic and diachronic, of conceptions of creation. Surveys of note include Stephanie Dalley, *Myths from Mesopotamia: Creation, the Flood, Gilgamesh and Others*, New York: Oxford University Press, 1989; Barbara C. Sproul, *Primal Myths: Creation Myths around the World*, San Francisco: HarperCollins, 1991.

[37] For the distinction, see Jayant V. Narlikar, "The Concepts of 'Beginning' and 'Creation' in Cosmology," *Philosophy of Science* 59 (1992): 361–71.

[38] See the discussions in Norman Kretzmann, "A General Problem of Creation: Why Would God Create Anything at all?" in Scott MacDonald (ed.), *Being and Goodness: The Concept of the Good in Metaphysics and Philosophical Theology*, pp. 208–49, Ithaca, NY: Cornell University Press, 1991; William J. Wainwright, "Jonathan Edwards, William Rowe and the Necessity of Creation," in Jeff Jordan and Daniel Howard-Snyder (eds), *Faith, Freedom and Rationality*, pp. 119–33, London: Rowman & Littlefield, 1996.

[39] Ludwig Köhler, *Theologie des Alten Testaments*, 3rd edn, Tübingen: Mohr, 1953, p. 71: "Die Schöpfung ist . . . nicht eine naturwissenschaftliche, sondern eine menschheitsgeschichtliche Aussage."

creation, and embodied in Christ.[40] There is thus a strongly Christological hue to the Christian vision of creation, which distinguishes it from its deist alternatives.[41]

In the third place, the Christian doctrine of creation *ex nihilo* stresses the capacity of God to be represented in the natural order.[42] Judaism, it may be noted, only developed this doctrine in the late fifteenth or early sixteenth century.[43] The Gnostic controversies of the second and third centuries highlighted the point that a doctrine of creation from pre-existent matter limited God's capacity for self-expression in creative actions. If God was obliged to fashion the world from existing material, it was argued, the divine imprint upon nature would be compromised or distorted by defects in the original material.[44] While making full allowance for the differences between the creator and creation, the possibility of some correspondence or analogy between the two was affirmed.

So how is the distinction between God and the creation to be maintained? What did Emil Brunner mean when he spoke of "such permanent capacity for revelation [*dauernde Offenbarungsmächigkeit*] as God has

---

[40] Key biblical texts in addition to the prologue to John's Gospel (John 1: 1–18) include Colossians 1: 15. On the former, see Gerard Siegwalt, "Der Prolog des Johannesevangeliums als Einführung in eine christliche Theologie der Rekapitulation," *Neue Zeitschrift für systematische Theologie und Religionsphilosophie* 24 (1981): 150–71.

[41] McGrath, *A Scientific Theology: 1 – Nature*, pp. 181–91.

[42] For this notion in Augustine, see N. Joseph Torchia, *Creatio ex nihilo and the Theology of St. Augustine: The Anti-Manichaean Polemic and Beyond*, New York: Peter Lang, 1999. Torchia argues that it is necessary to distinguish between *creatio ex nihilo* and *creatio de nihil*: the former corresponds to finite beings proceeding from nothing; the latter to that which proceeds from the divine substance, that is, God's *Verbum*.

[43] Hava Tirosh-Samuelson, "Theology of Nature in Sixteenth-Century Italian Jewish Philosophy," *Science in Context* 10 (1997): 529–70. Some scholars have recently suggested that the absence of an unambiguous doctrine of creation *ex nihilo* until such a relatively late date can be interpreted as evidence that ancient Judaism was not strictly monotheistic: see, for example, Peter Hayman, "Monotheism – A Misused Word in Jewish Studies?" *Journal of Jewish Studies* 42 (1992): 1–15. For some useful comments on the notion of "monotheism," see L. E. Goodman, *God of Abraham*, New York: Oxford University Press, 1996, pp. 3–36.

[44] See further McGrath, *A Scientific Theology: 1 – Nature*, pp. 159–66.

bestowed upon his works, in the traces of his own nature which he has expressed and made known in them"?[45] In what way can God be recognized as present within the creation, without being relegated to the natural order itself (a development which, it may be added, usually reflects theological carelessness rather than an intentional heterodox inclination)? The traditional Christian answer is that there is a relationship of analogy, not identity, between God and the created order. Augustine's classic statement of this relationship may be regarded as establishing the boundaries of the debate, without determining its conclusions: God fashioned the sensible things of this world to permit them to signify himself.[46]

This relationship has been construed in many ways during the long history of Christian reflection on the matter. Augustine's dictum was open to being interpreted in a neo-Platonic way, as is evident from Marsilio Ficino's doctrine of the resemblance between a symbol and its original, which rests on a Plotinian understanding of the relation of the world of senses and ideas.[47] Yet not all writers of this highly creative era subscribed to such an elaborate theory of analogy. Erasmus of Rotterdam, for example, tended to see analogies in a much more pragmatic manner; such analogies were rhetorically productive devices, which aided an appeal to the imagination.[48]

---

[45]   Emil Brunner, "Natur und Gnade," p. 345.

[46]   Augustine, *de Trinitate*, III.iv.10: "quid mirum si etiam in creatura caeli et terrae, maris et aeris, facit Deus quae vult sensibilia atque visibilia ad se ipsum in eis sicut oportere ipse novit significandum et demonstrandum, non ipsa sua qua est apparente substantia quae omnino incommutabilis est omnibusque spiritibus quos creavit interius secretiusque sublimior?"

[47]   Paul Oskar Kristeller, *The Philosophy of Marsilio Ficino*, New York: Columbia University Press, 1943, pp. 96–8. Ficino's Latin translation of Plotinus' *Enneads* (1492) is believed to have had a significant impact on the late Renaissance understanding of art. Several of Michelangelo's leading works can be interpreted as reflecting some such understanding of the relation of symbol and symbolized. See the analysis of Joanne Snow-Smith, "Michelangelo's Christian Neoplatonic Aesthetic of Beauty in his Early Oeuvre: The *Nuditas Virtualis* Image," in Francis Ames-Lewis and Mary Rogers (eds), *Concepts of Beauty in Renaissance Art*, pp. 147–62, Aldershot: Ashgate, 1998.

[48]   Jean-Claude Margolin, "L'analogie dans la pensée d'Erasme," *Archiv für Reformationsgeschichte* 69 (1978): 24–50.

The classic approach, usually referred to as *analogia entis*, asserts that there exists, on the one hand, a perceptible correspondence and, on the other, an ontological difference, between the creator and the creation.[49] God, though distinct from the creation, exists in an analogous relationship to it as a consequence of its origination. This idea is perhaps best known through the writings of Erich Przywara (1889–1972).[50] Przywara argued that Greek philosophy could be regarded as attempting to achieve an understanding of "being" which avoided the aporia of purely transcendental or immanentist modes of thought. For Przywara, this quest was unsuccessful. This conceptual dead end could only be avoided by developing a specifically Christian concept of the *analogia entis*, conceived in a dynamic, rather than static manner. On this reading, the *analogia entis* is based upon a rigorously Christian doctrine of creation which on the one hand affirms the absolute distinction between creator and creation, yet on the other posits a created capacity on the part of the analogy to model God.[51] The capacity of nature to signify the divine is thus affirmed, yet in a manner that precludes any understanding of nature possessing this capacity intrinsically and autonomously. Creation reveals God only when "seen" in this manner, characteristic of the Christian tradition, which establishes a link between nature and the divine.

Thus far, we have considered some aspects of the doctrine of creation. Yet one requires to be examined in much greater detail: the Christian understanding of human nature. Christian theology has much to say about both the observer and the observed in relation to natural theology. In what follows, we shall explore the core idea that humanity bears the "image of God."

---

[49]   For a contemporary trinitarian interpretation of this concept, see David Bentley Hart, *The Beauty of the Infinite: The Aesthetics of Christian Truth*, Grand Rapids, MI: Eerdmans, 2003, pp. 229–49.

[50]   See here Bernhard Gertz, *Glaubenswelt als Analogie: Die theologische Analogie-Lehre Erich Przywaras und ihr Ort in der Auseinandersetzung um die analogia fidei*, Düsseldorf: Patmos-Verlag, 1969; Rudolf Stertenbrink, *Ein Weg zum Denken: Die Analogia entis bei Erich Przywara*, Salzburg: Verlag Anton Pustet, 1971.

[51]   For an evaluation of Karl Barth's strident criticism of this theme, see H. G. Pöhlmann, *Analogia entis oder analogia fidei? Die Frage nach Analogie bei Karl Barth*, Göttingen: Vandenhoeck & Ruprecht, 1965; Martin Bieler, "Karl Barths Auseinandersetzung mit der *analogia entis* und der Anfang der Theologie." *Catholica* 40 (1986): 229–45.

Natural Theology and the Image of God

One of the central themes of the Christian tradition is that humanity is made "in the image of God" (Genesis 1: 26–7).[52] During the course of its extended engagement with this seminal text, the Christian church has come to see this as indicating that there is something intrinsic to human nature which enables it to discern, however dimly, the character of God in the created order. Hans Urs von Balthasar suggested that the relation between the creature and creator at this point could be understood as the "image reflecting on its prototype."[53] Part of the Christian understanding of human nature is its innate capacity, in consequence of its created status, of being able to recognize traces of the creator within the creation.

The idea that humanity has been made "in the image of God" has been interpreted in a number of ways within the Christian tradition.[54] One of these may be singled out for special comment, on account of its obvious resonances with natural theology. This is the long-standing view that the *imago Dei* designates the human capacity to reason – or, more accurately, to conform mentally to the patterns established by the divine *Logos* within creation – and hence to discern God, albeit partially and imperfectly.

---

[52] Friedrich Horst, "Der Mensch als Ebenbild Gottes," in *Gottes Recht: Gesammelte Studien zum Recht im Alten Testament*, pp. 222–34, Munich: Kaiser Verlag, 1961; James Barr, "The Image of God in the Book of Genesis: A Study of Terminology," *Bulletin of the John Rylands Library* 51 (1968): 11–26; David J. A. Clines, "The Image of God in Man," *Tyndale Bulletin* 19 (1968): 53–103; J. Maxwell Miller, "The 'Image' and 'Likeness' of God," *Journal of Biblical Literature* 91 (1972): 289–304; Tryggve N. D. Mettinger, "Abbild oder Urbild? 'Imago Dei' in traditions-geschichtlicher Sicht," *Zeitschrift für Alttestamentlicher Wissenschaft* 86 (1974): 403–24.

[53] Hans Urs von Balthasar, *Theo-Drama: Theological Dramatic Theory*, San Francisco: Ignatius, 1992, p. 417.

[54] For surveys, see David Cairns, *The Image of God in Man*, London: Collins, 1973; A. Jónsson Gunnlaugur and S. Cheney Michael, *The Image of God: Genesis 1:26–28 in a Century of Old Testament Research*, Stockholm: Almqvist & Wiksell International, 1988; Michael Welker, "Creation and the Image of God: Their Understanding in Christian Tradition and the Biblical Grounds," *Journal of Ecumenical Studies* 34 (1997): 436–48. In Jewish thought, the notion is often interpreted in terms of moral capacity and accountability: see David S. Shapiro, "The Doctrine of the Image of God and Imitatio Dei," in Menachem Kellner (ed.), *Contemporary Jewish Ethics*, pp. 127–51, New York: Sanhedrin, 1978.

The concept is developed within the Alexandrian theological tradition in such a way as to emphasize the correlation between the creation of humanity in the likeness of the divine *Logos* and the human capacity to shape one's ideas in a manner that was somehow "according to the *logos*" (logikos). The general approach can be found throughout the writings of Athanasius of Alexandria,[55] particularly his treatise *de incarnatione Verbi*. Athanasius here sets out his view that the divine *logos* is embedded within the structures of the created order – including, of course, human rationality – thus allowing humanity to gain at least some access to a knowledge of God through creation, as an anticipation and preparation for the recognition of the *logos* incarnate in Christ. The idea of humanity being made in the image of God plays a significant role in Athanasius's thought, in that he holds that it ultimately undergirds the human capacity to know God.[56] The relevance of this theme for a natural theology will be evident.

Perhaps the most important and influential discussion of the issue can be found in the tradition which identifies the *imago Dei* with human reason[57] – a resource which is meant to be used to seek and apprehend God. Augustine of Hippo, one of the most significant advocates of this position, suggests that humanity has been intentionally created with the capacity to discern the divine within nature.

> The image of the creator is to be found in the rational or intellectual soul of humanity . . . Although reason and intellect may at times be dormant, or may appear to be weak at some times, and strong at others, the human soul

---

[55] For background, see J. Rebecca Lyman, *Christology and Cosmology: Models of Divine Activity in Origen, Eusebius, and Athanasius*, Oxford: Clarendon Press, 1993, pp. 124–59. For the concept in Cyril of Alexandria, see the older, but still useful, study of Walter J. Burghardt, *The Image of God in Man According to Cyril of Alexandria*, Woodstock, MA: Woodstock Press, 1957.

[56] Athanasius, *de incarnatione Verbi*, iii, 10–11. For a further discussion, see Wolfgang A. Bienert, "Zur Logos-Christologie des Athanasius von Alexandrien in *Contra Gentes* und *De Incarnatione*," in E. A. Livingstone (ed.), *Papers Presented to the Tenth International Conference on Patristic Studies*, pp. 402–19, Louvain: Peeters, 1989.

[57] The term "reason" here should not be confused with its rationalist interpretations, characteristic of the Enlightenment: for this development, see Louis K. Dupré, *The Enlightenment and the Intellectual Foundations of Modern Culture*, New Haven, CT: Yale University Press, 2004.

cannot be anything other than rational and intellectual. It has been created according to the image of God in order that it may use reason and intellect in order to apprehend and behold God [*uti ratione atque intellectu ad intellegendum et conspiciendum Deum potest*].[58]

Human rationality thus bears a created, contingent relationship to – but is not identical with – divine rationality.

For Thomas Aquinas, the *imago Dei* is so closely associated with the notion of rationality that he holds that only intellectual beings – by which he means angels and humans – can be regarded as true image-bearers.[59] At the most basic level, Aquinas argues that all human beings may be said to possess this image, in that they possess a natural aptitude or capacity for understanding at least something of God, and responding to God in love. This capacity becomes an actuality through divine grace, when people "actually or habitually know and love God, even though imperfectly." Finally, the image may be said to be perfected when God is seen face to face, in the beatific vision.[60] However it is articulated, and however much it may be qualified, the theological consensus has long been that humanity, by virtue of being created in the "image of God," can discern at least something of the rationality of a world created with that rationality by God. We can make sense of it.

Protestant approaches to natural theology have also been shaped by their understandings of the *imago Dei*. John Calvin argued that Adam was not merely created with "right understanding" as a consequence of being created in the image of God. This distinction, he argued, also raised humanity above the level of all other creatures.[61] In that Christ is to be seen as the perfect *imago Dei*,[62] Calvin was able to forge a theological link between creation and redemption using the *imago Dei* as a theological *Leitmotif*. Calvin's affirmation of the legitimacy of a natural theology, subject to certain limits, rests on his fundamental belief that humanity, as

---

[58] Augustine, *de Trinitate*, XVI.iv.6. For comment, see John Sullivan, *The Image of God: The Doctrine of St. Augustine and its Influence*, Dubuque, IA: Priory Press, 1963.

[59] Aquinas, *Summa Theologiae*, Ia q. 93, aa. 2, 6.

[60] See further William J. Hoye, *Actualitas Omnium Actuum: Man's Beatific Vision of God as Apprehended by Thomas Aquinas*, Meisenheim: Hain, 1975.

[61] Calvin, *Institutes* I.xv.3.

[62] Randall Zachman, "Jesus Christ as the Image of God in Calvin's Theology," *Calvin Theological Journal* 25 (1990): 46–52.

the bearer of God's image, possesses at least some capability of discerning the presence and character of God from reflecting on the external order of the world, and the internal *sensus divinitatis*.[63]

The concept of the *imago Dei* played a significant role in the 1934 debate between Emil Brunner and Karl Barth on natural theology, especially the question of whether humanity possessed a capacity to discern God.[64] Brunner argued that two elements of the *imago Dei* were to be identified: its *formal* aspect, which distinguishes humanity from the remainder of God's creation; and its *material* aspect, which has to do with humanity's relationship with God, including the ability to "see" God within the natural order.[65] The divine–human encounter within history presupposes that humanity possesses a capability to respond to the personal, historical revelation of God in Christ, a capacity which Brunner terms *Angesprochsein und Sichansprechenlassen*.[66] Brunner envisages a direct correlation between the person who hears the word of God and the appearance of the word of God in Christ, effectively treating humanity as God's "conversation partner" (*Gesprächspartner*) in the continuum of history.[67]

---

[63] David Reiter, "Calvin's 'Sense of Divinity' and Externalist Knowledge of God," *Faith and Philosophy* 15 (1998): 253–70. See also the older study of Edward A. Dowey, *The Knowledge of God in Calvin's Theology*, New York: Columbia University Press, 1952, especially pp. 50–86.

[64] See the analysis in Joan O'Donovan, "Man in the Image of God: The Disagreement between Barth and Brunner Reconsidered," *Scottish Journal of Theology* 39 (1986): 433–59, especially pp. 444–7.

[65] For Brunner's definitive analysis of this concept, see Emil Brunner, *Der Mensch im Widerspruch: Die christliche Lehre vom wahren und vom wirklichen Menschen*, 4th edn, Zurich: Zwingli Verlag, 1965, pp. 85–210. Calvin did not use the terms "formal" and "material" when discussing the various components of his understanding of the *imago Dei*.

[66] For an analysis of these ideas, see Heinrich Leopold, *Missionarische Theologie: Emil Brunners Weg zur theologischen Anthropologie*, Gütersloh: Mohn, 1974; Roman Rössler, *Person und Glaube: Der Personalismus der Gottesbeziehung bei Emil Brunner*, Munich: Kaiser Verlag, 1965, pp. 19–20; Stephan Scheld, *Die Christologie Emil Brunners*, Wiesbaden: Franz Steinbeck, 1981, pp. 48–92.

[67] To use Robert Jenson's phrase, humanity is God's "conversational counterpart": Robert Jenson, *Systematic Theology*, 2 vols, New York: Oxford University Press, 1997–9, vol. 2, p. 95. For a critique of these volumes, see George Hunsinger, "Robert Jenson's *Systematic Theology*: A Review Essay," *Scottish Journal of Theology* 55 (2002): 161–200.

In responding to Brunner, Barth correctly pointed out that the notion of the "image of God" was susceptible to changing intellectual and social conventions, reflecting the prevailing assumptions of the age (such as the Enlightenment's emphasis on reason) to a significant degree.[68] Barth's own exposition of the notion is particularly linked with humanity as God's covenant partner. As bearer of this divine image, a human being is a partner of God, capable of dealings and of close relationship with God. The human person is thus someone whom God addresses as "Thou" and makes answerable as "I."[69] Barth regarded Brunner's distinction between the "formal" and "material" aspects of the image as intellectually unsustainable, and theologically valueless.[70] Barth concurs that, even as sinners, human beings remain human beings, instead of becoming tortoises.[71] But what, Barth asked, has this to do with the question of any natural receptivity towards the Word of God?

More recently, the encyclical *Veritatis Splendor* (1993) set out a series of insights essential to a properly Christian understanding of the foundation, methods, limits, and goals of a natural theology.

> The Splendour of Truth shines forth in all the works of the Creator and, in a special way, in man, created in the image and likeness of God (cf. Genesis 1: 26). Truth enlightens man's intelligence and shapes his freedom, leading him to know and love the Lord.[72]

Yet the encyclical goes beyond the idea that humanity is adequately defined theologically simply as the bearer of the *imago Dei*. In a significant move, humanity is defined within a broader understanding of the economy of salvation, as "made in the image of the Creator, redeemed by the Blood of Christ and made holy by the presence of the Holy Spirit."[73]

---

[68] *Church Dogmatics*, III/1, pp. 192–4.
[69] *Church Dogmatics*, III/1, p. 199. See also the earlier discussion at pp. 195–6.
[70] O'Donovan, "Man in the Image of God."
[71] John Baillie (ed.), *Natural Theology, Comprising "Nature and Grace" by Professor Dr. Emil Brunner and the reply "No!" by Dr. Karl Barth*, London: Geoffrey Bless, 1946, p. 79.
[72] *Veritatis Splendor*, Prooemium, 1.
[73] *Veritatis Splendor*, 10.

Any attempt to articulate a Christian understanding of the human observer of nature must take account of the processes of cognition and perception. It is therefore appropriate to consider these once more at this point, and reflect on how they may be integrated within, or correlated to, a theological understanding of human nature.

Such an approach can be applied to the notion of the *imago Dei*, which has in recent times been redeveloped and restated in terms of an innate human propensity to interpret the world in terms of the presence and agency of God. Some such adaptation of the notion can be seen in Mircea Eliade's concept of *homo religiosus*.[74] By this, Eliade intends us to understand the emergence of structures for the interpretation of human experience and the everyday world, which are to be seen as perennial aspects of human culture, not specific or limited to a given age or situation.[75] As J. Wentzel van Huyssteen argued, the concept of the "image of God" could be stated in terms of the emergence of a natural human tendency to believe in God.[76] This is not necessarily to be understood as something imprinted upon human nature, but can be interpreted as an emergent phenomenon, shaped by social and anthropological influences.[77]

The concept of the "image of God" could thus be developed further to mean a "cognitive perceptual bias" towards the truth. In this sense, the term could be understood to mean a set of acquired mental representations that underlie the perception of the world, which assist or enable humanity to discern the presence of God. The natural human facility to interpret the world in a religious manner has been the subject of much attention.[78] Although often pressed into the service of atheist apologetics,

---

[74] Mircea Eliade, *Patterns in Comparative Religion*, New York: Sheed and Ward, 1958.

[75] Ibid., pp. 144–5. For a critique of this idea, see John A. Saliba, *"Homo Religiosus" in Mircea Eliade: An Anthropological Evaluation*, Leiden: Brill, 1976.

[76] Wentzel J. van Huyssteen, *Alone in the World?: Human Uniqueness in Science and Theology*, Grand Rapids, MI: Eerdmans, 2006.

[77] As noted by Fritz Stolz, *Homo naturaliter religiosus: gehört Religion notwendig zum Mensch-Sein?* Bern: Peter Lang, 1997.

[78] See Pascal Boyer, *The Naturalness of Religious Ideas: A Cognitive Theory of Religion*, Berkeley, CA: University of California Press, 1994; Robert N. McCauley, "The Naturalness of Religion and the Unnaturalness of Science," in F. Keil and R. Wilson (eds), *Explanation and Cognition*, pp. 61–85, Cambridge, MA: MIT Press, 2000.

the recognition of the "naturalness" of belief in God is entirely consistent with a Christian natural theology.[79]

Yet it is also possible to understand the idea of the "image of God" in terms of the enactive nature of perception. In the Hebraic tradition, God is seen as *active* – one who does things. In contrast to more abstract Greek thought about the nature of the divine attributes, the Old Testament focuses on what God does to and for God's people, whether in the past or present – such as delivering them from bondage in Egypt or exile in Babylon, or shepherding them.[80] Christianity maintains this emphasis through the incarnation and redemption, both of which affirm God's action in history, directed towards humanity. To bear God's image could be understood in terms of the human replication of this divine activity, including the divine creativity.[81] The enactive nature of human cognition mirrors the enactive nature of God. God and humanity are not to be understood as mutual observers, but as mutual actors or agents.

We have often addressed the issue of discernment in this book, and it is important to note how this illuminates the Christian understanding of humanity. Most of the biblical material addressing this theme is visual, focused on the notion of "seeing." As we noted in our analysis of Jesus of Nazareth's parables of the kingdom, one can *see* nature without *perceiving* God. Yet some biblical material refers to auditory experiences, as in the case of Samuel (pp. 174–7), who hears God's voice, yet does not recognize it for what it really is. Both these images are brought together in a seminal statement concerning the capacity of the observer to grasp and discern the true meaning of reality: "They may indeed look, but not perceive, and may indeed listen, but not understand" (Mark 4: 12). This, however, is not to be seen simply as a comment on the limitations of human observation; it identifies a fundamental theme in any Christian understanding of human nature – a flawed capacity to discern.

So how is this flaw to be corrected? How are we to be enabled to see properly? Hans Urs von Balthasar, who emphasized that faith was itself a kind of seeing, argued that divine assistance was required if the signs of

---

[79] See, for example, John Henry Newman's discussion of "natural religion": John Henry Newman, *An Essay in Aid of a Grammar of Assent*, London: Longmans, Green & Co., 1903, pp. 396–9.

[80] Psalm 103 emphasizes both God's present and past actions on behalf of Israel.

[81] Think, for example, of John Dewey's constructivist account of human experience, discussed earlier (p. 56).

God within the world were to be seen and understood. Yet this does not take place by the supplementation of the natural order, so that it might point to God more powerfully; it comes about by the enhancement of the human capacity to discern.

> The spirit searching for meaning requires a higher light of grace in order to synthesize the signs . . . The light of grace comes to the aid of this natural inability; it strengthens and deepens the power of sight. It does not provide new clues or compensate for the inadequacy of the "scientific" arguments; rather, it bestows vision and makes the eye proportionate to what is being shown.[82]

The idea of "seeing without perceiving" is naturally linked with the idea of blindness. This has been a prominent theme in classic Christian discussions of the human situation – for example, in Augustine of Hippo's famous declaration of the task of the church:

> Our whole business in this life is to heal the eye of the heart [*sanare oculum cordis*], so that God might be seen. It is for this that the holy mysteries are celebrated, for this that the word of God is preached, and towards this end that the moral exhortations of the church are directed.[83]

Augustine here identifies the means by which the human mind is educated to "see" God as being through the sacraments, preaching, and directed action. His emphasis on the "healing of the eye of the heart" is, however, too easily understood in terms of blindness, considered as an ocular defect. Augustine's phrase "the eye of the heart" clearly indicates that he is aware that perception involves more than the human eye – a point that clearly merits further discussion.

We have already noted the importance of the phenomena of cortical blindness and visual agnosia in understanding the processes involved in

---

[82] Hans Urs von Balthasar, *The Glory of the Lord: A Theological Aesthetics*, 7 vols, Edinburgh: T&T Clark, 1982–9, vol. 1, pp. 175–6.

[83] Augustine of Hippo, *Sermo* 88, 5. The subject of the sermon is Mark 10: 46–52, the story of the healing of Bartimaeus, a blind man. A related point about the incapacity of humanity to see reality properly is made by Emil Brunner, *Offenbarung und Vernunft: Die Lehre von der christlichen Glaubenserkenntnis*, Zurich: Zwingli Verlag, 1941, pp. 76–8.

human perception (pp. 84–6); it is now appropriate to explore their theological implications in more detail. In the case of cortical blindness, the eyes function normally, and information is transmitted to the visual cortex. The visual cortex, however, is unable to process the information, and as a result, the individual cannot see. Yet perhaps more apposite to our reflections, visual agnosia is characterized by an ability to see individual aspects of an object, yet with an inability to make the connections needed to see the object as a whole. A green, shiny, round object with a stem sticking out at the top is seen; an apple is not seen.

In many ways, this corresponds to the dilemma of the human perception of nature, which identifies its constituent parts, yet fails to discern its meaning – the "big picture" which transcends its individual components. Observers may thus have all the evidence in front of their eyes, but cannot actually make sense of it. They may have all the information needed (including the necessary conceptual frameworks) to disclose the meaning of something – but are unable to link them together.

A biblical depiction of this is provided in the account provided in John's Gospel of a confrontation between Jesus and the Pharisees over the true meaning of the Old Testament. The Pharisees "search the Scriptures" (John 5: 39), yet fail to appreciate that they point to Jesus himself as their fulfillment. They have all the information, and the necessary conceptual schemes to make sense of it – but they are unable to discern its meaning, and its link with Jesus. They also have access to the visual data, in that they have seen Jesus and his works. The failure lies in their inability to make the connections necessary to "see" things correctly.

Augustine of Hippo spoke of the need for the "healing of the eye of the heart." Part of that healing is the provision of conceptual schemes (note his emphasis on the sacraments and preaching) which enable believers to perceive God enactively within nature. Yet there are deeper currents to Augustine's theology at this point, not least his emphasis on the capacity of divine grace to heal and restore human nature. We may therefore move on to consider the importance of the Christian understanding of salvation to natural theology.

Natural Theology and the Economy of Salvation

"If God made the world, he made a lousy job of it." This theme is widely encountered in atheist apologetics, and makes a not unreasonable point. Contrary to the rather blithe and breezy cosmic optimism which pervades

William Paley's account of the natural world, nature has its darker, more disturbing aspects – as seen, for example, in the massive destruction and loss of life resulting from the devastating tsunami of December 2004.[84] So how is a natural theology to account for these?

The style of natural theology which predominated during the era of the Enlightenment was essentially deistic, having little connection with the God whom the Christian tradition proclaims to have become incarnate in Jesus Christ. Deism offers a truncated and imaginatively impoverished version of the orthodox Christian economy of salvation, limiting the action and influence of its divinity to the primordial act of the creation of an ordered world, for which the best analogies were mechanical in nature.[85]

Although the movement generally known as "Deism" is perhaps less theologically coherent than has sometimes been assumed,[86] it is clear that it gave priority to the idea that God created the world, and endowed nature with the ability to develop and function without the need for God's continuing presence or interference. The "economy of salvation" was thus limited to the single action of creation, often disconnected from any notion of continuing providence.[87] To use the preferred metaphor of that age, the world was like a magnificent clock, showing clear evidence of design – in fact, being so well designed that it did not require maintenance of any kind. God seemed to have become an explanatory redundancy.[88] Having created a mechanical universe, God was able to step to

---

[84] See David Bentley Hart, *The Doors of the Sea: Where Was God in the Tsunami?* Grand Rapids, MI: Eerdmans, 2005.

[85] For a perceptive engagement with the impersonal deity of this movement and its impact on the social imagination of the West, see Charles Taylor, *A Secular Age*, Cambridge, MA: Belknap Press, 2007, pp. 270–95.

[86] See the comments in Peter A. Byrne, *Natural Religion and the Nature of Religion: The Legacy of Deism*, London: Routledge, 1989; David Pailin, "Should Herbert of Cherbury be Regarded as a 'Deist'?" *Journal of Theological Studies* 51 (2000): 113–49.

[87] For the subsequent re-establishment of this link, see Colin E. Gunton, *The Triune Creator*, pp. 182–4.

[88] See the analysis in Herbert H. Odom, "The Estrangement of Celestial Mechanics and Religion," *Journal of the History of Ideas* 27 (1966): 533–58; James E. Force, "The Breakdown of the Newtonian Synthesis of Science and Religion: Hume, Newton and the Royal Society," in R. H. Popkin and J. E. Force (eds), *Essays on the Context, Nature and Influence of Isaac Newton's Theology*, pp. 143–63, Dordrecht: Kluwer Academic Publishers, 1990.

one side – or be marginalized by natural philosophy – without any notice-able change in its functioning.[89]

This analogy served its apologetic purpose well while attention was focused on the ordering of the natural world. Yet within a generation of Newton's death, the merits of such an appeal to nature were being openly questioned. We have already seen how the "God" whose existence and attributes were inferred from natural processes bore a somewhat tangen-tial relationship to the God of Christian orthodoxy. The sense of unease was accentuated through a growing awareness of the disorder of the natural world, especially as this was revealed in natural disasters. The emerging Cartesian emphasis upon the "perfection" of God and God's works merely accentuated the magnitude of the problem, converting every apparent defect in nature into a demonstration of the incoherence of the God-hypothesis.[90] It was partly for this reason that the Lisbon earthquake and tsunami of 1755, in which some 75,000 people are thought to have perished, had such an impact on late Enlightenment thought, not least in regard to the merits of its concept of God.[91]

The problem of the apparent imperfections of the world was the topic of much discussion in the late seventeenth and early eighteenth centuries. In 1681, Thomas Burnet (1635–1715), chaplain to William III of Eng-land, and a cabinet officer, published his *Telluris Theoria Sacra*, or *The Sacred Theory of the Earth*, in which he argued that the world had been created perfectly proportioned, and without defect. Noah's flood, how-ever, changed everything. The smooth face of the earth was marred by mountains and scarred by the deep, uneven beds of rivers and seas.

---

[89] This underlies Thomas Hobbes's view that God can be compared to a retired constitutional monarch, having a certain role as a cosmic figurehead but divorced from any involvement in the day-to-day affairs of the universe. God's death would not be noticed. Interestingly, this points to rationalist styles of natural theology, at best suggesting that God once existed – but not that God continues to exist. See further Richard Tuck, "The 'Christian Atheism' of Thomas Hobbes," in Michael Hunter and David Wootton (eds), *Atheism from the Reformation to the Enlightenment*, pp. 102–20, Oxford: Clarendon Press, 1992.

[90] A point rightly emphasized by Michael J. Buckley, *At the Origins of Modern Atheism*, New Haven, CT: Yale University Press, 1987.

[91] For a careful analysis of this development on modern thought, see Susan Neiman, *Evil in Modern Thought: An Alternative History of Modern Philosophy*, Princeton, NJ: Princeton University Press, 2002.

There appearing nothing of Order, or any regular Design in the [earth's] Parts, it seems reasonable to believe that it was not the Work of Nature, according to her first Intention, or according to the first Model that was drawn in Measure and Proportion by the Line and by the Plummet, but a secondary Work, and the best that could be made of broken Materials. ... [Both earth and moon are] in my Judgment the Image or Picture of a great Ruin, and have the true aspect of a World lying in its Rubbish.[92]

Such views would now be regarded as virtually indefensible. Nevertheless, the cognitive dissonance and challenge that gave rise to them merits close attention. If the world was created "good," why is it presently so disordered? How can we speak of "natural evil"? The deist view of the natural world emphasizes that the world is the good creation of God, yet has no developed conceptual apparatus with which to engage its apparent degeneration, disruption, or decay.

This may be contrasted with the traditional Christian understanding of the "economy of salvation," which undergirds a trinitarian understanding of God.[93] The trajectory of the world does not begin and end with creation, but follows the more complex path of creation, fall, incarnation, redemption, and consummation. While each of these elements is open to a number of interpretations within the mainline Christian tradition, their concatenation to yield a coherent view of salvation history – and the God whose actions lie behind it – must be seen as an integral aspect of a distinctively and authentically Christian approach to reality, even if it is open to a number of interpretations.

---

[92] Marjorie Hope Nicolson, *Mountain Gloom and Mountain Glory: The Development of the Aesthetics of the Infinite*, Ithaca, NY: Cornell University Press, 1959, pp. 196–7. For further discussion of Burnet's treatise, see Stephen J. Gould, *Ever Since Darwin: Reflections in Natural History*, New York: Norton, 1977, pp. 141–6.

[93] For the concept in Irenaeus of Lyons, see the excellent extended analysis in Eric F. Osborn, *Irenaeus of Lyons*, Cambridge, UK: Cambridge University Press, 2001, pp. 51–141. Other ways of conceiving the idea ought to be noted: see, e.g., J. Patout Burns, "Economy of Salvation: Two Patristic Traditions," *Theological Studies* 37 (1976): 598–619. There are some important debates over whether Augustine's trinitarianism is adequately grounded in the "economy of salvation." For a judicious summary of the evidence, see Johannes Arnold, "Begriff und heilsökonomische Bedeutung der göttlichen Sendungen in Augustinus *De Trinitate*," *Recherches Augustiniennes* 25 (1991): 3–69.

Paul's appeal to creation as the basis of a knowledge of God needs careful consideration here. Although insistent that God can be known through the creation (Romans 1: 20), Paul speaks of the creation "groaning" (Romans 8: 22).[94] The created order is in transition, from what it once was to what it finally will become. Paul's statements can not only be interpreted in terms of the fall of creation from its original state, but also as an extension of the Old Testament prophetic theme of the hope of the future renewal and restoration of creation.[95]

This Pauline theme has major implications for natural theology, not least in that it clearly indicates that the present natural order is not to be seen as an order of "pure" nature, an apparently necessary assumption if the direct correlation of the "creation" with the "creator" is to be maintained. Christian doctrine has sought to develop and formalize this theme through the theological construction of the "fall."[96] This has been understood in different ways within the Christian tradition. For Irenaeus of Lyons, both the created order and humanity are subject to decay on account of their deflection from their true goals; for Augustine of Hippo, they have fallen from a primeval pristine state, and are now subject to corruption and degeneration. Both views have significant implications for natural theology.

In the understanding of the economy of salvation associated with Irenaeus of Lyons, the natural order of creation that was declared to be "good" by its creator has been deflected from its original path, now requiring redemption and renewal. The approach adopted by Augustine of Hippo holds that nature is to be considered as in some way defaced, degraded, or diminished as a consequence of the fall. On the basis of each approach, the enterprise of natural theology is faced with a significant obstacle – namely, that it cannot be assumed that the "nature" which is observed

---

[94] Jan Lambrecht, "The Groaning of Creation," *Louvain Studies* 15 (1990): 3–18.

[95] As argued by Laurie J. Braaten, "All Creation Groans: Romans 8:22 in Light of the Biblical Sources," *Horizons in Biblical Theology* 28 (2006): 131–59. Braaten argues that the cause of creation's "groaning" is not its own fall, but the impact of human sin.

[96] One of the best studies of this theme remains N. P. Williams, *The Ideas of the Fall and of Original Sin: A Historical and Critical Study,* London: Longmans, Green and Co., 1927. More recently, see the survey in Trevor Hart, "Redemption and Fall" in Colin E. Gunton (ed.), *Cambridge Companion to Christian Doctrine,* pp. 189–206, Cambridge, UK: Cambridge University Press, 1997.

directly corresponds to the state of nature which might be thought to bear the imprint of its creator.[97] Direct mapping from creation to the creator is thus rendered problematic.

This understanding of the economy of salvation extends to include the human observer, again with implications for natural theology. What if, as Anselm of Canterbury suggested, sin renders the human soul incapable of seeing the beauty of God, or discerning God's reality within the world?[98] Or if, as Calvin asserted, it is not merely nature itself, but the "natural" human capacity to interpret nature correctly that has been damaged by sin?[99]

The Christian concept of the "economy of salvation" helps account for the seemingly disordered, ugly, and evil aspects of nature. It allows us to make sense of what is observed, by offering a framework that is able to accommodate the darker side of nature. Yet this process of accommodation also renders nature impenetrable, in that it makes the interpretation of nature dependent on an understanding of what is "beautiful" and "ugly" which is not itself given in the observation of nature. Natural theology is about seeing nature in a certain way, reflecting assumptions which are brought to that observation rather than arising directly from it.

This is not a difficulty for the approach to natural theology that we defend in this volume, in that we propose viewing nature from within the Christian faith. On the other hand, the traditional approach to natural theology argues directly from the empirical world that we observe, and defines this empirical entity as "creation." The existence and characteristics of this "creation" are then transferred to the "creator," perhaps by a

---

[97] This theme has become of considerable importance within the environmental movement, which traces parallels between the biblical account of the "precipitous fall from Eden followed by a long, slow, upward attempt to recreate the Garden of Eden on earth" and the environmentalist's narrative of "a long, slow decline from a prehistoric past in which the world was ecologically more pristine and society was more equitable for all people and for both genders." Carolyn Merchant, *Reinventing Eden: The Fate of Nature in Western Culture*, London: Routledge, 2003, pp. 11–12.

[98] Anselm of Canterbury, *Proslogion*, 17. This spiritual obtuseness has important consequences for Anselm's views on the place of "proofs" of God's existence: see Eileen Sweeney, "Anselm's Proslogion: The Desire for the Word," *Saint Anselm Journal* 1 (2003): 17–31.

[99] Paul Helm, "John Calvin, the *Sensus Divinitatis* and the Noetic Effects of Sin," *International Journal of Philosophy of Religion* 43 (1998): 87–107.

Lockean process of extrapolation to infinity. Yet the theological fallacy entailed in this process cannot be overlooked: tensions, incoherencies, and contradictions within the realm of nature, which Christian theology classically attributes to the fall, are now, on account of the presuppositions of the traditional style of natural theology, *projected onto the concept of God*. The traditional approach to natural theology can offer only a limited defense of God at this point. In what follows, we shall focus on some specific issues to make the importance of this point clearer.

Natural theology, as we noted earlier, appeals to the orderedness of nature. Do not nature's laws point to a lawgiver? Is not cosmic orderliness itself a witness to God's ordering act of creation? The importance of such arguments is well-known,[100] and they continue to play an important role in natural theology. But what of the disorder that can be discerned within the natural world? It may be objected that the world may indeed be ordered, at least in some respects, and at some levels. Yet the world itself often seems chaotic, disorderly, unpredictable. How is this to be accounted for? Which is the real situation, and which the anomaly or shadow? Is the world really ordered, with patches of disorder? Or is it fundamentally chaotic, with occasional irruptions of structure? Are we to take a dualist route, and propose that there are two gods? Or to turn a blind eye to those aspects of nature that are inconsistent with the idea of a creator? Both routes have been taken in the past; yet both are unacceptable to Christians.

John Henry Newman's famous difficulties with the "argument from design" can be shown to rest on his belief that the creation was disordered on account of sin.[101] For Newman, both the natural order itself, and the human capacity to reflect upon it and discern its true significance, had to be considered, not as idealized entities, but as they were encountered and observed "actually and historically."[102] Human reason, "as it acts in fact and concretely in fallen man," proves incapable of perceiving the glory of God in the natural world. It was a matter of empirical observation, he asserted, that humanity, on inspecting nature, discerned

---

[100] See, for example, McGrath, *A Scientific Theology: 1 – Nature*, pp. 218–32.

[101] Noel Keith Roberts, "Newman on the Argument from Design," *New Blackfriars* 88 (2007): 56–66, especially pp. 64–5.

[102] John Henry Newman, *Apologia Pro Vita Sua*, London: Longmans, Green, & Co., 1864, pp. 335–6.

only "tokens so faint and broken of a superintending design" that the natural instinct and conclusion of the human mind was "towards a simple unbelief in matters of religion."

A distinctively Christian natural theology, such as that which we have explored and expounded in the present volume, has the capacity to address such tensions. It affirms that our concept of order presupposes an ultimate ground of order which transcends what we can observe in nature itself. Through providing a sophisticated interpretative framework for what we observe, it affirms that the world is indeed fundamentally ordered, while offering an account of its manifest disorder. The "economy of salvation" stresses the priority of order within creation, while noting on the one hand, the *actuality* of sin as disorder, and on the other the Christian *hope* of the ultimate restoration and renewal of order. As Thomas F. Torrance has argued, a fundamental belief in the primacy of divine ordering allows us to understand the presence of disorder within the universe, and anticipate its future elimination.

> The objective divine order of the good and rational does not merely negate evil, but lays hold of it in a re-creative and re-ordering movement with a view to mastering it, repairing what is disordered, and making it serve a fuller dimension of order than might have been possible any other way.[103]

There are important parallels here with John Dewey's notion of experience as *reconstruction* – the transformation of the indeterminate or underdetermined into the determinate and meaningful.[104]

Torrance's argument highlights the importance of a doctrine of salvation in restoring – or at least beginning the process of restoration – of a disordered creation. Such an "atoning reordering of creation" is to be understood as an engagement with the "source of disorder." The resurrection of Christ is understood as the means by which God "triumphs over all the forces of disintegration and disorder in the cosmos."[105]

---

[103] Thomas F. Torrance, *Divine and Contingent Order*, Oxford: Oxford University Press, 1981, p. 114.

[104] Michael Eldridge, *Transforming Experience: John Dewey's Cultural Instrumentalism*, Nashville, TN: Vanderbilt University Press, 1998. As we noted earlier (p. 195), this can be interpreted in terms of the concept of the "image of God" expressing humanity's mental creativity as reflecting that of God.

[105] Torrance, *Divine and Contingent Order*, p. 138.

Redemption can thus be understood as reordering – that is, restoring the God-given order in which the cosmos came into being. Torrance notes that the disorder which has crept into the universe affects human nature in particular; nevertheless, redemption must be understood to embrace the whole created order, which has now fallen into disorder, and not simply humanity. This theme is particularly associated with the Greek patristic tradition, which understood sin as the disordering of the cosmos, which required restoration to its original integrity through redemption.[106] Such an approach found much sympathy in the twentieth century, particularly from those theologians with a particular affinity with the Greek tradition.

And what of the appeal to the beauty of nature as a ground of belief in God? Many find this appeal deeply compelling. Yet for others it is deeply problematic. How are we to make sense of the ugly elements of nature? Once more, they may be ignored by using a principle of selective theological attention. Another strategy, particularly common amongst ecological writers, is to interpret natural ugliness as the outcome of inappropriate human intervention in nature, leading to the despoiling of its original integrity and beauty.[107] Yet each of these strategies is problematic.

A fully-orbed Christian theology has the potential to accommodate the moral and aesthetic ambivalence of nature, as it is presently encountered and observed, by locating its observation and interpretation within the economy of salvation. The creation stands in need of renewal from a God who will create all things anew (Revelation 21: 5). There is a profoundly eschatological dimension to an authentically Christian natural theology, in that it is to be interpreted in the light of its goal, not merely of its origin. The fading beauty and goodness of the world are to be interpreted in the light of the hope of their restoration and renewal. A Christian natural theology can thus be considered to concern, not simply some primordial creation, but the restoration of that creation as expressed in

---

[106] See the classic study of H. E. W. Turner, *The Patristic Doctrine of Redemption: A Study of the Development of Doctrine During the First Five Centuries*, London: Mowbray, 1952.

[107] Seyyed Hossein Nasr, *Religion and the Order of Nature*, Oxford: Oxford University Press, 1996, p. 272.

the Christian hope.[108] As Alexander Schmemann points out about the "world to come":

> This is not an "other" world, different from the one God has created and given to us. It is our same world, already perfected in Christ, but not yet in us. It is our same world redeemed and restored, in which Christ "fills all things with Himself."[109]

A Christian natural theology should therefore be able to offer theological stability to the notions of the beauty of the creation by setting our "seeing" of nature within its proper theological context, shaped by the "economy of salvation." The creation was brought into being as beautiful; it will be restored to that beauty; and traces of that beauty can still be discerned within its present state.[110] That beauty will be restored through redemption: thus Augustine of Hippo affirms that the purpose of Christ's incarnation and redemption was to heal the wounds of humanity, and restore its lost beauty.[111] Christian aesthetics can be understood as a discipleship of the mind, which intentionally sets out to discern and appreciate what is true, beautiful, and good in the world, recognizing that, like the field in the parable, it contains both wheat and tares, grain and weeds (Matthew 13: 24–30).

The same issues arise in relation to the goodness of creation. God created all things good; they will be restored to goodness; at present, good and evil coexist in the world, as wheat and weeds together in the same field. The theological framework set out in this book allows the good to

---

[108]   The classic study of such themes remains Jürgen Moltmann, *Theology of Hope: On the Ground and the Implications of a Christian Eschatology*, London: SCM, 1967. For discussion, see Randall E. Otto, *The God of Hope: The Trinitarian Vision of Jürgen Moltmann*, Lanham, MD: University Press of America, 1991; Richard Bauckham, *God Will Be All in All: The Eschatology of Jürgen Moltmann*, Edinburgh: T&T Clark, 1999.

[109]   Alexander Schmemann, *The World as Sacrament*, London: Darton, Longman & Todd, 1974, p. 51. His analysis of the concept of *anaphora* merits close reading on this point: pp. 43–53.

[110]   See, e.g., the analysis in David Bentley Hart, *The Beauty of the Infinite: The Aesthetics of Christian Truth*, Grand Rapids, MI: Eerdmans, 2003, pp. 318–94.

[111]   Augustine, *de musica*, VI.iv.7.

be identified with the wheat, and evil with the weeds, thus offering an interpretative apparatus for the "seeing" of nature. Once more, atonement is understood as the restoration of the original goodness of nature.[112] Nature, as an empirical reality, cannot be equated with its original state. Whether an Irenaean or Augustinian approach to the origin of evil is adopted,[113] the outcome for natural theology remains substantially the same – namely, that nature, *as presently observed*, cannot be assumed to be nature, *as originally created*.

The renewed natural theology set out in this work is grounded on an appeal to the human experience of nature, which requires to be interpreted within a theological framework shaped by the Christian vision of the economy of salvation. This framework points to the divine origins of nature, and the assurance that God is now at work renewing it. Nature is thus to be seen as a continual reminder and symbol of a renewed creation, a world which we do not yet know but believe to lie over the horizons of our human existence. It is as if we are homesick for a lost Eden, whose memory lingers, longing for a fulfillment that we know lies ahead of us, but have not yet found.

Just as John Keats saw the ornamentation on a Grecian urn as mirroring the great human longing for meaning, value, and beauty, we must learn to see the present beauty of nature as a sign and promise of the coming glory of God, its creator, redeemer, and consummator. It can be seen to point backwards to the Christ event, and forward to the coming "new heaven and new earth." Our sense of wonder at the beauty of nature heightens our awareness of our limits, while heightening our longing to enter into what it seems to promise. Nature is to be cherished and valued, not simply for what it *is*, but for what it *foreshadows* – a new creation, renewing and bringing to perfection the tired and wounded world that we know, inhabit, and seek to tend.

---

[112] For a rigorous discussion, see Mark Wynn, *God and Goodness: A Natural Theological Perspective*, London: Routledge, 1999, especially pp. 169–89.

[113] One of the best discussions remains John Hick, *Evil and the God of Love*, 2nd edn, London: Macmillan, 1985. For more recent reflections on these issues, see Eric Carlton, *Dancing in the Dark: Reflections on the Problem of Theodicy*, Madison, NJ: Fairleigh Dickinson University Press, 2005; Bruce A. Little, *A Creation-Order Theodicy: God and Gratuitous Evil*, Lanham, MD: University Press of America, 2005; Michael Stoeber, *Reclaiming Theodicy: Reflections on Suffering, Compassion and Spiritual Transformation*, Basingstoke: Palgrave Macmillan, 2005.

Natural Theology and the Incarnation

The figure of Jesus of Nazareth can be argued to be both the foundation and criterion of Christian theology. Although Christian theology has traditionally articulated his significance metaphysically, using the static Chalcedonian category of "being" to clarify his relationship to God, many would argue that this is better articulated dynamically, in terms of what God does for us through Christ. As Wolfhart Pannenberg remarked, "The divinity of Jesus and his freeing and redeeming significance for us are related in the closest possible way. To this extent, Melanchthon's famous sentence is appropriate: 'Who Jesus Christ is becomes known in his saving action'."[114] The importance of this point is accentuated through an understanding of the process of human perception.

As noted earlier, perception pays attention to significance (p. 98), being concerned with the importance or relevance of an object or event for the beholder. Reality is viewed through "significance spectacles," involving an assessment of the meaning of the environment for the observer. In the case of Jesus of Nazareth, this naturally leads to an assessment of his significance for us. What difference does he make? What is his relevance for existence? Such questions tend to prioritize soteriology over Christology, without in any way forcing their separation. So what is the significance of Jesus of Nazareth for natural theology?

An excellent starting point is provided by Hans Urs von Balthasar's extended reflection on the manifestation of God's glory in the world, in Christ, and in the church. For Balthasar, the Christian faith brings to fulfillment the natural longings and aspirations of the human race, fulfilling what is pure and filtering out what is distorted or confused. The gospel of the incarnation ". . . quenches and more than fulfils the human longing for love and beauty, a longing which, previous to and outside the sphere of revelation, exhausted itself in impotent and distorted sketches or such a desperately needed and yet unimaginable fulfilment."[115]

The Christian doctrine of creation provides an intellectual framework for seeing God *through* nature; the doctrine of the incarnation allows

---

[114] Wolfhart Pannenberg, *Jesus – God and Man*, Philadelphia: Westminster Press, 1968, pp. 38–9.

[115] Balthasar, *The Glory of the Lord*, vol. 1, p. 123. Balthasar here develops a line of thought found in Dionysius the Areopagite's *Divine Names*: see especially the discussion at pp. 122–3.

us to see God *in* nature, culminating in Christ himself. The encyclical *Veritatis Splendor,* addressed to the bishops of the Roman Catholic Church, affirms a strongly incarnational approach to the human quest for what is true, good, and beautiful: "The light of God's face shines in all its beauty on the countenance of Jesus Christ."[116] This Christological grounding of the church's engagement with nature has been characteristic of Christian orthodoxy down the ages, and has an important bearing on natural theology. For instance, in his 1871 Hulsean Lectures at Cambridge University, F. J. A. Hort made a comment of no small importance to our task: "The gospel itself can never be fully known till nature as well as man is fully known; and that the manifestation of nature as well of man in Christ is part of his manifestation of God."[117] Hort here argues that Christ is the point of convergence of the Christian vision of God, humanity, and the natural order. Hort's vision of the incarnation interconnects divinity, humanity, and the natural world, revealing a complex web of relationships that defies simple explanation, while finding its focus in Christ himself.

A similar point is made by Kierkegaard, who rightly pointed out that Jesus of Nazareth's command to attend to individual aspects of nature is actually an invitation to attend to the one to whom they point:

> "Consider the lilies of the field, behold the birds of the air." So He does not say, "No man can serve two masters . . . look at Me," no, He says, "No man can serve two masters . . . consider the lilies of the field, behold the birds of the air." He might have said with truth, with infinitely great truth, if thou wilt, "Look at Me." For lilies and birds do not literally express anything, and only He is the truth of that which the lilies and the birds symbolically denote.[118]

Earlier, we considered the way in which nature is used in the synoptic Gospels and the Johannine tradition. This might be taken to suggest that

---

[116] *Veritatis Splendor,* Prooemium, 2. For comment, see Gilbert Meilaender, "Veritatis Splendor: Reopening Some Questions of the Reformation," *Journal of Religious Ethics* 23 (1995): 225–38.

[117] F. J. A. Hort, *The Way, The Truth, The Life: The Hulsean Lectures for 1871,* Cambridge, UK: Cambridge University Press, 1893, p. 83.

[118] Søren Kierkegaard, *For Self-Examination, Judge for Yourselves! and Three Discourses, 1851,* trans. Walter Lowrie, London: Oxford University Press, 1941, p. 188.

Jesus of Nazareth's relationship to nature was essentially passive, as if he were no more than an observer of its patterns, or a shrewd teacher opportunistically exploiting convenient natural features to make a theological point. Yet there is something deeper here, as is indicated by another aspect of Jesus of Nazareth's relationship to the natural order – the miracles of creation. These disclose him as the master, not simply the interpreter, of nature.

The importance of the miracles is located both in what they reveal concerning Jesus of Nazareth's relationship to the natural order, and the impact they have on those who observe them.[119] Thus the healing of the paralytic, one of the earliest miracles recorded in the Gospel accounts (Mark 2: 1–12), evokes a response from the crowd, who were "all amazed and glorified God, saying, 'We have never seen anything like this!'" (Mark 2: 12). Similarly, the stilling of the storm on Lake Galilee (Mark 4: 35–41) gives rise to a sense of wonder on the part of those who witnessed it: "Who then is this, that even the wind and sea obey him?"[120]

The reference to the "wind and sea" is suggestive of the chaotic forces depicted in the opening verses of the book of Genesis;[121] these were subdued and controlled by the authoritative word of God – a pattern that is also found in the synoptic account of the stilling of the storm. These forces of chaos were also reified in the imagery of dragons and other monsters in the creation accounts found in the prophetic and wisdom writings.[122] The divine act of creation is often represented as the defeat of

---

[119]   A similar point could be made concerning the "signs" in John's Gospel, particularly the account of Jesus walking on the water. These "signs," like the "I am" sayings (see pp. 126–33), relate to elements of nature, as interpreted within the tradition of Israel. See, e.g., Willis Hedley Salier, *The Rhetorical Impact of the Semeia in the Gospel of John: A Historical and Hermeneutical Perspective*, Tübingen: Mohr Siebeck, 2004.

[120]   For the account found in Matthew's Gospel, see Günther Bornkamm, "The Stilling of the Storm in Matthew," in Günther Bornkamm, Gerhard Barth, and Heinz Joachim Held (eds), *Tradition and Interpretation in Matthew*, pp. 52–7, Philadelphia: Westminster Press, 1963.

[121]   David T. Tsumura, *The Earth and the Waters in Genesis 1 and 2: A Linguistic Investigation*, Sheffield: Sheffield Academic Press, 1989.

[122]   See John Day, *God's Conflict with the Dragon: Echoes of a Canaanite Myth in the Old Testament*, Cambridge, UK: Cambridge University Press, 1985; Susan Niditch, *Chaos to Cosmos: Studies in Biblical Patterns of Creation*. Chico, CA: Scholars Press, 1985.

the forces of chaos.[123] This reinforces the impression that this account of Jesus of Nazareth's stilling of the storm is to be understood as a demonstration of his authority over the forces of nature, with significant implications for the emerging understanding of the identity of Jesus as God incarnate.[124]

The Christian doctrine of the incarnation, however, is often interpreted in terms of the intellectual challenges and theological opportunities that arise from the fundamental idea that God enters into the world of time and space.[125] Yet the full import of the doctrine is better understood in terms of God entering into *place and history*, rather than *time and space*. God enters into a world shaped by memory, and invested with value and meaning – rather than into an abstract four-dimensional realm.[126] Walter Brueggemann articulates the difference between the notions of "place" and "space" as follows:

> Place is space which has historical meanings, where some things have happened which are now remembered and which provide continuity and identity across generations. Place is space in which important words have been spoken which have established identity, defined vocation, and envisioned destiny.[127]

Incarnation is thus about God inhabiting the place and history of humanity. It is a cultural and historical, not merely a physical, assertion. God enters and inhabits the world of human memories, symbols, and languages.

---

[123] For example, see Job 3: 8, 7: 12, 9: 13, 40: 15–32; Psalm 74: 13–15; Isaiah 27: 1, 51: 9–10.

[124] For this development, see Morna D. Hooker, "Chalcedon and the New Testament," in Sarah Coakley and David A. Pailin (eds), *The Making and Remaking of Christian Doctrine*, pp. 73–93, Oxford: Clarendon Press, 1993.

[125] For a classic engagement with these issues, see Thomas F. Torrance, *Space, Time and Incarnation*, London: Oxford University Press, 1969.

[126] For a discussion of the "loss of place" in modern theology, see Oliver O'Donovan, "The Loss of a Sense of Place," *Irish Theological Quarterly* 55 (1989): 39–58, especially as revised in Oliver O'Donovan and Joan Lockwood O'Donovan, *Bonds of Imperfection: Christian Politics, Past and Present*, pp. 296–320. Grand Rapids, MI: Eerdmans, 2004.

[127] Walter Brueggemann, *The Land: Place as Gift, Promise, and Challenge in Biblical Faith*, Philadelphia: Fortress Press, 2002, p. 5. See also John Inge, *A Christian Theology of Place*, Aldershot: Ashgate, 2003, pp. 33–58.

As we saw earlier (pp. 126–33), in offering an understanding of the significance of Jesus of Nazareth, the Johannine "I am" sayings mingle and meld natural symbols with their inherited cultural and cultic interpretations, to yield an understanding of "natural theology" that transcends William Paley's notion of the naive direct encounter of observer and the natural world. *Nature is "seen" and its meaning articulated from the standpoint of an interpretative tradition.* Yet this tradition invites us to see "nature," not simply as God's creation, but as a realm of place and history within which God chose to make a habitation. Once the doctrine of the incarnation is grasped and affirmed, the styles of natural theology associated with the Enlightenment are seen to fail to express and articulate the deeper understanding of nature that is integral to the Christian tradition, and its vision of God.

The idea of an incarnate God raises a critically important question for any attempt to construct a viable natural theology. If the God who is disclosed through the natural world is not the same God as that who is revealed in Christ, then it has little relevance to the tasks of Christian theology. If it is the same God, on the other hand, then the God who is found in nature must be the God of the Christian tradition, who became incarnate in Christ. The God who is known through nature must be ontologically identical to the God who is known through God's self-revelation; otherwise, Christian theology potentially finds itself following an intellectual pathway that leads to an ultimately Gnostic distinction between a creator god and a (different) redeemer god.[128] Christian theology has explored this pathway in the past, and has decisively rejected such a dualism as inconsistent with its vision of God, and especially its doctrine of creation.[129]

---

[128]   For the issue, see Kurt Rudolph, *Gnosis: The Nature and History of Gnosticism*, San Francisco: Harper & Row, 1987, pp. 57–8. For a classic study, with inevitable historical weaknesses, see Adolf von Harnack, *Marcion: das Evangelium vom fremden Gott. Eine Monographie zur Geschichte der Grundlegung der katholischen Kirche*, 2nd edn, Leipzig: Hinrichs, 1924.

[129]   See Robert M. Grant, *Irenaeus of Lyons*, London: Routledge, 1997, pp. 11–28. For more thorough analyses, see Alfred Bengsch, *Heilsgeschichte und Heilswissen: Eine Untersuchung zur Struktur und Entfaltung des theologischen Denkens im Werk "Adversus Haereses" des hl. Irenäus von Lyon*, Leipzig: St. Benno-Verlag, 1957; Norbert Brox, *Offenbarung, Gnosis und gnostischer Mythos bei Irenäus von Lyon: zur Charakteristik der Systeme*, Salzburg: Pustet Verlag, 1966.

Yet once this point is conceded, its retrospective force becomes apparent. If God is indeed incarnational, as the Christian tradition insists to be the case, this ontological affirmation has implications for epistemology. Ontology determines epistemology;[130] who God *is* determines how God *acts*. The somewhat static forms of natural theology found in some patristic writers, as well as in the Enlightenment, seem to assume that one can abstract or isolate God's existence from God's actions, ultimately leading to a deist conception of God, in effect if not intention.[131] If natural theology is to be a legitimate intellectual undertaking for the Christian theological community, it must have a correlation with the God who is disclosed in and through Jesus Christ. Yet once that correlation is established, and its incarnational and trinitarian implications explored, this understanding of God's nature and actions must be applied to the enterprise of natural theology. The incarnation knits together Christian thinking about the natural order and the person of Christ, refusing to allow them to be considered in isolation.

Truth, beauty, and goodness may be intimated in nature; they are, however, more fully disclosed through Christ. To use a characteristically Johannine way of speaking, Christ is not merely the one who reveals the truth; he *is* the truth.[132] He is not merely the one who teaches and commends goodness; he is goodness. The natural human quest for truth, beauty, and goodness is thus ultimately an unacknowledged quest for Christ. Such a quest may be prompted by nature; it cannot, however, be answered or fulfilled by nature – without being seen from an incarnational perspective.

Yet this brief theological analysis must be supplemented from the perspective of an understanding of human perception and cognition. Perception is egocentric; we always look at the world from a particular perspective.

---

[130] This insight is fundamental to the philosophy of the natural sciences, and my own "scientific theology" project: for its exposition and defense, see Alister E. McGrath, *A Scientific Theology: 2 – Reality*, London: T&T Clark, 2002, pp. 195–244, especially pp. 218–19.

[131] For a significant analysis, see Torrance, *Reality and Scientific Theology*, pp. 43–61. This criticism could also be directed beyond these specific forms of natural theology.

[132] For the best study, see Ignace de La Potterie, *La vérité dans saint Jean*, 2 vols, Rome: Biblical Institute Press, 1977. His later study should also be noted here: "Jésus, témoin de la vérité et roi par la vérité," *Studia Missionalia* 46 (1997): 21–41.

We have already seen how this insight undermines the unrealistic expectations of pure objectivity that is often associated with the Enlightenment; yet it is important to note that it resonates strongly with an incarnational theology. In his encounters with individuals, as related in the Gospels, Jesus can be seen to have entered into their egocentric perspectives, enabling them – like the man born blind (John 9) – to "see" things properly for the first time. He at once inhabits and expands their way of seeing things, in much the same way as the doctrine of the incarnation affirms that God chose to enter into history in order to encounter and engage humanity from our perspective.

This analysis could easily be extended to include other areas of Christian theology – for example, sacramentology. Any analysis of the way in which natural entities might be considered to point to the divine must note the potentially illuminating connections between a natural theology and the sacraments of the church. The capacity of nature to signify is integral to any understanding of the sacraments.[133] Many recent accounts of the theology of the sacraments explicitly acknowledge this point, as is particularly evident in John Macquarrie's "natural theology of sacramentality."[134] Macquarrie's starting point here is the notion that we live in "a sacramental universe," so that it is possible to know God's presence and activity through the "things" of the world.

Some have held that this capacity is intrinsic to the created order. Thus the early Syriac tradition took the view that the entire world was revelatory in nature, on account of its having been created by the *logos*.[135] Types, symbols, and mysteries were an integral part of the created order, of which sacramental theology was a natural extension. Others have held that it is the consequence of an imposed theological framework, which allows such natural symbols to be "seen" in a certain way. Thus Huldrych Zwingli's eucharistic theology rests on the assumption that the

---

[133] John H. McKenna, "Symbol and Reality: Some Anthropological Considerations," *Worship* 65 (1991): 2–27.

[134] John Macquarrie, *A Guide to the Sacraments*, London: SCM Press, 1997, pp. 1–33. Note especially Macquarrie's appeal to Paul Tillich's category of the "symbol" in his exploration of how every aspect of creation is potentially revelatory of divine presence.

[135] Seely Joseph Beggiani, "The Typological Approach of Syriac Sacramental Theology," *Theological Studies* 64 (2003): 543–57.

liturgical context creates the association between bread and the death of Christ.[136]

Yet this issue is not merely theological in nature, as it raises the essentially anthropological question of the place of symbols and signs in expressing and maintaining the identity of a community,[137] and the semiotic question of how natural signs come to express cultural ideas or values.[138] While a full discussion of such questions lies beyond the present work, even these brief comments indicate how important it is to explore further this theological link.

Conclusion to Part II

In the second part of this work, we have considered how a natural theology may be repositioned and regenerated by insisting that it is shaped and informed by the specific theological vision of the Christian tradition, rather than (as with the Enlightenment) the allegedly "universal" and autonomous truths of reason or common sense. There is an important parallel here with the historical development of scientific theories. Older theories, once regarded as normative and autonomous, are often found to represent "special cases" of more advanced theories.

Thus neither relativistic quantum mechanics nor quantum field theory can be said to invalidate classical mechanics;[139] rather, they provide a superior explanatory framework which creates conceptual space for the older approach, and clarifies the conditions under which it operates satisfactorily. The two approaches are thus shown to be interconnected, yet

---

[136] Alister E. McGrath, "The Eucharist: Reassessing Zwingli," *Theology* 93 (1990): 13–20; see further Michael Witczak, "The Manifold Presence of Christ in the Liturgy," *Theological Studies* 59 (1998): 680–702.

[137] See particularly Anthony P. Cohen, *The Symbolic Construction of Community*, London: Routledge, 1989.

[138] Richard J. Parmentier, *Signs in Society: Studies in Semiotic Anthropology*, Bloomington, IN: Indiana University Press, 1994, pp. 125–35; Jørgen D. Johansen and Svend E. Larsen, *Signs in Use: An Introduction to Semiotics*, London: Routledge, 2002, pp. 150–98.

[139] For those unfamiliar with this field, the best introduction is Richard W. Robinett, *Quantum Mechanics: Classical Results, Modern Systems and Visualized Examples*, New York: Oxford University Press, 1997.

distinct in terms of their domains of operation.[140] Relativistic quantum mechanics is the general theory; classical mechanics is its "special case," given its own distinct field of validity by the more universal theory.[141] In the same way, the approach to natural theology that we develop in this work explains the place of the type of natural theology associated with the Enlightenment, while identifying some of its limits.

The key point here is that a theory with considerable explanatory capacity is able to create conceptual space, valid under certain limiting yet significant conditions, for a theory which might, at first sight, appear to be quite independent – yet, on closer examination, turns out to be a special case of the higher-order theory.

In bringing this second part of this work to a close, we return to a point emphasized earlier: that perception takes place on the basis of "maps of meaning" or frameworks, which enable us to make sense of experience. This naturally raises the question of what sort of encounter with nature a Christian "map of meaning" makes possible. In the final part of this work, we shall move on to consider the form of natural theology that emerges from the theoretical framework developed up to this point.

---

[140] A. O. Bolivar, *Quantum-Classical Correspondence: Dynamical Quantization and the Classical Limit*. London: Springer, 2004.

[141] See, e.g., N. P. Landsman, *Mathematical Topics Between Classical and Quantum Mechanics*, New York: Springer, 1998, pp. 7–10; Franz Gross, *Relativistic Quantum Mechanics and Field Theory*, New York: Wiley, 1999, pp. 18–22.

PART III

Truth, Beauty, and Goodness: An Agenda for a Renewed Natural Theology

CHAPTER 9

Truth, Beauty, and Goodness: Expanding the Vision for Natural Theology

The major theme of the second part of this book has been the need to renew the vision for a natural theology on the basis of the Christian tradition. This, we have argued, lays a foundation for a vision of reality which creates conceptual space for the enterprise traditionally known as "natural theology" – while *at the same time* setting limits to its scope and validity. Such is the explanatory fecundity of the Christian vision of reality that it is able to account for both the capacity of the natural order to *point* to God, and the ability of the "baptized imagination" to achieve new levels of awareness and delight in viewing and encountering nature from a Christian standpoint.[1] This final part of our study explores the type of human responses to nature that might be appropriate to a renewed natural theology. It takes the basic themes of the Christian faith as given, and sets out to explore their implications for truth, beauty, and goodness.

Why truth, beauty, and goodness? Throughout this book, we have emphasized that natural theology is about *perceiving* nature in a certain way. The process of perception, as discussed earlier (pp. 80–110), involves thinking about (or "knowing"), affective responding to, and enactive interaction with the world. The three aspects of the natural world that

---

[1] On this, see David Tracy, *The Analogical Imagination: Christian Theology and the Culture of Pluralism*, New York: Crossroad, 1981, p. 177, referring to "a disclosure of a world of meaning and truth offering no certainty but promising some realized experience of the whole by the power of the whole."

particularly resonate with these three aspects of perception are truth, beauty, and goodness respectively. They also resonate with the subject matter of core philosophical areas of enquiry: metaphysics, aesthetics, and ethics.

This suggests that the triad of truth, beauty, and goodness – which already has a long history of use in this context[2] – might constitute a helpful scheme around which to organize a theological engagement with nature. This scheme can be understood as a matrix within which a Christian vision of nature, centered on the Word made flesh, can be explored. It reminds us that natural theology is not confined to *thinking about* nature, but extends to being touched emotionally by nature, and acting upon and within nature.

For William Paley, natural theology was essentially an intellectual analysis of the observation of nature. A fundamental contention of this work, however, is that neither the capacity of nature to disclose God, nor the capacity of the divine self-disclosure to illuminate nature, is to be understood simply in terms of propositional belief, as if the appeal and scope of the Christian faith were somehow limited to human intellectual inquiry.[3]

Deep within humanity lies a longing to make sense of things, to discern patterns within the fabric of life. Sometimes these puzzles are practical, of direct relevance to everyday life. When is the best time to sow my crops? Is there a piece missing from my self-assembly chair? Some, however, are metaphysical, even religious. Why are we here? What is life all about? How should we behave?[4] Natural theology is part of this general human enterprise of sense-making, while adopting its own distinctive approach.

---

[2]   One of the finest explorations of this theme is to be found in Victor Cousin, *Du vrai, du beau et du bien*, 8th edn, Paris: Didier, 1860.

[3]   This is not in any way to diminish the importance of such detached attempts to offer objective understandings of reality. These are based on one of the most ancient and persistent human beliefs – that there exists some order of things, some meaning embedded deep within reality, which can be grasped, appreciated, and acted upon by humanity: see Gerard Naddaf, *The Greek Concept of Nature*, Albany, NY: State University of New York Press, 2005. Intellectual reflection on the structure of created reality has been thought by many to be a way to truth, beauty, and goodness. Though often rejected, this idea has never been adequately refuted; though periodically dismissed as an obsolete irrelevance, it regularly returns.

[4]   For the limits of the sciences in attempting to address these questions, see Peter B. Medawar, *The Limits of Science*, Oxford: Oxford University Press, 1985, p. 66.

Yet no adequate account of the human encounter with nature can be given, if this is prematurely restricted to a cool, considered, disengaged attempt to explain.[5]

As we stressed in Chapter 5, human cognition is concerned with *significance* – significance in terms of physical survival, but also psychological survival through establishing meaning in life, personal identity, and value.[6] Yet too often, the lingering influence of the Enlightenment leads to natural theology being conceptualized simply as a type of intellectual outlook. Against this, we insist that natural theology should be understood in terms of "hot cognition" rather than "cool consideration." "Sense-making" involves more than giving a rational, logical account of the way things are. It is about the affect-laden human engagement with life and nature, often expressed in such questions as "Why I am here?" "What is really important?" "Can I make a difference to things?" and "Do I matter?"[7]

The approach to natural theology that we have outlined in the second part of this work offers a framework that enables us to perceive nature as God's creation. This leads us to assess the implications of this foundational schema for our understanding of our place in the universe, and our responsibilities towards the environment – and the appropriate actions and attitudes that ensue. To come to see nature as God's creation may involve a schema change as significant as coming to see the birth of Jesus of Nazareth in terms of the incarnation, or his empty tomb in terms of the resurrection.[8] Its implications, as we have seen, require careful analysis.

---

[5] Note Hannah Arendt's reflections on the challenges faced by the human mind when it is forced to operate "outside a pre-established frame of references": Kimberley Curtis, *Our Sense of the Real: Aesthetic Experience and Arendtian Politics*, Ithaca, NY: Cornell University Press, 1999, pp. 111–12.

[6] Roy Baumeister, *Meanings of Life*, New York: Guilford, 1991, pp. 3–206.

[7] Ibid, pp. 32–47. Baumeister organizes his analysis around the concepts of purpose, value, personal efficacy, and self-worth.

[8] In adult life, just as in childhood, psychological growth occurs when new information results in schema change that involves the interplay of assimilation and accommodation so that schemas become more differentiated, nuanced, or expansive. This process may involve the radical shattering and reconstitution of schemas through trauma: see Ronnie Janoff-Bulman, *Shattered Assumptions: Towards a New Psychology of Trauma*, New York: Free Press, 1992. For the case of the resurrection in particular, see Joanna Collicutt McGrath, "Post-Traumatic Growth and the Origins of Early Christianity," *Mental Health, Religion and Culture* 9 (2006): 291–306.

Yet those implications extend beyond confirming an existing or establishing a new rational explanation of the world as God's creation. Natural theology also addresses questions of significance – questions such as "What is my place in the universe?" or "How should I live?" These are questions about *value*, that are better seen as relating to the quest for goodness, rather than for truth. The Christian faith provides a resilient structure of meaning for life,[9] which includes the articulation of a vision of human nature, and its place within the natural order.[10] As Stanley Hauerwas has emphasized, the ultimate basis of Christian ethics in the world is a specific way of *seeing* the world.[11] A natural theology must therefore embrace questions which are often considered under the category of "natural law," yet are clearly concerned with the question of whether seeing nature as God's creation entails certain forms of action, ways of living, or ethical attitudes within the realm of nature.

The need to reconceive natural theology in terms of a broader range of human responses than simply rational understanding or explanation is also indicated by the persistent and abiding human interest in the transcendent. In the first part of this work, we observed that this was generally experienced and conceptualized as fleeting and elusive, while being held to be desirable and of profound importance. Transcendent experiences, while welcomed on their own terms, are often regarded as conferring insights that may help us answer the ultimate questions of human existence. However, the human engagement with the transcendent cannot be restricted to this single element. As we noted earlier, such experiences are held to possess qualities which cannot adequately be expressed or conveyed in terms of their intellectual content. William James's suggestion that mystical experiences involve "states of insight into depths of truth unplumbed by the discursive intellect,"[12] or Rudolf Otto's insistence upon

---

[9] Baumeister, *Meanings of Life*, pp. 196–201. For a more extended study, see Israela Silberman, "Religion as a Meaning System: Implications for the New Millennium," *Journal of Social Issues* 61 (2005): 641–63.

[10] See, e.g., the specific vision set out in Reinhold Niebuhr, *The Nature and Destiny of Man: A Christian Interpretation*, 2 vols, London: Nisbet, 1941.

[11] Stanley Hauerwas, *Vision and Virtue: Essays in Christian Ethical Reflection*, Notre Dame, IN: Fides Publishers, 1974.

[12] William James, *The Varieties of Religious Experience*, London: Longmans, Green & Co., 1902, pp. 380–1.

their "inexpressible" or "ineffable" character,[13] strongly indicate that these involve an appeal which goes far beyond the "rational."

Jonathan Edwards (1703–58), writing in response to the Enlightenment's emphasis on rational evaluations of nature, stressed both the importance of discerning the *beauty* of God within creation, and the incapacity of rational analysis to convert individuals – a process that he held to depend upon an "apprehension of the spiritual beauty and glory of divine things."[14] For Edwards, a truly Christian natural theology affirmed the discernment of divine beauty and glory within nature, an aesthetic response that goes beyond identifying its rationality structures.

The rise of Romanticism was also in part a cultural reaction against the aesthetically and emotionally attenuated responses to nature associated with the Enlightenment. Thus John Keats's complex poem "Lamia" (1820) can be seen in part as a protest against rationalizing accounts of the wonders of nature, which threatened to reduce the "awful" rainbow to the "dull catalogue of common things." For Keats, the scientific drive to explain nature lost sight of and became decoupled from a deeper, *imaginative* engagement with the world, in which reality was apprehended as much in terms of beauty as of truth. In Keats's view, nature elicits a response from humanity that is both emotional *and* intellectual. This emotional-intellectual response includes but also extends beyond the desire to make sense of things, to experiences of awe, admiration, elevation, or fear. The vision for a natural theology must therefore be expanded beyond what is traditionally termed "dogmatics" or "systematic theology" to embrace worship and spirituality.[15]

---

[13] Rudolf Otto, *The Idea of the Holy*, London: Oxford University Press, 1977, p. 5.

[14] Jonathan Edwards, *Treatise on the Religious Affections*, New Haven, CT: Yale University Press, p. 307. See further Roland Delattre, *Beauty and Sensibility in the Thought of Jonathan Edwards,* Yale University Press, New Haven, CT, 1968. For the connection between beauty and ethics in Edwards, see Roland A. Delattre, "Aesthetics and Ethics: Jonathan Edwards and the Recovery of Aesthetics for Religious Ethics," *Journal of Religious Ethics* 31 (2003): 277–97.

[15] This point is stressed by many writers in the field of spirituality, including Thomas Merton, *Seeds of Contemplation*, Wheathampstead: Anthony Clarke, 1972, pp. 197–8.

The importance of this point can be appreciated by reflecting on one of these human responses to nature – that of awe. "Awe" is not easily defined, but can be thought of as a sense of the magnificence and mystery of certain phenomena. The concept of "awe" has featured prominently in religious, sociological, and psychological accounts of the human engagement with nature. As noted earlier, Rudolph Otto spoke of the "numinous" – a *mysterium tremendum* which inspired awe on the part of those who experienced it.[16] Such an experience can be both profoundly positive and terrifyingly negative, and frequently reduces the subject to a state of silence or confusion. More recently, the concept has begun to attract the attention of experimental psychologists,[17] who have stressed the importance of "vastness" in triggering a sense of awe, together with the dominance of accommodation (wonder) over assimilation (sense-making).

It is not our intention to engage with the psychology of awe further here; we shall return to this later (p. 279). The point is that natural theology must be able to express a richer, more expansive, and more comprehensive range of human responses to the natural order than the insight, typically encountered in the writings of Paley, that it is logically supportive of the existence of a wise and benevolent God. Rational explanation must here be supplemented by adoration and worship, responding to the sense of awe in the presence of God's creation. The concluding part of this book therefore sets out a Christian approach to natural theology which allows engagement with nature at every level – intellectual, affective, and enactive – offering a robust and comprehensive platform for the appreciation of the natural world from within the Christian tradition. While important in its own right and on its own terms, the enterprise has added significance on account of recent atheist criticisms of Christianity, which assert that it leads to an impoverished

---

[16]   Otto, *The Idea of the Holy.*

[17]   Richard S. Lazarus, *Emotion and Adaptation*, New York: Oxford University Press, 1991; Paul Ekman, "An Argument for Basic Emotions," *Cognition and Emotion* 6 (1992): 169–200; Dacher Keltner and Jonathan Haidt, "Approaching Awe, a Moral, Spiritual and Aesthetic Emotion," *Cognition and Emotion* 17 (2003): 297–314; Michelle Shiota, Belinda Campos, and Dacher Keltner, "The Faces of Positive Emotion: Prototype Displays of Awe, Amusement, and Pride," *Annals of the New York Academy of Science* 1000 (2003): 296–9.

view of nature, which contrasts sharply with the superior approach of the natural sciences.

This is particularly evident in the persistent complaint of the antireligious polemicist Richard Dawkins, himself a significant critic of Paley, to the effect that a religious view of the world is imaginatively and aesthetically deficient.

> The universe is genuinely mysterious, grand, beautiful, awe-inspiring. The kinds of views of the universe which religious people have traditionally embraced have been puny, pathetic, and measly in comparison to the way the universe actually is. The universe presented by organized religions is a poky little medieval universe, and extremely limited.[18]

Dawkins' criticisms, however misguided and misinformed they may be,[19] make the need for an all-embracing Christian approach to the natural world all the more important and urgent.

To indicate the potential richness of such a renewed natural theology, we have chosen to use a framework shaped by the three interrelated notions of truth, beauty, and goodness. As noted at the opening of this chapter, the choice of this tripartite framework accords with our emphasis on contemporary accounts of human perception and discernment. Yet it must be noted that the conceptual interlocking of the notions of truth, beauty, and goodness has an ancient provenance in pre-Enlightenment Christian theology. In the high Middle Ages, for example, the idea of "intelligible beauty" was seen as a way of expressing an important aspect of the Christian vision of reality. A theology of creation laid the foundations of what Umberto Eco has termed a "pancalistic vision of the

---

[18] Richard Dawkins, "A Survival Machine," in John Brockman (ed.), *The Third Culture*, pp. 75–95, New York: Simon & Schuster, 1996. For Dawkins' critique of Paley, see Richard Dawkins, *The Blind Watchmaker: Why the Evidence of Evolution Reveals a Universe Without Design*, New York: W. W. Norton, 1986.

[19] See the criticisms of his position in Alister E. McGrath, *Dawkins' God: Genes, Memes and the Meaning of Life*, Oxford: Blackwell, 2004, pp. 140–58. It may be noted that most philosophical accounts of the human aesthetic engagement with nature seem to assume that, if anything, an absence of belief in God diminishes the aesthetic value of such an encounter.

cosmos," grounded in a "feeling for intelligible beauty" characteristic of this formative age.[20] Rationality, beauty, and goodness were each facets of the same creator, reflected in the divine creation, and discerned, if at times dimly, by humanity, who had been created in the image of that same God. As T. S. Eliot (1888–1965) put it: "O greater Light, we thank thee for the less."[21]

The linking together of truth, beauty, and goodness during the eighteenth century was associated with the rise of Romanticism, helping to articulate its dissatisfaction with severely rationalist approaches to nature. Often referred to as the "Platonic triad,"[22] these concepts played an

---

[20] Umberto Eco, *Art and Beauty in the Middle Ages*, New Haven, CT: Yale University Press, 2002, pp. 4–5, 17–19. For the concept of "order" as a link between *veritas* and *pulchritudo* in the theology of Augustine of Hippo, see Josef Rief, *Der Ordobegriff des jungen Augustinus*, Paderborn: Schoningh, 1962, pp. 344–8.

[21] T. S. Eliot, "Choruses from the Rock," in T. S. Eliot, *Collected Poems, 1909–1962*, London: Faber, 1963, p. 183. One of the poem's leading themes is how the "greater light" which is "too bright for mortal vision" adapts itself to the human capacity to perceive it. As noted earlier (p. 109 n.75), this concept is expressed in the theological notion of "accommodation." This should not be confused with the synonymous yet conceptually different Piagetian notion.

[22] Plato himself does not appear to have linked these ideas in this manner. Plato uses the phrase *sophos kagathos* ("the wise and good"), perhaps basing this on the earlier stock phrase *kalos kagathos* ("the beautiful and good") – on which see Walter Donlan, "The Origins of *kalos kagathos*," *American Journal of Philology* 94 (1973): 365–74. See further the detailed study of Félix Bourriot, *Kalos kagathos – kalokagathia: d'un terme de propagande de sophistes à une notion sociale et philosophique: étude d'histoire athénienne*, Hildesheim: Olms, 1995. Nor is the notion found in later Platonism, although a "neo-Platonic triad" of Being, Life, and Intellect is well-attested. See, for example, D. N. Bell, "*Esse, vivere, intellegere*. The Noetic Triad and the Image of God," *Recherches de théologie ancienne et médiévale* 52 (1985): 5–43. Mark J. Edwards, "Porphyry and the Intelligible Triad," *Journal of Hellenic Studies* 60 (1990): 14–24. For its later development, see Cornelio Fabro, "The Overcoming of the Neoplatonic Triad of Being, Life, and Intellect by Thomas Aquinas," in Dominic J. O'Meara (ed.), *Neoplatonism and Christian Thought*, pp. 97–108. Albany, NY: State University of New York Press, 1981. The issue remains important in modern theology, as pointed out by Wayne J. Hankey, "*Theoria* versus *Poesis*: Neoplatonism and Trinitarian Difference in Aquinas, John Milbank, Jean-Luc Marion and John Zizioulas," *Modern Theology* 15 (1999): 387–415.

important role in providing intellectual underpinnings for the Romantic exploration of the human encounter with nature. Thus Johann Gottfried Herder (1744–1803) regularly appealed to this natural triad – which he unashamedly referred to as his "holy trinity" – as something approaching a self-evident truth.[23] Similarly, Johann Wolfgang von Goethe (1749–1832) claimed that all of Plato's ideas related to an eternal whole, consisting of truth, goodness, and beauty.[24]

In choosing to adopt this traditional framework as a means of unfolding the potential of a renewed natural theology, I must stress that my intention is to catalyze further discussion of the issues, not to limit it to these categories, helpful though they may be. What is offered in the final part of this work is little more than a foray into these broad areas, opening up questions for further discussion and exploration, which I hope will offer an expanded and useful framework for retrieving and developing a natural theology. It is, however, hoped that this preliminary skirmish will be helpful in identifying some useful landmarks.

Yet a further point must be made before turning to a more extended exploration of these motifs. The vision for natural theology set out in this work affirms that our experience of the rationality, beauty, or goodness of the cosmos has the potential to elicit the quest for the divine, or intimate the nature of God. Yet perhaps more importantly, it offers a theological framework which provides a degree of conceptual stability to these notions, partly by grounding them in something still more fundamental – the nature of God – and partly by insisting that the human capacity to recognize and respond to them is grounded in humanity possessing the image of God, even if in a weakened and attenuated form. Within such a theological framework, as we have argued (pp. 198–209), the all-important notion of the "economy of salvation" offers at least a partial explanation of both the apparent partial irrationality, ugliness, and evil of the world, and the human failure to respond appropriately

---

[23] See Johann Gottfried Herder, *Ideen zur Philosophie der Geschichte der Menschheit*, 4 vols, Riga: Johann Friedrich Hartknoch, 1784.

[24] See especially his essay "Die Geschichte der Farbenlehre," in Johann Wolfgang von Goethe, *Gedenkausgabe der Werke, Briefe und Gespräche*, ed. Ernst Rudolf Beutler, 27 vols, Zurich: Artemis-Verlag, 1948–71, vol. 16, p. 346.

to what can be known of the rationality, beauty, and goodness of the world.[25]

The importance of this point can be seen from John Ruskin's somewhat melancholy lecture "The Storm Cloud of the Nineteenth Century," delivered in 1884, in which he sets out a dark, despondent view of nature, lacking the vitality and exhilaration of his earlier period. Something has been lost, according to Ruskin – the instinctive human sense of the divinity mediated by nature. Earlier generations possessed this; now it has gone. Humanity is now alienated from both God and nature – and thus ultimately from itself.

> In the entire system of the Firmament, thus seen and understood, there appeared to be, to all the thinkers of those ages, the incontrovertible and unmistakable evidence of a Divine Power in creation, which had fitted, as the air for human breath, so the clouds for human sight and nourishment – the Father who was in heaven feeding day by day the souls of his children with marvels, and satisfying them with bread, and so filling their hearts with food and gladness.[26]

For Ruskin, humanity has lost any sense of its place within the universe. With this metaphysical loss has come "a web of hesitating sentiment, pathetic fallacy, and wandering fancy."[27]

---

[25] Augustine of Hippo is one of many writers to address these issues. See Peter R. L. Brown, "Saint Augustine and Political Society," in Dorothy F. Donnelly (ed.), *The City of God: A Collection of Critical Essays*, pp. 17–35. New York: Peter Lang, 1995:

> Augustine is acutely aware of the juxtaposition of these two elements. On the one hand, there is the self-evidence of a divine order of supreme beauty, to be contemplated in nature and in the absolute certainties of the laws of thought: on the other hand, the fact that, in this beautiful universe, the human soul tends to disperse itself in a baffling multiplicity of intense but partial loves. Such human loves only hint at a lost harmony: and it is the reestablishment of this harmony, by finding man's proper place and rhythm, that constitutes, for Augustine, the sum total of Christian behaviour.

[26] John Ruskin, *Works*, ed. E. T. Cook and A. Wedderburn, 39 vols, London: Allen, 1903–12, vol. 34, pp. 10–11. For comment on the theme of alienation within this work, see Brian J. Day, "The Moral Intuition of Ruskin's 'Storm-Cloud'," *Studies in English Literature* 45 (2005): 917–34.

[27] Ruskin, *Works*, vol. 5, p. 231. For a recent account of the emergence of this attitude, see Charles Taylor, *A Secular Age*, Cambridge, MA: Belknap Press, 2007, pp. 377–419.

The restored ontology of creation that is an integral part of a Christian natural theology allows us, to use Ruskin's phrase, to "love a stone for a stone's sake, and a cloud for a cloud's"[28] – precisely because of what they are understood, in the first place, to *be*, and in the second, to *signify*. A Christian natural theology thus opens up the possibility of restoring this sense of place and position, allowing nature to be seen in this richly textured and modulated way. Both the observer and the observed are thus seen in a new light, with important implications for how we engage with what is seen – a matter which we shall now turn to explore in more detail.

---

[28] Ruskin, *Works*, vol. 25, p. 219.

CHAPTER 10

Natural Theology and Truth

Much traditional natural theology has been concerned with making rational sense of our experience of the world. What explanation of the world may be offered, on the basis of what may be perceived? We have already noted the limitations of the styles of natural theology that were associated with the Enlightenment (pp. 165–70). These were shaped, to a greater or lesser extent, by the movement's emphasis upon rational demonstration and a strongly rationalist notion of truth.[1] This chapter explores the place of sense-making for a natural theology, affirming its significance, yet contesting its finality.

The word "truth" is used here in a loose sense, intended to emphasize that the process of "seeing" involves (but only as one of its elements) intellectual, propositional thinking. In using this term, we wish to draw attention to the importance of assimilation in enabling the human mind to develop schemas – mental maps of the world, or sets of rules or scripts for negotiating the world. The process of "seeing" is not, of course, limited to this, and we shall consider its affective and enactive aspects in subsequent chapters.

---

[1] For reflections on the contested legacy of such a notion of truth, see Simon Blackburn, *Truth: A Guide for the Perplexed*, London: Allen Lane, 2005.

Resonance, Not Proof: Natural Theology and Sense-Making

The great Boyle Lectures of the eighteenth century set out to prove the truth of the Christian faith, especially in the face of the rising challenge of atheism.[2] The "public confutation of atheism" associated with the early Boyle lectures rested on the demonstration of the intellectual necessity and explanatory fecundity of a creator God. There is unquestionably much that is to be valued in this insight. A Christian natural theology holds that the *logos* through which the world was created is embedded in the structures of the created order, above all the human person, and incarnated in Christ.[3]

Yet this insight does not mean that we can "prove" God's existence on the basis of an appeal to nature, thus conceiving natural theology as an intellectually autonomous attempt to establish the existence and character of God.[4] Rather, as we have argued, natural theology is the approach to nature that arises from the inhabitation of the Christian faith, leading to nature being "seen" in a certain way.

Natural theology, as we have presented it in this work, cannot be regarded as "proving" God's existence. Rather, it insists that the existence of a God such as that proposed by the Christian tradition makes sense of what may be observed of the world. Such an approach holds that there is an accumulation of considerations which, though not constituting logical proof (how could experience *prove* anything in such a way?), is at the very least consistent with the existence of a creator God. This is the kind of argument set forth by F. R. Tennant (1886–1957) in his important study *Philosophical Theology*.[5] This does not mean that such considerations

---

[2] John J. Dahm, "Science and Apologetics in the Early Boyle Lectures," *Church History* 19 (1970): 172–86.

[3] For the relation of the anthropological and Christological aspects of the *imago Dei* in early Christianity, see Peter Schwanz, *Imago Dei als christologisch-anthropologisches Problem in der Geschichte der Alten Kiche von Paulus bis Clemens von Alexandrien*, Halle: Niemeyer, 1970.

[4] Michael Ruse, "The Argument from Design: A Brief History," in William A. Dembski and Michael Ruse (eds), *Debating Design: From Darwin to DNA*, pp. 13–31. Cambridge, UK: Cambridge University Press, 2004.

[5] Frederick R. Tennant, *Philosophical Theology*, 2 vols, Cambridge, UK: Cambridge University Press, 1930, vol. 2, p. 79.

constitute irrefutable evidence for the existence or character of a creator God; they are, however, consistent with such a theistic worldview, and reinforce the plausibility of such a worldview for those who are already committed to them.[6] The agenda is not therefore "proof" of core Christian beliefs, but the demonstration of resonance between theory and observation, leading to an enhanced commitment to the theory that is able to explain and account for so much that is observed.

Traditional approaches to natural theology, witnessing to the influence of the Enlightenment, focus on demonstrating that belief in God offers the best explanation of the world. This does not amount to a "proof" of the existence of God, as some versions of natural theology, responding to the challenges of the Enlightenment, unwisely suggested. Again, we must emphasize that there can be no question of the natural world ever functioning as a "proof" of any worldview, religious or otherwise.[7] These things simply cannot be resolved empirically, despite the insistence of certain empiricists that all theories be subject to this criterion:

> Among empirical theorists there is a philosophically naive but utterly entrenched inclination to suppose that a theory's empirical check is also a *reality* check for it; that a theory is objectively right in its claims to the extent that it "checks out" empirically.[8]

Yet there is a valid question which may still be asked: what is the best explanation of what may be observed? Does belief in God – especially the

---

[6] Keith Ward, *God, Chance and Necessity*, Oxford: One World, 1996, pp. 50–60.

[7] See the arguments put forward in D. H. Mellor, *The Warrant of Induction*, Cambridge, UK: Cambridge University Press, 1988. The fundamental issue is that empirical evidence cannot provide the necessary proofs for "abstract reasoning," as pointed out by John Woods, *Paradox and Paraconsistency: Conflict Resolution in the Abstract Sciences*, Cambridge, UK: Cambridge University Press, 2003, pp. 1–39. Note especially his comment: "In a rough and ready way, theories divide into those for which the criterion of empirical adequacy is a legitimate standard, if not always a fulfilled one, and those for which this standard is made inappropriate by subject matter and method" (p. 2).

[8] Woods, *Paradox and Paraconsistency*, p. 2.

---

specific God of the Christian faith – represent the best, or at the least a viable, explanation of what is known of the world?

Interest in the method of "inference to the best explanation" first developed in the 1960s, through the work of Gilbert Harman.[9] The idea was not new; the same basic principles can be found in the works of the American pragmatist philosopher Charles Peirce, who used the concept of "abduction" (or "retroduction") to refer to the same process of inferring the best account of multiple observations.[10] "Abduction" is to be understood as inference from the observed consequences of a postulated hypothesis to the explanatory antecedents contained within that hypothesis. This inference is based on the explanatory success or fruitfulness of a hypothesis in accounting for, and offering a better understanding of, what is actually observed. It is entirely possible to argue that this method underlies the natural sciences, constituting a core element of the scientific method.[11] Yet the approach is open to criticism on account of its vagueness concerning how one determines which of a set of competing explanations is to be declared "the best." What criteria are appropriate to such an adjudication?

This is not an easy question to answer, in that the criteria by which the "best" explanation might be identified are themselves contested.[12] The standard model of "inference to the best explanation" appeals to various

---

[9] See Harman's three canonical essays: Gilbert Harman, "The Inference to the Best Explanation," *Philosophical Review* 74 (1965): 88–95; "Detachment, Probability, and Maximum Likelihood," *Noûs* 1 (1967): 401–11; "Knowledge, Inference, and Explanation," *American Philosophical Quarterly* 5 (1968): 164–73.

[10] Tomis Kapitan, "Peirce and the Structure of Abductive Inference," in N. Houser, D. D. Roberts, and J. Van Evra (eds), *Studies in the Logic of Charles Sanders Peirce*, pp. 477–96, Bloomington, IN: Indiana University Press, 1997; Ilkka Niiniluoto, "Defending Abduction," *Philosophy of Science* 66 (Proceedings) (2000): S436–51.

[11] See Ernan McMullin, *The Inference that Makes Science*, Milwaukee, WI: Marquette University Press, 1992; Stathos Psillos, "Simply the Best: A Case for Abduction," in Robert Kowalski, Antonis C. Kakas and Fariba Sadri (eds), *Computational Logic: Logic Programming and Beyond*, pp. 605–25, Berlin: Springer, 2002.

[12] For a discussion, see Paul R. Thagard, "The Best Explanation: Criteria for Theory Choice," *Journal of Philosophy* 75 (1976): 76–92; Peter Lipton, *Inference to the Best Explanation*, 2nd edn, London: Routledge, 2004, pp. 55–64.

"epistemic virtues," such as simplicity, elegance,[13] consilience, and concision. In recent years, attempts have been made to give added resilience to the approach, by incorporating Bayesian probability theory into the assessment of competing explanations.[14] Yet the approach remains imprecise and undefined, leading its critics to suggest that it rests on intuitions rather than rigorous analysis. There will always be at least a degree of uncertainty attending any assertion that a given explanation is indeed the best. Yet this does not prevent such discussion taking place, either in relation to the epistemic virtues themselves, or the outcome of their application.

Notwithstanding these difficulties, however, it remains an entirely legitimate judgment that the scientific method itself ultimately represents an abductive engagement with the observation of the world. One may entirely reasonably extend this to argue that an acceptable degree of "empirical fit" or "empirical adequacy" is a necessary yet not adequate condition for holding a belief.[15] An empiricist method, it must be stressed, can accommodate without difficulty the transcendent in general, and belief in God in particular.[16]

Although Christianity can rightly be argued to be primarily concerned with human salvation, it is important to note that there is nevertheless an explanatory supervenience to this message of salvation. Richard Swinburne's classic work *The Existence of God* may be regarded as one of the most important twentieth-century affirmations of the explanatory

---

[13] See here the important essay of Eric Barnes, "Inference to the Loveliest Explanation," *Synthese* 103 (1995): 251–78. Recently the concept of "virtue epistemology" has been advanced to account for the unity of foundationalist epistemic principles through the appeal to the notion of "intellectual virtue" as a means of subsuming foundationalist sources of epistemic justification: see especially Linda Zagzebski, *Virtues of the Mind*, Cambridge, UK: Cambridge University Press, 1997; John Greco, "Two Kinds of Intellectual Virtue," *Philosophy and Phenomenological Research* 60 (2000): 179–84.

[14] Timothy McGrew, "Confirmation, Heuristics, and Explanatory Reasoning," *British Journal for Philosophy of Science* 54 (2003): 553–67.

[15] The idea of "empirical adequacy" is especially associated with Bas van Fraassen: see Bas van Fraassen, *The Scientific Image*, Oxford: Oxford University Press, 1980. For a response, see Stathis Psillos, "On van Fraassen's Critique of Abductive Reasoning," *Philosophical Quarterly* 46 (1996): 31–47; Alasdair Richmond, "Between Abduction and the Deep Blue Sea," *Philosophical Quarterly* 49 (1999): 86–91.

[16] See the recent discussion in Bas C. van Fraassen, *The Empirical Stance*, New Haven, CT: Yale University Press, 2002, pp. 189–90.

capacity of theism. An important aspect of his argument concerns the potential of the Christian understanding of God to make sense of the ordering of the world.[17]

So what is it that requires to be explained? Natural theology engages a number of features of the world that call out for explanation, including the following:[18]

1   The apparent ordering of the universe, which is accessible and intelligible to the human mind;
2   A fruitful cosmic history, including the suggestion that it is "fine-tuned" for the emergence of life;
3   The interconnectedness of the universe, which resists reduction to its individual parts;
4   The coexistence of disorder and order within the world;
5   A generalized human awareness of the transcendent.

We have already noted how the Christian doctrine of creation, set within the context of the "economy of salvation," has an emergent explanatory elegance and fecundity (pp. 198–209). On the basis of a Christian doctrine of creation, the universe is both inherently intelligible and inherently contingent, its intelligibility reflecting its contingent origins in the rationality of God.[19] This point can be seen as lying behind both James Clerk Maxwell's insistence that there exists an inner relation between the laws of the mind and the laws of nature, and Albert Einstein's belief in a "pre-established harmony" between the intelligibility of the independent world and the perceiving subject.

A natural theology thus affirms and explains the created capacity of the human mind to make sense of its surroundings. As already emphasized, this does not mean that such a natural theology is restricted to, still less defined by, such a sense-making exercise. It is, however, to recognize that such an undertaking is an integral, yet not defining, aspect of its task.

---

[17]   Richard Swinburne, *The Existence of God*, Oxford: Clarendon Press, 1979, p. 136.

[18]   See, e.g., John Polkinghorne, "Physics and Metaphysics in a Trinitarian Perspective," *Theology and Science* 1 (2003): 33–49, who outlines six slightly different features of the universe that demand explanation.

[19]   Thomas F. Torrance, "Divine and Contingent Order," in A. R. Peacocke (ed.), *The Sciences and Theology in the Twentieth Century*, pp. 81–97, Notre Dame, IN: University of Notre Dame Press, 1981.

Traditionally, such a natural theology is understood to make sense of the physical world we inhabit. However, it is also capable of making sense of alternative attempts to make sense of that world, by demonstrating its capacity to locate them on an intellectual map, based on its own distinctive reading and structuring of the world.

The Big Picture, Not the Gaps: Natural Theology and Observation of the World

From what has just been said, it will be clear that a renewed Christian natural theology is partly concerned with offering an explanation of what may be observed, in the belief that the quality and comprehensiveness of its account will surpass that of its alternatives. We have emphasized the importance of grasping the "big picture," stressing that the explicability of the world itself requires an explanation. While there are gaps in a scientific understanding of the world, the approach that we adopt does not focus on such gaps, but upon the importance of accounting for what may be observed of reality as a whole. It must, however, be conceded that some forms of natural theology chose to focus on gaps in scientific understanding, in effect converting these into evidence of God's existence.

This older habit of proposing a "God of the gaps" has now been widely discarded as useless, being seen by many as potentially a liability. The approach, which tends now to be found primarily in more popular writings, including the movement widely known as "intelligent design," argues that science is unable to offer a complete account of the world. There are significant gaps in our understanding.[20] These explanatory deficits, it is argued, can be remedied by an appeal to God. Such an approach, however, is intensely vulnerable, mainly because the inexorable advance of the scientific enterprise means that gaps tend to get filled. The core assumptions of the approach inevitably entail that God is squeezed into smaller and fewer gaps. In addition to its obvious historical vulnerability,

---

[20] This point is made forcibly in the work often regarded as marking the origins of this approach: Michael J. Behe, *Darwin's Black Box: The Biochemical Challenge to Evolution*, New York: Free Press, 1996. For rival evaluations of intelligent design, see Thomas Woodward, *Doubts About Darwin: A History of Intelligent Design*, Grand Rapids, MI: Baker Books, 2003; Niall Shanks, *God, the Devil, and Darwin: A Critique of Intelligent Design Theory*, Oxford: Oxford University Press, 2004.

it is theologically unacceptable on account of its implicit exclusion of God's activity from the remainder of creation. This approach associates God primarily with gaps and thereby excludes appealing to God from the parts of creation that *are* scientifically understood – or from the bigger explanatory picture that emerges overall.[21]

One of the most significant critics of such an approach was Charles Coulson (1910–74), Oxford University's first professor of theoretical chemistry, noted for his concern to advance a dialogue between science and Christian theology. Coulson's concerns were both historical and theological. His unitary vision of reality led him to reject the notion of strictly demarcated "scientific" and "religious" domains of reality.

> This is a fatal step to take. For it is to assert that you can plant some sort of hedge in the country of the mind to mark the boundary where a transfer of authority takes place. Its error is twofold. First it presupposes a dichotomy of existence which would be tolerable if no scientist were ever a Christian, and no Christian ever a scientist, but which becomes intolerable while there is one single person owning both allegiances. And second it invites "science" to discover new things and thence gradually to take possession of that which "religion" once held.[22]

History makes clear that science advances, and has a marked propensity to fill gaps once held to be "religious" in nature. "There is no 'God of the gaps' to take over at those strategic places where science fails; and the reason is that gaps of this sort have the unpreventable habit of shrinking."[23] Yet why look to the gaps in scientific understanding? For Coulson, reality as a whole demanded explanation. "Either God is in the whole of Nature, with no gaps, or He's not there at all."[24]

---

[21]   For comment, see Jack Collins, "Miracles, Intelligent Design, and God-of-the-Gaps," *Perspectives on Science and Christian Faith* 55 (2003): 22–9.

[22]   Charles A. Coulson, *Science and Christian Belief*, Chapel Hill, NC: University of North Carolina Press, 1958, p. 19. For comment on Coulson's views, see David J. Hawkin and Eileen Hawkin, *The Word of Science: The Religious and Social Thought of C. A. Coulson*, London: Epworth, 1989, pp. 23–48. The views criticized by Coulson re-emerged in Steven Jay Gould's notion of "non-overlapping magisteria": see Stephen Jay Gould, *Rocks of Ages: Science and Religion in the Fullness of Life*, New York: Ballantine Books, 1999, pp. 65–70.

[23]   Coulson, *Science and Christian Belief*, p. 20.

[24]   Ibid., p. 22.

This unsatisfactory "God of the gaps" approach can be extended further, by arguing that there are "supernatural" breaches or fissures in the natural realm, which are not open to scientific or rational analysis. By definition, some would argue, there are aspects of experience which must be tagged as "supernatural," and hence lying beyond the scope of the scientific method. While conceding that there are indeed important limits to the scientific method, which must be identified and respected, this does not entail that there are explanatory gaps in a scientific understanding of reality which can only be explained by an appeal to the "supernatural."

Rather than suggesting that God offers an explanation of what the natural sciences are currently unable to explain, more recent theistic writers have stressed the importance of belief in God in explaining the "big picture" – that is to say, the overall patterns of ordering which are discerned within the universe. The British philosopher of religion Richard Swinburne insists that the explanatory aspects of theism are not limited to the fine details of reality, but extend far beyond these to embrace the great questions of life – those things that are either "too big" or "too odd" for science to explain.[25] The reliability of such explanations is, of course, open to challenge; there is, however, no doubt that such explanations are being offered, and are seen as important.

An obvious example of "big" and "odd" things about the universe that demand an explanation are what are now widely described as "anthropic phenomena," to which we now turn.

Natural Theology, Counterintuitive Thinking, and Anthropic Phenomena

In recent years, considerable attention has been paid to what are now widely known as "anthropic phenomena." The term "anthropic principle" was introduced by Brandon Carter in 1974, to express the idea that the fundamental constants of the universe were such that they appeared to have been "designed" to allow life to come into existence.[26] It was an

---

    25   Swinburne, *The Existence of God*, p. 71.

    26   Brandon Carter, "Large Number Coincidences and the Anthropic Principle," in M. S. Longair (ed.), *Confrontation of Cosmological Theories with Observational Data*, pp. 291–8, Boston: D. Reidel, 1974. For the interesting but somewhat problematic suggestion that such lines of argument predate the emergence of modern cosmology,

unfortunate choice of term; Carter meant to imply that the universe appeared to possess an innate propensity to encourage the emergence of life, rather than *homo sapiens.*

Perhaps the language of an older generation is to be preferred here. In 1913, Lawrence J. Henderson (1878–1942), Professor of Biological Chemistry at Harvard University, raised the question of whether the nature of the physical world, particularly the process of evolution, was biocentric. "The whole evolutionary process," he wrote, "both cosmic and organic, is one, and the biologist may now rightly regard the universe in its very essence as biocentric."[27]

The langue of "fine-tuning" has increasingly been found appropriate to express the idea that the universe appears to have possessed certain qualities from the moment of its inception for the production of intelligent life on Earth at this point in cosmic history, capable of reflecting on the implications of its existence. Nature's fundamental constants turn out to possess reassuringly life-friendly values. The existence of carbon-based life on Earth depends upon a delicate balance of physical and cosmological forces and parameters, which are such that were any one of these quantities to be slightly altered, the balance would be destroyed and life would not exist.[28] The smallest variation in the constant of universal gravitation, or the mass

---

see Milan Cirkovic, "Ancient Origins of a Modern Anthropic Cosmological Argument," *Astronomical and Astrophysical Transactions* 22 (2003): 879–86.

[27]   Lawrence J. Henderson, *The Fitness of the Environment: An Inquiry Into the Biological Significance of the Properties of Matter,* Boston: Beacon Press, 1913, p. 312. On Henderson's approach, see Iris Fry, "On the Biological Significance of the Properties of Matter: L. J. Henderson's Theory of the Fitness of the Environment," *Journal of the History of Biology* 29 (1996): 155–96. For similar ideas more recently, see Michael Denton, *Nature's Destiny: How the Laws of Biology Reveal Purpose in the Universe,* New York: Free Press, 1998. Note the references to "biocentric adaptations in the design of the cosmos" (p. 14), and the assertion that "the universe is profoundly biocentric and gives every appearance of having been specially designed for life" (p. 16).

[28]   For standard discussions of these ideas, see John D. Barrow and Frank J. Tipler, *The Cosmological Anthropic Principle,* Oxford: Oxford University Press, 1986; George Greenstein, *The Symbiotic Universe: Life and Mind in the Cosmos,* New York: Morrow, 1988; John Gribbin and Martin Rees, *Cosmic Coincidences: Dark Matter, Mankind and Anthropic Cosmology,* New York: Bantam Books, 1989; Paul Davies, *The Goldilocks Enigma: Why Is the Universe Just Right for Life?* London: Allen Lane, 2006.

of the neutron, or the charge of the electron, would have changed everything, making the emergence of human observers impossible. Initially, anthropic phenomena were identified within cosmology, especially the values of
the fundamental constants of nature. Yet in recent years, similar phenomena
have been identified in chemistry, biochemistry, and evolutionary biology.[29]
Our concern here is not to provide further examples of such phenomena, but to assess their significance for natural theology. While the existence of "fine-tuning" or "anthropic" phenomena is both conceded and
widely discussed within both the scientific and philosophical communities,
there is no consensus on how these phenomena are best to be interpreted.
Some writers, for example, are cautious about drawing any metaphysical
conclusions about anthropic matters, suggesting that the delicate balance
of values might be an inevitable consequence of a deep natural structure
which has yet to be uncovered.[30] Others suggested that an ensemble of
universes exists, of which ours happens to have the conditions necessary
for life. Force strengths, particle masses, expansion speeds, and so on vary
from universe to universe. Sooner or later, it is argued, conditions in one
of these universes will be just right to permit life to evolve.[31]
An alternative approach is to consider the perspective of the observer.
The philosopher Nick Bostrom has argued that the anthropic principle
is best accounted for by "observation selection effects."[32] Substantially
the same point was made earlier by Brandon Carter, who noted that our
data depend upon the existence of a suitably positioned observer to have
access to the data in the first place.[33] Others have argued that anthropic

---

[29] See, e.g., Simon Conway Morris, *Life's Solution: Inevitable Humans in a Lonely Universe*, Cambridge, UK: Cambridge University Press, 2003; R. J. P. Williams and J. J. R. Fraústo da Silva, *The Chemistry of Evolution: The Development of Our Ecosystem*, London: Elsevier, 2006.

[30] String theory is a particular favorite: see Gordon L. Kane, Malcolm J. Perry, and Anna N. Zytkow, "The Beginning of the End of the Anthropic Principle," *New Astronomy* 7 (2002): 45–53.

[31] For an excellent collection of essays dealing with these questions, see Bernard Carr (ed.), *Universe or Multiverse?* Cambridge, UK: Cambridge University Press, 2007.

[32] See especially Nick Bostrom, *Anthropic Bias: Observation Selection Effects in Science and Philosophy*, London: Routledge, 2002, pp. 11–58.

[33] Brandon Carter, "The Anthropic Principle and its Implications for Biological Evolution," *Philosophical Transactions of the Royal Society* A 310 (1983): 347–63.

phenomena represent a clear confirmation of the fundamental theistic hypothesis of a creator God.[34]

In many ways, the approach to natural theology which we set out in this work is ideally adapted to engage with anthropic phenomena. It is not argued that such phenomena represent a "proof" of the existence of a creator God,[35] but that they are consistent with the view of God encountered and practiced within the Christian faith. On this approach, the observation of anthropic phenomena resonates with the core themes of the Christian vision of reality.[36] The importance of this point can be further appreciated from the perspective of counterfactual thinking, which has recently become significant as a conceptual tool in historical understanding.[37]

Counterfactual thinking takes its starting point from the belief that things need not be as they are. By conducting "thought experiments," it is possible to construct alternative scenarios, which allow the roles of specific actors, factors, and agencies and the generalities of happenstance in bringing about an existing situation to be better understood.[38] What would have happened if Charles I had avoided the Civil War? If there had been no American Revolution? If Nazi Germany had defeated the Soviet Union during World War II?

---

[34] For an important example of such a discussion, sensitive to the complexities of the issue, see John Polkinghorne, *Belief in God in an Age of Science*, New Haven, CT: Yale University Press, 1998.

[35] For this approach, see the well-argued essay by Robin Collins, "A Scientific Argument for the Existence of God: The Fine-Tuning Design Argument," in Michael J. Murray (ed.), *Reason for the Hope Within*, pp. 47–75, Grand Rapids, MI: Eerdmans, 1999.

[36] For a similar approach, see Polkinghorne, "Physics and Metaphysics in a Trinitarian Perspective."

[37] See Philip Tetlock and Aaron Belkin (eds), *Counterfactual Thought Experiments in World Politics: Logical, Methodological, and Psychological Perspectives*, Princeton, NJ: Princeton University Press, 1996. At a more popular level, see Niall Ferguson (ed.), *Virtual History: Alternatives and Counterfactuals*, London: Picador, 1997.

[38] Denis J. Hilton, John I. McClure, and Ben R. Slugowski, "The Course of Events: Counterfactuals, Causal Sequences, and Explanation," in David R. Mandel, Denis J. Hilton, and Patrizia Catellani (eds), *The Psychology of Counterfactual Thinking*, pp. 44–60, London: Routledge, 2005.

The approach allows us to begin to consider alternative scenarios, and evaluate them theologically. A good example of this is C. S. Lewis's fictional work *Perelandra*, which invites us to imagine a world which has not fallen, partly in order to understand our own more profoundly.[39] From the point of view of natural theology, counterfactual thinking highlights the aspects of the world which cause natural theology to be such a plausible and fruitful means of engaging with the world. Consider the following questions, each of which requires us to imagine theologically significant alternative worlds.

What if the strong nuclear force were 10 percent weaker? Or if the explosive force of the original "big bang" were 1 percent greater? What if the quantum-mechanically determined chemical properties of carbon were such that complex macromolecules could not form? Without proteins, life cannot reproduce; without DNA, it cannot transmit genetical information. What if the physical properties of water were slightly different? What if we could not understand the physical world, or if it possessed a rationality inaccessible to us? What if we were not here to observe the world, and raise these questions?

All of these are scientifically and metaphysically significant questions. Yet many would argue that the finely tuned fruitfulness of the world and the intelligibility of the world, though both insights that arise from science, nevertheless call for some explanation and understanding which, by its very nature, is likely to go beyond what science itself can provide. It is possible that these things are nothing more than remarkable coincidences and fortunate accidents, or evidence that we happen to have come into being in one of a vast number of universes which is capable of developing in a biofriendly manner. But it also corresponds to a Christian understanding of the nature of God. These observations make sense within such a framework. This is not a repristinated version of Paley's argument from design, but a scientifically and theologically informed variant of "inference to the best explanation" (Harman) or "abduction to the best explanation" (Peirce), discussed earlier (pp. 233–8).

In this section, we have considered one aspect of natural theology's capacity to make sense of things. We shall now move on to consider a further specific aspect of this "big picture" – the surprising, even amazing, capacity of mathematics to represent reality.

---

[39] Sanford Schwarz, "Paradise Reframed: Lewis, Bergson, and Changing Times on Perelandra," *Christianity and Literature* 51 (2002): 569–600.

Natural Theology and Mathematics:
A "Natural" Way of Representing Reality

Does nature have a language, that human beings can read and interpret? Is there a cosmic Linear B, capable of being deciphered by those with an intuition for its basic forms, so that we might be able to read the secrets of the universe? The very idea of a "natural theology" is often framed in terms of the grammar and syntax of its distinctive language, which in turn reflect its own distinct rationality. For many, this language is that of mathematics.

There is widespread agreement of the ability of mathematics to describe the patterns and symmetries found at every level of the created order.[40] One of the most distinctive features of the scientific revolution of the sixteenth and seventeenth centuries was a growing realization of the power of mathematics, and especially geometry, to describe what experimental observation was disclosing concerning the motion of celestial bodies.[41]

Johann Kepler (1571–1639), noted for his demonstration of the elliptical orbits of the planets, argued that the ability of mathematics to describe celestial mechanics was to be grounded theologically. Since geometry had its origins in the mind of God, it was only to be expected that the created order would conform to its patterns:

> In that geometry is part of the divine mind from the origins of time, even from before the origins of time (for what is there in God that is not also from God?) it has provided God with the patterns for the creation of the world, and has been transferred to humanity with the image of God.[42]

Kepler's statement is strongly reminiscent of Augustine's conception of the "image of God." There is a resonance between the rationality of God, of the universe, and of humanity – and the natural language in which this rationality can be expressed, represented, and communicated is mathematics. Mathematics is able to represent experimental observation, and

---

[40] Ian Stewart, *Nature's Numbers: Discovering Order and Pattern in the Universe*, London: Weidenfeld & Nicolson, 1995.

[41] Joella G. Yoder, *Unrolling Time: Christiaan Huygens and the Mathematization of Nature*, Cambridge, UK: Cambridge University Press, 1988.

[42] Johann Kepler, *Gesammelte Werke*, ed. Max Caspar, Munich: C. H. Beck, 1937–83, vol. 6, p. 233.

the universe cannot be comprehended quantitatively without recourse to mathematical formulae.

So what is the basis of this remarkable, perhaps even unreasonable, effectiveness of mathematics in representing reality?[43] As Paul Davies comments, the importance of this question is too easily overlooked: "No one who is closed off from mathematics can ever grasp the full significance of the natural order that is woven so deeply into the fabric of physical reality."[44] Why is mathematics, sometimes regarded as a free creation of the human mind, able to do this? Both fractals and string theory must be regarded as free creations of the human mind; yet both appear to have an inbuilt propensity to describe the natural order.[45]

In his account of a mathematical view of modern physics, Roger Penrose stresses how such theories – including Newtonian dynamics, Maxwellian electrodynamics, special and general relativity, thermodynamics and quantum electrodynamics – have a "superb" ability to mirror nature.[46] On the basis of his careful analysis of the theory and practice of mathematics, Penrose concludes that three worlds exist, which must somehow be correlated in the human quest for knowledge and understanding. These are the world of "our conscious perceptions," the physical world outside us, and the "Platonic world of mathematical forms."[47] This third world is populated with such entities as Maxwell's electrodynamic equations, the algebra of complex numbers, and Lagrange's theorem. So how do these

---

[43] See the classic paper of Eugene Wigner, "The Unreasonable Effectiveness of Mathematics," *Communications on Pure and Applied Mathematics* 13 (1960): 1–14.

[44] Paul Davies, *The Mind of God: Science and the Search for Ultimate Meaning*, London: Penguin, 1992, p. 93. See further Roger Penrose, *Shadows of the Mind*, London: Vintage, 1995.

[45] John Briggs, *Fractals: The Patterns of Chaos. Discovering a New Aesthetic of Art, Science, and Nature*, London: Thames & Hudson, 1992; Benoit B. Mandelbrot, *The Fractal Geometry of Nature*, New York: W. H. Freeman, 1982; Joe Rosen, *Symmetry Discovered: Concepts and Applications in Nature and Science*, Cambridge, UK: Cambridge University Press, 1975.

[46] Roger Penrose, "The Modern Physicist's View of Nature," in John Torrance (ed.), *The Concept of Nature*, pp. 117–66. Oxford: Oxford University Press, 1992.

[47] Penrose, *Shadows of the Mind*, pp. 411–20. The background to Penrose's phrase "the three mysteries" will be found in such works as Emil Heinrich du Bois-Reymond, *Über die Grenzen des Naturerkennens: Die sieben Welträtsel – Zwei Vortrage*, Leipzig: Veit, 1907.

worlds relate? We have already seen the remarkable correspondence be-tween mathematics and the physical world, and could provide significant examples to develop this point further (Penrose provides an analysis of Einstein's theory of general relativity as a classic instance of this point).[48]

Penrose offers the following account of the mystery of how the three worlds – Platonic, physical, and mental – coinhere and correlate.

> There is the mystery of why such precise and profoundly mathematical laws play such an important role in the behaviour of the physical world. Somehow the very world of physical reality seems almost mysteriously to emerge out of the Platonic world of mathematics . . . Then there is the second mystery of how it is that perceiving beings can arise from out of the physical world. How is it that subtly organized material objects can mysteriously conjure up mental entities from out of its material substance? . . . Finally, there is the mystery of how it is that mentality is able seemingly to "create" mathematical concepts . . . and thereby enable our minds to gain entry, by understanding, into the Platonic mathematical realm.[49]

For Penrose, these considerations are resolved – or at least correlated – by a Platonic approach to mathematics – which holds that there is an inter-action, almost a *perichoresis*, between the real world of mathematical ideas, the physical world that we observe, and the mental world that we construct in the representation of that world.[50]

Yet the Christian tradition offers another way of understanding the remarkable properties of mathematics, especially its resonance with the real world, which avoids what some have called the "epistemological bankruptcy" of Platonic approaches.[51] The theological foundation of such an approach is a created correspondence between the world and the mind, reflecting the fact that both are the creation of the same God, expressing

---

[48]   Penrose, *Shadows of the Mind*, p. 415.

[49]   Ibid., pp. 413–16. See also the extended discussion in M. S. Longair and Roger Penrose, *The Large, The Small, and The Human Mind*, Cambridge, UK: Cambridge University Press, 1999.

[50]   For Plato's views, see J. R. Lucas, *The Conceptual Roots of Mathematics: An Essay on the Philosophy of Mathematics*, London: Routledge, 2000, pp. 1–32.

[51]   A concern explored by Bob Hale, "Is Platonism Epistemologically Bankrupt?" in Matthias Schirn (ed.), *The Philosophy of Mathematics Today*, pp. 77–98, Oxford: Clarendon, 1998.

the same divine *logos*. The "unreasonable effectiveness of mathematics" can be argued to be retrodicted by a Christian doctrine of creation, resonating strongly with some core elements of that doctrine.

This point has been argued by a number of Christian theologians with a particular interest in both natural theology and the natural sciences. Thomas F. Torrance is of particular interest at this point. In 1993, he pointed out how the capacity of mathematics to represent reality illustrated "the comprehensive presupposition upon which the whole contingent order of things reposes in order to be what it is" – yet which "cannot be established in any way from within the rational frame of the contingent order" itself, in that this is essentially incomplete. Its significance can only be established and sustained "from beyond itself."[52] There is an essential harmony between the Christian vision of the world, and what may actually be known of it.

In developing this point, we would argue that Christian theology provides an ontological foundation which confirms and consolidates otherwise fleeting, fragmentary glimpses of a greater reality, gained from the exploration of nature without an attending theoretical framework. A traditional natural theology can be thought of as drawing aside a veil briefly, partially, and tantalizingly, eliciting an awareness of potential insight, and creating a longing to be able to grasp and possess whatever is being intimated. What is transient and fragmentary is clarified and consolidated from within the standpoint of the Christian tradition, which is able to affirm whatever can be known in this tantalizing manner, while clarifying it and placing it upon a firmer foundation in the divine *logos*.

Truth, Natural Theology, and Other Religious Traditions

The specific understanding of Christian natural theology set out in this work speaks from within the Christian tradition, and from a specifically Christian perspective. As we have already seen (pp. 177–216), it offers a means by which natural intuitions and instincts of the divine may be explained and developed. Yet it also offers a specific vantage point from

---

[52] Thomas F. Torrance, "The Transfinite Significance of Beauty in Science and Theology," in Luz García Alonso, Evanghelos Moutsopoulos, and Gerhard Seel (eds), *L'art, la science et la métaphysique: Études offertes à André Mercier*, pp. 393–418, Berne: Peter Lang, 1993.

which other aspects of the common human intellectual landscape may be charted and explored.

Although specific to the Christian tradition, this style of natural theology has aspirations to universality. It offers a coherent organizing logic which is able to account, not only for its own existence, but also for that of its intellectual and spiritual rivals. In short: natural theology offers and embodies a tradition-specific yet trans-traditional rationality, which is grounded in the particularities of the Christian tradition alone. It provides insights into both the existence of the Christian tradition and that of its rivals. Christians believe these claims to be true and warranted, while recognizing that there is no means of *proving* these claims by universally accepted criteria – precisely because there *are* no universally accepted criteria.

Once more, the importance of the failure of the Enlightenment dream of universal criteria of rationality and judgment must be noted. There are a number of areas in which a natural theology offers a coherent and illuminating account of commonalities which exist with other traditions, religious and secular, while at the same time offering a plausible account of how those rival traditions might arise.[53] The Christian tradition thus possesses two advantages over its alternatives:

1 It offers an explanation of the world which is internally coherent, and an explanation of the externally observable fact that related insights may be held, at least to some extent, outside the Christian tradition;
2 It holds that what may be known of God through the publicly accessible reality of nature, although in a fragmentary and potentially inconsistent manner, may be clarified and extended through the Christian revelation, which is *specific* to the Christian tradition.

A Christian natural theology can therefore be said to function as a meta-traditional device. We are not speaking here of the Enlightenment's hypothetical "tradition-transcendent rationality" so effectively critiqued by Alasdair MacIntyre (see pp. 167–8), but of a *tradition-specific rationality* with an explanatory power allowing it to extend its scope to other traditions so that for the Christian community it functions as a "tradition-transcendent rationality." This rationality argues for the

---

[53] For a full analysis, see Alister McGrath, *A Scientific Theology: 2 – Reality*, London: T&T Clark, 2002, pp. 78–97.

intelligibility of the universe and the intelligence of humanity as its observer and interpreter – and thus offers an explanation of why such rival traditions exist.

Yet a Christian natural theology is not simply affirming that other religious traditions may contain hints of the truth of the full revelation of the gospel. A fully orbed natural theology extends far beyond the limited realm of ideas, embracing images, narratives, and values. In every respect, the Christian vision of reality affirms that echoes, hints, rumors, and anticipations of the gospel will be found outside the domain of the church. For the Oxford literary critic and philologist J. R. R. Tolkien, all religions and worldviews rest on myths – an attempt to account for reality, expressed in many different ways, as splintered fragments of light, each reflecting only some aspects of a greater whole. For Tolkien, Christianity takes the structural form of such a myth – but is the *real* myth, to which all other myths only approximate. His Oxford colleague C. S. Lewis (1898–1963) took a similar view. In a paper entitled "Is Theology Poetry?" delivered to the Socratic Club at Oxford in 1945, Lewis insisted that occasional similarities between Christianity and other religions is to be expected, on the basis of the overarching nature of the Christian view of reality.

> Theology, while saying that a special illumination has been vouchsafed to Christians and (earlier) to Jews, also says that there is some divine illumination vouchsafed to all men. The Divine light, we are told, "lighteneth every man." We should, therefore, expect to find in the imagination of great Pagan teachers and myth-makers some glimpse of that theme which we believe to be the very plot of the whole cosmic story – the theme of incarnation, death and rebirth.[54]

Lewis's argument is that Christianity offers a grand narrative which makes sense of all things, and which gives rise to subnarratives that are incomplete, occasionally distorted, refractions of its greater whole. The gospel tells the whole truth, the whole story, setting out a narrative account of reality that allows these subnarratives to be positioned and explained, while indicating that these only find their completion and fulfillment in that one grand narrative of the Christian gospel.

---

[54] C. S. Lewis, "Is Theology Poetry?" in *Essay Collection and Other Short Pieces*, pp. 1–21. London: HarperCollins, 2000; quote pp. 15–16.

Truth is incarnate. And "incarnate" is here more than a metaphor. It is not an accidental resemblance that what, from the point of view of being, is stated in the form "God became Man", should involve, from the point of view of human knowledge, the statement "Myth became Fact". The essential meaning of all things came down from the "heaven" of myth to the "earth" of history. In so doing, it partly emptied itself of its glory, as Christ emptied Himself of His glory to be Man.[55]

Lewis's analysis, it will be noted, extends the domain of natural theology from the realm of ideas to that of narratives, while simultaneously affirming the centrality of incarnation – both as historical actuality and as theological foundation – for an authentically Christian natural theology.

On the basis of this analysis, it can be argued that a Christian natural theology affirms the existence of partial and fragmentary – yet *real* – insights into the world outside the Christian tradition, while holding that this tradition itself represents their full disclosure, to the extent that they may be known at all. These insights have been developed and deployed in many ways within the Christian tradition, perhaps most notably in the "fulfillment theology" of mission, which holds that the divine *logos* is at work in other faiths, offering bridges and gateways which the Christian missionary must identify and develop.[56]

This approach to understanding the place of other faiths, and the best methods of entering into dialogue with their adherents, was adopted by the great Edinburgh mission conference of 1910. The leading Protestant practitioners and theorists of mission at Edinburgh declared that Jesus Christ represented the true goal of humanity, and was hence the "fulfillment of other religions." Holding that "all religions await their fulfillment in Christ," the Conference gave its missionaries a mandate to respect and engage with native cultures, seeing these as capable of being fulfilled in and through Christ.[57] This led to a new interest

---

[55] Ibid., p. 16.

[56] For the emergence of this theology in writers such as Brooke Foss Westcott (1825–1901) and their application in the Indian missionary context, see Martin Maw, *Visions of India: Fulfilment Theology, the Aryan Race Theory, and the Work of British Protestant Missionaries in Victorian India*, Frankfurt am Main: Peter Lang, 1990.

[57] The best study is Eric J. Sharpe, *Not to Destroy but to Fulfil: The Contribution of J. N. Farquhar to Protestant Missionary Thought in India Before 1914*, Lund: Gleerup, 1965.

in finding "points of contact" between indigenous cultures and the gospel.[58]

There are significant limits to any theological account of the existence and specific characteristics of other religious, not least as a result of the influence of cultural factors on the shaping of both ideas and actions. Nevertheless, the type of natural theology that we have explored in the present work unquestionably lays a foundation upon which a theology of religions may be constructed.

Up to this point, we have been focusing on the capacity of the Christian faith to illuminate the structures of the world. There is clearly much to affirm here, above all the explanatory fecundity of the Christian vision of reality, and its capacity to illuminate the natural order. Yet this limits the scope of a natural theology to intellectual, propositional thinking. In later chapters, we shall insist that natural theology also extends to the realms of beauty and goodness. Yet at this point, we need to consider whether the concept of "truth" can be restricted to this very intellectual account of things. In the two sections that follow, we shall make a case for natural theology embracing a deeper and richer vision of truth.

On Retrieving the Richness of Truth

Protesting against the excessively rationalist conceptions of truth gaining influence in England in the nineteenth century, John Henry Newman (1801–90) argued for the rediscovery of an older notion of truth, appealing beyond the narrow confines of the human faculty of reason.[59] Truth,

---

[58] For an excellent study of this approach, see Sung-Deuk Oak, "Shamanistic *Tan'gun* and Christian *Hananim*: Protestant Missionaries' Interpretation of the Korean Founding Myth, 1805–1934," *Studies in World Christianity* 7 (2001): 42–57.

[59] See M. Jamie Ferreira, "The Grammar of the Heart: Newman on Faith and Imagination," in Gerard Magill (ed.), *Discourse and Context: An Interdisciplinary Study of John Henry Newman*, pp. 129–43, Carbondale, IL: Southern Illinois University Press, 1993. There are interesting parallels here with Pascal's *raisons du cœur*: See Blaise Pascal, *Pensées*, 277: "Le cœur a ses raisons que la raison ne connaît point." See also 248: "La foi est différente de la preuve; l'une est humaine, l'autre est le don de Dieu. Justus ex fide vivit Ro.1:17 c'est de cette foi que Dieu lui-même met dans le cœur, dont la preuve est souvent l'instrument, fides ex auditu Ro.10:17, mais cette foi est dans le cœur, et fait dire non scio, mais credo."

he argued, is apprehended by a complex act of perception, which involves, while nevertheless transcending, the human reason.[60] "The heart," Newman suggested, is "commonly reached, not through the reason, but through the imagination, by means of direct impressions, by the testimony of facts and events, by description."[61] For this reason, Newman insists that the dogmatic teaching of the church appeals to both the imagination and the reason. "It is discerned, rested in, and appropriated as a reality, by the religious imagination; it is held as a truth, by the theological intellect."[62]

For Newman, there was clearly a danger that an excessively rationalist conception of natural theology would conceive the outcome of the human encounter with nature in terms similar to solving a crossword puzzle. The limitations of the approach that so troubled Newman were subsequently explored by Gabriel Marcel (1889–1973), who drew a pointed distinction between what he termed "problems" and "mysteries."[63] The world of the problematical was addressed by the natural sciences, which represented its structures and relationships mathematically; the world of the ontological mystery was not accessible to such a simple analysis. To treat reality as a "problem" is to define reality in terms of what the human mind can conceptualize as a problem, and hence solve and represent in a formula.

Marcel's distinction was developed with a more specifically theological agenda in mind by Austin Farrer (1904–68), who defined the realm of the problematic as "the field in which there are right answers." To treat reality as a "problem" is to "approach the world with a fixed measuring instrument, whether of the literal and physical, or of the conceptual sort." The realm of mystery, however, involves engagement with reality at such a level that it cannot be investigated in terms of "determinate and soluble problems." To use Farrer's terms, natural theology cannot be restricted to

---

[60] John Henry Newman, *An Essay in Aid of a Grammar of Assent*, 2nd edn, London: Burns & Oates, 1870, pp. 87–8.

[61] Ibid., pp. 89–90.

[62] Ibid., p. 95.

[63] Gabriel Marcel, *Être et avoir*, Paris: Aubier Éditions Montaigne, 1935. The distinction was developed further in his 1949–50 Gifford Lectures: Gabriel Marcel, *The Mystery of Being*, London: Harvill Press, 1950. For a careful study of Marcel's approach, see Roger Troisfontaines, *De l'existence à l'être: la philosophie de Gabriel Marcel*, 2 vols, Louvain: Nauwelaerts, 1953.

exploring the "limited and manageable relation" between a theory and one aspect of reality; rather, it is confronted "with the object itself, in all its fullness," which we experience "not as a cluster of problems but as a single though manifold mystery."[64]

Yet the difficulties with such a rationalist approach to truth extend beyond the notion of mystery. The concept of truth possesses relational overtones, which were either filtered out or marginalized through the Enlightenment's emphasis on notional correctness.[65] The relational aspects of truth were explored by Emil Brunner in his short yet significant work *Wahrheit als Begegnung* ("Truth as Encounter"), based on lectures delivered in Sweden in 1937.[66] The German title draws on the dialogical notion of "encounter" (*Begegnung*) in a manner explicitly reminiscent of the personalist approach of Martin Buber.[67] This work, with its distinctive emphasis upon truth within the context of a relationship with God, was frequently cited by Brunner as his most definitive and programmatic thesis. For Brunner, revelation is directed towards the goal of establishing a personal relationship between the God who reveals, and humanity which receives this revelation.[68] Brunner argues that faith is primarily a personal encounter with the God who meets us personally in Jesus Christ. The anti-intellectualism of this concept of divine revelation will be evident. This reflects Brunner's conviction that the early church misunderstood revelation as the divine impartation of doctrinal truth about God, rather than the personal self-revelation of God.

For Brunner, "truth" is itself a personal concept, and the subject–object dichotomy a destructive element within Christian theology. The biblical revelation lies "beyond objectivism and subjectivism," in that revelation is

---

[64] Austin Farrer, *The Glass of Vision*, London: Dacre Press, 1948, p. 67.

[65] This was pointed out, partly in response to William James's more pragmatic account of truth, by Edmund Jacobson, "The Relational Account of Truth," *Journal of Philosophy, Psychology and Scientific Methods* 7 (1910): 253–61.

[66] Emil Brunner, *Wahrheit als Begegnung*. Zürich: Zwingli Verlag, 1963. The original English translation (1943) was misleadingly entitled *The Divine–Human Encounter*; this was revised and reissued in 1964 as *Truth as Encounter*.

[67] For Buber's approach as a critique of religion, see Nicholas Lash, *Easter in Ordinary: Reflections on Human Experience and the Knowledge of God*, Charlottesville, VA: University Press of Virginia, 1988, pp. 178–98.

[68] Roman Rössler, *Person und Glaube: Der Personalismus der Gottesbeziehung bei Emil Brunner*, Munich: Kaiser Verlag, 1965, pp. 19–20.

understood to be an event in history. This should not be interpreted to mean that history reveals God, but that God's self-revelation takes place within the historical process. By the phrase "personal correspondence" (*personale Korrespondenz*, or, less frequently, *personhafte Korrespondenz*), employed extensively in this work, Brunner intends to convey the fact that revelation cannot be conceived as purely propositional or intellectual, but must be understood as an act of God, and supremely the act of Jesus Christ.

On this approach to truth, natural theology can be seen as part of the enterprise of establishing a correct relationship between humanity and the natural order. It does not merely augment information, but changes attitudes. This immediately points to a connection between natural theology and the human relationship with the environment. How we see the natural order determines our attitude towards it. We shall return to consider this further in Chapter 12, dealing with natural theology and ethics.

The need for intellectual recalibration of the concept of truth is also emphasized by the Greek Orthodox writer John Zizioulas, who points out how the interaction of the Christian gospel with Hellenistic philosophy forced theologians of the patristic era to develop a highly nuanced account of truth.[69] For Zizioulas, truth is certainly about a responsible way of thinking, attentive to the divinely implanted structures of reality; it is also, however, about a way of living, and especially a form of gathering together in communion. The discernment of truth is not a solitary occupation; it is something that is discovered in fellowship with Christ and in communion with one another. Similar concerns are regularly expressed by Hans Urs von Balthasar in the course of his extended programmatic attempt to reinstate the concept of beauty within a "theological aesthetics,"[70] a theme we shall consider further in the following chapter.

Truth and a Natural Theology of the Imagination

Nature makes us wonder. It makes us wonder why things are the way they are, or, indeed, why they are there at all. It stimulates our imaginations,

---

[69] John D. Zizioulas, *Being as Communion: Studies in Personhood and the Church*, Crestwood, NY: St Vladimir's Seminary Press, 1993, pp. 67–122.

[70] See especially Aidan Nichols, *The Word Has Been Abroad: A Guide Through Balthasar's Aesthetics*, Edinburgh: T&T Clark, 1998, pp. 1–22.

forcing us to ask questions, propose provisional answers, and devise strategies by which these might be answered. Although these questions can often be classified as "scientific," concerned with making sense of the world, they often penetrate to the imaginative depths of human nature, raising questions that the sciences cannot hope to answer.[71]

Thus far in this chapter, we have generally colluded with the notion that truth primarily concerns sense-making, in that this has allowed us to explore the importance of natural theology in this important intellectual domain. We must now return to the anxieties expressed earlier in this final part of this volume, to the effect that such an approach to truth diminishes the notion, failing to take into account the richer vision of "truth" characteristic of Christianity in the past. How can we develop a Christian approach to nature – that is to say, a natural theology or a theology of nature – which is not *limited* to intellectual or explanatory matters? Natural theology cannot be allowed to note a sense of awe or wonder in the presence of nature, while then proceeding to disregard that awe in its headlong rush to understand what is being experienced. A fundamental reconnection between experience and understanding, between perception and cognition, is to be sought. On a Christian understanding of things, a truly natural theology appeals to the human imagination, not simply the human reason.

This line of thought naturally raises the question of what the Christian writer most associated with the notion of a "baptized imagination" might have to contribute to a discussion of natural theology. C. S. Lewis was adamant that nature was characterized by its ordering, which the human mind could discern and grasp: "Unless all that we take to be knowledge is illusion, we must hold that in thinking we are not reading rationality into an irrational universe but responding to a rationality with which the universe has always been saturated."[72] We can see here a classic approach to natural theology – the initial discernment of the rationality of the universe, which then becomes the basis of an argument for the existence of God which holds that such a rationality cannot adequately be explained on the basis of a purely naturalist account of

---

[71] For an important exploration of this issue, see Mary Midgley, *Science and Poetry*, London: Routledge, 2001.
[72] C. S. Lewis, *Christian Reflections*, Grand Rapids, MI: Eerdmans, 1967, p. 65.

reality.[73] Yet, important though this appeal to reason may be for Lewis's approach as a whole, it was supplemented by something more elusive, and in Lewis's view, more fundamental and compelling – an appeal to the imagination.

Lewis thus insisted that nature is possessed of a rationality; yet it is saturated with something deeper, something that touches parts of the human soul that a cold, clinical analysis of the structures of the world misses. Reason and imagination both have their part to play in any comprehensive account of reality. In an important essay on the nature of metaphorical language entitled "Bluspels and Flalansferes," Lewis explained how he understood these faculties to be related: "I am a rationalist. For me, reason is the natural organ of truth; but imagination is the organ of meaning. Imagination, producing new metaphors or revivifying old, is not the cause of truth, but its condition."[74]

A natural theology should, following the classical English tradition, exult in being able to discern and interpret the "rationality with which the universe has always been saturated." Yet Lewis's words point to the possible recovery of an imaginative approach to natural theology – one that acknowledges and affirms the ordering of the world, and its appeal to the human reason, but nevertheless insists on the full recognition of the role of the imagination in any human response to the world. The world, for Lewis, points to something beyond it which needs to be engaged with the imagination, rather than the intellect.

Such questions had been explored long before Lewis appreciated their significance. Augustine of Hippo's exploration of the relation of *signum* and *significatum* began as early as the 390s, but is best seen in the later

---

[73] Lewis sets out such an argument at several points in his writings. For the most celebrated, see C. S. Lewis, *Miracles: A Preliminary Study*, New York: Macmillan, 1978, pp. 12–24. This edition of this work includes a revised version of its third chapter, in response to certain criticisms of Lewis's position made by Elizabeth Anscombe at the Oxford Socratic Club early in 1947. See also Stanley L. Jaki, *The Origin of Science and the Science of its Origin*, Edinburgh: Scottish Academic Press, 1978, p. 21, offering such an argument on the basis of "the fact that since the world was rational it could be comprehended by the human mind, but as the product of the Creator it could not be derived from the mind of man, a creature."

[74] C. S. Lewis, *Rehabilitations and Other Essays*, London: Oxford University Press, 1939, p. 158.

work *de doctrina Christiana*. Here, Augustine draws a distinction between "natural signs" (*signa naturalia*) which make something other than themselves known without any conscious agency of their own,[75] and "given signs" (*signa data*), which are consciously produced in order to convey meaning.[76] Augustine's recognition of the communicative aspects of signs is widely regarded as ground-breaking, and is clearly relevant to our discussion of natural theology: for Augustine, God has left traces of the divine identity, character, and nature in the created order, in addition to the explicit, ostensive acts of revelation, culminating in Jesus Christ. While it might reasonably be argued that God intended to leave such traces impressed upon the natural order, these *signa naturalia* are clearly distinct from the *signa data* of divine revelation. And both genres elicit attention, engagement, and a sense of wonder, stimulating both mind and imagination.

Augustine also draws a distinction between the *usus* and *fruitio* of a sign.[77] To enjoy a sign is to love it for its own sake – for what it is in itself. To use a sign is to exploit its capacity to attain what is loved – in other words, to use the *signum* as a gateway to its *significatum*.[78] And for Augustine, the one who is to be loved and enjoyed in this way is none other than God himself,[79] who has provided us with a richly textured and signed world which we may enjoy, while at the same time allowing it to denote and signify its original creator and its ultimate goal.

---

[75] As, for example, a fire creates smoke, or the footprint left by a passing animal (*vestigium transeuntis animantis*).

[76] Augustine, *de doctrina Christiana* II.i.1–2. For analysis, see Geoffrey Galt Harpham, "The Fertile Word: Augustine's Ascetics of Interpretation," *Criticism* 38 (1986): 237–54; Alexander L. Zachary, "Interpretative Desire: Augustine's Semiotics and the Transcendental Signified," *Columbia Journal of Literary Criticism* 2 (2004): 25–34.

[77] Augustine, *de doctrina Christiana*, I.iii.3–iv.4. For discussion, see Oliver O'Donovan, "*Usus* and *Fruitio* in Augustine, *De Doctrina Christiana* I," *Journal of Theological Studies* 33 (1982): 361–97; Clifford Ando, "Augustine on Language," *Revue des études augustiniennes* 40 (1994): 45–78; James K. A. Smith, *Speech and Theology: Language and the Logic of Incarnation*, London: Routledge, 2002, pp. 114–50.

[78] Augustine, *de doctrina Christiana*, I.iv.4. "Frui est enim amore inhaerere alicui rei propter seipsam. Uti autem, quod in usum venerit ad id quod amas obtinendum referre, si tamen amandum est."

[79] Augustine, *de doctrina Christiana*, I.xxii.21.

This distinction between *usus* and *fruitio* would be exploited by Lewis in his 1941 sermon "The Weight of Glory," to which we shall return presently. Yet Lewis was aware that signs possess a capacity to capture the imagination, rather than merely inform the reason. Lewis, perhaps under the influence of J. R. R. Tolkien, appreciated how an engagement with the natural world could be the basis of the construction of a world of the imagination – a world which, though rooted in the real, reaches upwards and beyond it. Lewis regarded himself as being one of those, who, "on a wakeful night, entertain themselves with invented landscapes." In his mind, he would use nature as the model for fantasy, tracing "great rivers from where the gulls scream at the estuary, through the windings of ever narrower and more precipitous gorges, up to the barely audible tinkling of their source in a ford of the moors."[80] The natural was used as a sign to an imaginary world. But what relation, other than visual semblance, might such an imaginary world bear to its natural prototype?

This question is central to Tolkien's theory of *mythopoeia*, the science of myth-making.[81] The word "myth" requires comment. Tolkien described the myth writer as a "subcreator," whose work was inspired by God as creator, and is to be seen as an imitation of the world of this supreme Creator through the making of worlds no less complex yet no less proportioned and hierarchical than that which we see around us. For Tolkien:

> The significance of a myth is not easily to be pinned on paper by analytical reasoning. It is at its best when it is presented by a poet who feels rather than makes explicit what his theme portends; who presents it incarnate in the world of history and geography.[82]

The subcreator is able to create worlds of order, beauty, and goodness, which are only a pale reflection of the ideal world of the divine – but are

---

[80] C. S. Lewis, *An Experiment in Criticism*, Cambridge, UK: Cambridge University Press, 1961, p. 52.

[81] See Christopher Garbowski, *Recovery and Transcendence for the Contemporary Mythmaker: The Spiritual Dimension in the Works of J. R. R. Tolkien*, Lublin, Poland: Marie Curie-Sklodowska University Press, 2000.

[82] J. R. R. Tolkien, "Beowulf: The Monsters and the Critics," in Christopher Tolkien (ed.), *The Monsters and the Critics and Other Essays*, pp. 5–48, London: HarperCollins, 1997; quote at p. 15.

nevertheless based upon it, even if they are at best pale copies of its beauty and splendor.[83]

A discussion of truth, then, leads into an exploration of the place of beauty in natural theology – a topic that merits much greater consideration in its own right.

---

[83] There are important parallels here with Owen Barfield's ideas about the function of poetry in disclosing meaning through the imagination – see, e.g, Owen Barfield, *Poetic Diction: A Study in Meaning*, Middletown, CT: Wesleyan University Press, 1973, pp. 178–81.

CHAPTER 11

Natural Theology and Beauty

In the previous chapter, we affirmed both the legitimacy and limits of characterizing the human perception of nature solely in terms of an essentially intellectual process of sense-making. It has long been recognized that this encounter also has affective dimensions, which ought to find expression in a Christian natural theology. Human responses to nature include the emotions of "wonder," "awe," "fear," and "beauty." None of these can be identified with, or reduced to, the intellectualized response to nature that was characteristic of the Enlightenment. As the literary critic Terry Eagleton points out, beauty is involved in "the whole region of human perception and sensation, in contrast to the more rarified domain of conceptual thought."[1]

There is now growing interest in the place of beauty in a scientific account of the natural world. In recent years, for example, the biological importance of the aesthetic has become increasingly recognized, and its implications for reproduction and evolution noted. "Beauty is one of the ways life perpetuates itself, and love of beauty is deeply rooted in our biology."[2] While it is possible to identify possible biological roots for

---

[1] Terry Eagleton, *The Ideology of the Aesthetic*, Oxford: Blackwell, 1990, p. 13.

[2] Nancy L. Etcoff, *Survival of the Prettiest: The Science of Beauty*, New York: Doubleday, 2000, p. 234.

aesthetic experiences,[3] many have argued that these cannot provide an adequate account of the richness of such experiences, nor the significance that individuals attach to them.[4]

In the present chapter, we shall use the category of "beauty" to explore this affective engagement with nature, and how it can be incorporated into natural theology. It is in some ways a difficult notion to discuss, not least on account of difficulties concerning definition[5] and the question of objectivity of aesthetic judgment.[6] While these questions cannot be resolved in this chapter, we maintain that the idea of "beauty" clearly continues to be found meaningful. We begin by considering how the idea of beauty can be retrieved in a natural theology.

Recovering the Place of Beauty in Natural Theology

An emphatic assertion of the beauty of the world and its theological importance is found in most writers of the patristic and medieval periods, who celebrated this beauty as something that is intrinsically delightful, while at the same time affirming its potential to lead those questing for a fuller disclosure of that beauty to discover its source and culmination in God.[7]

It is a theme that echoes throughout Augustine's *Confessions*. The love of beauty is a transposed love for God. Augustine writes of his late

---

[3] For example, E. O. Wilson's suggestion that humans evolved as creatures deeply enmeshed with the intricacies of nature, and that this affinity with nature (which he terms "biophilia") remains ingrained in our genotype. See Edward O. Wilson, *Biophilia: The Human Bond with Other Species*, Cambridge, MA: Harvard University Press, 1984.

[4] See the evaluations assembled by Stephen R. Kellert and Edward O. Wilson (eds), *The Biophilia Hypothesis*, Washington, DC: Island Press, 1993.

[5] For some of the issues, see Malcolm Budd, "Kant's Aesthetics of Nature," in *The Aesthetic Appreciation of Nature*, pp. 24–89, Oxford: Oxford University Press, 2005.

[6] For the debate, see Miller's defense and Goldman's critique of aesthetic objectivity: Richard W. Miller, "Three Versions of Objectivity: Aesthetic, Moral, and Scientific," in Jerrold Levinson (ed.), *Aesthetics and Ethics: Essays at the Intersection*, pp. 26–58, Cambridge, UK: Cambridge University Press, 1998; Alan H. Goldman, *Aesthetic Value*, Boulder, CO: Westview Press, 1995, pp. 36–9.

[7] For an excellent collection of citations and references, see James Schaefer, "Appreciating the Beauty of Earth," *Theological Studies* 61 (2001): 23–52.

discovery of an ancient beauty, already planted deep within him, which inflamed him with desire to know it truly and fully.[8] Augustine's extraordinary vision of divinely created beauty leads him to find God within himself; yet in so doing, he also finds himself far from God, in a strange place of interior exile (*in regione dissimilitudinis*).[9] Self-knowledge has its place; it is, however, the precondition for, not an alternative to, redemption.

Beauty became a leading theme of Augustine's mature writings.[10] This beauty, simultaneously transcendent and immanent, is expressed in the ordering of creation. To appreciate the beauty of God's creation is to appreciate the greater beauty of God. Each aspect of the creation merits detailed study for this reason: "If I were to take each one of them individually, and unwrap them, as it were, and examine them, along with all the rich blessings contained within them, how long it would take!"[11]

It is a theme that has resonated throughout Christian theology.[12] Earlier generations of theologians had a strong sense of the importance of the category of beauty, and its role in an understanding of the capacity of nature to disclose the divine. This was especially the case during the Middle Ages, characterized by a profound concern to do justice to the aesthetic dimensions of both faith and theology. In his detailed studies of medieval aesthetics, Umberto Eco has analyzed the factors which led to this emphasis upon beauty.[13] We may note two of his observations.

---

[8] Augustine, *Confessiones*, X.xxvii.38.

[9] Ibid., VII.x.16. Augustine mentions writing two or three books on the notion of beauty (IV.xii.20); these do not appear to have survived, if indeed they were ever written.

[10] See the detailed analysis in Carol Harrison, *Beauty and Revelation in the Thought of Saint Augustine*, Oxford: Oxford University Press, 1992.

[11] Augustine, *de civitate Dei*, xx.24.

[12] The detailed observation and interpretation of various aspects of nature in the poems of Gerald Manley Hopkins illustrate this particularly well: see James Finn Cotter, "Hopkins and Augustine," *Victorian Poetry* 39 (2001): 69–82. For an analysis of Hopkins's aesthetic and theological emphasis on recapturing every aspect of individuality and symbolism within nature, and thus recalling creation's divine origin, see Hilary Fraser, *Beauty and Belief. Aesthetics and Religion in Victorian Literature*, Cambridge, UK: Cambridge University Press, 1986, pp. 67–106.

[13] See Umberto Eco, *Art and Beauty in the Middle Ages*, New Haven, CT: Yale University Press, 1986; *The Aesthetics of Thomas Aquinas*, Cambridge, MA: Harvard University Press, 1988.

In the first place, a number of biblical texts, especially from within the wisdom tradition, spoke of the world being created in an ordered manner. The most important of these was Wisdom 11: 20: "you have arranged all things by measure and number and weight." This verse was widely interpreted to mean that the natural order was characterized by a *modus*, *forma*, and *ordo* which could be seen as embodiments of beauty and goodness.

Secondly, the writings of Dionysius the Areopagite proved a highly fertile source of reflection on the importance of beauty, and were widely read during this era. Thomas Aquinas, for example, is first thought to have encountered the ideas of Dionysius in a lecture series given by Albertus Magnus at Cologne around 1250. Dionysius's *Divine Names* presents the world "as a cascade of beauties springing forth from the First Principle, a dazzling radiance of sensuous splendours which diversify in all created being."[14] Aquinas's argument that the beauty of the created order arises directly from the beauty of God as its creator can be seen both as an attempt to impose conceptual unity on Dionysius's expansive reflections on the divine beauty, and also as a means of affirming his own theological agenda – the analogy between God and the creation.

Recent decades have witnessed the rediscovery of the significance of beauty,[15] even if its implications for a natural theology have yet to be explored fully. Just as Karl Barth is widely credited with the recovery of trinitarian theology in the twentieth century, it is likely that Hans Urs von Balthasar will be seen as having stimulated and resourced the recent renewal of a theology of beauty. In a tightly argued analysis, Balthasar developed the point that beauty requires form in order to be grasped and appreciated. It has to be presented to the human senses in a manner that can be assimilated. This immediately accentuates the theological significance of the concepts of creation and incarnation, in that both propose a correlation and connection between the character of God and the

---

[14]   Eco, *The Aesthetics of Thomas Aquinas*, p. 23.

[15]   See Frank Burch Brown, *Religious Aesthetics: A Theological Study of Making and Meaning*, Princeton, NJ: Princeton University Press, 1989; Patrick Sherry, *Spirit and Beauty: An Introduction to Theological Aesthetics*, Oxford: Clarendon Press, 1992; Richard Viladesau, *Theological Aesthetics: God in Imagination, Beauty and Art*, New York: Oxford University Press, 1999; David Bentley Hart, *The Beauty of the Infinite: The Aesthetics of Christian Truth*, Grand Rapids, MI: Eerdmans, 2003.

tangible, visible world.[16] "Only that which has form can snatch one up into a state of rapture. Only through form can the lightning-bolt of eternal beauty flash."[17] The Christian doctrines of creation and incarnation both propose a theologically significant link between the forms that we observe, and the character of God. Both nature and Christ disclose, in their specific ways, the divine *logos* – to those who have eyes to see. We have already noted the interconnection of these doctrines in the prologue to John's Gospel; Balthasar's analysis reinforces this critical point.

When observed from within the Christian faith, the natural world can be "seen" in a new light, leading to a deeper appreciation of its beauty. A natural theology is thus sensitive and affirming of the beauty of the natural order, seeing this as an aspect of its God-given character. To appreciate the importance of this aspect of natural theology, we shall consider an incident in the life of John Ruskin, which points to the intrinsic theological danger of excluding beauty from any account of the Christian vision of reality.

The Neglect of Beauty: The "Deconversion" of John Ruskin

John Ruskin (1819–1900), one of the most significant figures in English Victorian culture, was noted for his emphasis on seeing things as they really are: "we want, in this sad world of ours, very often to see in the dark – that's the greatest gift of all – but at any rate to see; no matter by what light, so only we can see things as they are."[18] For Ruskin, the category of "beauty" played an important role in this process of discernment.[19] This can be seen from what appears to have been an epiphanic experience of the transcendent at Schaffhausen in 1832, when Ruskin saw, in

---

[16] Hans Urs von Balthasar, *The Glory of the Lord: A Theological Aesthetics*, 7 vols, Edinburgh: T&T Clark, 1982–9, vol. 1, pp. 23–34.

[17] Ibid., pp. 32–3.

[18] From Ruskin's inaugural lecture at Cambridge for the College of Fine Art in 1858; John Ruskin, *Works*, ed. E. T. Cook and A. Wedderburn, 39 vols, London: Allen, 1903–12, vol. 16, p. 171.

[19] Robert Hewison, *John Ruskin: The Argument of the Eye*, Princeton, NJ: Princeton University Press, 1976, pp. 54–64.

the spectacle of an alpine sunset, "the revelation of the beauty of the earth . . . the opening of the first page of its volume."[20]

The first volume of Ruskin's landmark work *Modern Painters* was devoted to an examination of the truths of nature. This work is notable for its championing of the style of J. M. W. Turner (1775–1851), at a time when his style was detested by most contemporary British art critics. Why did Ruskin lionize Turner? The answer lay in his fidelity to nature. Others, Ruskin commented, "copied [nature] like children, drawing what they knew to be there, but not what they saw there."[21] Where others represented what they intellectually knew to be present within nature, Turner saw the world in a different, more insightful manner, and chose to draw what he actually saw. Art is not about the imitation of natural objects or phenomena; it reveals the truth concerning them. "The word Truth, applied to art, signifies the faithful statement, either to the mind or senses, of any fact of nature."[22] And this led to an appreciation of the beauty of nature itself, expressed in beautiful forms.[23] Art was to be understood as a way of representing things as they actually were, drawing out their inherent beauty and composition, not imposing human conventions of beauty upon them.[24] Ruskin's idea implies the need to approach and experience nature directly, without the need for accommodation or intermediate constructions.

Ruskin's early evangelical faith appears to have led him to consider things of beauty as potentially idolatrous. In 1858, while visiting Turin, he attended a local Waldesian church. Religious liberty only having recently been restored to that region, this Protestant church was a new and somewhat inelegant construction, which compared unfavorably with the great architectural and artistic masterpieces he saw around him – such as Paolo Veronese's "Queen of Sheba," which he spent hours copying. When he reflected on the beauty of this painting, on brilliant music, on everything that constituted what he called the "gorgeousness of life," he found

---

[20] Tim Hilton, *John Ruskin*, New Haven, CT: Yale University Press, 2002, p. 26.

[21] Ruskin, *Works*, vol. 3, p. 309.

[22] Ibid., vol. 3, p. 104. Note also his 1856 lecture "The Two Paths," which contrasts a naturalism which "represents God's truth" with a formalism which "repeats men's errors."

[23] Ruskin, *Works*, vol. 4, p. 94.

[24] Hilton, *John Ruskin*, pp. 68–9.

himself forced to ask whether such power and beauty could conceivably be adverse to the honor of its creator.

> Has God made faces beautiful and limbs strong, and created these strange, fiery, fantastic energies, and created the splendour of substance and the love of it; created gold, and pearls, and crystal, and the sun that makes them gorgeous; and filled human fancy with all splendid thoughts; and given to the human touch its power of placing and brightening and perfecting, only that all these things may lead His creatures away from Him?[25]

A crisis was clearly building up in Ruskin's mind, torn between his Protestant suspicion of beauty as the source of idolatry and the aesthetic wonder he experienced in contemplating Turin's rich heritage of art and architecture. His faith, as he later described it, took the form of a restrictive, limiting set of beliefs, somewhat cerebral in nature. So what could he do, when confronted by a beauty and wonder which seemed to proclaim the aesthetic inadequacy of his Protestant faith?[26] In a bold act of "deconversion," he chose to follow beauty, and left Protestantism behind.[27] "I came out of the chapel, in sum of twenty years of thought, a conclusively unconverted man." His later works reflect his growing belief that the categories of Christianity were not sufficient to express his emotional response to nature.[28]

But why? How did Ruskin find himself in such a position? Why did he believe that reason pulled in one direction, and beauty and the imagination

---

[25] From a letter to his father, cited by Hilton, *John Ruskin*, p. 256. Note that Ruskin later offered a number of accounts of his "deconversion," with subtly different emphases: see George P. Landow, *The Aesthetic and Critical Theories of John Ruskin*, Princeton, NJ: Princeton University Press, 1971.

[26] Barbour rightly stresses the importance of the aesthetic deficiency of Protestantism in this matter: John D. Barbour, *Versions of Deconversion: Autobiography and the Loss of Faith*, Charlottesville, VA: University Press of Virginia, 1994, pp. 53–85.

[27] For the best account of this event, see Hilton, *John Ruskin*, pp. 254–7. On the concept of "deconversion" at this time, see Barbour, *Versions of Deconversion*, 34–52.

[28] See, e.g., his "Cestus of Aglaia" (1866) and "The Queen of the Air" (1869), *Works*, vol. 19. The title of the former is taken from the 14th book of the *Iliad*; Ruskin takes the "cestus" to represents the spiritual power of art. Ruskin returned to some form of Christian belief in 1875.

in another?[29] If all originate in God, why should not all lead to God? Why should not the human quest for truth, beauty, and goodness converge on God, instead of conspiring against one another to create confusion, or collaborating to lead away from their ultimate source and origin? There is no reason, save the Enlightenment's misplaced emphasis upon the priority of reason, which should lead anyone to conceive of natural theology solely in terms of the observed rationality of the natural order.[30]

To explore this point further, we may consider the important criticism of William Paley's influential approach to natural theology developed by Hugh Miller (1802–56).

Hugh Miller on the Aesthetic Deficiencies of Sense-Making

Many Victorian church leaders regarded William Paley's achievements as a natural theologian as being of lasting importance. In his 1871 lecture "The Natural Theology of the Future," Charles Kingsley praised Paley as a great natural theologian, and argued that Darwin's theory of evolution merely clarified the mechanism of divine creation: "We knew of old that God was so wise that He could make all things: but behold, He is so much wiser than even that, that He can make all things make themselves."[31] Every clergyman, Kingsley suggested, ought to be qualified in at least

---

[29] For some reflections, see John B. Beer, *Providence and Love: Studies in Wordsworth, Channing, Myers, George Eliot, and Ruskin*, Oxford: Oxford University Press, 1998, pp. 233–312.

[30] Indeed, contemplation of the "sublime" could even be argued to "advance our sense-making pursuits" – a point argued by Kirk Pillow, *Sublime Understanding: Aesthetic Reflection in Kant and Hegel*, Cambridge, MA: MIT Press, 2000, 2–4. For reflections on the theological importance of the Kantian notion of the sublime, see Clayton Crockett, *A Theology of the Sublime*, London: Routledge, 2001, pp. 99–112.

[31] Charles Kingsley, "The Natural Theology of the Future," in *Westminster Sermons*, London: Macmillan, 1874, pp. v–xxxiii; quote at p. xxvii. For the place of Darwinian natural selection in Kingsley's natural theology, see David Levy and Sandra Peart, "Charles Kingsley and the Theological Interpretation of Natural Selection," *Journal of Bioeconomics* 8 (2006): 197–218.

one physical science, so that they could appreciate the power of Paley's argument.

While acknowledging the intrinsic beauty of nature in his *Natural Theology*, Paley's interests ultimately lay elsewhere. Nature, he argued, was to be considered primarily as a "contrivance" – that is, something that has been designed and manufactured. Paley's language and imagery here reflects his basic belief that the world is best considered as a carefully designed and constructed machine. His use of the famous analogy of the watch depends upon clear evidence of design within its mechanisms as a testimony to the wisdom of its designer, and the skill of its constructor. Contrivance implies purpose. Natural theology is best undertaken by considering the world as a superbly designed and carefully fabricated machine.

Yet machines can be ugly. How could the beauty of the natural world be adequately accommodated and expressed through such a flawed analogy? That was the judgment of the Scottish geologist Hugh Miller who, though remembered as one of the outstanding scientific popularizers of his day,[32] was also an important advocate of natural theology.[33] He saw such a theology as both an apologetic weapon of no small importance for the church in a time of uncertainty, and as an appropriate intellectual response to the wonder and intricacy of the natural order. Yet where others had emphasized the ordering and intelligibility of nature, Miller chose to focus on what he called "the poetry of nature," which science inspired and illuminated. "Nature is a vast tablet, inscribed with signs," he wrote, which "become poetry in the mind when read."[34]

Miller's particular contribution to the redirecting of natural theology in the generations following Paley lay in his interpretation of the human appropriation of nature. It had long been noted that humans imitated nature in their art, using the beauty of nature to stimulate and shape the artistic endeavor. Aristotle, for example, held that human art consciously

---

[32]   For an excellent assessment of his importance, see Simon J. Knell and Michael A. Taylor, "Hugh Miller: Fossils, Landscapes, and Literary Geology," *Proceedings of the Geologists' Association* 117 (2006): 85–98.

[33]   The best study of this aspect of Miller's thought is John Hedley Brooke, "Like Minds: The God of Hugh Miller," in Michael Shortland (ed.), *Hugh Miller and the Controversies of Victorian Science*, pp. 171–86, Oxford: Clarendon Press, 1996. Miller was a major force in the creation of the Free Church of Scotland in 1843.

[34]   Brooke, "Like Minds," p. 176.

imitated nature, and offered the beginnings of an explanation of this trend.[35] In his *Testimony of the* Rocks (1857),[36] Miller took this same observation, and offered a radically different interpretation. Human art reflected the same fundamental architectonic principles as those mani- fested in the natural world. There was a convergence between the mind of the creator, and that of the human observer of nature. But why?

Miller's argument was that this consonance or resonance was not acquired, but was intrinsic to human rationality as a consequence of having been created in the image of God. The patterns of nature were to be regarded as a divine creation, appealing to an admiration of correlated patterns that were somehow built into or impressed upon the human mind. For Miller, the intricacy and beauty of the shells of the ammonite or *Murchisonia bigranulosa* far exceeded those of any human design – even the exquisite designs of Westminster Abbey or Canterbury Cathedral.

Miller's natural theology has generally been neglected for entirely under- standable reasons. It is widely perceived to be linked, perhaps irredeem- ably, to his pre-Darwinian understanding of biological evolution. The scientific developments that so fatally wounded Paley were assumed to inflict at least as much damage upon Miller's approach. Yet Miller raised a question that remains both pertinent and controversial: how are we to account for the seeming synergy between human taste and the natural order?

For example, it is known that landscapes often evoke a powerful aes- thetic response in humans.[37] One possible explanation is that this has been hard-wired into the human brain as a consequence of evolution. If humanity originated in the tropical African savannah,[38] might our origins continue to shape our responses to alternative environments? Might we actually be making functional judgments about the habitability of a

[35] Herbert Granger, "Aristotle on the Analogy between Action and Nature," *Classical Quarterly* 43 (1993): 168–76. For an influential discussion of the relation of art and nature, see Arthur O. Lovejoy, " 'Nature' as Aesthetic Form," *Modern Language Notes* 42 (1927): 444–50.

[36] Hugh Miller, *The Testimony of the Rocks; or, Geology in its Bearings on the Two Theologies, Natural and Revealed*, Ann Arbor, MI: Scholarly Publishing Office, University of Michigan Library, 2005.

[37] Simon Bell, *Landscape: Pattern, Perception, and Process*, New York: Spon, 1999, 63–96.

[38] John D. Barrow, *The Artful Universe: The Cosmic Source of Human Creativity*, Harmondsworth: Penguin, 1995, pp. 91–101.

landscape, believing that we are making an aesthetic judgment concerning its alleged beauty? And might it be possible to translate a judgment about the beauty of a landscape to a practical decision as to what needs to be done to preserve it, and thus indirectly to preserve ourselves?[39] Interesting though such speculations might be, they generally lack a rigorous evidential basis. Nevertheless, they point once more to the importance of incorporating the aesthetic dimension of the human response to the natural world into any responsible account of natural theology.

John Ruskin and the Representation of Nature

We have already noted Ruskin's concern to "see" nature properly, and his belief in the aesthetic importance of such vision. Ruskin's attitude to nature is that its accurate representation in art or noninterventionist science (such as natural history and geology) provides a true aesthetic that gives access to the transcendent.[40] In this way the glory of God can be encountered almost directly through nature, which is to be seen as a symbol, message, or gift of the creator. While there is nothing specifically Christian in this approach, it can easily be given a theological foundation, such as that noted earlier (pp. 185–90). Yet Ruskin's account of perception places an emphasis on the observer's ability to encounter nature *directly*, without the intervention of intermediaries.

Ruskin wanted to get as close to natural phenomena as possible by minimizing the intrusiveness of the observer. Although Ruskin appeared willing to acknowledge, at least implicitly, that the observer is a participant in the process of observation, rather than being detached from it, it is clear that he finds this an uncomfortable thought. Ruskin wished to attain

---

[39]   Holmes Rolston, "From Beauty to Duty: Aesthetics of Nature and Environmental Ethics," in Arnold Berleant (ed.), *Environment and the Arts: Perspectives on Environmental Ethics*, pp. 127–41, Aldershot: Ashgate, 2002. Holmes's approach seems vulnerable to at least some of the general criticisms of aesthetic approaches to environmentalism set out in J. Robert Loftis, "Three Problems for the Aesthetic Foundations of Environmental Ethics," *Philosophy in the Contemporary World* 10 (2003): 41–50.

[40]   Compare the views of Charles Kingsley, which give much greater emphasis to the sciences on this point: John C. Hawley, "Charles Kingsley and the Book of Nature," *Anglican and Episcopal History* 61 (1991): 461–79.

truth, understood as a simple correspondence with sense data and perception, for its own sake. He also wanted to see and represent beauty, believing that this is primarily inherent in the phenomena.[41] Yet Ruskin clearly regarded any recognition of the role of social construction in human perception as a potential distorter of reality, and hence as a subverter of his theory of beauty and truth.

The difficulty with Ruskin's approach can be summarized in a line from T. S. Eliot's *Four Quartets*: "... human kind/Cannot bear very much reality."[42] Reality needs to be adapted to our capacity to cope with it. As we noted in our account of human perception and cognition (pp. 86–92), this involves the use of schemas to organize and analyze the complexities of experience. Ruskin, however, insists upon encountering the natural world directly, without any such intermediaries.

Ruskin's criticism of Romanticism and his promotion of Turner's art reflected his desire to get back to nature by attempting to observe it without the encumbrance of *a priori* mental or cultural categories. His fear of distorting the reality of nature led him to insist that the perceptual process should be as free from construction as far as possible. His concern to get as close as possible to the phenomena led him to minimize the intrusiveness of the observer. In the end, it led to Ruskin's psychological breakdown, in that psychological schemata have an important functional role to play in the maintenance of mental stability by making the environment ordered and predictable.[43] In particular, Ruskin does not appear to have appreciated the importance of paradox in holding together the tensions created by a sense of awe at nature's wonders.

One can have sympathy with Ruskin's anxieties about the potential distortion of the beauty of nature that might arise from the interposition of theoretical representations. Yet his attempt to "see" the complexity of nature directly led not to an enhanced perception of nature, but to an

---

[41]   However, Ruskin allows for the creative interpretation of phenomena if this is explicitly recognized as such.

[42]   T. S. Eliot, *Burnt Norton*, I, ll. 44–5. For reflections, see W. Dow Edgerton, "Words and the Word," *Theological Studies* 44 (1988): 462–78.

[43]   Kay Redfield Jamison, *Touched with Fire: Manic Depressive Illness and the Artistic Temperament*, New York: Free Press, 1993, pp. 110–14. On Ruskin's breakdown, see especially John D. Rosenberg, *The Darkening Glass: A Portrait of Ruskin's Genius*, London: Routledge & Kegan Paul, 1963; Jay Fellows, *Ruskin's Maze: Mastery and Madness in his Art*, Princeton, NJ: Princeton University Press, 1981.

overwhelming of his own capacity to perceive it. Ruskin simply could not cope with his own demands for direct access to the phenomena.

As we have seen, the process of perception demands such intermediaries, if the mind is not to be engulfed with a tidal wave of sensory conflicts and confusions. The role of theories in the natural sciences can be seen as paralleling the place of schemas in perception. In recent years there has been growing appreciation of how these theoretical representations of reality are beautiful in themselves, thus adding another level to the human aesthetic engagement with nature. We shall consider this in what follows.

The Beauty of Theoretical Representations of Nature

The importance of beauty as a criterion in the development and evaluation of scientific theories has long been recognized, even if the debate remains open as to how theoretical elegance is to be ranked as an explanatory virtue. For example, aesthetic considerations played a significant role in consolidating the acceptance of both the Copernican model of the solar system and the theory of special relativity. Some have argued that the conformity of a scientific theory to metaphysical preconceptions should be considered as an essentially aesthetic quality of that theory, and hence be an indicator of its validity. This is not without its difficulties, not least because each age has its own ideas as to what is metaphysically plausible or indeed self-evident. Yet there is little doubt that a case can be made for proposing that "harmony between theory and preconception yields gratification of a *prima facie* aesthetic kind."[44]

There is no doubt that the conceptual elegance of Euclidean geometry was regarded as one of its chief virtues, catalyzing its acceptance as the foundation of the theory of space of the ancient Greek physicists. In more recent times, the dynamic equations set out in the seventeenth century by Isaac Newton were regarded as both simple and graceful in their own time, even if their extraordinary elegance would not be fully revealed until

---

[44] James W. McAllister, "Truth and Beauty in Scientific Reason," *Synthese* 78 (1989): 25–51; quote at p. 35. For further reflection, see Eric Barnes, "Inference to the Loveliest Explanation," *Synthese* 103 (1995): 251–78.

the advent of the symplectic geometry of the Hamiltonian or Lagrangian formalisms.[45]

The elegance of James Clerk Maxwell's electromagnetic equations,[46] especially when reformulated from their original quaternion format into a simple vector format, has often been noted, as has the sheer beauty of Einstein's mathematical formulation of the theory of general relativity. Many others could easily be added to this potentially endless list, including the extraordinary mathematical elegance of Dirac's relativistic wave equation. This has led some philosophers of science to argue that, since aesthetic properties such as elegance are of such importance in evaluating scientific theories, particularly in cases when competing theories are equally empirically adequate, those aesthetic properties must be regarded as intrinsic to the theories themselves.[47]

A more restrained approach may be found in the writings of Michael Polanyi, who emphasizes the empirical correlation between beauty and truth. "The affirmation of a great scientific theory is in part an expression of delight. The theory has an inarticulate component acclaiming its beauty, and this is essential to the belief that it is true."[48] The "sense of scientific beauty" is directly linked to a coherent vision of reality, which recognizes that the real is also the beautiful. Polanyi sees this supremely displayed in mathematics, whose "intellectual beauty," he argues, "betokens the reality of its conceptions and the truth of its assertions."[49] It is, he insists, the "intellectual beauty" of mathematical representations of reality that points to its capacity to reveal universal truth.[50] There is a clear connection here with G. H. Hardy's assertion of the beauty of mathematics, which is set out in unmistakably Platonic terms:

---

[45] Roger Penrose, *The Road to Reality: A Complete Guide to the Laws of the Universe*, London: Jonathan Cape, 2004, pp. 483–91.

[46] For the original form in which they were stated, see James Clerk Maxwell, "A Dynamical Theory of the Electromagnetic Field," *Philosophical Transactions of the Royal Society of London* 155 (1865): 459–512.

[47] Eddy M. Zemach, *Real Beauty*, University Park, PA: Pennsylvania State University Press, 1997.

[48] Michael Polanyi, *Personal Knowledge: Towards a Post-Critical Philosophy*, London: Routledge & Kegan Paul, 1958, p. 133. For the emergence of the ideas in this work, see William Taussig Scott and Martin X. Moleski, SJ, *Michael Polanyi: Scientist and Philosopher*, Oxford: Oxford University Press, 2005, pp. 211–36.

[49] Polanyi, *Personal Knowledge*, p. 192.

[50] Ibid., p. 189.

A mathematician, like a painter or a poet, is a maker of patterns. If his patterns are more permanent than theirs, it is because they are made with *ideas*. . . . The mathematician's patterns, like the painter's or the poet's, must be *beautiful*: the ideas, like the colours of words, must fit together in a harmonious way. Beauty is the first test: there is no place for ugly mathematics. . . . It may be very hard to *define* mathematical beauty, but . . . that does not prevent us from recognizing [it].[51]

Polanyi argues that the intellectual elegance of a theory is an indicator of its correspondence with reality. In what one hopes is an illuminating overstatement, he suggests that "no scientific theory is beautiful if it is false."[52] This perhaps gives less weight than it should to the cultural location of notions of elegance or beauty. Many historians would argue that most aesthetic convictions held by scientists, such as the Aristotelian doctrine that uniform circular motion is the most beautiful of all, ended up actually impeding the advance of knowledge. Some major innovations like Kepler's elliptical planetary orbits or quantum mechanics have appeared conceptually ugly, forcing their defenders to emphasize their predictive success rather than their beauty.

But why should beauty be a criterion of any sort for the truth? After all, aesthetic judgments are notoriously subject to change over time. Which is the more beautiful: Ptolemy's geocentric, or Copernicus's heliocentric model of the solar system? And what of Kepler: are ellipses really more elegant than circles?[53] Although there are clear difficulties in using such an approach, it could still be argued that "beauty is a sign of truth" if it is the case that "the beauty of our theories shows that we are nearing the fundamental laws of nature." Yet the real difficulty is that there is as yet little evidence that the natural sciences have identified which aesthetic properties might indicate the truth of scientific theories, or how such criteria might be incorporated within the process of theory-testing and selection.[54]

---

[51] G. H. Hardy, *A Mathematician's Apology*, Cambridge, UK: Cambridge University Press, 1941, p. 24.

[52] Polanyi, *Personal Knowledge*, p. 195.

[53] For the argument, see James W. McAllister, *Beauty and Revolution in Science*, Ithaca, NY: Cornell University Press, 1999.

[54] James W. McAllister, "Is Beauty a Sign of Truth in Scientific Theories?" *American Scientist* 86 (1998): 174–83.

One explanation of the role of beauty in the natural sciences was put forward in 2002 by Theo Kuipers, who argued that the human mind established associations between recurring features of science that are not conceptually connected with empirical success.[55] On this model, scientists associate "beauty" with "truth" on account of previous exposure to theoretical situations in which this connection proved fruitful. The association in question is therefore not arbitrary, in that it is grounded in the features of past successful theories. Paul Thagard, on the other hand, argues that the perception of "beauty" in relation to a theory is a direct response to its coherence. "Scientists find theories with such features pleasurable because of their contribution to coherence, which is intrinsically pleasurable."[56]

Others are more skeptical. James McAllister points out that the concept of "beauty" is contested. As a result, every property of a theory that has at some date been seen as aesthetically attractive has at other times been judged as displeasing, or objectively neutral. Theories gain acceptance on the basis of essentially rational criteria, with aesthetic criteria being involved subsequently, often as retrodictive explanations of the success of a theory. Beauty, he argues, is a harbinger of probability only in retrospect: "A revolution is occasioned by the eminently rational decision by certain scientists to pursue indicators of truth in disregard of beauty."[57]

Although such discussions are inconclusive, they nevertheless reflect a deep-seated intuition within the scientific community that beauty is indeed a guide to truth, even if the mechanism and validation of this relationship is unclear. The potential of such an approach for a new natural theology will be obvious. If both the world and humanity can be seen as embodying the same divine architectonics, we should perhaps not be

---

[55] Theo A. F. Kuipers, "Beauty, a Road to the Truth," *Synthese* 131 (2002): 291–328.

[56] Paul R. Thagard, "Why is Beauty a Road to Truth?" in R. Festa, A. Aliseda, and J. Pejnenburg (eds), *Cognitive Structures in Scientific Inquiry*, pp. 365–70, Amsterdam: Rodopi, 2005.

[57] McAllister, "Truth and Beauty in Scientific Reason," p. 45.

surprised that true theories reflect the beauty of the "mind of God," to which they bear witness both through their truth and beauty.[58]

Beauty, Awe, and the Aesthetic Engagement with Nature

Until recently, aesthetics was dominated by a generalized philosophical, deductive approach to the topic, such as that found in the writings of Alexander Gottlieb Baumgarten (1714–60). Baumgarten introduced the category of the "aesthetic" in 1750 to refer to human knowledge expressed in the form of feeling or emotion, as opposed to that expressed in logic.[59] Although Baumgarten might be considered to be a critic of Enlightenment rationalism at this point, his real intention appears to have been to expand the notion of "rationality" to include human sensual experiences. The human experience of reality was far greater than logical analysis conceded; finding a place for the experience of beauty seemed essential if rationalism was to avoid becoming little more than an agglomerate of abstracted generalizations.[60]

Yet this theoretical approach paid little attention to the empirical question of what people find to be attractive. It was for this reason that Gustav Theodor Fechner (1801–87) set out, not entirely successfully, to develop an empirical, or inductive, approach to aesthetics. Fechner argued that "aesthetics from above" sought to disengage a general principle of beauty from the objects of aesthetic experience and the facts of aesthetic enjoyment. As a corrective, Fechner set out to develop what he termed an "aesthetics from below," based on empirical analysis of what people actually found to be beautiful.[61] Although this has not resolved the

---

[58] Thomas Dubay, *The Evidential Power of Beauty: Science and Theology Meet*, San Francisco: Ignatius Press, 1999, p. 45.

[59] Kai Hammermeister, *The German Aesthetic Tradition*, Cambridge, UK: Cambridge University Press, 2002, pp. 3–13.

[60] Ibid., p. 10.

[61] For a discussion of Fechner's approach, see Marilyn Marshall, "Physics, Metaphysics, and Fechner's Psychophysics," in William R. Woodward and Mitchell G. Ash (eds), *The Problematic Science: Psychology in Nineteenth-Century Thought*, pp. 65–87, New York: Praeger, 1982.

question of what determines beauty, it has encouraged a growing interest in the biological and psychological aspects of beauty,[62] leading to an increased awareness of its importance in engaging the natural world.

Aesthetics has been surprisingly slow to engage with the beauty of nature. Even in the relatively recent past, aesthetics was often understood to be limited to the philosophy of art, apparently overlooking the importance of the human response to the natural order itself. In a landmark article of 1966, Ronald Hepburn asserted the importance of the aesthetic engagement with the natural order, and set out two ways in which he believed that human experiences of nature differed from experiences of art.[63] First, the observer often interacts with the natural world in a special way that encourages an immersion of the spectator in the aesthetic object. Second, the natural world itself is unframed and unbounded, challenging the spectator to integrate his or her experience with what is observed.

In recent years, partly in response to a growing realization of the beauty of nature as a motive for environmental responsibility, increased theoretical attention has been paid to how the human aesthetic appreciation of nature is to be understood. Some have emphasized the aesthetical importance of the immersion of the observer in nature; others have suggested that aesthetics is better interpreted in terms of the natural world generating emotional "arousal" within the observer. A third approach is of particular interest: here, it is argued that a proper engagement with nature leads to an "appreciative

---

[62] See, e.g., Judith H. Langlois, Lisa Kalakanis, Adam J. Rubinstein, Andrea Larson, Monica Hallam, and Monica Smoot, "Maxims or Myths of Beauty? A Meta-Analytic and Theoretical Review," *Psychological Bulletin* 126 (2000): 390–423. The neurological basis of human aesthetic judgments has also received considerable attention in recent years, with particular attention being paid to changes in aesthetic preferences following brain damage: see Dahlia W. Zaidel, *Neuropsychology of Art: Neurological, Cognitive and Evolutionary Perspectives*, New York: Psychology Press, 2005, pp. 23–48, 87–120.

[63] A point made in an important article by Ronald W. Hepburn, "Contemporary Aesthetics and the Neglect of Natural Beauty," in Bernard Williams and Alan Montefiore (eds), *British Analytical Philosophy*, pp. 285–310, London: Routledge and Kegan Paul, 1966.

incomprehension."[64] The category of "mystery" is thus an appropriate response to the inability of the human mind fully to grasp what is being observed, provoking its capacity for imagination as much as for analysis in shaping a response.[65]

This theme has featured in recent analysis of the emotion of "awe," which has important aesthetic, moral, and religious aspects.[66] In their psychological analysis of the family of concepts linked to awe, Keltner and Haidt argue that two features are central to an experience of awe: "perceived vastness" and "accommodation." The perceptually orientated term "vastness" highlights the impact of the sheer physical size of the natural realm, and the resulting human awareness of being overwhelmed. This experience of vastness leads to accommodation – the Piagetian process of adjusting mental structures which cannot assimilate a new experience.

> The concept of accommodation brings together many insights about awe, such as that it involves confusion (St Paul) and obscurity (Burke), and that it is heightened in times of crisis, when extant traditions and knowledge structures do not suffice (Weber). We propose that prototypical awe involves a challenge to or negation of mental structures when they fail to make sense of an experience of something vast. . . . They may also involve feelings of enlightenment and even rebirth, when mental structures expand to accommodate truths never before known. We stress that awe involves a *need* for accommodation, which may or may not be satisfied.[67]

---

[64] See Stan Godlovitch, "Icebreakers: Environmentalism and Natural Aesthetics," *Journal of Applied Philosophy* 11 (1994): 15–30. This provocative analysis argues for the parochial nature of human aesthetical judgments in relation to nature, and asserts that the smashing of ice blocks by the flux of a river should be seen as no less aesthetically offensive than bulldozing the Navaho Sandstone Castles of Monument Valley, Arizona.

[65] For some important reflections, see Emily Brady, "Imagination and the Aesthetic Appreciation of Nature," *Journal of Aesthetics and Art Criticism* 56 (1998): 139–47; Robert S. Fudge, "Imagination and the Science-Based Aesthetic Appreciation of Unscenic Nature," *Journal of Aesthetics and Art Criticism* 59 (2001): 275–85.

[66] For what follows, see Dacher Keltner and Jonathan Haidt, "Approaching Awe, a Moral, Spiritual and Aesthetic Emotion," *Cognition and Emotion* 17 (2003): 297–314.

[67] Ibid., p. 304. The authors suggest that the term "surprise" could be used to refer to experiences that involve accommodation without vastness.

This important analysis of the core themes of the experience of "awe" allows us to distinguish it psychologically from the enterprise of sense-making, discussed in the previous chapter. Awe is about *accommodation*; sense-making is about *assimilation*.

This naturally leads us to consider what triggers such an experience of awe. Keltner and Haidt note that many such triggers (or "elicitors") can be identified. Many of these are physical, such as landscapes or other grand vistas, or natural phenomena such as tornados.[68] This clearly establishes a link between awe and natural theology. Yet Keltner and Haidt note that the same type of experience is elicited by other stimuli – including large buildings, a grand theory, or an encounter with God. This suggests that there might be important potential links between natural theology and worship, for example, in that both relate to substantially the same psychological response. This is clearly an area that needs further exploration.

Aesthetics and the "Seeing" of Beauty

One of the most persistent themes in contemporary aesthetic reflection is that the appreciation of nature depends on an understanding of *what nature actually is*. Aesthetic appreciation (and judgment) needs to be "objective" in the sense that it needs to be a response to the proper nature of the aesthetic object.[69] An appreciation of the beauty of an aesthetic object is governed by its identity – that is to say, seeing it for what it really is.[70] For this reason, some have argued that the natural sciences are essential to any aesthetic engagement with nature, in that they disclose its true character, and hence enhance the quality of the human aesthetic response.[71]

---

[68]   Ibid., p. 305.

[69]   Allen Carlson, *Aesthetics and the Environment: The Appreciation of Nature, Art, and Architecture*, London: Routledge, 2000, pp. 54–71.

[70]   Mihaly Csikszentmihalyi, *The Art of Seeing: An Interpretation of the Aesthetic Encounter*, Oxford: Oxford University Press, 1991.

[71]   Noel Carroll, "On Being Moved by Nature: Between Religion and Natural History," in Salim Kemal and Ivan Gaskell (eds), *Landscape, Natural Beauty, and the Arts*, pp. 244–66, Cambridge, UK: Cambridge University Press, 1993, pp. 254–60.

This is a leading theme of the writings of the British philosopher Frank Sibley (1923–96). Aesthetics, for Sibley, is about how we *see* things. There are certain qualities of an art object, Sibley holds, that are not discernible to the untrained eye. One might thus be said to see, and yet not see, at one and the same time. Aesthetics is about a heightened form of perception, in which things are *seen* in a certain way.[72] The central task of aesthetics, for Sibley, was for artists to enable people "to see what they see." There is indeed something there to be seen – but the act of beholding and discerning requires certain competencies, which have to be acquired.[73]

This represents a significant reaffirmation of the importance of "seeing" things correctly in order to appreciate them properly. An ontology of nature – an understanding of what nature actually is – can thus be argued to play a critical role in shaping and guiding human aesthetic responses to the natural world. But how is such an ontology to be established? Some have argued that it is to be based solely upon the natural sciences. Yet while these disciplines may well offer descriptions and explanations of nature *at a certain level*, this does not necessarily mean that they are capable of a greater disclosure.[74] As has often been noted, their "explanations" might lead to nature being viewed in a manner that dulled the human mind to certain aspects of its beauty, even if they clarified or enhanced others.

This was certainly the concern expressed by writers such as Goethe and John Keats, who held that science offered a reductionist account of nature, which threatened to diminish its intrinsic wonder by offering what amounted to little more than a "dull catalogue of common things."[75] In particular, Keats argued that Isaac Newton had destroyed the poetry of

---

[72] See especially Frank Sibley, "Aesthetics and the Looks of Things," *Journal of Philosophy* 56 (1959): 905–15; "Analysing Seeing," in Frank Sibley (ed.), *Perception: A Philosophical Symposium*, pp. 81–132, London: Methuen, 1971. For a critique of Sibley's approach, see Ted Cohen, "A Critique of Sibley's Position," *Theoria* 39 (1973): 113–52; Peter Kivy, "Aesthetic Concepts: Some Fresh Considerations," *Journal of Aesthetics and Art Criticism* 37 (1979): 423–32.

[73] See the development of this idea in Mihaly Csikszentmihalyi, *The Art of Seeing*.

[74] See the issues raised in Peter Lipton, "What Good is an Explanation?" in John Cornwell (ed.), *Explanations: Styles of Explanation in Science*, pp. 1–21, Oxford: Oxford University Press, 2004.

[75] Keats, "Lamia," Part II, l. 233.

the rainbow by reducing it to the prismatic colors (a process he referred to as "unweaving"). While this is a clear example of poetic overstatement, not without a touch of petulance, its exaggerations must not be allowed to obscure the danger that Keats discerned. By reducing nature to its assembly of constituent parts, is there not a risk of missing the aesthetic impact which it makes overall – as a total entity, rather than its individual constituents?[76]

The recognition of the beauty of nature is significant in itself; yet it also has importance in terms of what it intimates and suggests. From a Christian perspective, an appreciation of the beauty of nature can be interpreted as a transitory intuition of what is eternal, the experience *signifying* yet not *delivering* something of immense and transformative importance, and thus creating a sense of absence, a feeling of longing, within the human soul. We shall explore this point further in the final section of this chapter.

Beauty, Natural Theology, and Christian Apologetics

The importance of natural beauty in commending the Christian faith has long been appreciated.[77] Charles Baudelaire (1821–67) wrote of an "immortal instinct for the beautiful" which prompts us to see the world as "nature exiled in the imperfect," and thus creates a longing for a "revealed paradise" that we can enter and possess.[78] Baudelaire's fundamental theme is that the experience of beauty within the world awakens a deeper instinct within human nature, which longs for the consummation of that beauty, thus creating an "insatiable thirst for all that lies

---

[76] For an excellent account of both the risks and opportunities arising from scientific reductionism, see John Cornwell (ed.), *Nature's Imagination: The Frontiers of Scientific Vision*, Oxford: Oxford University Press, 1995.

[77] For a neglected contribution to this discussion, see Thomas F. Torrance, "The Transfinite Significance of Beauty in Science and Theology," in Luz García Alonso, Evanghelos Moutsopoulos and Gerhard Seel (eds), *L'art, la science et la métaphysique: Études offertes à André Mercier*, pp. 393–418, Berne: Peter Lang, 1993.

[78] Charles Baudelaire, *L'art romantique*, Paris: Calmann-Lévy, 1885, p. 167.

beyond." Beauty can be held to call us, seeking a response: "Beautiful, *kalon*, is what comes from a call, *kalein*."[79]

Looking back on his days as a young, impressionable teacher of rhetoric, Augustine recalled his fascination with beauty. Beauty, it seemed, had the capacity to attract, bypassing the faculty of reason (*why* should we be attracted to this?) on account of the intrinsic loveliness of the beautiful. He recalled the questions he used to ask himself, constantly searching for the key to the meaning of beauty, which elicited so significant a response from those who behold it:

> Now do we love anything, unless it is beautiful? So what, then, is beautiful? What is beauty? What is it that allures us and delights us in those things that we love? Unless there were grace and elegance in them, they could not possibly draw us to themselves.[80]

The apologetic importance of Augustine's comments will be obvious. If God, Jesus Christ, or the ideas of the gospel can be considered to be "beautiful," they will possess an intrinsic capacity to attract, in advance of any appeal that they might make to the human intellect.

The recognition of the beauty of nature is a common insight of humanity;[81] it is not an insight or judgment that is limited or restricted to the Christian faith.[82] Indeed, there is ample evidence of a renewed interest in beauty within culture at large, and particularly within philosophical circles, since about 1980. Mary Mothersill's reaffirmation of the

---

[79] Jean-Louis Chrétien, *The Call and the Response*, New York: Fordham University Press, 2004, p. 7. See also his earlier comment: "Things and forms do not beckon us because they are beautiful in themselves, for their own sake, as it were. Rather, we call them beautiful precisely because they call us and recall us" (p. 3).

[80] Augustine, *Confessiones*, IV.xiii.20.

[81] Carroll, "On Being Moved by Nature."

[82] Contrary to Richard Dawkins, it may also be pointed out that Christian faith does not diminish, but augments, the aesthetic appreciation of nature. For Dawkins' unsubstantiated, but influential, assertions, see Richard Dawkins, *Unweaving the Rainbow: Science, Delusion and the Appetite for Wonder*, London: Penguin Books, 1998. For some apposite comments on the role of the sciences on the perception of beauty, see Holmes Rolston, "Does Aesthetic Appreciation of Landscapes Need to be Science-Based?" *British Journal of Aesthetics* 33 (1995): 374–86.

importance of the concept of beauty, which she defines as "a disposition to produce pleasure in virtue of aesthetic properties,"[83] generated considerable discussion. And, just as perceptions of the ordering or rationality of nature, which are similarly not limited to Christianity, may act as a conduit to belief in God as the origin and consummator of such orderedness, so the recognition of beauty can equally provide the basis of an informed Christian apologetic.[84] So how?

In his Leslie Stephen Memorial Lecture at the University of Cambridge in November 1985, Georg Steiner pointed out how a natural theology, grounded in a Christian doctrine of creation, provided the basis of a meta-traditional appeal to beauty: "there is aesthetic creation because there is *creation*."[85] A similar point is made by Robert Jenson in exploring the way in which Jonathan Edwards finds a close correlation, if not outright identity, between God's holiness and beauty, with highly significant implications for Edwards' encounter with (and reading of) the "book of nature."[86]

Edwards' vision of God focuses on the beauty of God on the one hand, and God's desire to be known on the other.[87] God is distinguished from all other things by divine beauty; yet God is not content with self-absorption or self-contemplation. Emphasizing the role of Christ as *logos* in creation, Edwards agues that the world mirrors the divine beauty.

When we are delighted with flowery meadows and gentle breezes of wind, we may consider that we only see the emanations of the sweet benevolence of Jesus Christ; when we behold the fragrant rose and lily, we see his love and purity. So the green trees and fields, and singing of birds, are emanations of his infinite joy and benignity; the easiness and naturalness of trees

---

[83] Mary Mothersill, *Beauty Restored*, Oxford: Clarendon Press, 1984, p. 349.

[84] See the important discussion of "beauty as a way to God" in Viladesau, *Theological Aesthetics*, pp. 103–40.

[85] George Steiner, *Real Presences: Is There Anything in What We Say?* London: Faber, 1991, p. 67. See also Jeremy S. Begbie, *Voicing Creation's Praise: Towards a Theology of the Arts*, Edinburgh: T&T Clark, 1991, pp. 224–8.

[86] Robert W. Jenson, *America's Theologian: A Recommendation of Jonathan Edwards*, New York: Oxford University Press, 1988, pp. 15–18.

[87] Beldan C. Lane, "Jonathan Edwards on Beauty, Desire and the Sensory World," *Theological Studies* 65 (2004): 44–68.

and vines are shadows of his infinite beauty and loveliness; the crystal rivers and murmuring streams have the footsteps of his sweet grace and bounty.[88]

God desires the divine beauty to be known and enjoyed by God's creatures, and thus chooses to communicate that beauty through the creation, that all might see, acknowledge, and respond to it.[89] Nature is *meant* to disclose the beauty of God, functioning as a school of desire in which humanity may learn how to perceive God's glory, and respond in faith and awe.

So what are the apologetic implications of Edwards' emphasis on the beauty of God? For Edwards, rational argument has a valuable and important place in Christian apologetics. But it is certainly not the sole, and perhaps not even the chief, resource of the apologist. The real resource is an apprehension of divine glory, which arises through a perception of the beauty of God:

> Though great use may be made of external arguments, they are not to be neglected, but highly prized and valued; for they may be greatly serviceable to awaken unbelievers, and bring them to serious consideration, and to confirm the faith of true saints; yea, they may be in some respect subservient to the begetting of a saving faith in men. Though what was said before remains true, that there is no spiritual conviction of the judgment, but what arises from an apprehension of the spiritual beauty and glory of divine things.[90]

Edwards' argument is significant, and merits close consideration. The heart of his analysis is that *rational arguments* do not convert. They may remove obstacles to conversion, but in themselves and of themselves they do not possess the capacity to transform humanity. Instead, we must aim to convey or bring about "an apprehension of the spiritual beauty and glory of divine things." Divine revelation is about capturing the human

---

[88] Jonathan Edwards, *The Miscellanies*, New Haven, CT: Yale University Press, 1994, p. 279.

[89] Avihu Zakai, "Jonathan Edwards and the Language of Nature: The Re-Enchantment of the World in the Age of Scientific Reasoning," *Journal of Religious History* 26 (2002): 15–41.

[90] Jonathan Edwards, *Treatise on the Religious Affections*, New Haven, CT: Yale University Press, 1959, p. 307.

imagination with glimpses of glory, not simply persuading the mind with impressions of rationality.[91] Edwards' appeal to the beauty of nature *as an apologetic strategy* has much to commend it.

But need such a strategy be limited to the natural world? What about human culture, and the attempts to create – not merely observe – beauty? It is one of the more significant achievements of Hans Urs von Balthasar to have demonstrated that such an approach can be extended far beyond an encounter with the purely natural world to embrace the world of human culture, focused on the notion of "beauty."[92] As Richard Viladesau has rightly pointed out, the capacity of both art and music to point to, or create a longing for, the transcendent can both be given a rigorous theological foundation, and found an appropriate apologetic application.[93] The beauty of the world cannot be finally satisfying in itself, but calls for completion in some deeper manner and mode.

This theme is found in the writings of John Henry Newman. In one of his greatest university sermons, Newman pointed to the capacity of music to signify beauty, and intensify the human longing for an encounter with the true source of the traces of the beauty observed within the world. Why is music, supposedly a human creation, capable of evoking such a response, unless it has a deeper, more fundamental, connection with the order of things?

> Can it be that those mysterious stirrings of heart, and keen emotions, and strange yearnings after we know not what, and awful impressions from we know not whence, should be wrought in us by what is unsubstantial, and comes and goes, and begins and ends in itself? It is not so; it cannot be. No; they have escaped from some higher sphere; they are the outpourings of eternal harmony in the medium of created sound; they are echoes from our Home; they are the voice of Angels, or the Magnificat of Saints, or the living laws of Divine Governance, or the Divine Attributes; something are

---

[91] See Alister E. McGrath, "Towards the Restatement and Renewal of a Natural Theology: A Dialogue with the Classic English Tradition," in Alister McGrath (ed.), *The Order of Things: Explorations in Scientific Theology*, pp. 63–96, Oxford: Blackwell Publishing, 2006, especially p. 95.

[92] For an analysis, see Noel O'Donaghue, "A Theology of Beauty," in John Riches (ed.), *The Analogy of Beauty: The Theology of Hans Urs von Balthasar*, pp. 1–10, Edinburgh: T&T Clark, 1986.

[93] Viladesau, *Theological Aesthetics*, pp. 148–77. See also the earlier discussion at pp. 103–40.

they besides themselves, which we cannot compass, which we cannot utter, though mortal man, and he perhaps not otherwise distinguished above his fellows, has the gift of eliciting them.[94]

Perhaps the most significant apologetic strategy based on the human quest for beauty – irrespective of whether that beauty is sought in nature or culture – is due to C. S. Lewis. Even Lewis's earlier writings show an interest in the concept of beauty, and its capacity to lead towards – or away from – God (a theme encountered in *The Pilgrim's Regress*). One of his later writings, *Till We Have Faces: A Myth Retold*, also shows a preoccupation with beauty,[95] particularly its corruption and possible renewal.

The human quest for beauty is, for Lewis, an important point of contact for the Christian gospel, and it is a central theme of arguably his most important shorter work – the 1941 sermon "The Weight of Glory."[96] Like Baudelaire, Lewis argues that we possess an instinct of transcendence, stimulated by beauty – a "desire for our own far-off country, which we find in ourselves even now."[97] For Lewis, beauty evokes an ideal that is more real than anything we encounter in this transitory world, evoking a sense of longing for a half-remembered realm from which we are presently exiled. It is a desire "for something that has never actually appeared in our experience,"[98] yet which is constantly suggested and intimated by what we do experience. Lewis suggests that we tend to use a highly expedient way of dealing with this desire: we call it "beauty," and believe

---

[94] John Henry Newman, *Fifteen Sermons Preached Before the University of Oxford*, London: Longmans, Green, & Co., 1909, pp. 346–7.

[95] For the basic outline of the novel, see Clyde S. Kilby, "*Till We Have Faces*: An Interpretation," in Peter J. Schakel (ed.), *The Longing for a Form: Essays on the Fiction of C. S. Lewis*, pp. 171–81, Kent, OH: Kent State University Press, 1977. Kilby does not sufficiently appreciate the importance of beauty to the narrative. For more reflective approaches, see Peter J. Schakel, *Reason and Imagination in C. S. Lewis: A Study of Till We Have Faces*, Grand Rapids, MI: Eerdmans, 1984; and especially Carla A. Arnell, "On Beauty, Justice and the Sublime in C. S. Lewis's *Till We Have Faces*," *Christianity and Literature* 52 (2002): 23–34.

[96] C. S. Lewis, "The Weight of Glory," in *Screwtape Proposes a Toast, and Other Pieces*, pp. 94–110, London: Fontana, 1965.

[97] Ibid., p. 97.

[98] Ibid.

that by naming it, we have tamed it. Categorization of the experience is the easiest way of neutralizing its potency.

But the experience does not, will not, go away. The "quest for beauty" is actually a quest for the *source* of that beauty, which is mediated through the things of this world, not contained within them. "The books or the music in which we thought the beauty was located will betray us if we trust to them; it was not *in* them, it only came *through* them, and what came through them was longing."[99] For Lewis, the desire, the sense of longing, remains with us, "still wandering and uncertain of its object."[100]

At this point, Lewis then shows how a natural theology can be deployed in an apologetic manner, focusing on the sense of longing evoked by beauty. Recognizing beauty, we follow it – and find ourselves astonished and dismayed when that quest ends in frustration or despair. "Beauty has smiled, but not to welcome us."[101] We catch a glimpse of that "indescribable something" of which beauty is the messenger, presently believing it to be the message itself – yet re-evaluating this perception, as its failure to deliver what we believed it to promise suggests that there is another interpretation.

So the truth dawns upon us. The "authoritative imagery" of the Christian tradition addresses the longing that we *know*, that we *experience*, while promising to reveal what presently lies concealed – "what we do not yet know and need to know."[102] What Christianity offers is able to satisfy the original desire, while at the same time revealing an element in that desire which had, until that point, remained unnoticed.[103] This desire turns out to be the "truest index of our real situation." It is to be understood as "our longing to be reunited with something in the universe from which we now feel cut off, to be on the inside of some door which we have always seen from the outside."[104] The desire is a summons "to pass in through Nature, beyond her, into that splendour which she fitfully reflects."[105] Nature turns out to be "the first sketch," "only the image, the symbol,"[106] of that greater reality to which it points.

---

[99] C. S. Lewis, "The Weight of Glory," p. 98.
[100] Ibid., p. 99.
[101] Ibid., p. 105.
[102] Ibid., p. 100.
[103] Ibid., pp. 104–5.
[104] Ibid., p. 106.
[105] Ibid., p. 108.
[106] Ibid., pp. 107–8.

The trajectory of Lewis's approach is thus clear, as is its grounding in the Augustinian distinction between the *usus* and *fruitio* of a sign. The issue is primarily that of discernment, in which we are called upon to grasp the true meaning of this wandering, indescribable sense of longing as "the scent of a flower we have not found."[107] Though a "good image of what we really desire," we mistake it for the "thing itself." Beauty reveals truth by pointing to a realm beyond the visible world of particulars. It allows us to see beyond a door that is presently closed, to anticipate opening it and crossing its threshold: "We cannot mingle with the splendours we see. But all the leaves of the New Testament are rustling with the rumour that it will not always be so. Some day, God willing, we shall get *in*."[108]

"Consider the lilies of the field" (Matthew 6: 28). Those lilies are part of an ephemeral order, whose beauty will ultimately fade. Yet the approach to natural theology that we have set out in this volume allows that transitory moment of beauty to be preserved and appreciated, and its deeper significance grasped. But there is more to beauty than the appreciation of nature, and an anticipation of entering into a fuller experience of what is presently known only in part. In his *Critique of Judgement* (1790) Immanuel Kant suggested that beauty can be regarded as a symbol of the good, opening up the question of the relationship between them.

More recently, the philosopher Elaine Scarry, while insisting upon the importance of beauty, sees its pursuit as demanding a "constant perceptual acuity" that sharpens our attentiveness towards the world.[109] The perception of beauty brings about a "quality of heightened attention" that demands and permits a more committed, thoughtful, and principled engagement with the world.

---

[107] Ibid., p. 98.

[108] Ibid., p. 107.

[109] Elaine Scarry, *On Beauty and Being Just*, Princeton, NJ: Princeton University Press, 1999, p. 62. Scarry argues for a link between perception of beauty and the pursuit of justice (pp. 91–5). Furthermore, she suggests that beauty "decenters" the self, thus acting as an important corrective to the individual's narcissistic tendency to see oneself as the center of all things (pp. 111–13). Scarry's thesis is highly controversial, with some significant weak points – see, e.g., the critical and insightful assessment in Denis Dutton, "Mad about Flowers: Elaine Scarry on Beauty," *Philosophy and Literature* 24 (2000): 249–60.

It is as though beautiful things have been placed here and there throughout the world to serve as small wake-up calls to perception, spurring lapsed alertness back to its most acute level. Through its beauty, the world continually recommits us to a rigorous standard of perceptual care: if we do not search it out, it comes and finds us.[110]

When we behold the beautiful, we learn to be attentive to the world; and when we are attentive to the world, we notice injustice. As Scarry observes, this leads to the recognition of a link between beauty and justice – and thus naturally leads us to consider the place of goodness in a natural theology.

---

[110] Scarry, *On Beauty and Being Just*, p. 81.

CHAPTER 12

Natural Theology and Goodness

Humanity tries to make sense of the world, partly through a quest for a rational explanation of what may be observed, and partly through a search for significance, value, and meaning. Although these two quests are clearly related, they are not the same. Our understanding of the meaning of life has a profound influence on fundamental questions of existence, both ethical and spiritual. In this final chapter to deal with the Platonic triad of truth, beauty, and goodness, we shall use the category of "goodness" to explore the enactive aspects of natural theology. What difference does seeing the natural world, including ourselves, from within the perspective of the Christian faith make to our attitudes and actions?

A central theme of this work has been the need to see things as they really are. This extends beyond our desire to make rational sense of things and to appreciate them properly at the aesthetic level, embracing the essentially ethical question of how right action within the world depends upon rightly seeing that world in the first place. This point underlies Iris Murdoch's insistence, noted earlier (pp. 46–9), upon the permanent place of metaphysics, especially the notion of the transcendent, in any sustainable account of morality. Morality depends upon an acquired capacity to see things as they really are. (Indeed, one could make the related point that divine judgment can be understood as our being forced to see ourselves as we actually are, all illusions and pretences having finally been exposed and removed.) The way in which we "see" the world shapes the moral vision that informs how we act within the world. In what follows, we shall explore this point in greater detail.

The Moral Vision of Reality

Goodness, Murdoch argued, is inextricably connected with knowledge of reality – not an impersonal "quasi-scientific" account of the world, but a deeper knowledge of the reality that we inhabit.[1] "As moral beings," Murdoch points out, "we are immersed in a reality which transcends us." The foundation of morality is a capacity to see this reality as it really is, so that "moral progress consists in awareness of this reality and submission to its purposes."[2] This point underlies a natural theology of goodness, which is seen to rest on discerning and acting upon a specific way of "seeing" the world.

For many writers, the concept of "goodness" is of critical importance to any account of human identity, or the basis of social existence. As Charles Taylor argued in his *Sources of the Self*, "selfhood and good, or in another way selfhood and morality, turn out to be inextricably intertwined themes."[3] And however the question of the nature and function of "goodness" is configured, an engagement with nature is inevitable, precisely because humanity exists within nature, possessing natural characteristics – even if these are to be transcended and overcome.[4]

For this reason, Terry Eagleton rightly points out that the universal basis of morality does not lie in some fictional "universal rationality," but in the universal biological nature of humanity, no matter how much this may be shaped by cultural constraints.[5] While Eagleton's analysis is not

---

[1] Iris Murdoch, *The Sovereignty of Good*, London: Routledge, 1970, p. 37.

[2] Iris Murdoch, "Vision and Choice in Morality," *Proceedings of the Aristotelian Society*, supplementary vol. 30 (1956): 32–58; quote at p. 56. For comment, see Lawrence Blum, "Iris Murdoch and the Domain of the Moral," *Philosophical Studies* 50 (1986): 343–67. On the general issue, see Michael DePaul, "Argument and Perception," *Journal of Philosophy* 85 (1988): 552–65.

[3] Charles Taylor, *Sources of the Self: The Making of the Modern Identity*, Cambridge, UK: Cambridge University Press, 1989, p. 3.

[4] One of the best recent discussions of these issues is to be found in Robert Merrihew Adams, *Finite and Infinite Goods: A Framework for Ethics*, New York: Oxford University Press, 2002.

[5] Terry Eagleton, *After Theory*, London: Allen Lane, 2003, pp. 115–16. The argument of Marc Hauser, to the effect that human evolution has created a universal moral grammar within our brains that enables us to make rapid decisions about ethical dilemmas, should also be noted here: Marc D. Hauser, *Moral Minds: How Nature Designed Our Universal Sense of Right and Wrong*, New York: Ecco, 2006.

without its difficulties, it indicates unequivocally the need to locate goodness within any account of natural theology. The notions of truth, beauty, and goodness are simply too tightly bound together to allow them to be disconnected, in theory or practice.[6]

Traditionally, any attempt to discern morality within the natural order has been categorized as "natural law." Although subject to all kinds of theoretical and practical criticisms, the notion that nature might be able to disclose an ethic independent of human *fiat* has proved remarkably resilient, for reasons we shall note later. Yet one of its most significant weaknesses is that it is ultimately dependent upon a theory of nature which nature itself cannot supply. What is "natural"?[7] How is this human perception of what is "natural" shaped by historical, cultural, and psychological factors?[8]

A Christian natural theology appeals to an understanding of the economy of salvation which allows the foundations to be laid for a concept of natural law.[9] A viable natural theology of goodness is determined and undergirded by a Christian understanding of nature. For this reason, a natural theology of goodness – in common with its counterparts of truth and beauty – is shaped by the contours of the Christian theological tradition.[10]

So what aspects of the Christian vision of nature are of importance to such a natural theology of goodness? A fundamental theme of a Christian doctrine of creation is that the world is *ordered*. This ordering is not limited to the physical structures of the world, capable of being analyzed

---

[6] See the important argument of Elaine Scarry, *On Beauty and Being Just*, Princeton, NJ: Princeton University Press, 1999, pp. 1–53.

[7] Yves R. Simon, *The Tradition of Natural Law: A Philosopher's Reflections*, New York: Fordham University Press, 1992, pp. 41–54. Note especially Simon's comments (pp. 53–4) on the distinction between "native" and "natural," found in the writings of Louis de Bonald (1754–1840).

[8] See the discussion of Philip E. Devine, *Natural Law Ethics*, Westport, CT: Greenwood, 2000, pp. 49–65.

[9] Similar ideas are found in the important study of Jean Porter, *Natural and Divine Law: Reclaiming the Tradition for Christian Ethics*, Grand Rapids, MI: Eerdmans, 1999, who stresses that Scripture itself provides the means for determining which concept of nature is to be considered as normative.

[10] Rufus Black, *Christian Moral Realism: Natural Law, Narrative, Virtue, and the Gospel*, Oxford: Oxford University Press, 2000.

and represented by the natural sciences,[11] in that the notion of the "ordering of reality" clearly possesses both aesthetic and moral dimensions. As medieval theologians regularly pointed out, beauty was partly defined in terms of symmetry and proportionality.[12] Similarly, the concept of ordering has strong moral and legal overtones. Has the world been created with certain norms – a "natural law" – built into its very fabric? This brings us to the intensely controversial question of natural law, which is an integral element of our vision for a renewed natural theology.

Natural Theology and Natural Law

The notion of "natural law" has captivated the imagination of humanity since the dawn of civilization. An integral aspect of pre-Socratic philosophy was the notion that the world embodied certain values, which the wise could identify and use as the basis for living out the good life. The Sophists, for example, tended to treat nature (*physis*) as the ultimate basis of morality, as opposed to human convention (*homologia* or *symbola*). Similarly, Aristotle makes an appeal to the order of nature in determining what forms of human laws and constitutions are to be followed.[13]

The Old Testament shows particular interest in this idea, with the notion of "conformity to a norm" playing a highly significant role in Israel's reflections on the nature of righteousness (Hebrew: *sdq*).[14] The

---

[11] For the immense importance of this idea, especially in relation to the rise of the natural sciences in a Christian context, see Francis Oakley, *Omnipotence, Covenant and Order: An Excursion in the History of Ideas from Abelard to Leibniz*, Ithaca, NY: Cornell University Press, 1984; Thomas F. Torrance, *The Christian Frame of Mind: Reason, Order, and Openness in Theology and Natural Science*, 2nd edn, Colorado Springs: Helmers & Howard, 1989; Seyyed Hossein Nasr, *Religion and the Order of Nature*, Oxford: Oxford University Press, 1996.

[12] Umberto Eco, *Art and Beauty in the Middle Ages*, New Haven, CT: Yale University Press, 2002, pp. 28–42.

[13] Fred D. Miller, *Nature, Justice and Rights in Aristotle's Politics*, Oxford: Clarendon Press, 1995, pp. 27–66.

[14] See, e.g., Otto Kaiser, "Dike und Sedaqa. Zur Frage nach der sittlichen Weltordnung. Ein theologische Präludium," *Neue Zeitschrift für systematische Theologie und Religionsphilosophie* 7 (1965): 251–75; Heinrich H. Schmid, *Gerechtigkeit als Weltordnung. Hintergrund und Geschichte des alttestamentlichen Gerechtigkeitsbegriffes*, Tübingen: Mohr, 1968.

world is understood to be ordered in a certain way as a result of its divine creation; to act "rightly" is thus to act in accordance with this patterning of structures and events. Emphasis has often been placed on the idea that the divine act of creation involves the imposition of order upon chaos; such ideas can be found throughout the wisdom literature of the ancient Near East.[15] The "ordering of the world," established by God in creation, acts as a theological bridge between natural righteousness and the "righteousness of the law."[16]

The idea that human morality might ultimately be grounded in something built into the fabric of the universe itself has obstinately refused to die out. It possesses a certain intuitive plausibility, even if its conceptual clarification has proved to be immensely difficult. Anselm of Canterbury, for example, saw a fundamental relationship between truth and justice: both, he argued, were grounded in the fundamental notion of rectitude, which was itself grounded in the divinely ordained structures of reality.[17] On this reading, truth could be regarded as metaphysical rectitude, and justice as volitional rectitude. John Calvin held that, despite sin, the human conscience was able to discern the fundamental structures of natural law. "The law of God," he wrote, "is nothing else than that natural law and that conscience which God has engraved within the human mind."[18] The role of natural law in shaping the Christian ethics of the

---

[15] See Heinrich H. Schmid, "Jahweglaube und altorientalisches Weltordnungsgedanken," in *Altorientalische Welt in der alttestamentlichen Theologie*, pp. 31–63, Zurich: Theologischer Verlag, 1974; Stefan M. Maul, "Der assyrische König: Hüter der Weltordnung," in Kazuko Watanabe (ed.), *Priests and Officials in the Ancient Near East*, pp. 201–14. Heidelberg: Universitätsverlag C. Winter, 1999; Michaela Bauks, " 'Chaos' als Metapher für die Gefärdung der Weltordnung," in Bernd Janowski, Beate Ego, and Annette Krüger (eds), *Das biblische Weltbild und seine altorientalischen Kontexte*, pp. 431–64. Tübingen: Mohr Siebeck, 2001.

[16] An important issue explored in David Novak, *Natural Law in Judaism*, Cambridge, UK: Cambridge University Press, 1998.

[17] Gottlieb Söhngen, "Rectitudo bei Anselm von Canterbury als Oberbegriff von Wahrheit und Gerechtigkeit," in H. Kohlenberger (ed.), *Sola Ratione*, pp. 71–7, Stuttgart: Friedrich Frommann Verlag, 1970.

[18] Calvin, *Institutes*, IV.xx.16. For detailed discussion of this important affirmation of natural law, discerned through the conscience rather than through the reason, see Susan E. Schreiner, "Calvin's Use of Natural Law," in Michael Cromartie (ed.), *A Preserving Grace: Protestants, Catholics, and Natural Law*, pp. 51–76, Grand

Caroline Divines – widely regarded as representing a "Golden Age" of Anglican moral theology – has often been noted.[19]

Yet the concept of natural law was at its most potent when used as a weapon against the exaggerated power of human institutions, and particularly tyrannous monarchs. Francisco Suárez (1548–1617) developed a sophisticated theory of natural law, which he applied to issues of political consent and conformity, the question of just wars, and the right of the people to revolt against unjust political systems.

By the end of the nineteenth century, however, the utility of the notion of natural law was being questioned. In 1897, Oliver Wendell Holmes argued that the real issue was to understand how the courts administered law; there was nothing to be gained from philosophical or metaphysical speculation of any kind. Law could be defined rather neatly as "the prediction of what the courts will do." In 1918, he went further. In his essay "Natural Law," he argued that those jurists who "believe in natural law" existed in a rather "naïve state of mind that accepts what has been familiar and accepted by them and their neighbors as something that must be accepted by all men everywhere."[20] Holmes's views were typical of his age. Natural law was to be regarded as an outmoded intellectual abstraction from an outdated, static notion of nature, called into question by Darwin's theory of evolution. No longer could nature be seen as a permanent entity, embodying values; rather, it was in a state of flux, within

Rapids, MI: Eerdmans, 1997. Older studies remain valuable: see, e.g., Gunter Gloede, *Theologia naturalis bei Calvin*, Stuttgart: Kohlhammer, 1935, pp. 103–34; Jürgen Baur, *Gott, Recht und weltliches Regiment im Werke Calvins*, Bonn: Bouvier, 1965, pp. 46–9.

[19] See especially Iain M. MacKenzie, *God's Order and Natural Law: The Works of the Laudian Divines*, Aldershot: Ashgate, 2002. Nevertheless, the period also witnessed increasing secularization of the notion in England: Linda Kirk, *Richard Cumberland and Natural Law: Secularisation of Thought in Seventeenth-Century England*, Cambridge. UK: James Clarke & Co., 1987. For the wider picture of the fortunes of natural law in the early Enlightenment, see T. J. Hochstrasser, *Natural Law Theories in the Early Enlightenment*, Cambridge, UK: Cambridge University Press, 2000, pp. 1–37.

[20] Oliver Wendell Holmes, *Collected Legal Papers*, New York: Harcourt, Brace, and Howe, 1920, p. 312.

which humanity was free to make its own creative (and fundamentally pragmatic) adjustments.[21]

Yet the rise of Nazism in Germany changed all of this – partly by demonstrating the need for a ground of moral judgment that lay beyond arbitrary human convention, and partly by forcing many leading German legal theorists to leave Germany, and settle elsewhere, above all in the United States of America, where they helped forge new approaches to traditional questions. With these developments, a new interest in natural law emerged, which is still a living force today. We shall consider this development in what follows.

The Eternal Return of Natural Law

In 1933, the Nazis seized power in Germany, and promptly set about using the law to impose totalitarian rule. The story of how this happened is of enormous interest, demonstrating how laws established for an essentially democratic purpose could be subverted to other ends, given the necessary political will.[22] As Ernst Wolf remarks in his study of German Protestant attitudes towards these developments, the traditional Protestant notion that law was somehow grounded in objective realities of the world or in social consensus was utterly incapable of responding to the arbitrary enforcement of power by the Third Reich.[23] What could be done? What intellectual opposition could be offered to these developments? Those positivists who defined justice in terms of predicting the judgments of the courts found themselves unable to challenge their legality, precisely because they had lost interest in the moral foundations and goals of positive law.

---

[21] For the development of such criticisms, see Pauline Westerman, *The Disintegration of Natural Law Theory: Aquinas to Finnis*, Leiden: Brill, 1998.

[22] For an outstanding analysis of the issues, see Peter L. Lindseth, "The Paradox of Parliamentary Supremacy: Delegation, Democracy, and Dictatorship in Germany and France, 1920s–1950s," *Yale Law Journal* 113 (2004): 1341–1417.

[23] Ernst Wolf, "Zum protestantischen Rechtsdenken," in *Peregrinatio II: Studien zur reformatorischen Theologie, zum Kirchenrecht, und zur Sozialethik*, pp. 191–206, Munich: Kaiser Verlag, 1965.

In 1936, a professional lawyer published a criticism of this trend. Heinrich Rommen (1897–1967) published *Die ewige Wiederkehr des Naturrechts* ("The eternal return of natural law").[24] Rommen, who had been imprisoned briefly by the Nazis for his work with a Roman Catholic social action group, pointed out that Germany's modern dictators were "masters of legality," able to use the legal and judicial systems to pursue their own political agendas. Germany's legal professionals, he argued, were so used to thinking about law in purely positivist terms that they were left intellectually defenseless in the face of the National Socialist threat. In this dire situation, one needed to appeal to a higher authority than the state. Natural law offered precisely the intellectual lifeline that was so badly needed.

It may, not unreasonably, be pointed out that Nazi Germany represents a somewhat extreme situation, which cannot be used to justify the renewal of what, to its critics, is an essentially outmoded theory of law. While there is merit in this observation, the situation in Germany at this time merely highlights an issue which cannot be ignored – namely, whether there are transcendent grounds for concepts of justice and due process, which are not merely the product of human convention. Nor is the relevance of the Nazi situation limited to legal developments of the 1930s; related issues emerged when the Allies sought retribution for those events in the postwar era. The desire to prosecute war criminals at Nuremberg for "crimes against humanity" gave rise to a new interest in natural law. As Anthony Lisska points out, if the notion of crimes against humanity was to have a theoretical foundation, it required a "radically different account of the nature of law from that proposed by the then reigning theory, legal positivism."[25]

Yet the disturbing questions raised by the rise of the Third Reich and its aftermath have not gone away. They are raised again by a "pragmatic" approach to morality, such as that associated with Richard Rorty. On this reading of things, humanity creates its own values and ideas, and is not accountable to any external objectivity (natural law) or internal subjectivity (conscience) for the outcome of this creative process. "We figure out what practices to adopt first, and then expect our philosophers

---

[24] Heinrich Rommen, *Die ewige Wiederkehr des Naturrechts*, Leipzig: Hegner, 1936.

[25] Anthony J. Lisska, *Aquinas's Theory of Natural Law: An Analytic Reconstruction*, Oxford: Clarendon Press, 1996, pp. 8–9.

to adjust the definition of 'human' or 'rational' to suit."[26] Rorty argues that a consequence of this communitarian or pragmatic approach to truth must be the recognition that

> ... there is nothing deep down inside us except what we have put there ourselves, no criterion that we have not created in the course of creating a practice, no standard of rationality that is not an appeal to such a criterion, no rigorous argumentation that is not obedience to our own conventions.[27]

Truth and morality are thus matters of social convention, created by human communities. Yet if Rorty is right, what justification could be given for opposing Nazism? Rorty finds himself unable to offer a persuasive justification for the moral or political rejection of totalitarianism. If this is indeed the case, Rorty admits, then it has to be acknowledged that:

> When the secret police come, when the torturers violate the innocent, there is nothing to be said to them of the form "There is something within you which you are betraying. Though you embody the practices of a totalitarian society, which will endure forever, there is something beyond those practices which condemns you."[28]

For Rorty, the truth of moral values depends simply upon their existence and acceptance within society. This view has been severely criticized as adopting an uncritical approach concerning prevailing social conventions. As Richard Bernstein points out, Rorty appears to have done little more than reify social practices, and treat these as being synonymous with "truth," "goodness," or "justice."[29] Or, as Philip Devine notes, Rorty seems incapable of offering a criterion that stands *above* human practice, by which the latter can be judged.[30]

---

[26] Richard Rorty, *Contingency, Irony and Solidarity*, Cambridge. UK: Cambridge University Press, 1989, 194–5, n. 6.

[27] Richard Rorty, *The Consequences of Pragmatism*, Minneapolis, MN: University of Minneapolis Press, 1982, p. xlii.

[28] Ibid.

[29] Richard J. Bernstein, *Philosophical Profiles: Essays in a Pragmatic Mode*, Philadelphia: University of Pennsylvania Press, 1986, pp. 53–4.

[30] Philip E. Devine, *Natural Law Ethics*, Westport, CT: Greenwood, 2000, pp. 32–4.

Natural law faces a host of intellectual difficulties, which at times seem overwhelming.[31] Yet Rommen's arguments suggest that it will never cease to appeal to the human imagination, above all in situations of manifest legal corruption, political violence, or cultural manipulation. The idea that there exist standards of justice and goodness which are above those determined, and often invented, by human beings and human institutions represents far more than "metaphysical comfort" (Nietzsche): it constitutes the basis for criticism and reform of otherwise potentially arbitrary or self-serving notions of "the good."

So can those values be identified by direct observation of nature? Although some such vision has always been perceived as attractive, it encounters considerable difficulties, as we shall see in the next section.

The Moral Ambivalence of Nature

The casual reader of William Paley's *Natural Theology* encounters a paean of praise for the goodness of the natural order, deftly – though somewhat selectively – illustrated by luminous examples of the wisdom of God in establishing such an excellent creation. The darker side of nature is conspicuously absent. To be fair to Paley, this was the wisdom of his age. Many writers of the late eighteenth and early nineteenth century were enthralled by the notion of the moral purity of nature, and hailed its potential to instruct and inspire.[32] The discovery of Tahiti had a profound influence on this debate, with the islands of the South Pacific being widely depicted as a naturalist paradise, perhaps reflecting a golden age in the history of humanity which could be recovered even in an increasingly industrialized England.[33]

---

[31]   For example, consider the intractable question, much debated among contemporary Thomists, as to whether we apprehend the human good by theoretical or practical reason. On this debate, see Patrick Lee, "Is Thomas's Natural Law Theory Naturalist?" *American Catholic Philosophical Quarterly* 71 (1997): 567–87.

[32]   Niels Bugge Hansen, *That Pleasant Place: The Representation of Ideal Landscape in English Literature from the 14th to the 17th Century*, Copenhagen: Akademisk Forlag, 1973.

[33]   Bernard Smith, *European Vision and the South Pacific, 1768–1850*, London: Oxford University Press, 1960.

Yet the darker side of nature could not be ignored. Where Wordsworth and other Romantics saw nature as a moral educator, Tennyson argued that the only ethic evident within nature was that of the struggle for survival. The familiar lines from Canto 5 of his *In Memoriam* make this point powerfully:

> Man . . .
> Who trusted God was love indeed
> And love Creation's final law –
> Though Nature, red in tooth and claw
> With ravine, shrieked against his creed.[34]

Tennyson's point was simple: those who spoke naively and sentimentally of God's love being expressed in nature had to offer a convincing explanation of its vicious cycles of violence, pain, and suffering. The so-called "naturalist" tradition in modern American fiction also reflects this recognition of a deep moral ambivalence within nature itself; nature is represented as a destructive, mechanistic Darwinian world within which it was assumed that most modern Americans struggled to prosper and survive.[34]

The changing views of John Ruskin on the beauty and moral goodness of nature are an especially important testimony to this growing awareness of the moral ambiguity of nature.[35] In the 10 years intervening between the publication of the second volume of his *Modern Painters* (1846) and the third (1856), Ruskin began to be troubled by the darker side of nature. In his earlier period, he expressed a Wordsworthian optimism towards nature, quoting the famous lines from *Tintern Abbey*: "Nature never did betray/The heart that loved her." Yet as he looked at nature, Ruskin began to see different things. Where once he had seen glory, now he saw gloom – a presaging of the dark, pessimistic, brooding, tone of his *Storm-Cloud of the Nineteenth Century*. The "great cathedrals of the earth" have become a wasteland, a symbol of doubt and metaphysical terror. As John Rosenberg points out, it is clear that a major shift has taken place in how nature was "seen":

---

[34] V. L. Partington, *The Beginnings of Critical Realism in America*, New York: Harcourt, Brace, 1930, p. 327.

[35] The best account of this is found in John D. Rosenberg, *The Darkening Glass: A Portrait of Ruskin's Genius*, New York: Columbia University Press, 1986, pp. 22–45.

The tone of the first two volumes is pious and lyrical; that of the later volumes is humanistic and tragic. In *Modern Painters* I and II, Ruskin looked at the peaks of mountains and saw God; in *Modern Painters* III, IV, and V he looks at their bases and sees shattered rocks and impoverished villages. The face of the Creator withdraws from the creation, and in its place man emerges as a tragic figure in the foreground of a still potent, but flawed, nature.[36]

Ruskin's concerns cannot be dismissed at this point. His own changing attitude to the natural order merely reinforces the importance of his own emphasis on the importance of "seeing" nature – a nature which turns out to be highly ambiguous, open to multiple interpretations. This is evident in the final volume of his *Modern Painters*, in which Ruskin mounts a deft yet decisive criticism of Paley's natural theology – perhaps one of the most powerful ever to have been penned. Ruskin invites his readers to reflect on the goodness of God, as seen from a landscape in the Scottish highlands:

It is a little valley of soft turf, enclosed in its narrow oval by jutting rocks and broad flakes of nodding fern. From one side of it to the other winds, serpentine, a clear brown stream, drooping into quicker ripple as it reaches the end of the oval field, and then, first islanding a purple and white rock with an amber pool, it dashes away into a narrow fall of foam under a thicket of mountain-ash and alder. The autumn sun, low but clear, shines on the scarlet ash-berries and on the golden birch-leaves, which, fallen here and there, when the breeze has not caught them, rest quiet in the crannies of the purple rock.

Thus far, Ruskin might be taken to expound a little simplistically, if elegantly, the capacity of nature to witness to God's goodness. Although the style may be Ruskin's, the ideas are Paley's. Yet abruptly, the passage breaks into a more somber reflection on the less attractive aspects of that same rural scene:

Beside the rock, in the hollow under the thicket, the carcase of a ewe, drowned in the last flood, lies nearly bare to the bone, its white ribs protruding through the skin, raven-torn; and the rags of its wool still flickering from the branches that first stayed it as the stream swept it down.[37]

---

[36] Rosenberg, *The Darkening Glass*, p. 22.
[37] John Ruskin, *Works*, ed. E. T. Cook and A. Wedderburn, 39 vols, London: Allen, 1903–12, vol. 7, p. 268.

The dead sheep is a potent symbol of the darker side of nature, the seeming irrationality, ugliness, and wastefulness of life, glossed over by Paley – yet demanding to be accommodated convincingly by any viable natural theology.[38]

The tensions caused by the apparent moral ambivalence of nature was exacerbated by the rise of Darwinism. Darwin himself found the existence of pain and suffering in the world to be an unbearable intellectual and moral burden, particularly in the light of his own protracted (and still unexplained) illness.[39] The death of his daughter Annie at the tender age of 10 unquestionably deepened his feeling of moral outrage over this issue.[40]

In 1961, Donald Fleming put forward the important thesis that Darwin's experience of suffering was an integral element of his own loss of faith. Fleming held that Darwin came to believe that "modern man would rather have senseless suffering than suffering warranted to be intelligible because willed from on high."[41] Pain and suffering were to be accepted as the meaningless outcome of the evolutionary process; this, however disagreeable, seemed preferable to the alternative – namely, that God either inflicted suffering himself, or permitted it to be inflicted by others.

The idea that evolution took place according to certain general principles or laws, with the precise details left to chance, never entirely satisfied Darwin, seeming to leave many intellectual loose ends and open up difficult moral issues – not least, the immense wastage of life attending the process of natural selection. But it seemed to Darwin to be less troubling than the alternative – that "a beneficent and omnipotent God would

---

[38]   The issues raised by the problem of evil for the Victorian era are well summarized by James Moore, "Theodicy and Society: The Crisis of the Intelligentsia," in Richard J. Helmstadter and Bernard Lightman (eds), *Victorian Faith in Crisis: Essays in Continuity and Change in Nineteenth-Century Religious Belief*, pp. 153–86, Basingstoke: Macmillan, 1990.

[39]   For a study of the causes of Darwin's illness, characterized by intermittent "excitement, violent shivering and vomiting attacks," see Ralph E. Colp, *To Be an Invalid: The Illness of Charles Darwin*, Chicago: University of Chicago Press, 1977.

[40]   This has been beautifully documented by Randal Keynes, *Annie's Box: Charles Darwin, His Daughter and Human Evolution*, London: Fourth Estate, 2001.

[41]   Donald Fleming, "Charles Darwin, the Anaesthetic Man," *Victorian Studies* 4 (1961): 219–36.

have designedly created the *Ichneumonidae* with the express intention of their feeding within the living bodies of caterpillars."[42] At least this could be put down to an accident of nature, rather than purposeful divine design.

Responses may, of course, be made to these concerns. John Haught, for example, offers a response to the moral dilemmas emerging from a Darwinian view of life, appealing to a "self-emptying God" who "participates fully in the world's struggle and pain."

> The picture of an incarnate God who suffers along with creation [affirms] that the agony of living beings is not undergone in isolation from the divine eternity, but is taken up everlastingly and redemptively into the very "life-story" of God.[43]

It is a thoroughly incarnational, trinitarian vision of God,[44] which offers Christians a framework by which they may view and even make limited sense of the complex Darwinian picture of an emergent, suffering world.

The eschatological aspects of the Christian tradition also provide at least a modicum of illumination of the situation. As noted earlier (pp. 198–209), the concept of the "economy of salvation" challenges the implicit assumption that we may directly map the empirical world, observed around us, onto the idea of "God's good creation." Nature must be observed through "significance spectacles," which allow us to see the natural world as decayed and ambivalent – not as immoral, but as a morally variegated entity whose goodness is often opaque and hidden, at times overshadowed by darker and less comfortable insights, yet illuminated by the hope of transformation.

---

[42] Letter to Asa Gray (1860): *The Life and Letters of Charles Darwin*, 3 vols, London: John Murray, 1887, vol. 2, pp. 310–12.

[43] John Haught, *God After Darwin: A Theology of Evolution*, Boulder, CO: Westview Press, 2001, pp. 49–50.

[44] Marilyn McCord Adams points out the conceptual richness of such an approach to evil, noting its "pedagogical advantage of displaying the nuance and texture of Christianity's theological resources, as well as exhibiting its explanatory power": Marilyn McCord Adams, *Horrendous Evils and the Goodness of God*, Ithaca, NY: Cornell University Press, 1999, especially pp. 155–202; quote at pp. 205–6.

This theme is perhaps best explored liturgically, rather than theologically or philosophically.[45] The liturgy of Advent weaves together the great themes of Christology, soteriology, and eschatology, by focusing on Christ's double "advent" to deliver the world from its bondage to sin and decay. At Advent the church celebrates Christ's first coming and awaits his second, affirming God's justice and presence in spite of the apparent absence of justice and divine presence in the world. The Old Testament prophets clearly recognized the natural consequences of sin, and looked forward to the Messianic Age as an era of both ecological and social purity. This expectation was subsequently expanded into Christian eschatology, which affirmed that Christ's ministry was marked by signs of his coming victory over natural decay and corruption (Luke 7: 18–23, John 11: 17–27).

At Advent, the church thus looks backward to Christ's earthly ministry, undertaken in this morally ambivalent world, while also looking forward to the full renewal of heaven and earth, to the making of all things new, and to the coming divine presence that will finally bring about the restoration of goodness and the ending of suffering and pain (Revelation 21: 1–5).

Yet the issue here is not so much about the intellectual difficulties raised by the moral ambivalence of nature. It is about how we may "see" nature in a way that expands and enhances our moral vision, enabling us to act correctly both in relation to nature, and within the natural order. Herbert Spencer (1820–1903) elevated alleged biological facts (such as the struggle for existence, natural selection, and the survival of the fittest) to prescriptions for human moral conduct.[46] The outcome was Social Darwinism, now regarded, despite its early popularity, as intellectually indefensible and ethically unacceptable.[47] Spencer believed that nature disclosed the "good" by moving towards it, so that, in a certain sense, it might be said that "evolution is a process which, in itself, generates

---

[45]   For what follows, see the study of Telford Work, "Advent's Answer to the Problem of Evil," *International Journal of Systematic Theology* 2 (2000): 100–11.

[46]   Michael Ruse, *Evolutionary Naturalism*, London: Routledge, 1995, pp. 225–31.

[47]   Peter G. Woolcock, "The Case Against Evolutionary Ethics Today," in Jane Maienschein and Michael Ruse (eds), *Biology and the Foundation of Ethics*, pp. 276–306, Cambridge, UK: Cambridge University Press, 1999.

value."[48] Similarly, Julian Huxley (1887–1975) tried to develop an ethical system based on what he regarded as Darwinian evolution's more progressive aspects.[49] Neither Spencer nor Huxley managed to evade the trap of G. E. Moore's "naturalistic fallacy," which argues that moral values cannot be held to rest upon natural observables.[50]

The point here is that we cannot trace a straight and narrow trajectory, proceeding directly from the present empirical reality that we call "nature" and the ideal that we call "the good," identifying observation of natural patterns and processes with explicit moral values or norms.[51] In order to function as a moral resource, nature therefore needs to be "seen" and interpreted in a certain way, which is disclosed by and enacted within the Christian faith. As we have emphasized, the Christian "sees" nature through a lens which is shaped by the fundamental themes of the Christian faith.

The optimism of earlier thinkers, who believed that nature disclosed patterns of excellence and morality that exceeded any devised by human lawmakers, has now been left behind. The question is no longer "How may we imitate natural patterns?" but "How may we transcend them?" We shall consider this further in the next section.

The Knowability of Goodness in Nature

Earlier, we noted how the idea of a transcendent good plays a significant role in providing stability and authorization for human ethics. Instead of being bound to concepts of justice or goodness that had achieved tem-

---

[48] Ruse, *Evolutionary Naturalism*, p. 231.

[49] See here Paul L. Farber, *The Temptations of Evolutionary Ethics*, Berkeley, CA: University of California Press, 1994, p. 136. Farber comments that Huxley's "ethics was a projection of his values onto the history of man," so that his "naturalism assumed the vision he pretended to discover."

[50] For a more comprehensive discussion, see R. J. McShea and D. W. McShea, "Biology and Value Theory," in Jane Maienschein and Michael Ruse (eds), *Biology and the Foundation of Ethics*, pp. 307–27, Cambridge, UK: Cambridge University Press, 1999.

[51] See, e.g., the approach in Hugh Rice, *God and Goodness*, Oxford: Oxford University Press, 2000, pp. 48–63.

porary cultural predominance, or were being enforced by those in power, an ethic could be articulated which, at least in principle, resonated with the deeper structures of the universe.

This, however, raises the question that has pervaded the present work: how may the natural order be interpreted, in order to disclose the identity of the good? Nature is open to multiple interpretations at the moral, as well as at the intellectual and aesthetic, level.[52] Any attempt to construct or develop a concept of good by the mere observation of nature will yield a perplexingly inconsistent variety of notions. This is especially evident from the ultimately abortive attempts to construct ethics on the basis of Darwinism, in the belief that this somehow represents an authentically natural moral system.[53] Nature can be "read" in ways that appear to endorse such morally questionable notions as oppression, violence, and eugenics.[54]

Yet unless there is an alternative, coherent way of "reading" nature, humanity will simply end up by imitating its patterns. For this reason, it is important to return to a central theme of this work: that the Christian tradition offers a way of seeing nature, which allows its goodness to be discerned. It offers a way of making sense of the apparent moral diversity within nature, by insisting that we view it through the interpretative framework of the economy of salvation. As Oliver O'Donovan argues, if morality is about the human "participation in the created order," then Christian morality is about humanity's "glad response to the deed of God

---

[52] George C. Williams, "Mother Nature Is a Wicked Old Witch!" in Matthew H. Nitecki and Doris V. Nitecki (eds), *Evolutionary Ethics*, pp. 217–31, Albany, NY: State University of New York Press, 1995.

[53] See Farber, *The Temptations of Evolutionary Ethics*, p. 136. Farber comments that Huxley's "ethics was a projection of his values onto the history of man," so that his "naturalism assumed the vision he pretended to discover." For further comment, see Michael Ruse, "Is Rape Wrong on Andromeda?" in *The Darwinian Paradigm: Essays on Its History, Philosophy, and Religious Implications*, pp. 209–46, London: Routledge, 1989.

[54] The emergence of "social Darwinism" is especially significant in this connection: see Robert C. Bannister, *Social Darwinism: Science and Myth in Anglo-American Social Thought*, Philadelphia: Temple University Press, 1979. For the suggestion that such ideas can be found in Darwin himself, see Richard Weikart, "A Recently Discovered Darwin Letter on Social Darwinism," *Isis* 86 (1995): 609–11.

which has restored, proved and fulfilled that order."[55] Yet that process of restoration is ongoing, not complete. Nature is not perfect, but it in the process of being transformed – a transformation which may be discerned by the eye of faith.

The Christian tradition insists that all that is true, beautiful, and good finds its fulfillment in Jesus Christ. O'Donovan rightly points out that the incarnation of the Word is presented as "creation restored and renewed,"[56] thus offering a means of "seeing" nature in a certain moral way. This is not an alien or external way of seeing things, forced upon nature; it is about allowing nature to be viewed and understood from the standpoint of its *Urbild*, "through whom all things were made."

This is a point that will be familiar to the readers of Stanley Hauerwas. Even as early as 1971, Hauerwas had come to appreciate the importance of acting within a world which was accessible to the senses – a world that could be seen. In an important critique of "situation ethics," Hauerwas appropriated Iris Murdoch's observation that we can act only in a world that we can see.[57] Hauerwas thus argues that we need a framework or lens through which we may "see" the world of human behavior.[58] This, he insists, is provided by sustained, detailed, extended reflection on the Christian narrative:

> The primary task of Christian ethics involves an attempt to help us see. For we can only act within the world we can see, and we can only see the world rightly by being trained to see. We do not come to see just by looking, but by disciplined skills developed through initiation into a narrative.[59]

---

[55] Oliver O'Donovan, *Resurrection and Moral Order*, Grand Rapids, MI: Eerdmans, 1986, p. 76.

[56] Ibid., p. 143.

[57] Iris Murdoch, "Vision and Choice in Morality."

[58] See Stanley Hauerwas, *Vision and Virtue: Essays in Christian Ethical Reflection*, Notre Dame, IN: Fides Publishers, 1974. For Hauerwas on this point, see Arne Rasmusson, *The Church as Polis: From Political Theology to Theological Politics as Exemplified by Jürgen Moltmann and Stanley Hauerwas*, Lund: Lund University Press, 1994, especially pp. 190–351.

[59] Stanley Hauerwas, "The Demands of a Truthful Story: Ethics and the Pastoral Task," *Chicago Studies* 21 (1982): 59–71; quote at pp. 65–6.

As a result of exercising this discipline of "seeing" things as they really are, Hauerwas argues, "the church serves the world by giving the world the means to see itself truthfully."[60] Once more, we discern the pattern of thought that we have argued to be fundamental to a renewed natural theology: the Christian tradition, focusing and culminating in Jesus Christ, as the lens through which nature is to be seen.

The outcomes of such ways of looking at nature can be illustrated from the ministry of Francis of Assisi (1181–1226), widely regarded as the most popular of Catholic saints. Although it would be an exaggeration to suggest that Francis's attitude to nature was informed by a well-developed theology, there is no doubt that certain controlling insights governed his thought, especially in relation to the created order. Francis's celebrated love for flowers and animals must never be confused with an infantile sentimentality, but is to be seen as an expression of a theology of creation that affirms both the goodness of creation, and the interconnectedness of the entire created order.[61] Each aspect of nature is affirmed, and its value to humanity noted:

> Be praised, my Lord, by brother fire
> By him we are lightened at night
> And he is fair and cheerful and sturdy and strong.
>
> Be praised, my Lord, by our sister, mother earth
> She sustains and governs us
> And brings forth many fruits and colored flowers and plants.[62]

---

[60] Stanley Hauerwas, *The Peaceable Kingdom: A Primer in Christian Ethics*, Notre Dame, IN: University of Notre Dame Press, 1983, pp. 101–2.

[61] Francis here reacts against contemporary forms of dualism that held that matter was intrinsically evil, and was thus to be shunned by those pursuing the spiritual life. See Claire Taylor, *Heresy in Medieval France: Dualism in Aquitaine and the Agenais, 1000–1249*, London: Royal Historical Society, 2005. See further Thomas B. Stratman, "St. Francis of Assisi: Brother to All Creatures," *Spirituality Today* 34 (1982): 222–32; Per Binde, "Nature in Roman Catholic Tradition," *Anthropological Quarterly* 74 (2001): 15–27.

[62] Francis of Assisi, "Canticum fratris solis vel Laudes creaturarum," in Kajetan Esser, OFM., *Die opuskula des hl. Franziskus von Assisi*, Neue textkritische edn, Rome: Editiones Collegii S. Bonaventurae ad Claras aquas, 1976, pp. 128–9; my translation.

The use of the language of "brother" and "sister" to refer to aspects of nature expresses an understanding of value and interdependence, grounded in a unitary vision of reality.

Thus far, we have explored how the Christian faith allows us to retrieve a meaningful account of the goodness of nature. Yet in closing, it is also important to note how this allows us to blunt the force of one of the challenges often brought against a theistic ethics – the so-called "Euthyprho Dilemma."

The Discernment of Goodness: The Euthyphro Dilemma

As we have already stressed, a Christian natural theology allows the trans-traditional human quest for goodness to be understood, and its limits identified.[63] The general human quest for truth, beauty, and goodness is easily accommodated within such a natural theology, which is able to offer an account of its origins, and a prescription for how it might find its goal. The generalized category of "nature" itself is incapable of bearing the metaphysical weight that is required if it is to be the foundation of a notion of "goodness." However, if nature is "seen" as creation, the situation is somewhat different. This recognition entails the acceptance of a new ontology, which holds that things in general, and above all human beings, possess a *telos* or purpose other than one which they conceptually set for themselves.

The importance of a Christian natural theology for an engagement with the notion of goodness can be illustrated from the resolution which it enables of the so-called "Euthyphro dilemma."[64] This is formulated and explored in Plato's dialogue of that same name, which explores the basis of morality and sanctity. The dialogue tells of Socrates meeting Euthyphro, a young theologian, at the entrance to the law courts. It turns out that Euthyphro – like Socrates himself – has been charged with "impiety" on account of a case that he is bringing against his father, who he alleged to have murdered a laborer on their estate at Naxos. A discussion ensues about what is "good" or "sacred." Euthyphro suggests a criterion:

---

[63] See Alister E. McGrath, *A Scientific Theology: 2 – Reality*, London: T&T Clark, 2002, pp. 92–7.

[64] Alister E. McGrath, *A Scientific Theology: 1 – Nature*, Edinburgh: T&T Clark, 2001, pp. 214–18.

"what is pleasing to the gods is holy, and what is not pleasing to them is unholy." Socrates responds that the gods might differ about what they consider right and wrong, so that what will be pleasing to one god might be displeasing to others. This point, of course, reflects the polytheism of the era, and cannot be transferred with conviction to a monotheist context.

Euthyphro then offers a new definition: "holiness is what the gods all love, and its opposite, unholiness, is what the gods all hate." Socrates then responds with the famous question: "Is that which is holy loved by the gods because it is holy, or is it holy because it is loved by the gods?"[65] In other words, do the gods endorse a standard of morality that already exists, and is independent of their will; or do the gods create those standards of morality? The usual formulation of this dilemma takes a slightly different form, as follows:[66]

Either: a right action is right because God approves (or commands) it;
Or: God approves (or commands) a right action because it is right.

If the "dilemma" is to have any force, the alternatives presented here are clearly intended to exhaust the options. The first approach asserts the dependence of a moral action on God, the second its independence.

Yet the dilemma gains its force precisely because we are asked to consider the relationship between two allegedly independent entities: what *human beings* recognize as good, and what *God* recognizes as good. The dilemma forces us, through the terms in which it is posited, to choose between human and divine conceptions of goodness or justice. But if these can be shown to be related to each other in any way, the force of the dilemma is lost. The choice we are forced to make is then seen as false. As we have seen in our exploration of the Christian reflection on the

---

[65] Plato, *Euthyphro*, 10a. For the text, see John C. Hall, "Plato: *Euthyphro* 10a1–11a10'," *Philosophical Quarterly*, 18 (1968): 1–11; Richard Sharvy, "Euthyphro 9b–11b: Analysis and Definition in Plato and Others," *Noûs*, 6 (1972), 119–37.

[66] See Paul Faber, "The *Euthyphro* Objection to Divine Normative Theories: A Response," *Religious Studies* 21 (1985): 559–72; Peter Geach, "Plato's *Euthyphro*: An Analysis and Commentary," *Monist*, 50 (1966): 369–82; Mark McPherran, "Socratic Piety in the 'Euthyphro'," *Journal of the History of Philosophy* 23 (1985): 283–310.

implications of creation in relation to the *imago Dei* (pp. 190–7), there is a congruence between divine notions of truth, beauty, and goodness and proper human notions of the same on account of the creaturely status of humanity.[67]

Conclusion to Part III

In this chapter, we have laid an emphasis upon "seeing" good, linking this with our overall vision of natural theology as seeing things as they actually are. Nature may seem mysterious, even unknowable; the natural theology we have developed in this work declares that nature, though ultimately unknowable, is still capable of being known to be good. The fundamental argument of this work is that the Christian tradition makes it possible to "see" or "behold" nature in such a way that its otherwise opaque or ambiguous truth, beauty, and goodness may be perceived.

Natural theology is fundamentally the specific human perception of nature that is enabled and elicited by the Christian theological vision. This act of tradition-informed "seeing" cannot be limited to a rational explanation of what is observed, but extends beyond this to include its impact upon the human imagination and emotion. Our rational, aesthetic, and moral visions are all shaped by the Christian tradition, and brought into contact with the world of the here and now, which is to be observed and appreciated, and within which we are called to act.

Iris Murdoch once spoke of "the calming, whole-making tendencies of human thought," which, while respecting singularities, is able to transcend these through generating a comprehensive vision of the world.[68] A renewed Christian natural theology provides us with such a conceptual net to throw over our experience of the world – whether rational, moral, or aesthetic – in order that we may at least live with its seeming contradictions, and yearn for its future transfiguration. It enables us to affirm and value the singularities of nature, while at the same time disclosing the

---

[67] For some interesting Jewish responses to the dilemma, see Michael J. Harris, *Divine Command Ethics: Jewish and Christian Perspectives*, London: Routledge, 2003, pp. 3–25.

[68] Iris Murdoch, *Metaphysics as a Guide to Morals*, London: Penguin, 1992, p. 7. On the importance of such singularities, see Alister E. McGrath, *A Scientific Theology: 3 – Theory*, London: T&T Clark, 2003, pp. 34–43.

deeper patterns of truth and reality that lie beneath its surface. To use Isaac Newton's engaging image, which serves as an epigraph for this work: we should indeed examine and appreciate the beauty of individual pebbles and shells on the shoreline, while realizing that a great ocean of truth lies beyond.[69]

---

[69] David Brewster, *Life of Sir Isaac Newton*, new edn, revised W. T. Lynn, London: Tegg, 1875, p. 303.

CHAPTER 13

Conclusion

In this volume, we have begun to explore how an approach to natural theology that is securely grounded in a trinitarian vision of God offers an enriched and fulfilling engagement with the natural world, transcending the limits of merely making sense of things. As we have stressed, this book is an essay – an attempt to open conversations, redirect thinking, and explore new options. It is a foray into new territory, rather than a comprehensive and exhaustive exploration of the possibilities it offers. Although we have only explored some of the many aspects of our themes, it would seem that the approach here outlined has considerable potential, offering an enhanced means of understanding and appreciating nature. While further exploration and examination is clearly necessary, it is not unreasonable to suggest that natural theology can be extricated from at least some of its present difficulties, and given a new and profitable lease of life.

The approach to natural theology that we defend and commend in this volume mandates an attentive engagement with the natural realm, encouraging us to see it afresh. As John Ruskin insisted, "to see clearly is poetry, prophecy, and religion – all in one."[1] Nature may indeed be an "open secret"; but those who possess the key to its mysteries can unlock

---

[1] John Ruskin, *Works*, ed. E. T. Cook and A. Wedderburn, 39 vols, London: Allen, 1903–12, vol. 5, p. 333.

its hidden meaning, seeing it as it really is. A Christian natural theology gives a robust theoretical foundation to this process of beholding, understanding, and appreciating nature, by providing an intellectual framework that affirms and legitimates a heightened attentiveness to the world around us.

The approach we have set out has obvious implications for the increasingly important dialogue between Christian theology and the natural sciences. It offers the possibility of a shared engagement with the natural world from different starting points and different presumptions, with the possibility of enhanced intellectual enrichment and creative discernment on both sides. Natural theology, as we have defined the concept and articulated its application, can bring together the poet's imaginative engagement with the world, the scientist's meticulous observation of nature, and the theologian's vision of God, leading to a whole which is greater than the sum of its parts. This expanded vision for natural theology might hold the key to the reconnection of discussions and debates that have long gone their separate ways.

In describing his memory of looking at a wood near Fontainebleau in 1842, John Ruskin spoke of an epiphanic moment of illumination, in which scientific and theological streams of perception flowed together, to yield a significant moment of transcendent insight. It is fitting to end this work with a remark from this neglected visionary who appreciated, perhaps more than most, the true importance of "seeing" nature for what it really was, and brought imaginative, scientific, and theological concerns together in his writings:

The woods, which I had only looked on as wilderness, fulfilled, I then saw, in their beauty the same laws which guided the clouds, divided the light, and balanced the wave. "He hath made everything beautiful, in his time," became for me thenceforward the interpretation of the bond between the human mind and all visible things; and I returned along the wood-road feeling that it had led me far – farther than ever fancy had reached, or theodolite measured.[2]

---

[2] Ruskin, *Works*, vol. 35, p. 315. The biblical quote is Ecclesiastes 3: 11, which continues with the words "He has set eternity in their hearts." The historical basis of Ruskin's recollection is, it ought to be said, somewhat vulnerable: see, e.g., Clive Wilmer, "Back to Nature: Ruskin's Aspen and an Art in the Service of the Given," *Times Literary Supplement*, 1 December 1995, pp. 3–4.

Bibliography

Abraham, William J. *Divine Revelation and the Limits of Historical Criticism.* Oxford: Oxford University Press, 1982.

Adams, J., D. Graham, and B. Jennet. "The Neuropathology of the Vegetative State After an Acute Brain Insult." *Brain* 123 (2000): 1327–38.

Adams, Marilyn McCord. *Horrendous Evils and the Goodness of God.* Ithaca, NY: Cornell University Press, 1999.

Adams, Robert Merrihew. *Finite and Infinite Goods: A Framework for Ethics.* New York: Oxford University Press, 2002.

Ainsworth, M., M. Biehar, E. Waters, and S. Wall. *Patterns of Attachment: A Psychological Study of the Strange Situation.* Hillsdale, NJ: Erlbaum, 1978.

Aleaz, K. P. "The Gospel According to Lesslie Newbigin: An Evaluation." *Asia Journal of Theology* 13 (1999): 172–200.

Alexander, Thomas M. *John Dewey's Theory of Art, Experience, and Nature: The Horizons of Feeling.* Albany, NY: State University of New York Press, 1987.

Allen, Diogenes, and Eric O. Springsted. *Spirit, Nature, and Community: Issues in the Thought of Simone Weil.* Albany, NY: State University of New York Press, 1994.

Allen, Paul L. *Ernan McMullin and Critical Realism in the Science–Theology Dialogue.* Aldershot: Ashgate, 2006.

Allen, Ward. *Translating for King James: Notes Made by a Translator of King James' Bible.* Nashville, TN: Vanderbilt University Press, 1969.

Alston, William P. *Perceiving God: The Epistemology of Religious Experience.* Ithaca, NY: Cornell University Press, 1991.

Ambrozic, Aloysius M. *The Hidden Kingdom: A Redactional-Critical Study of the References to the Kingdom of God in Mark's Gospel.* Washington, DC: Catholic Biblical Association of America, 1972.

Ando, Clifford. "Augustine on Language." *Revue des études augustiniennes* 40 (1994): 45–78.

Andrews, Stephen. "The Ambiguity of Capacity: A Rejoinder to Trevor Hart." *Tyndale Bulletin* 45 (1994): 169–79.

Antes, Peter. "What Do We Experience if We Have Religious Experience?" *Numen* 49 (2002): 336–42.

Antonaccio, Maria. "Imagining the Good: Iris Murdoch's Godless Theology." *Annual of the Society of Christian Ethics* 16 (1996): 223–42.

Arbel, Vita Daphna. *Beholders of Divine Secrets: Mysticism and Myth in the Hekhalot and Merkavah Literature*. Albany, NY: State University of New York Press, 2003.

Arbib, Michael. "Interaction of Multiple Representations of Space in the Brain." In J. Paillard (ed.), *Brain and Space*, pp. 379–403. Oxford: Oxford University Press, 1991.

Archer, Margaret, Andrew Collier, and Douglas V. Porpora (eds). *Transcendence: Critical Realism and God*. London: Routledge, 2004.

Arnell, Carla A. "On Beauty, Justice and the Sublime in C. S. Lewis's *Till We Have Faces*." *Christianity and Literature* 52 (2002): 23–34.

Arnold, Johannes. "Begriff und heilsökonomische Bedeutung der göttlichen Sendungen in Augustinus *De Trinitate*." *Recherches Augustiniennes* 25 (1991): 3–69.

Aslin, R., J. Saffran, and E. Newport. "Computation of Conditional Probability Statistics by 8-Month-Old Infants." *Psychological Science* 9 (1998): 321–4.

Bailey, Kenneth E. *Poet and Peasant: A Literary-Cultural Approach to the Parables in Luke*. Grand Rapids: Eerdmans, 1976.

Baillie, John (ed.). *Natural Theology, comprising "Nature and Grace" by Professor Dr. Emil Brunner and the reply "No!" by Dr. Karl Barth*. London: Geoffrey Bless, 1946.

Bak, Hans, and Walter W. Holbling. *"Nature's Nation" Revisited: American Concepts of Nature from Wonder to Ecological Crisis*. Amsterdam: VU Press, 2003.

Balantine, Samuel E. *The Hidden God: The Hiding Face of God in the Old Testament*. Oxford: Oxford University Press, 1983.

Balashov, Yuri. "Duhem, Quine, and the Multiplicity of Scientific Tests." *Philosophy of Science* 61 (1994): 608–28.

Ball, David Mark. *"I Am" in John's Gospel: Literary Function, Background and Theological Implications*. Sheffield: Sheffield Academic Press, 1996.

Balthasar, Hans Urs von. *The Glory of the Lord: A Theological Aesthetics*, 7 vols. Edinburgh: T&T Clark, 1982–9.

Balthasar, Hans Urs von. *Theo-Drama: Theological Dramatic Theory*. San Francisco: Ignatius, 1992.

Balthasar, Hans Urs von. *Presence and Thought: An Essay on the Religious Philosophy of Gregory of Nyssa*. San Francisco: Ignatius Press, 1995.

Bandt, Hellmut. *Luthers Lehre vom Verborgenen Gott: Eine Untersuchung zu dem offenbarungsgeschichtlichen Ansatz seiner Theologie.* Berlin: Evangelische Verlagsanstalt, 1958.

Bannister, Robert C. *Social Darwinism: Science and Myth in Anglo-American Social Thought.* Philadelphia: Temple University Press, 1979.

Barbeau, Jeffrey W. "Newman and the Interpretation of Inspired Scripture." *Theological Studies* 63 (2002): 53–68.

Barbour, John D. *Versions of Deconversion: Autobiography and the Loss of Faith.* Charlottesville, VA: University Press of Virginia, 1994.

Barfield, Owen. *Poetic Diction: A Study in Meaning.* Middletown, CT: Wesleyan University Press, 1973.

Barker, Margaret. *The Great Angel: A Study of Israel's Second God.* London: SPCK, 1992.

Barnes, Eric. "Inference to the Loveliest Explanation," *Synthese* 103 (1995): 251–78.

Barnes, T. R. *English Verse: Voice and Movement.* Cambridge, UK: Cambridge University Press, 1967.

Barr, James. "The Image of God in the Book of Genesis: A Study of Terminology." *Bulletin of the John Rylands Library* 51 (1968): 11–26.

Barr, James. "Do We Perceive the Speech of the Heavens? A Question in Psalm 19." In Jack C. Knight and Lawrence A. Sinclair (eds), *The Psalms and Other Studies on the Old Testament,* pp. 11–17. Nashotah, WI: Nashotah House Seminary, 1990.

Barr, James. *Biblical Faith and Natural Theology.* Oxford: Clarendon Press, 1993.

Barrell, John. *The Political Theory of Painting from Reynolds to Hazlitt: The Body of the Public.* New Haven, CT: Yale University Press, 1986.

Barrell, John. *Painting and the Politics of Culture: New Essays on British Art, 1700–1850.* Oxford: Clarendon Press, 1992.

Barrett, Justin L. *Why Would Anyone Believe in God?* Lanham, MD: AltaMira Press, 2004.

Barrett, Justin L. "The Naturalness of Religious Concepts: An Emerging Cognitive Science of Religion." In P. Antes, A. Geertz and R. R. Warne (eds), *New Approaches to the Study of Religion. Volume 2: Textual, Comparative, Sociological, and Cognitive Approaches,* pp. 401–18. Berlin: de Gruyter, 2004.

Barrow, John D. *The Artful Universe: The Cosmic Source of Human Creativity.* Harmondsworth: Penguin, 1995.

Barrow, John D. and Frank J. Tipler, *The Cosmological Anthropic Principle.* Oxford: Oxford University Press, 1986.

Barth, Karl. "Die Gerechtigkeit Gottes." In *Das Wort Gottes und die Theologie,* pp. 5–17. Munich: Kaiser Verlag, 1925.

Barth, Karl. *Römerbrief.* Zurich: Zollikon, 8th edn, 1947.

Barton, John. "The Messiah in Old Testament Theology." In John Day (ed.), *King and Messiah in Israel and the Ancient Near East,* pp. 365–79. Sheffield: Sheffield Academic Press, 1998.

Barton, Stephen C. "Parables on God's Love and Forgiveness (Luke 15:1–32)." In Richard N. Longenecker (ed.), *The Challenge of Jesus' Parables*, pp. 199–216. Grand Rapids, MI: Eerdmans, 2000.

Batstone, David. *From Conquest to Struggle: Jesus of Nazareth in Latin America.* Albany, NY: State University of New York Press, 1991.

Bauckham, Richard. *God Will Be All in All: The Eschatology of Jürgen Moltmann.* Edinburgh: T&T Clark, 1999.

Baudelaire, Charles. *L'art romantique.* Paris: Calmann-Lévy, 1885.

Bauks, Michaela. " 'Chaos' als Metapher für die Gefärdung der Weltordnung." In Bernd Janowski, Beate Ego, and Annette Krüger (eds), *Das biblische Weltbild und seine altorientalischen Kontexte*, pp. 431–64. Tübingen: Mohr Siebeck, 2001.

Baumeister, Roy. *Meanings of Life.* New York: Guilford, 1991.

Baur, Jürgen. *Gott, Recht und weltliches Regiment im Werke Calvins.* Bonn: Bouvier, 1965.

Beauregard, Mario, and Vincent Paquette. "Neural Correlates of a Mystical Experience in Carmelite Nuns." *Neuroscience Letters* 405 (2006): 186–90.

Beer, John B. *Providence and Love: Studies in Wordsworth, Channing, Myers, George Eliot, and Ruskin.* Oxford: Oxford University Press, 1998.

Begbie, Jeremy S. *Voicing Creation's Praise: Towards a Theology of the Arts.* Edinburgh: T&T Clark, 1991.

Beggiani, Seely Joseph. "The Typological Approach of Syriac Sacramental Theology." *Theological Studies* 64 (2003): 543–57.

Behe, Michael J. *Darwin's Black Box: The Biochemical Challenge to Evolution.* New York: Free Press, 1996.

Beiser, Frederick C. *The Fate of Reason: German Philosophy from Kant to Fichte.* Cambridge, MA: Harvard University Press, 1987.

Beiser, Frederick C. *The Sovereignty of Reason: The Defense of Rationality in the Early English Enlightenment.* Princeton, NJ: Princeton University Press, 1996.

Beja, Morris. *Epiphany in the Modern Novel.* London: Owen, 1971.

Bell, D. N. "*Esse, vivere, intellegere.* The Noetic Triad and the Image of God." *Recherches de théologie ancienne et médiévale* 52 (1985): 5–43.

Bell, Simon. *Landscape: Pattern, Perception, and Process.* New York: Spon, 1999.

Bengsch, Alfred. *Heilsgeschichte und Heilswissen: Eine Untersuchung zur Struktur und Entfaltung des theologischen Denkens im Werk "Adversus Haereses" des hl. Irenäus von Lyon.* Leipzig: St. Benno-Verlag, 1957.

Benin, Stephen D. *The Footprints of God: Divine Accommodation in Jewish and Christian Thought.* Albany: State University of New York, 1993.

Bennett, Max R., and Peter M. S. Hacker. *Philosophical Foundations of Neuroscience.* Oxford: Blackwell, 2003.

Berger, Peter. *A Rumor of Angels: Modern Society and the Rediscovery of the Supernatural.* Garden City, NY: Doubleday, 1969.

Berger, Peter L., and Thomas Luckmann. *The Social Construction of Reality: A Treatise in the Sociology of Knowledge.* Harmondsworth: Penguin Books, 1971.

Bernstein, Richard J. *Philosophical Profiles: Essays in a Pragmatic Mode.* Philadelphia: University of Pennsylvania Press, 1986.

Bernstein, Richard J. *Beyond Objectivism and Relativism: Science, Hermeneutics, and Praxis.* Philadelphia: University of Pennsylvania Press, 1991.

Bhaskar, Roy. *From East to West: Odyssey of a Soul.* New York: Routledge, 2000.

Bhaskar, Roy. *Meta-Reality: Creativity, Love and Freedom.* London: Sage Publications, 2002.

Bhaskar, Roy. *Reflections on Meta-Reality: Transcendence, Emancipation and Everyday Life.* London: Sage Publications, 2002.

Bidney, Martin. *Patterns of Epiphany: From Wordsworth to Tolstoy, Pater, and Barrett Browning.* Carbondale, IL: Southern Illinois University Press, 1997.

Bieler, Martin. "Karl Barths Auseinandersetzung mit der *analogia entis* und der Anfang der Theologie." *Catholica* 40 (1986): 229–45.

Bienert, Wolfgang A. "Zur Logos-Christologie des Athanasius von Alexandrien in *Contra Gentes* und *De Incarnatione.*" In E. A. Livingstone (ed.), *Papers Presented to the Tenth International Conference on Patristic Studies*, pp. 402–19. Louvain: Peeters, 1989.

Binde, Per. "Nature in Roman Catholic Tradition." *Anthropological Quarterly* 74 (2001): 15–27.

Black, Rufus. *Christian Moral Realism: Natural Law, Narrative, Virtue, and the Gospel.* Oxford: Oxford University Press, 2000.

Blackburn, Simon. *Truth: A Guide for the Perplexed.* London: Allen Lane, 2005.

Blum, Lawrence. "Iris Murdoch and the Domain of the Moral." *Philosophical Studies* 50 (1986): 343–67.

Boden, Margaret. "Consciousness and Human Identity: An Interdisciplinary Perspective." In J. Cornwell (ed.), *Consciousness and Human Identity*, pp. 1–20. Oxford: Oxford University Press, 1998.

Boeve, Lieven, Hans Geybels, and Stijn van den Bossche (eds). *Encountering Transcendence: Contributions to a Theology of Christian Religious Experience.* Leuven: Peeters, 2005.

Boeve, Lieven, and Laurence Paul Hemming. *Divinising Experience: Essays in the History of Religious Experience from Origen to Ricoeur.* Leuven: Peeters, 2004.

Boggs, Rebecca Melora Corinne. "Poetic Genesis, the Self and Nature's Things in Hopkins." *Studies in English Literature* 37 (1997): 831–55.

Boisvert, Raymond D. *Dewey's Metaphysics.* New York: Fordham University Press, 1988.

Bolivar, A. O. *Quantum-Classical Correspondence: Dynamical Quantization and the Classical Limit.* London: Springer, 2004.

Boller, Paul F. *American Transcendentalism, 1830–1860: An Intellectual Inquiry.* New York: Putnam, 1974.

Borella, Jean. *Le sens du surnaturel.* Geneva: Editions ad Solem, 1996.

Borg, Marcus J. *Meeting Jesus Again for the First Time: The Historical Jesus and the Heart of Contemporary Faith.* San Francisco: Harper, 1994.

Borig, Rainer. *Der wahre Weinstock: Untersuchungen zu Jo 15, 1–10.* Munich: Kösel Verlag, 1967.

Bornkamm, Günther. "The Stilling of the Storm in Matthew." In Günther Bornkamm, Gerhard Barth, and Heinz Joachim Held (eds), *Tradition and Interpretation in Matthew*, pp. 52–7. Philadelphia: Westminster Press, 1963.

Bornstein, B., H. Sroka, and H. Munitz. "Prosopagnosia with Animal Face Agnosia." *Cortex* 5 (1969): 164–9.

Bostrom, Nick. *Anthropic Bias: Observation Selection Effects in Science and Philosophy.* London: Routledge, 2002.

Bourriot, Félix. *Kalos kagathos – kalokagathia: d'un terme de propagande de sophistes à une notion sociale et philosophique: étude d'histoire athénienne.* Hildesheim: Olms, 1995.

Bower, T. G. R., and J. Patterson. "The Separation of Place, Movement and Time in the World of the Infant." *Journal of Experimental Child Psychology* 15 (1973): 161–8.

Bower, T. G. R. *Development in Infancy*, 2nd edn. San Francisco: W. H. Freeman, 1982.

Bowker, John W. *The Sacred Neuron: Extraordinary New Discoveries Linking Science and Religion.* London: I. B. Tauris, 2005.

Bowlby, John. *Attachment and Loss, Volume I: Attachment.* London, Hogarth Press, 1969.

Boyarin, Daniel. *Intertextuality and the Reading of Midrash.* Bloomington, IN: Indiana University Press, 1990.

Boyer, Pascal. *The Naturalness of Religious Ideas: A Cognitive Theory of Religion.* Berkeley, CA: University of California Press, 1994.

Boyle, Robert. *The Works of the Honourable Robert Boyle*, ed. Thomas Birch, 2nd edn, 6 vols. London: Rivingtons, 1772.

Braaten, Laurie J. "All Creation Groans: Romans 8:22 in Light of the Biblical Sources." *Horizons in Biblical Theology* 28 (2006): 131–59.

Brady, Emily. "Imagination and the Aesthetic Appreciation of Nature." *Journal of Aesthetics and Art Criticism* 56 (1998): 139–47.

Brewer, William F., and Bruce L. Lambert. "The Theory-Ladenness of Observation and the Theory-Ladenness of the Rest of the Scientific Process." *Philosophy of Science* 68 (2001): S176–86.

Brewster, David. *Life of Sir Isaac Newton*, new edn, revised W. T. Lynn. London: Tegg, 1875.

Briggs, John. *Fractals: The Patterns of Chaos. Discovering a New Aesthetic of Art, Science, and Nature.* London: Thames & Hudson, 1992.

Brinkschmidt, Egon. *Martin Buber und Karl Barth: Theologie zwischen Dialogik und Dialektik.* Neukirchen-Vluyn: Neukirchener Verlag, 2000.

Brooke, John Hedley. *Science and Religion: Some Historical Perspectives*. Cambridge, UK: Cambridge University Press, 1991.

Brooke, John Hedley. "Like Minds: The God of Hugh Miller." In Michael Shortland (ed.), *Hugh Miller and the Controversies of Victorian Science*, pp. 171–86. Oxford: Clarendon Press, 1996.

Brooke, John Hedley, and Ian McLean (eds). *Heterodoxy in Early Modern Science and Religion*. Oxford: Oxford University Press, 2006.

Brower, Reuben Arthur. *The Fields of Light: An Experiment in Critical Reading*. Oxford: Oxford University Press, 1951.

Brown, Frank Burch. *Religious Aesthetics: A Theological Study of Making and Meaning*. Princeton, NJ: Princeton University Press, 1989.

Brown, James. *Subject and Object in Modern Theology*. London: SCM Press, 1955.

Brown, Peter R. L. "Saint Augustine and Political Society." In Dorothy F. Donnelly (ed.), *The City of God: A Collection of Critical Essays*, pp. 17–35. New York: Peter Lang, 1995.

Brown, Warren S., Nancey C. Murphy, and H. Newton Malony (eds). *Whatever Happened to the Soul? Scientific and Theological Portraits of Human Nature*. Minneapolis: Fortress Press, 1998.

Brox, Norbert. *Offenbarung, Gnosis und gnostischer Mythos bei Irenäus von Lyon: zur Charakteristik der Systeme*. Salzburg: Pustet Verlag, 1966.

Brueggemann, Walter. *The Land: Place as Gift, Promise, and Challenge in Biblical Faith*. Philadelphia: Fortress Press, 2002.

Brunner, Emil. *Offenbarung und Vernunft: Die Lehre von der christlichen Glaubenserkenntnis*. Zurich: Zwingli Verlag, 1941.

Brunner, Emil. "The New Barth: Observations on Karl Barth's Doctrine of Man." *Scottish Journal of Theology* 4 (1951): 123–35.

Brunner, Emil. *Wahrheit als Begegnung*. Zürich: Zwingli-Verlag, 1963.

Brunner, Emil. *Der Mensch im Widerspruch: Die christliche Lehre vom wahren und vom wirklichen Menschen*, 4th edn. Zurich: Zwingli Verlag, 1965.

Brunner, Emil. "Natur und Gnade: Zum Gespräch mit Karl Barth." In Rudolf Wehrli (ed.), *Ein offenes Wort. Vorträge und Aufsätze 1917–1934*, pp. 333–66. Zürich: Theologischer Verlag, 1981.

Buckley, Michael J. *At the Origins of Modern Atheism*. New Haven, CT: Yale University Press, 1987.

Budd, Malcolm. "Kant's Aesthetics of Nature." In *The Aesthetic Appreciation of Nature*, pp. 24–89. Oxford: Oxford University Press, 2005.

Bultmann, Rudolf. "Is Exegesis without Presuppositions Possible?" In Kurt Mueller-Vollmer (ed.), *The Hermeneutics Reader: Texts of the German Tradition from the Enlightenment to the Present*, pp. 241–8. Oxford: Blackwell, 1986.

Burghardt, Walter J. *The Image of God in Man According to Cyril of Alexandria*. Woodstock, MA: Woodstock Press, 1957.

Burnet, Gilbert (ed.). *The Boyle Lectures (1692–1732): A Defence of Natural and Revealed Religion, Being an Abridgement of the Sermons Preached at the Lectures Founded by Robert Boyle*, 4 vols. Bristol: Thoemmes Press, 2000.

Burns, J. Patout. "Economy of Salvation: Two Patristic Traditions." *Theological Studies* 37 (1976): 598–619.

Burrow, J. W. *The Crisis of Reason: European Thought, 1848–1914*. New Haven, CT: Yale University Press, 2000.

Byrne, Peter A. *Natural Religion and the Nature of Religion: The Legacy of Deism*. London: Routledge, 1989.

Cairns, David. *The Image of God in Man*. London: Collins, 1973.

Campbell, Joseph. *The Flight of the Wild Gander: Explorations in the Mythological Dimension*. New York: Viking Press, 1969.

Campbell, Joseph. *The Power of Myth*. New York: Doubleday, 1988.

Campbell, Joseph. *The Hero's Journey: Joseph Campbell on His Life and Work*. Shaftesbury: Element, 1999.

Carafiol, Peter. *Transcendent Reason: James Marsh and the Forms of Romantic Thought*. Tallahassee, FL: University Presses of Florida, 1982.

Carlson, Allen. *Aesthetics and the Environment: The Appreciation of Nature, Art, and Architecture*. London: Routledge, 2000.

Carlton, Eric. *Dancing in The Dark: Reflections on the Problem of Theodicy*. Madison, NJ: Fairleigh Dickinson University Press, 2005.

Carr, Bernard (ed.). *Universe or Multiverse?* Cambridge, UK: Cambridge University Press, 2007.

Carroll, Noel. "On Being Moved by Nature: Between Religion and Natural History." In Salim Kemal and Ivan Gaskell (eds), *Landscape, Natural Beauty, and the Arts*, pp. 244–66. Cambridge, UK: Cambridge University Press, 1993.

Carter, Brandon. "Large Number Coincidences and the Anthropic Principle." In M. S. Longair (ed.), *Confrontation of Cosmological Theories with Observational Data*, pp. 291–8. Boston: D. Reidel, 1974.

Carter, Brandon. "The Anthropic Principle and its Implications for Biological Evolution." *Philosophical Transactions of the Royal Society* A 310 (1983): 347–63.

Casalengo, Alberto. "La parabola del franello di senape (Mc 4,30–32)." *Rivista biblica* 26 (1978): 139–61.

Cassiday, K., R. McNally, and S. Zeitlin. "Cognitive Processing of Trauma Cues in Rape Victims with Post-Traumatic Stress Disorder." *Cognitive Therapy and Research* 16 (1992): 283–95.

Casteras, Susan P. (ed.). *John Ruskin and the Victorian Eye*. New York: Harry N. Abrams, 1993.

Cebulj, Christian. *Ich bin es: Studien zur Identitätsbildung im Johannesevangelium*. Stuttgart: Verlag Katholisches Bibelwerk, 2000.

Chapman, Edgar L. "From Rebellious Rationalist to Mythmaker and Mystic: The Religious Quest of Philip José Farmer." In Robert Reilly (ed.), *The Transcendent Adventure: Studies of Religion in Science Fiction/Fantasy*, pp. 127–44. Westport, CT: Greenwood Press, 1985.

Cherry, Conrad. *Nature and Religious Imagination: From Edwards to Bushnell.* Philadelphia: Fortress Press, 1980.

Chester, Andrew. "Jewish Messianic Expectations and Mediatorial Figures and Pauline Christology." In Martin Hengel and Ulrich Heckel (eds), *Paulus und das antike Judentum*, pp. 17–89. Tübingen: J. C. B. Mohr, 1991.

Cheung, Leo K. C. "Showing, Analysis and the Truth-Functionality of Logical Necessity in Wittgenstein's *Tractatus.*" *Synthese* 139 (2004): 81–105.

Chittick, William C. *The Self-Disclosure of God: Principles of Ibn al-'Arabi's Cosmology.* Albany, NY: State University of New York Press, 1998.

Chomsky, Noam. *Aspects of the Theory of Syntax.* Cambridge, MA: MIT Press, 1965.

Chrétien, Jean-Louis. *The Call and the Response.* New York: Fordham University Press, 2004.

Churchland, Patricia S. *Neurophilosophy: Toward a Unified Science of the Mind-Brain.* Cambridge, MA: MIT Press, 1986.

Cirkovic, Milan. "Ancient Origins of a Modern Anthropic Cosmological Argument." *Astronomical and Astrophysical Transactions* 22 (2003): 879–86.

Clarke, Elizabeth. *Theory and Theology in George Herbert's Poetry: "Divinitie and Poesy Met".* Oxford: Clarendon Press, 1997.

Clarke, Peter B., and Peter Byrne. *Religion Defined and Explained.* London: St Martin's Press, 1993.

Clayton, Philip, and A. R. Peacocke (eds). *In Whom We Live and Move and Have Our Being: Panentheistic Reflections on God's Presence in a Scientific World.* Grand Rapids, MI: Eerdmans, 2004.

Clines, David J. A. "The Image of God in Man." *Tyndale Bulletin* 19 (1968): 53–103.

Cohen, Anthony P. *The Symbolic Construction of Community.* London: Routledge, 1989.

Cohen, Morris R. "Some Difficulties in Dewey's Naturalistic Metaphysics." *Philosophical Review* 49 (1940), 196–220.

Cohen, Ted. "A Critique of Sibley's Position." *Theoria* 39 (1973): 113–52.

Collicutt McGrath, Joanna. "Post-traumatic Growth and the Origins of Early Christianity." *Mental Health, Religion and Culture* 9 (2006): 291–306.

Collier, Andrew. *Critical Realism: An Introduction to Roy Bhaskar's Philosophy.* London: Verso, 1994.

Collins, Adela Y. *Cosmology and Eschatology in Jewish and Christian Apocalypticism.* Leiden: E. J. Brill, 1996.

Collins, Jack. "Miracles, Intelligent Design, and God-of-the-Gaps." *Perspectives on Science and Christian Faith* 55 (2003): 22–9.

Collins, John J. *Apocalypticism in the Dead Sea Scrolls*. London: Routledge, 1997.

Collins, Robin. "A Scientific Argument for the Existence of God: The Fine-Tuning Design Argument." In Michael J. Murray (ed.), *Reason for the Hope Within*, pp. 47–75. Grand Rapids, MI: Eerdmans, 1999.

Colp, Ralph E. *To Be an Invalid: The Illness of Charles Darwin*. Chicago: University of Chicago Press, 1977.

Combrink, H. J. B. "A Social-Scientific Perspective on the Parable of the 'Unjust' Steward (Lk 16:1–8a)." *Neotestamentica* 30 (1996): 281–306.

Conradi, Peter J. *Iris Murdoch: A Life*. London: HarperCollins, 2001.

Conway Morris, Simon. *Life's Solution: Inevitable Humans in a Lonely Universe*. Cambridge, UK: Cambridge University Press, 2003.

Conzelmann, Hans. "The Address of Paul on the Areopagus." In L. E. Keck and J. L. Martyn (eds), *Studies in Luke-Acts: Essays in Honor of Paul Schubert*, pp. 217–30. Nashville, TN: Abingdon Press, 1966.

Cornwell, John (ed.). *Nature's Imagination: The Frontiers of Scientific Vision*. Oxford: Oxford University Press, 1995.

Cotter, James Finn. "Hopkins and Augustine." *Victorian Poetry* 39 (2001): 69–82.

Coudert, Allison. "Some Theories of a Natural Language from the Renaissance to the Seventeenth Century." In Albert Heinekamp and Dieter Mettler (eds), *Magia Naturalis und die Entstehung der modernen Naturwissenschaften*, pp. 56–118. Wiesbaden: Steiner, 1978.

Coulson, Charles A. *Science and Christian Belief*. Chapel Hill, NC: University of North Carolina Press, 1958.

Cousin, Victor. *Du vrai, du beau et du bien*, 8th edn. Paris: Didier, 1860.

Crick, Francis H. C. *The Astonishing Hypothesis: The Scientific Search for the Soul*. London: Simon & Schuster, 1994.

Crockett, Clayton. *A Theology of the Sublime*. London: Routledge, 2001.

Crossan, John Dominic. *In Parables: The Challenge of the Historical Jesus*. New York: Harper & Row, 1973.

Crossan, John Dominic. *Finding is the First Act: Trove Fairytales and Jesus' Treasure Parable*. Philadelphia: Fortress Press, 1979.

Crossan, John Dominic. *Cliffs of Fall: Paradox and Polyvalency in the Parables of Jesus*. New York: Seabury, 1980.

Crossan, John Dominic. *The Dark Interval: Towards a Theology of Story*. Sonoma, CA: Eagle, 1988.

Crossan, John Dominic. *The Historical Jesus: The Life of a Mediterranean Jewish Peasant*. San Francisco: HarperSanFrancisco, 1991.

Csikszentmihalyi, Mihaly. *The Art of Seeing: An Interpretation of the Aesthetic Encounter*. Oxford: Oxford University Press, 1991.

Csikszentmihalyi, Mihaly. *Creativity: Flow and the Psychology of Discovery and Invention*. New York: Harper Collins, 1996.

Culler, Jonathan D. *Structuralist Poetics: Structuralism, Linguistics and the Study of Literature.* London: Routledge, 2002.

Curtis, Kimberley. *Our Sense of the Real: Aesthetic Experience and Arendtian Politics.* Ithaca, NY: Cornell University Press, 1999.

Dahm, John J. "Science and Apologetics in the Early Boyle Lectures." *Church History* 19 (1970): 172–86.

Daiches, David. *The King James Version of the Bible.* Chicago: University of Chicago Press, 1941.

Dallal, Ahmad. "Ghazali and the Perils of Interpretation: Review Essay of *Al-Ghazali and the Ash'arite School,* by Richard M. Frank." *Journal of the American Oriental Society* 122 (2002): 773–87.

Dalley, Stephanie. *Myths from Mesopotamia: Creation, the Flood, Gilgamesh and Others.* New York: Oxford University Press, 1989.

Damasio, Antonio R. *Descartes' Error: Emotion, Reason, and the Human Brain.* New York: Putnam, 1994.

Daniel, Clay. "Milton's Neo-Platonic Angel?" *Studies in English Literature* 44 (2004): 173–88.

Danto, Arthur C. *The Transfiguration of the Commonplace: A Philosophy of Art.* Cambridge, MA: Harvard University Press, 1981.

d'Aquili, Eugene G., and Andrew B. Newberg. *The Mystical Mind: Probing the Biology of Religious Experience.* Minneapolis: Fortress Press, 1999.

Darwin, Charles. *The Life and Letters of Charles Darwin,* 3 vols. London: John Murray, 1887.

Dasenbrock, Reed Way. "Accounting for the Changing Certainties of Interpretative Communities." *MLN* 101 (1986): 1022–41.

Davies, Paul. *The Mind of God: Science and the Search for Ultimate Meaning.* London: Penguin, 1992.

Davies, Paul. *The Goldilocks Enigma: Why Is the Universe Just Right for Life?* London: Allen Lane, 2006.

Davies, Oliver. "Soundings: Towards a Theological Poetics of Silence." In Oliver Davies and Denys Turner (eds), *Silence and the Word: Negative Theology and Incarnation,* pp. 201–22. Cambridge, UK: Cambridge University Press, 2002.

Davis, Caroline Franks. *The Evidential Force of Religious Experience.* Oxford: Clarendon Press, 1989.

Dawkins, Richard. *The Blind Watchmaker: Why the Evidence of Evolution Reveals a Universe Without Design.* New York: W. W. Norton, 1986.

Dawkins, Richard. *River Out of Eden: A Darwinian View of Life.* London: Phoenix, 1995.

Dawkins, Richard. "A Survival Machine." In John Brockman (ed.), *The Third Culture,* pp. 75–95. New York: Simon & Schuster, 1996.

Dawkins, Richard. *Unweaving the Rainbow: Science, Delusion and the Appetite for Wonder.* London: Penguin, 1998.

Day, Brian J. "The Moral Intuition of Ruskin's 'Storm-Cloud'." *Studies in English Literature* 45 (2005): 917–34.

Day, John. *God's Conflict with the Dragon: Echoes of a Canaanite Myth in the Old Testament*. Cambridge, UK: Cambridge University Press, 1985.

De la Potterie, Ignace. *La vérité dans saint Jean*, 2 vols. Rome: Biblical Institute Press, 1977.

De la Potterie, Ignace. "Jésus, témoin de la vérité et roi par la vérité." *Studia Missionalia* 46 (1997): 21–41.

Delattre, Roland. *Beauty and Sensibility in the Thought of Jonathan Edwards*. New Haven, CT: Yale University Press, 1968.

Delattre, Roland. "Aesthetics and Ethics: Jonathan Edwards and the Recovery of Aesthetics for Religious Ethics." *Journal of Religious Ethics* 31 (2003): 277–97.

Delaura, David J. *Hebrew and Hellene in Victorian England: Newman, Arnold, and Pater*. Austin, TX: University of Texas Press, 1969.

Denton, Michael. *Nature's Destiny: How the Laws of Biology Reveal Purpose in the Universe*. New York: Free Press, 1998.

DePaul, Michael. "Argument and Perception." *Journal of Philosophy* 85 (1988): 552–65.

Derrida, Jacques. *La dissemination*. Paris: Editions du Seuil, 1972.

Dessain, Charles Stephen, and Thomas Gornall (eds). *The Letters and Diaries of John Henry Newman*, 31 vols. Oxford: Clarendon Press, 1963–2006.

Deutsch, Nathaniel. *Guardians of the Gate: Angelic Vice-Regency in Late Antiquity*. Leiden: Brill, 1999.

Devine, Philip E. "On the Definition of 'Religion'." *Faith and Philosophy* 3 (1986): 270–84.

Devine, Philip E. *Natural Law Ethics*. Westport, CT: Greenwood, 2000.

Devlin, Christopher. "The Image and Word." *The Month* 3 (1950): 199–201.

Dewey, John. "The Postulate of Immediate Empiricism." *Journal of Philosophy* 2 (1905): 393–9.

Dewey, John. "Does Reality Possess Practical Character?" In *Essays Philosophical and Psychological in Honor of William James*, pp. 53–80. New York: Longmans, Green, and Co., 1908.

Dewey, John. *A Common Faith*. New Haven, CT: Yale University Press, 1934.

Dewey, John. *Experience and Nature*, 2nd edn. New York: Dover, 1958.

Dierksmeier, Claus. *Das Noumenon Religion: eine Untersuchung zur Stellung der Religion im System der praktischen Philosophie Kants*. Berlin: de Gruyter, 1998.

Dillon, Richard I. "Towards a Tradition-History of the Parables of the True Israel (Mt 21.33–22.14)." *Biblical Research* 47 (1966): 1–42.

Dinges, William D. "Joseph Campbell and the Contemporary American Spiritual Milieu." In Lawrence Madden (ed.), *The Joseph Campbell Phenomenon*, pp. 9–40. Washington, DC: Pastoral, 1992.

Dodd, C. H. *The Parables of the Kingdom*. New York: Charles Scribner's Sons, 1961.

Dombrowski, Daniel A. *Analytic Theism, Hartshorne, and the Concept of God*. Albany, NY: State University of New York Press, 1996.

Donaldson, Margaret C. *Children's Minds*. London: Fontana Press, 1987.

Donlan, Walter. "The Origins of *kalos kagathos*." *American Journal of Philology* 94 (1973): 365–74.

Douglas, Ann. "Heaven our Home: Consolation Literature in the Northern United States, 1830–1880." In Philippe Ariès and David E. Stannard (eds), *Death in America*, pp. 49–68. Philadelphia: University of Pennsylvania Press, 1975.

Dowey, Edward A. *The Knowledge of God in Calvin's Theology*. New York: Columbia University Press, 1952.

Dubay, Thomas. *The Evidential Power of Beauty: Science and Theology Meet*. San Francisco: Ignatius Press, 1999.

Du Bois-Reymond, Emil Heinrich. *Über die Grenzen des Naturerkennens: Die sieben Welträtsel – Zwei Vortrage*. Leipzig: Veit, 1907.

Duff, Jeremy, and Joanna Collicutt McGrath. *Meeting Jesus: Human Responses to a Yearning God*. London: SPCK, 2006.

Dulles, Avery R. *Models of Revelation*. Maryknoll, NY: Orbis Books, 1992.

Dupré, Louis K. *Passage to Modernity: An Essay in the Hermeneutics of Nature and Culture*. New Haven, CT: Yale University Press, 1993.

Dupré, Louis K. *Religious Mystery and Rational Reflection*. Grand Rapids, MI: Eerdmans, 1998.

Dupré, Louis K. *The Enlightenment and the Intellectual Foundations of Modern Culture*. New Haven, CT: Yale University Press, 2004.

Durckheim, Karlfried Graf. *The Way of Transformation: Daily Life as Spiritual Exercise*. London: Allen & Unwin, 1988.

Durkheim, Emile. *The Elementary Forms of Religious Life*. New York: Free Press, 1995.

Dutton, Denis. "Mad about Flowers: Elaine Scarry on Beauty." *Philosophy and Literature* 24 (2000): 249–60.

Eagleton, Terry. "Nature and the Fall in Hopkins: A Reading of 'God's Grandeur'." *Essays in Criticism* 23 (1973): 68–75.

Eagleton, Terry. *The Ideology of the Aesthetic*. Oxford: Blackwell, 1990.

Eagleton, Terry. *After Theory*. London: Allen Lane, 2003.

Earle, Bo. "Involuntary Narration, Narrating Involition: Proust on Death, Repetition and Self-Becoming." *MLN* 117 (2002): 943–70.

Earle, Bo. "'Tarrying with the Negative': Baudelaire, Mallarmé, and the Rhythm of Modernity." *MLN* 118 (2003): 1015–42.

Ebeling, Gerhard. *Kirchengeschichte als Geschichte der Auslegung der Heiligen Schrift*. Tübingen: Mohr, 1947.

Eco, Umberto. *Art and Beauty in the Middle Ages*. New Haven, CT: Yale University Press, 1986.

Eco, Umberto. *The Aesthetics of Thomas Aquinas*. Cambridge, MA: Harvard University Press, 1988.

Edgerton, W. Dow. "Words and the Word." *Theological Studies* 44 (1988): 462–78.

Edwards, Jonathan. *Treatise on the Religious Affections*. New Haven, CT: Yale University Press, 1959.

Edwards, Jonathan. *The Miscellanies*. New Haven, CT: Yale University Press, 1994.

Edwards, Mark J. "Porphyry and the Intelligible Triad." *Journal of Hellenic Studies* 60 (1990): 14–24.

Ekman, Paul. "An Argument for Basic Emotions." *Cognition and Emotion* 6 (1992): 169–200.

Eldridge, Michael. *Transforming Experience: John Dewey's Cultural Instrumentalism*. Nashville, TN: Vanderbilt University Press, 1998.

Eldridge, Richard. "Kant, Hölderlin, and the Experience of Longing." In *The Persistence of Romanticism: Essays in Philosophy and Literature*, pp. 31–51. Cambridge, UK: Cambridge University Press, 2001.

Eldridge, Richard. "Plights of Embodied Soul: Dramas of Sin and Salvation in Augustine and Updike." In *The Persistence of Romanticism: Essays in Philosophy and Literature*, 205–28. Cambridge, UK: Cambridge University Press, 2001.

Eliade, Mircea. *Patterns in Comparative Religion*. New York: Sheed and Ward, 1958.

Eliot, T. S. *Collected Poems, 1909–1962*. London: Faber. 1963.

Ellrodt, Robert. *Seven Metaphysical Poets: A Structural Study of the Unchanging Self*. Oxford: Oxford University Press, 2000.

Emmet, Dorothy. *The Role of the Unrealisable: A Study in Regulative Ideals*. New York: St. Martin's Press, 1994.

Erikson, Erik H. *Identity and the Life Cycle*. New York: W. W. Norton, 1980.

Eskola, Timo. *Messiah and the Throne: Jewish Merkabah Mysticism and the Early Christian Exaltation Discourse*. Tübingen: Mohr, 2001.

Etcoff, Nancy L. *Survival of the Prettiest: The Science of Beauty*. New York: Doubleday, 2000.

Evans, Craig A. "Parables in Early Judaism." In Richard N. Longecker (ed.), *The Challenge of Jesus' Parables*, pp. 51–75. Grand Rapids, MI: Eerdmans, 2000.

Evernden, Neil. *The Social Creation of Nature*. Baltimore, MD: Johns Hopkins University Press, 1992.

Evola, Julius. *Meditations on the Peaks: Mountain Climbing as Metaphor for the Spiritual Quest*. Rochester, VT: Inner Traditions, 1998.

Faber, Paul. "The *Euthyphro* Objection to Divine Normative Theories: A Response." *Religious Studies* 21 (1985): 559–72.

Fabian, Johannes. *Moments of Freedom: Anthropology and Popular Culture*. Charlottesville, VA: University Press of Virginia, 1998.

Fabro, Cornelio. "The Overcoming of the Neoplatonic Triad of Being, Life and Intellect by Thomas Aquinas." In Dominic J. O'Meara (ed.), *Neoplatonism and Christian Thought*, pp. 97–108. Albany, NY: State University of New York Press, 1981.

Fantz, Robert L. "The Origin of Form Perception." *Scientific American* 203 (1961): 66–72.

Farber, Paul L. *The Temptations of Evolutionary Ethics*. Berkeley, CA: University of California Press, 1994.

Farrer, Austin. *The Glass of Vision*. London: Dacre Press, 1948.

Faulconer, James E. (ed.). *Transcendence in Philosophy and Religion*. Bloomington, IN: Indiana University Press, 2003.

Fellows, Jay. *Ruskin's Maze: Mastery and Madness in His Art*. Princeton, NJ: Princeton University Press, 1981.

Ferguson, Niall (ed.). *Virtual History: Alternatives and Counterfactuals*. London: Picador, 1997.

Ferreira, M. Jamie. "The Grammar of the Heart: Newman on Faith and Imagination." In Gerard Magill (ed.), *Discourse and Context: An Interdisciplinary Study of John Henry Newman*, pp. 129–43. Carbondale, IL: Southern Illinois University Press, 1993.

Ferris, David. "Where Three Paths Meet: History, Wordsworth, and the Simplon Pass." *Studies in Romanticism* 30 (1991): 391–438.

Ffrench, Patrick. "'Tel Quel' and Surrealism: A Re-evaluation. Has the Avant-Garde Become a Theory?" *The Romantic Review* 88 (1997): 189–96.

Fiddes, Paul S. "'Where Shall Wisdom Be Found?' Job 28 as a Riddle for Ancient and Modern Readers." In John Barton and David Reimer (eds), *After the Exile: Essays in Honor of Rex Mason*, pp. 171–90. Macon, GA: Mercer University Press, 1996.

Fiorenza, Elisabeth Schüssler. *Wisdom Ways: Introducing Feminist Biblical Interpretation*. Maryknoll, NY: Orbis Books, 2001.

Fisch, Harold. "The Scientist as Priest: A Note on Robert Boyle's Natural Theology." *Isis* 44 (1953): 252–65.

Fischer, Balthasar. "Eine Predigt Johann Henry Newmans aus dem Jahre 1840 zur Frage des christlichen Psalmenverständnisses." In Ernst Haag (ed.), *Freude an der Weisung des Herrn: Beiträge zur Theologie der Psalmen*, pp. 69–79. Stuttgart: Katholisches Bibelwerk, 1986.

Fischer, Michael. *Does Deconstruction Make Any Difference? Poststructuralism and the Defense of Poetry in Modern Criticism*. Bloomington, IN: Indiana University Press, 1985.

Fish, Stanley E. *Is There a Text in this Class? The Authority of Interpretive Communities*. Cambridge, MA: Harvard University Press, 1980.

Fish, Stanley E. *Surprised By Sin: The Reader in Paradise Lost*, 2nd edn. London: Macmillan, 1997.

Fleissner, Robert F. *Sources, Meaning, and Influences of Coleridge's Kubla Khan: Xanadu Re-Routed: A Study in the Ways of Romantic Variety.* Lewiston, NY: Edwin Mellen, 2000.

Fleming, Donald. "Charles Darwin, the Anaesthetic Man." *Victorian Studies* 4 (1961): 219–36.

Flieger, Verlyn. *Splintered Light: Logos and Language in Tolkien's World,* rev. edn. Kent, OH: Kent State University, 2002.

Force, James E. "The Breakdown of the Newtonian Synthesis of Science and Religion: Hume, Newton and the Royal Society." In R. H. Popkin and J. E. Force (eds), *Essays on the Context, Nature and Influence of Isaac Newton's Theology,* pp. 143–63. Dordrecht: Kluwer Academic Publishers, 1990.

Foster, Richard J. *Celebration of Discipline: The Path to Spiritual Growth.* London: Hodder and Stoughton, 1989.

Fott, David. *John Dewey: America's Philosopher of Democracy.* Lanham, MD: Rowman and Littlefield, 1998.

Fraassen, Bas C. van. *The Scientific Image.* Oxford: Oxford University Press, 1980.

Fraassen, Bas C. van. *The Empirical Stance.* New Haven, CT: Yale University Press, 2002.

Francis of Assisi. "Canticum fratris solis vel Laudes creaturarum." In Kajetan Esser, OFM., *Die opuskula des hl. Franziskus von Assisi,* Neue textkritische edn. Rome: Editiones Collegii S. Bonaventurae ad Claras aquas, 1976, pp. 128–9.

Frank, Richard M. *Al-Ghazali and the Ash'arite School.* Durham, NC: Duke University Press, 1994.

Fraser, Hilary. *Beauty and Belief. Aesthetics and Religion in Victorian Literature.* Cambridge, UK: Cambridge University Press, 1986.

Fredrikson, Paula. *From Jesus to Christ: The Origins of the New Testament Images of Jesus.* New Haven, CT: Yale University Press, 1988.

Freeman, Walter J. *Societies of Brains: A Study in the Neuroscience of Love and Hate.* Hillsdale, NJ: Lawrence Erlbaum Associates, 1995.

Freeman, Walter J. *How Brains Make Up Their Minds.* New York: Columbia University Press, 2000.

Fry, Iris. "On the Biological Significance of the Properties of Matter: L. J. Henderson's Theory of the Fitness of the Environment," *Journal of the History of Biology* 29 (1996): 155–96.

Fudge, Robert S. "Imagination and the Science-Based Aesthetic Appreciation of Unscenic Nature." *Journal of Aesthetics and Art Criticism* 59 (2001): 275–85.

Fyfe, Aileen. "The Reception of William Paley's *Natural Theology* in the University of Cambridge." *British Journal for the History of Science* 30 (1997): 321–35.

Gadamer, Hans-Georg, and Jean Grondin. "Looking Back with Gadamer Over His Writings and Their Effective History." *Theory, Culture and Society* 23 (2006): 85–100.

Gallagher, Shaun. *How the Body Shapes the Mind*. Oxford: Clarendon Press, 2005.

Garbowski, Christopher. *Recovery and Transcendence for the Contemporary Mythmaker: The Spiritual Dimension in the Works of J. R. R. Tolkien*. Lublin, Poland: Marie-Curie-Sklodowska University Press, 2000.

Gardner, W. H. "A Note on Hopkins and Duns Scotus." *Scrutiny* 5 (1936): 61–70.

Garland, Ken. *Mr Beck's Underground Map*. Harrow Weald: Capital Transport, 1994.

Gärtner, Bertil. *The Areopagus Speech and Natural Revelation*. Uppsala: Gleerup, 1955.

Gascoigne, John. "From Bentley to the Victorians: The Rise and Fall of British Newtonian Natural Theology." *Science in Context* 2 (1988): 219–56.

Gavin, William J. and James O. Pawelski. "James's 'Pure Experience' and Csikszentmihalyi's 'Flow': Existential Event or Methodological Postulate?" *Streams of William James* 6/2 (2004): 11–16.

Gazzaniga, Michael S. *The Mind's Past*. Berkeley, CA: University of California Press, 1998.

Gazzaniga, Michael S. *The Cognitive Neurosciences*, 3rd edn. Cambridge, MA: MIT Press, 2004.

Geach, Peter. "Plato's *Euthyphro*: An Analysis and Commentary." *Monist*, 50 (1966): 369–82.

Geertz, Clifford. *The Interpretation of Cultures: Selected Essays*. London: Fontana, 1973.

Gerhardsson, Birger. "The Narrative Meshalim in the Synoptic Gospels: A Comparison with the Narrative Meshalim in the Old Testament." *New Testament Studies* 34 (1988): 339–63.

Gertz, Bernhard. *Glaubenswelt als Analogie: Die theologische Analogie-Lehre Erich Przywaras und ihr Ort in der Auseinandersetzung um die analogia fidei*. Düsseldorf: Patmos-Verlag, 1969.

Ghosh, Kantik. *The Wycliffite Heresy: Authority and the Interpretation of Texts*. Cambridge, UK: Cambridge University Press, 2002.

Gibson, Arthur. *Metaphysics and Transcendence*. London: Routledge, 2003.

Gillespie, Neal C. "Divine Design and the Industrial Revolution: William Paley's Abortive Reform of Natural Theology." *Isis* 81 (1990): 214–29.

Gloede, Gunter. *Theologia naturalis bei Calvin*. Stuttgart: Kohlhammer, 1935.

Gnuse, Robert K. *The Dream Theophany of Samuel: Its Structure in Relation to Ancient Near Eastern Dreams and Its Theological Significance*. Lanham, MD: University Press of America, 1984.

Godlovitch, Stan. "Icebreakers: Environmentalism and Natural Aesthetics." *Journal of Applied Philosophy* 11 (1994): 15–30.

Goethe, Johann Wolfgang von. *Gedenkausgabe der Werke, Briefe und Gespräche*, ed. Ernst Rudolf Beutler, 27 vols. Zurich: Artemis-Verlag, 1948–71.

Goldman, Alan H. *Aesthetic Value*. Boulder, CO: Westview Press, 1995.

Goodacre, Mark S. *The Synoptic Problem: A Way Through the Maze*. London: Sheffield Academic Press, 2001.

Goodman, L. E. *God of Abraham*. New York: Oxford University Press, 1996.

Gopnik, A., A. Meltzoff, and P. Kuhl. *The Scientist in the Crib: What Early Learning Tells Us About the Mind*. New York, Harper Collins, 2001.

Gouinlock, James. *John Dewey's Philosophy of Value*. New York: Humanities Press, 1972.

Gould, Stephen J. *Ever Since Darwin: Reflections in Natural History*. New York: Norton, 1977.

Gould, Stephen J. *Rocks of Ages: Science and Religion in the Fullness of Life*. New York: Ballantine Books, 1999.

Grandy, R. E. (ed.). *Theories and Observation in Science*. Englewood Cliffs, NJ: Prentice-Hall, 1973.

Granger, Herbert. "Aristotle on the Analogy between Action and Nature." *Classical Quarterly* 43 (1993): 168–76.

Granger, John. *Looking for God in Harry Potter*. Wheaton, IL: SaltRiver, 2004.

Grant, Edward. *The Foundations of Modern Science in the Middle Ages: Their Religious, Institutional and Intellectual Contexts*. Cambridge, UK: Cambridge University Press, 1996.

Grant, Robert M. *Irenaeus of Lyons*. London: Routledge, 1997.

Gray, Francine du Plessis. *Simone Weil*. New York: Viking, 2001.

Grean, Stanley. "Elements of Transcendence in Dewey's Naturalistic Humanism." *Journal of the American Academy of Religion* 52 (1984): 263–88.

Greco, John. "Two Kinds of Intellectual Virtue." *Philosophy and Phenomenological Research* 60 (2000): 179–84

Greenfield, P. M., and C. P. Childs. "Understanding Sibling Concepts: A Developmental Study of Kin Terms in Zinacantan." In P. Dasen (ed.), *Piagetian Psychology: Cross-Cultural Contributions*, pp. 335–58. New York: Gardner Press, 1977.

Greenstein, George. *The Symbiotic Universe: Life and Mind in the Cosmos*. New York: Morrow, 1988.

Greetham, D. C. *Theories of the Text*. Oxford: Oxford University Press, 1999.

Gribbin, John, and Martin Rees. *Cosmic Coincidences: Dark Matter, Mankind and Anthropic Cosmology*. New York: Bantam Books, 1989.

Gross, Franz. *Relativistic Quantum Mechanics and Field Theory*. New York: Wiley, 1999.

Gross, Rita M., and Terry C. Muck. *Christians Talk About Buddhist Meditation, Buddhists Talk About Christian Prayer*. London: Continuum, 2003.

Gunnlaugur, A. Jónsson, and S. Cheney Michael. *The Image of God: Genesis 1:26–28 in a Century of Old Testament Research*. Stockholm: Almqvist & Wiksell International, 1988.

Gunton, Colin E. *The Triune Creator: A Historical and Systematic Study*. Edinburgh: Edinburgh University Press, 1998.

Gunton, Colin E. *The Christian Faith: An Introduction to Christian Doctrine.* Oxford: Blackwell, 2002.

Hacking, Ian. *The Social Construction of What?* Cambridge, MA: Harvard University Press, 1999.

Haldane, John. "Admiring the High Mountains: The Aesthetics of Environment," *Environmental Values* 3 (1994): 97–106.

Haldane, John. "Philosophy, the Restless Heart, and the Meaning of Theism." *Ratio* 19 (2006): 421–40.

Hale, Bob. "Is Platonism Epistemologically Bankrupt?" In Matthias Schirn (ed.), *The Philosophy of Mathematics Today*, pp. 77–98. Oxford: Clarendon, 1998.

Hall, John C. "Plato: *Euthyphro* 10a1–11a10', *Philosophical Quarterly*, 18 (1968): 1–11.

Hall, Ronald L. *The Human Embrace: The Love of Philosophy and the Philosophy of Love: Kierkegaard, Cavell, Nussbaum.* University Park, PA: Pennsylvania State University Press, 2000.

Halperin, David J. *The Faces of the Chariot: Early Jewish Responses to Ezekiel's Vision.* Tübingen: Mohr, 1988.

Hamilton, Gordon J. "Augustine's Methods of Biblical Interpretation." In H. A. Meynell (ed.), *Grace, Politics and Desire: Essays on Augustine*, pp. 103–19. Calgary, AB: University of Calgary Press, 1990.

Hamlyn, D. W. *Sensation and Perception: A History of the Philosophy of Perception.* London: Routledge & Kegan Paul, 1961.

Hammermeister, Kai. *The German Aesthetic Tradition.* Cambridge, UK: Cambridge University Press, 2002.

Hampshire, Stuart. *Innocence and Experience.* Cambridge, MA: Harvard University Press, 1989.

Hankey, Wayne J. "*Theoria* versus *Poesis*: Neoplatonism and Trinitarian Difference in Aquinas, John Milbank, Jean-Luc Marion and John Zizioulas." *Modern Theology* 15 (1999): 387–415.

Hansen, Niels Bugge. *That Pleasant Place: The Representation of Ideal Landscape in English Literature from the 14th to the 17th Century.* Copenhagen: Akademisk Forlag, 1973.

Hanson, N. R. *Patterns of Discovery: An Inquiry into the Conceptual Foundations of Science.* Cambridge, UK: Cambridge University Press, 1958.

Hardy, Alister C. *The Spiritual Nature of Man: A Study of Contemporary Religious Experience.* Oxford: Clarendon Press, 1980.

Hardy, G. H. *A Mathematician's Apology.* Cambridge, UK: Cambridge University Press, 1941.

Harman, Gilbert. "The Inference to the Best Explanation." *Philosophical Review* 74 (1965): 88–95.

Harman, Gilbert. "Detachment, Probability, and Maximum Likelihood." *Noûs* 1 (1967): 401–11.

Harman, Gilbert. "Knowledge, Inference, and Explanation." *American Philosophical Quarterly* 5 (1968): 164–73.

Harnack, Adolf von. *Marcion: das Evangelium vom fremden Gott. Eine Monographie zur Geschichte der Grundlegung der katholischen Kirche*, 2nd edn. Leipzig: Hinrichs, 1924.

Harpham, Geoffrey Galt. "The Fertile Word: Augustine's Ascetics of Interpretation." *Criticism* 38 (1986): 237–54.

Harris, Michael J. *Divine Command Ethics: Jewish and Christian Perspectives.* London: Routledge, 2003.

Harrison, Carol. *Beauty and Revelation in the Thought of Saint Augustine.* Oxford: Oxford University Press, 1992.

Harrison, Peter. *"Religion" and the Religions in the English Enlightenment.* Cambridge, UK: Cambridge University Press, 1990.

Hart, David Bentley. *The Beauty of the Infinite: The Aesthetics of Christian Truth.* Grand Rapids, MI: Eerdmans, 2003.

Hart, David Bentley. *The Doors of the Sea: Where Was God in the Tsunami?* Grand Rapids, MI: Eerdmans, 2005.

Hart, John W. *Karl Barth vs. Emil Brunner: The Formation and Dissolution of a Theological Alliance, 1916–1936.* New York: Peter Lang, 2001.

Hart, Kevin. *The Trespass of the Sign.* Cambridge, UK: Cambridge University Press, 1989.

Hart, Ray L. *Unfinished Man and the Imagination: Toward an Ontology and a Rhetoric of Revelation.* New York: Herder & Herder, 1968.

Hart, Trevor. "A Capacity for Ambiguity? The Barth–Brunner Debate Revisited." *Tyndale Bulletin* 44 (1993): 289–305.

Hart, Trevor. "Redemption and Fall" In Colin E. Gunton (ed.), *Cambridge Companion to Christian Doctrine*, pp. 189–206. Cambridge, UK: Cambridge University Press, 1997.

Hartshorne, Charles. *The Divine Relativity: A Social Conception of God*, New Haven, CT: Yale University Press, 1948.

Hauerwas, Stanley. *Vision and Virtue: Essays in Christian Ethical Reflection.* Notre Dame, IN: Fides Publishers, 1974.

Hauerwas, Stanley. "The Demands of a Truthful Story: Ethics and the Pastoral Task." *Chicago Studies* 21 (1982): 59–71.

Hauerwas, Stanley. *The Peaceable Kingdom: A Primer in Christian Ethics.* Notre Dame, IN: University of Notre Dame Press, 1983.

Hauerwas, Stanley. "Murdochian Muddles: Can We Get Through Them If God Does Not Exist?" In Maria Antonaccio and William Schweiker (eds), *Iris Murdoch and the Search for Human Goodness*, pp. 190–208. Chicago: University of Chicago Press, 1996.

Hauerwas, Stanley. *With the Grain of the Universe: The Church's Witness and Natural Theology.* London: SCM Press, 2002.

Haught, John. *God After Darwin: A Theology of Evolution*. Boulder, CO: Westview Press, 2001.

Hauser, Marc D. *Moral Minds: How Nature Designed Our Universal Sense of Right and Wrong*. New York: Ecco, 2006.

Havel, Václav. "The Need for Transcendence in the Postmodern World." *The Futurist* 29 (1995): 46–9.

Hawkin, David J., and Eileen Hawkin. *The Word of Science: The Religious and Social Thought of C. A. Coulson*. London: Epworth, 1989.

Hawley, John C. "Charles Kingsley and the Book of Nature." *Anglican and Episcopal History* 61 (1991): 461–79.

Hay, David. *Something There: The Biology of the Human Spirit*. London: Darton, Longman and Todd, 2006.

Hayman, Peter. "Monotheism – A Misused Word in Jewish Studies?" *Journal of Jewish Studies* 42 (1992): 1–15.

Hefner, Philip J. *The Human Factor: Evolution, Culture, and Religion*. Minneapolis: Fortress Press, 1993.

Helm, Paul. "John Calvin, the *Sensus Divinitatis* and the Noetic Effects of Sin." *International Journal of Philosophy of Religion* 43 (1998): 87–107.

Helmholtz, Hermann von. *Handbuch der physiologischen Optik*. Leipzig: Voss, 1867.

Henderson, Lawrence J. *The Fitness of the Environment: An Inquiry Into the Biological Significance of the Properties of Matter*. Boston: Beacon Press, 1913.

Hepburn, Ronald W. "Contemporary Aesthetics and the Neglect of Natural Beauty." In Bernard Williams and Alan Montefiore (eds), *British Analytical Philosophy*, pp. 285–310. London: Routledge and Kegan Paul, 1966.

Herder, Johann Gottfried. *Ideen zur Philosophie der Geschichte der Menschheit*, 4 vols. Riga: Johann Friedrich Hartknoch, 1784.

Herder, Johann Gottfried. *Kalligone*, 3 vols. Leipzig: Hartknoch, 1800.

Heusel, Barbara Stevens. *Iris Murdoch's Paradoxical Novels: Thirty Years of Critical Reception*. Rochester, NY: Camden House, 2001.

Hewison, Robert. *John Ruskin: The Argument of the Eye*. Princeton, NJ: Princeton University Press, 1976.

Hick, John. *Evil and the God of Love*, 2nd edn. London: Macmillan, 1985.

Hick, John. *An Interpretation of Religion: Human Responses to the Transcendent*, 2nd edn. Basingstoke: Palgrave Macmillan, 2004.

Higgins, Lesley. " 'To Prove Him With Hard Questions': Answerability in Hopkins' Writings." *Victorian Poetry* 37 (2001): 37–68.

Hill, Peter C. "Giving Religion Away: What the Study of Religion Offers Psychology." *International Journal for the Psychology of Religion* 9 (1999): 229–49.

Hilton, Denis J., John I. McClure, and Ben R. Slugowski. "The Course of Events: Counterfactuals, Causal Sequences, and Explanation." In David R. Mandel,

Denis J. Hilton, and Patrizia Catellani (eds), *The Psychology of Counterfactual Thinking*, pp. 44–60. London: Routledge, 2005.

Hilton, Tim. *John Ruskin*. New Haven, CT: Yale University Press, 2002.

Hobbs, R. Gerald. "How Firm a Foundation: Martin Bucer's Historical Exegesis of the Psalms." *Church History* 53 (1984): 477–91.

Hochstrasser, T. J. *Natural Law Theories in the Early Enlightenment*. Cambridge, UK: Cambridge University Press, 2000.

Hocking, William Ernest. "Dewey's Concepts of Experience and Nature." *Philosophical Review* 49 (1940): 228–44.

Holmes, Oliver Wendell. *Collected Legal Papers*. New York: Harcourt, Brace, and Howe, 1920.

Holyoak, Keith J., and Paul Thagard. *Mental Leaps: Analogy in Creative Thought*. Cambridge, MA: MIT Press, 1995.

Hood, Ralph W. "The Facilitation of Religious Experience". In R. W. Hood (ed.), *Handbook of Religious Experience*, pp. 569–97. Birmingham, AL: Religious Education Press, 1995.

Hooker, Morna D. "Chalcedon and the New Testament." In Sarah Coakley and David A. Pailin (eds), *The Making and Remaking of Christian Doctrine*, pp. 73–93. Oxford: Clarendon Press, 1993.

Hopkins, Gerard Manley. *Sermons and Devotional Writings of Gerard Manley Hopkins*, ed. Christopher Devlin. London: Oxford University Press, 1959.

Horkheimer, Max. *Die Sehnsucht nach dem ganz Anderen. Ein Interview mit Kommentar von Helmut Gumnior*. Hamburg: Furche-Verlag, 1971.

Horst, Friedrich. "Der Mensch als Ebenbild Gottes." In *Gottes Recht: Gesammelte Studien zum Recht im Alten Testament*, pp. 222–34. Munich: Kaiser Verlag, 1961.

Hort, F. J. A. *The Way, The Truth, The Life: The Hulsean Lectures for 1871*. Cambridge, UK: Cambridge University Press, 1893.

Hough, Graham. *The Last Romantics*. New York: Barnes & Noble, 1961.

Hoye, William J. *Actualitas Omnium Actuum: Man's Beatific Vision of God as Apprehended by Thomas Aquinas*. Meisenheim: Hain, 1975.

Hoyningen-Huene, Paul. *Reconstructing Scientific Revolutions: Thomas S. Kuhn's Philosophy of Science*. Chicago: University of Chicago Press, 1993.

Hubbard, Moyer V. *New Creation in Paul's Letters and Thought*. Cambridge, UK: Cambridge University Press, 2002.

Hull, Richard. "Sent Meaning vs. Attached Meaning: Two Interpretations of Interpretation in *The Scarlet Letter*." *American Transcendental Quarterly* 14 (2000): 143–58.

Hultgren, Arland J. *The Parables of Jesus: A Commentary*. Grand Rapids, MI: Eerdmans, 2000.

Humphries, Simon. " 'All by Turn and Turn About': The Indeterminacy of Hopkins' 'Epithalamion'." *Victorian Poetry* 38 (2000): 343–63.

Hunsinger, George. "Robert Jenson's *Systematic Theology*: A Review Essay." *Scottish Journal of Theology* 55 (2002): 161–200.

Hunt, Shelby D. "A Realist Theory of Empirical Testing Resolving the Theory-Ladenness/Objectivity Debate." *Philosophy of the Social Sciences* 24 (1994): 133–58.

Hurtado, Larry W. *Lord Jesus Christ: Devotion to Jesus in Earliest Christianity*. Grand Rapids, MI: Eerdmans, 2003.

Huxley, Aldous. *The Doors of Perception*. London: Chatto & Windus, 1954.

Huyssteen, Wentzel J. van. *Alone in the World? Human Uniqueness in Science and Theology*. Grand Rapids, MI: Eerdmans, 2006.

Inge, John. *A Christian Theology of Place*. Aldershot: Ashgate, 2003.

Inge, William R. *Personal Idealism and Mysticism*, 2nd edn. London: Longmans, Green, 1913.

Ireland, Dennis J. *Stewardship and the Kingdom of God: An Historical, Exegetical, and Contextual Study of the Parable of the Unjust Steward in Luke 16:1–13*. Leiden: Brill, 1992.

Irlam, Shaun. *Elations: The Poetics of Enthusiasm in Eighteenth-Century Britain*. Stanford, CA: Stanford University Press, 1999.

Israel, Jonathan I. *Radical Enlightenment: Philosophy and the Making of Modernity 1650–1750*. Oxford: Oxford University Press, 2001.

Israel, Jonathan I. *Enlightenment Contested: Philosophy, Modernity, and the Emancipation of Man 1670–1752*. Oxford: Oxford University Press, 2006.

Jacobson, David. *Emerson's Pragmatic Vision: The Dance of the Eye*. University Park, PA: Pennsylvania State University Press, 1993.

Jacobson, Edmund. "The Relational Account of Truth." *Journal of Philosophy, Psychology and Scientific Methods* 7 (1910): 253–61.

Jaki, Stanley L. *The Origin of Science and the Science of its Origin*. Edinburgh: Scottish Academic Press, 1978.

James, E. O. *The Ancient Gods: The History and Diffusion of Religion in the Ancient Near East and the Eastern Mediterranean*. London: Phoenix, 1999.

James, William. *The Varieties of Religious Experience*. London: Longmans, Green & Co., 1902.

James, William. "What Pragmatism Means." In *Pragmatism: A New Name for Some Old Ways of Thinking*, pp. 17–32. New York: Longman Green and Co., 1907.

James, William. *Essays in Radical Empiricism*. Cambridge, MA: Harvard University Press, 1976.

Jamison, Kay Redfield. *Touched with Fire: Manic Depressive Illness and the Artistic Temperament*. New York: Free Press, 1993.

Janoff-Bulman, Ronnie. *Shattered Assumptions: Towards a New Psychology of Trauma*. New York: Free Press, 1992.

Janz, Paul D. *God, the Mind's Desire: Reference, Reason and Christian Thinking*. Cambridge, UK: Cambridge University Press, 2004.

Jenson, Robert W. *America's Theologian: A Recommendation of Jonathan Edwards*. New York: Oxford University Press, 1988.

Jenson, Robert W. *Systematic Theology*, 2 vols. New York: Oxford University Press, 1997–9.

Johansen, Jørgen D. and Svend E. Larsen. *Signs in Use: An Introduction to Semiotics*. London: Routledge, 2002.

John of the Cross. *Obras Completas*. Burgos: Editorial Monte Carmelo, 2000.

Johnson, Mark. *The Body in the Mind: The Bodily Basis of Meaning, Imagination, and Reason*. Chicago: University of Chicago Press, 1987.

Johnson, William A. *The Search for Transcendence: A Theological Analysis of Nontheological Attempts to Define Transcendence*. New York: Harper & Row, 1974.

Jowers, Dennis W. "The Reproach of Modalism: A Difficulty for Karl Barth's Doctrine of the Trinity." *Scottish Journal of Theology* 36 (2003): 231–46.

Jüngel, Eberhard. *Gottes Sein ist im Werden: Verantwortliche Rede vom Sein Gottes bei Karl Barth: eine Paraphrase*. Tübingen: Mohr, 1965.

Kabat-Zinn, J. "Mindfulness-Based Interventions in Context: Past, Present, and Future." *Clinical Psychology: Science and Practice* 10 (2003): 144–56.

Kähler, Martin. *Der sogenannte historische Jesus und der geschichtliche, biblische Christus*. Munich: Kaiser Verlag, 1953.

Kaiser, Christopher B. "Climbing Jacob's Ladder: John Calvin and the Early Church on our Eucharistic Ascent to Heaven." *Scottish Journal of Theology* 56 (2003): 247–67.

Kaiser, Otto. "Dike und Sedaqa. Zur Frage nach der sittlichen Weltordnung. Ein theologische Präludium." *Neue Zeitschrift für systematische Theologie und Religionsphilosophie* 7 (1965): 251–75.

Kanarfogel, Ephraim. *Peering Through the Lattices: Mystical, Magical and Pietistic Dimensions in the Tosafist Period*. Detroit: Wayne State University Press, 2000.

Kane, Gordon L., Malcolm J. Perry, and Anna N. Zytkow. "The Beginning of the End of the Anthropic Principle." *New Astronomy* 7 (2002): 45–53.

Kapitan, Tomis. "Peirce and the Structure of Abductive Inference." In N. Houser, D. D. Roberts, and J. Van Evra (eds), *Studies in the Logic of Charles Sanders Peirce*, pp. 477–96. Bloomington, IN: Indiana University Press, 1997.

Katz, Marylin A. *Penelope's Renown: Meaning and Indeterminacy in the Odyssey*. Princeton, NJ: Princeton University Press, 1991.

Kaylor, Michael M. "'Beautiful Dripping Fragments:' A Whitmanesque Reading of Hopkins' 'Epithalamion'." *Victorian Poetry* 40 (2002): 157–87.

Keck, David. *Angels and Angelology in the Middle Ages*. Oxford: Oxford University Press, 1998.

Kee, Alistair. *The Way of Transcendence: Christian Faith Without Belief in God*. Harmondsworth: Pelican, 1971.

Kellert, Stephen R., and Edward O. Wilson (eds). *The Biophilia Hypothesis*. Washington, DC: Island Press, 1993.

Kelly, Thomas A. F. *Language and Transcendence: A Study in the Philosophy of Martin Heidegger and Karl-Otto Apel.* Berne: Peter Lang, 1994.

Keltner, Dacher, and Jonathan Haidt. "Approaching Awe, a Moral, Spiritual and Aesthetic Emotion." *Cognition and Emotion* 17 (2003): 297–314.

Kepler, Johann. *Gesammelte Werke,* ed. Max Caspar. Munich: C. H. Beck, 1937–83.

Kerr, Fergus. *Immortal Longings: Versions of Transcending Humanity.* London: SPCK, 1997.

Kestenbaum, Victor. *The Grace and Severity of the Ideal: John Dewey and the Transcendent.* Chicago: University of Chicago Press, 2002.

Keynes, Randal. *Annie's Box: Charles Darwin, His Daughter and Human Evolution.* London: Fourth Estate, 2001.

Kierkegaard, Søren. *For Self-Examination, Judge for Yourselves! and Three Discourses, 1851,* trans. Walter Lowrie. London: Oxford University Press, 1941.

Kilby, Clyde S. "*Till We Have Faces:* An Interpretation." In Peter J. Schakel (ed.), *The Longing for a Form: Essays on the Fiction of C. S. Lewis,* pp. 171–81. Kent, OH: Kent State University Press, 1977.

Kilby, Karen. *Karl Rahner: Theology and Philosophy.* London: Routledge, 2004.

Kingsley, Charles. "The Natural Theology of the Future." In *Westminster Sermons,* pp. v–xxxiii. London: Macmillan, 1874.

Kirk, Linda. *Richard Cumberland and Natural Law: Secularisation of Thought in Seventeenth-Century England.* Cambridge, UK: James Clarke & Co., 1987.

Kivy, Peter. "Aesthetic Concepts: Some Fresh Considerations." *Journal of Aesthetics and Art Criticism* 37 (1979): 423–32.

Kleeman, Terry F. "Mountain Deities in China: The Domestication of the Mountain God and the Subjugation of the Margins." *Journal of the American Oriental Society* 114 (1994): 226–38.

Kloppenborg, John S. *The Formation of Q: Trajectories in Ancient Wisdom Collections.* Philadelphia: Fortress Press, 1987.

Knell, Simon J., and Michael A. Taylor. "Hugh Miller: Fossils, Landscapes, and Literary Geology." *Proceedings of the Geologists' Association* 117 (2006): 85–98.

Knorr-Cetina, Karin. *Epistemic Cultures: How the Sciences Make Knowledge.* Cambridge, MA: Harvard University Press, 1999.

Koch, Klaus. *The Rediscovery of Apocalyptic.* Napierville, IL: Alec R. Allenson, 1972.

Kock, Christoph. *Natürliche Theologie: Ein evangelischer Streitbegriff.* Neukirchen-Vluyn: Neukirchener, 2001.

Köhler, Ludwig. *Theologie des Alten Testaments,* 3rd edn. Tübingen: Mohr, 1953.

Kolakowski, Leszek. "Concern about God in an Apparently Godless Age." In *My Correct Views on Everything,* ed. Zbigniew Janowski, pp. 173–83. South Bend, IN: St. Augustine's Press, 2005.

Kretzmann, Norman. "A General Problem of Creation: Why Would God Create Anything at all?" In Scott MacDonald (ed.), *Being and Goodness: The Concept of the Good in Metaphysics and Philosophical Theology*, pp. 208–49. Ithaca, NY: Cornell University Press, 1991.

Kretzmann, Norman. *The Metaphysics of Creation: Aquinas's Natural Theology in Summa Contra Gentiles II*. Oxford: Clarendon Press, 1999.

Kristeller, Paul Oskar. *The Philosophy of Marsilio Ficino*. New York: Columbia University Press, 1943.

Kugel, James L. "The Ladder of Jacob." *Harvard Theological Review* 88 (1995): 209–27.

Kuhn, Thomas S. *The Structure of Scientific Revolutions*, 2nd edn. Chicago: University of Chicago Press, 1970.

Kuipers, Theo A. F. "Beauty, a Road to the Truth," *Synthese* 131 (2002): 291–328.

Kulling, Heinz. *Geoffenbartes Geheimnis: Eine Auslegung von Apostelgeschichte 17, 16–34*. Zurich: Theologischer Verlag, 1993.

Kulp, Christopher B. *The End of Epistemology: Dewey and His Current Allies on the Spectator Theory of Knowledge*. Westport, CT: Greenwood Press, 1992.

Kurz, W. S. "Hellenistic Rhetoric in the Christological Proofs of Luke-Acts." *Catholic Biblical Quarterly* 42 (1980): 171–95.

Lackey, Michael. " 'God's Grandeur': Gerard Manley Hopkins' Reply to the Speculative Atheist." *Victorian Poetry* 39 (2001): 83–90.

Lakoff, George, and Mark Johnson. *Philosophy in the Flesh: The Embodied Mind and its Challenge to Western Thought*. New York: Basic Books, 1999.

Lambrecht, Jan. "The Groaning of Creation." *Louvain Studies* 15 (1990): 3–18.

Landow, George P. *The Aesthetic and Critical Theories of John Ruskin*. Princeton, NJ: Princeton University Press, 1971.

Landsman, N. P. *Mathematical Topics Between Classical and Quantum Mechanics*. New York: Springer, 1998.

Lane, Belden C. *The Solace of Fierce Landscapes: Exploring Desert and Mountain Spirituality*. New York: Oxford University Press, 1998.

Lane, Belden C. "Jonathan Edwards on Beauty, Desire and the Sensory World." *Theological Studies* 65 (2004): 44–68.

Lang, Helen S. *The Order of Nature in Aristotle's Physics: Place and the Elements*. Cambridge, UK: Cambridge University Press, 1998.

Langbaum, Robert. "The Epiphanic Mode in Wordsworth and Modern Literature." *New Literary History* 14 (1983): 335–21.

Langlois, Judith H., Lisa Kalakanis, Adam J. Rubinstein, Andrea Larson, Monica Hallam, and Monica Smoot. "Maxims or Myths of Beauty? A Meta-Analytic and Theoretical Review." *Psychological Bulletin* 126 (2000): 390–423.

Lash, Nicholas. *Easter in Ordinary: Reflections on Human Experience and the Knowledge of God*. Charlottesville, VA: University Press of Virginia, 1988.

Laudan, Larry, and Jarrett Leplin. "Empirical Equivalence and Underdetermination." *Journal of Philosophy* 88 (1991): 449–72.

Lazarus, Richard S. *Emotion and Adaptation*. New York: Oxford University Press, 1991.

LeDoux, Joseph E. *The Emotional Brain: The Mysterious Underpinnings of Emotional Life*. New York: Simon & Schuster, 1996.

Lee, Patrick. "Is Thomas's Natural Law Theory Naturalist?" *American Catholic Philosophical Quarterly* 71 (1997): 567–87.

Leeming, David Adams. *A Dictionary of Creation Myths*. New York: Oxford University Press, 1995.

Lefrançois, Guy R. *Theories of Human Learning*, 3rd edn. Pacific Grove, CA: Brooks/Cole Publishers, 1995.

Leopold, Heinrich. *Missionarische Theologie: Emil Brunners Weg zur theologischen Anthropologie*. Gütersloh: Mohn, 1974.

Lesses, Rebecca Macy. *Ritual Practices to Gain Power: Angels, Incantations, and Revelation in Early Jewish Mysticism*. Harrisburg, PA: Trinity Press International, 1998.

Levin, Jonathan. *The Poetics of Transition: Emerson, Pragmatism, & American Literary Modernism*. Durham, NC: Duke University Press, 1999.

Levine, Michael P. *Pantheism: A Non-Theistic Concept of Deity*. London: Routledge, 1994.

Levy, David and Sandra Peart. "Charles Kingsley and the Theological Interpretation of Natural Selection." *Journal of Bioeconomics* 8 (2006): 197–218.

Lewellen, Ted C. *The Anthropology of Globalization: Cultural Anthropology Enters the 21st Century*. Westport, CT: Bergin & Garvey, 2002.

Lewis, C. S. *Rehabilitations and Other Essays*. London: Oxford University Press, 1939.

Lewis, C. S. *Surprised by Joy*. London: Collins, 1959.

Lewis, C. S. *An Experiment in Criticism*. Cambridge, UK: Cambridge University Press, 1961.

Lewis, C. S. "The Weight of Glory." In *Screwtape Proposes a Toast, and Other Pieces*, pp. 94–110. London: Fontana, 1965.

Lewis, C. S. *Christian Reflections*. Grand Rapids, MI: Eerdmans, 1967.

Lewis, C. S. *Miracles: A Preliminary Study*. New York: Macmillan, 1978.

Lewis, C. S. "Is Theology Poetry?" In *Essay Collection and Other Short Pieces*, pp. 10–21. London: HarperCollins, 2000.

Libet, Benjamin, Anthony Freeman, and Keith Sutherland (eds). *The Volitional Brain: Towards a Neuroscience of Free Will*. Thorverton, UK: Imprint Academic, 1999.

Lillard, Angeline S. "Ethnopsychologies: Cultural Variations in Theory of Mind." *Psychological Bulletin* 123 (1998): 2–32.

Lindberg, David C., and Ronald L. Numbers. "Beyond War and Peace: A Reappraisal of the Encounter between Christianity and Science." *Church History* 55 (1984): 338–54.

Linden, Stanton J. Darke *Hierogliphicks: Alchemy in English Literature from Chaucer to the Restoration*. Lexington, KY: University Press of Kentucky, 1996.

Lindseth, Peter L. "The Paradox of Parliamentary Supremacy: Delegation, Democracy, and Dictatorship in Germany and France, 1920s–1950s." *Yale Law Journal* 113 (2004): 1341–417.

Lipton, Peter. *Inference to the Best Explanation*, 2nd edn. London: Routledge, 2004.

Lipton, Peter. "What Good is an Explanation?" In John Cornwell (ed.), *Explanations: Styles of Explanation in Science*, pp. 1–21. Oxford: Oxford University Press, 2004.

Lisska, Anthony J. *Aquinas's Theory of Natural Law: An Analytic Reconstruction*. Oxford: Clarendon Press, 1996.

Little, Bruce A. *A Creation-Order Theodicy: God and Gratuitous Evil*. Lanham, MD: University Press of America, 2005.

Liu, Alan. "Local Transcendence: Cultural Criticism, Postmodernism, and the Romanticism of Detail." *Representations* 32 (1990): 75–113.

Lloyd, Geoffrey E. R. "Greek Antiquity: The Invention of Nature." In John Torrance (ed.), *The Concept of Nature*, pp. 1–24. Oxford: Oxford University Press, 1992.

Locke, John. *The Works of John Locke*. 10 vols. London: Thomas Tegg, 1823.

Loe, Thomas. "'The Dead' as Novella." *James Joyce Quarterly* 28 (1991): 485–97.

Loftis, J. Robert. "Three Problems for the Aesthetic Foundations of Environmental Ethics." *Philosophy in the Contemporary World* 10 (2003): 41–50.

Long, Eugene Thomas. "Quest for Transcendence." *Review of Metaphysics* 52 (1998): 3–19.

Longair, M. S., and Roger Penrose. *The Large, The Small, and The Human Mind*. Cambridge, UK: Cambridge University Press, 1999.

Lovejoy, Arthur O. "'Nature' as Aesthetic Form." *Modern Language Notes* 42 (1927): 444–50.

Lovejoy, Arthur O., and George Boas. *Primitivism and Related Ideas in Antiquity*. New York: Octagon Books, 1973.

Lubac, Henri de. *Surnaturel: études historiques*. Paris: Aubier, 1946.

Lucas, J. R. *The Conceptual Roots of Mathematics: An Essay on the Philosophy of Mathematics*. London: Routledge, 2000.

Luiza, Robert M. "The Tower of Babel: *The Wanderer* and the Ruins of History." *Studies in the Literary Imagination* 36 (2003): 1–35.

Lyman, J. Rebecca. *Christology and Cosmology: Models of Divine Activity in Origen, Eusebius, and Athanasius*. Oxford: Clarendon Press, 1993.

Mach, Michael. *Entwicklungsstudien des jüdischen Engelglaubens in vorrabbinischer Zeit*. Tübingen: J. C. B. Mohr, 1992.

Macierowski, E. M., and R. F. Hassing. "John Philoponus on Aristotle's Definition of Nature: A Translation from the Greek with Introduction and Notes." *Ancient Philosophy* 8 (1988): 73–100.

MacIntyre, Alasdair. *After Virtue*, 2nd edn. Notre Dame, IN: University of Notre Dame Press, 1984.

MacIntyre, Alasdair. *Whose Justice? Which Rationality?* Notre Dame, IN: University of Notre Dame Press, 1988.

MacKenzie, Iain M. *God's Order and Natural Law: The Works of the Laudian Divines*. Aldershot: Ashgate, 2002.

Mackie, J. L. *Ethics: Inventing Right and Wrong*. London: Penguin Books, 1977.

Macquarrie, John. *A Guide to the Sacraments*. London: SCM Press, 1997.

Makdisi, George. *Ibn 'Aqil: Religion and Culture in Classical Islam*. Edinburgh: Edinburgh University Press, 1997.

Mandelbrot, Benoit B. *The Fractal Geometry of Nature*. New York: W. H. Freeman, 1982.

Manuel, Frank E. *The Religion of Isaac Newton*. Oxford: Clarendon Press, 1974.

Marcel, Gabriel. *Être et avoir*. Paris: Aubier Éditions Montaigne, 1935.

Marcel, Gabriel. *The Mystery of Being*. London: Harvill Press, 1950.

Margolin, Jean-Claude. "L'analogie dans la pensée d'Erasme." *Archiv für Reformationsgeschichte* 69 (1978): 24–50.

Marshall, James D. "On What We May Hope: Rorty on Dewey and Foucault." *Studies in Philosophy and Education* 13 (1994): 307–23.

Marshall, Marilyn. "Physics, Metaphysics, and Fechner's Psychophysics." In William R. Woodward and Mitchell G. Ash (eds), *The Problematic Science: Psychology in Nineteenth-Century Thought*, pp. 65–87. New York: Praeger, 1982.

Masuzawa, Tomoko. *In Search of Dreamtime: The Quest for the Origin of Religion*. Chicago: University of Chicago Press, 1993.

Mather, Cotton. *The Christian Philosopher*, ed. Winton U. Solberg. Urbana, IL: University of Illinois Press, 1994.

Maul, Stefan M. "Der assyrische König: Hüter der Weltordnung." In Kazuko Watanabe (ed.), *Priests and Officials in the Ancient Near East*, pp. 201–14. Heidelberg: Universitätsverlag C. Winter, 1999.

Maw, Martin. *Visions of India: Fulfilment Theology, the Aryan Race Theory, and the Work of British Protestant Missionaries in Victorian India*. Frankfurt am Main: Peter Lang, 1990.

Maxwell, James Clerk. "A Dynamical Theory of the Electromagnetic Field." *Philosophical Transactions of the Royal Society of London* 155 (1865): 459–512.

McAllister, James W. "Truth and Beauty in Scientific Reason." *Synthese* 78 (1989): 25–51.

McAllister, James W. "Is Beauty a Sign of Truth in Scientific Theories?" *American Scientist* 86 (1998): 174–83.

McAllister, James W. *Beauty and Revolution in Science*. Ithaca, NY: Cornell University Press, 1999.

McCauley, Robert N. "The Naturalness of Religion and the Unnaturalness of Science." In F. Keil and R. Wilson (eds), *Explanation and Cognition*, pp. 61–85. Cambridge, MA: MIT Press, 2000.

McGrath, Alister E. "Karl Barth als Aufklärer? Der Zusammenhang seiner Lehre vom Werke Christi mit der Erwählungslehre." *Kerygma und Dogma* 30 (1984): 273–83.

McGrath, Alister E. *Luther's Theology of the Cross: Martin Luther's Theological Breakthrough*. Oxford: Blackwell, 1985.

McGrath, Alister E. "The Eucharist: Reassessing Zwingli." *Theology* 93 (1990): 13–20.

McGrath, Alister E. *In the Beginning: The Story of the King James Bible*. New York: Doubleday, 2001.

McGrath, Alister E. *A Scientific Theology: 1 – Nature*. Edinburgh: T&T Clark, 2001.

McGrath, Alister E. *A Scientific Theology: 2 – Reality*. London: T&T Clark, 2002.

McGrath, Alister E. *A Scientific Theology: 3 – Theory*. London: T&T Clark, 2003.

McGrath, Alister E. *The Intellectual Origins of the European Reformation*, 2nd edn. Oxford: Blackwell, 2003.

McGrath, Alister E. *Dawkins' God: Genes, Memes and the Meaning of Life*. Oxford: Blackwell, 2004.

McGrath, Alister E. *The Twilight of Atheism: The Rise and Fall of Disbelief in the Modern World*. New York: Doubleday, 2004.

McGrath, Alister E. "Assimilation in the Development of Doctrine: The Theological Significance of Jean Piaget." In Alister E. McGrath (ed.), *The Order of Things: Explorations in Scientific Theology*, pp. 169–82. Oxford: Blackwell Publishing, 2006

McGrath, Alister E. "Towards the Restatement and Renewal of a Natural Theology: A Dialogue with the Classic English Tradition." In Alister E. McGrath (ed.), *The Order of Things: Explorations in Scientific Theology*, pp. 63–96. Oxford: Blackwell Publishing, 2006.

McGrath, Alister E. "Stratification: Levels of Reality and the Limits of Reductionism." In *The Order of Things: Explorations in Scientific Theology*, pp. 97–116. Oxford: Blackwell Publishing, 2006.

McGrath, Alister E. (ed.). *The Order of Things: Explorations in Scientific Theology*. Oxford: Blackwell Publishing, 2006.

McGrath, Alister E. "Spirituality and Well-Being: Some Recent Discussions." *Brain* 129 (2006): 278–82.

McGrath, Alister E. *Christian Theology: An Introduction*, 4th edn. Oxford: Blackwell, 2007.

McGrath, Alister E. *Christianity's Dangerous Idea: The Protestant Revolution.* San Francisco: HarperOne, 2007.

McGrath, F. C. *The Sensible Spirit: Walter Pater and the Modernist Paradigm.* Tampa, FL: University Presses of Florida, 1986.

McGrath, James F. *John's Apologetic Christology: Legitimation and Development in Johannine Christology.* Cambridge, UK: Cambridge University Press, 2001.

McGrew, Timothy. "Confirmation, Heuristics, and Explanatory Reasoning." *British Journal for Philosophy of Science* 54 (2003): 553–67.

McGuire, J. E. "Boyle's Conception of Nature." *Journal of the History of Ideas* 33 (1972): 523–42.

McKenna, John H. "Symbol and Reality: Some Anthropological Considerations." *Worship* 65 (1991): 2–27.

McKenna, John H. "Eucharistic Presence: An Invitation to Dialogue." *Theological Studies* 60 (1999): 294–332.

McKinnon, Andrew. "Sociological Definitions, Language Games and the 'Essence' of Religion." *Method and Theory in the Study of Religion* 14 (2002): 61–83.

McMullin, Ernan. *The Inference that Makes Science.* Milwaukee, WI: Marquette University Press, 1992.

McNeil, J. and E. Warrington. "Prosopagnosia: A Face-Specific Disorder." *Quarterly Journal of Experimental Psychology* 46 (1993): 1–10.

McPherran, Mark. "Socratic Piety in the 'Euthyphro'." *Journal of the History of Philosophy* 23 (1985): 283–310.

McShea, R. J. and D. W. McShea. "Biology and Value Theory." In Jane Maienschein and Michael Ruse (eds), *Biology and the Foundation of Ethics*, pp. 307–27. Cambridge, UK: Cambridge University Press, 1999.

Medawar, Peter B. *The Limits of Science.* Oxford: Oxford University Press, 1985.

Meilaender, Gilbert. "Veritatis Splendor: Reopening Some Questions of the Reformation." *Journal of Religious Ethics* 23 (1995): 225–38.

Mellor, D. H. *The Warrant of Induction.* Cambridge, UK: Cambridge University Press, 1988.

Menand, Louis. *The Metaphysical Club: A Story of Ideas in America.* New York: Farrar, Straus, and Giroux, 2001.

Merchant, Carolyn. *Reinventing Eden: The Fate of Nature in Western Culture.* London: Routledge, 2003.

Mercier, André. *Thought and Being: An Inquiry into the Nature of Knowledge.* Basle: Verlag für Recht und Gesellschaft, 1959.

Merleau-Ponty, Maurice. *The Primacy of Perception and Other Essays on Phenomenological Psychology, the Philosophy of Art, History and Politics*, ed. James M. Edie, trans. William Cobb. Evanston, IL: Northwestern Univ. Press, 1964.

Merton, Thomas. *Disputed Questions.* New York: Farrar, Straus and Cudahy, 1960.

Merton, Thomas. *Seeds of Contemplation*. Wheathampstead: Anthony Clarke, 1972.

Merton, Thomas. *The Inner Experience: Notes on Contemplation*. San Francisco: HarperSanFrancisco, 2003.

Mettinger, Tryggve N. D. "Abbild oder Urbild? 'Imago Dei' in traditionsgeschichtlicher Sicht." *Zeitschrift für Alttestamentlicher Wissenschaft* 86 (1974): 403–24.

Miall, David S. "Wordsworth and *The Prelude*: the Problematics of Feeling." *Studies in Romanticism* 31 (1992): 233–53.

Miall, David S. "Mark Johnson, Metaphor, and Feeling." *Journal of Literary Semantics* 26 (1997): 191–210.

Midgley, Mary. *Science and Poetry*. London: Routledge, 2001.

Midgley, Mary. *Evolution as a Religion: Strange Hopes and Stranger Fears*, 2nd edn. London: Routledge, 2002.

Milbank, John. *The Suspended Middle: Henri de Lubac and the Debate Concerning the Supernatural*. London: SCM Press, 2005.

Millar, J. Hillis. *The Disappearance of God: Five Nineteenth-Century Writers*. Cambridge, MA: Harvard University Press, 1963.

Miller, David L. "The Flight of the Wild Gander: The Postmodern Meaning of 'Meaning'." In Daniel C. Noel (ed.), *Paths to the Power of Myth: Joseph Campbell and the Study of Religion*, pp. 108–17. New York: Crossroad, 1990.

Miller, Fred D. *Nature, Justice and Rights in Aristotle's Politics*. Oxford: Clarendon Press, 1995.

Miller, Hugh. *The Testimony of the Rocks; or, Geology in its Bearings on the Two Theologies, Natural and Revealed*. Ann Arbor, MI: Scholarly Publishing Office, University of Michigan Library, 2005.

Miller, J. Maxwell. "The 'Image' and 'Likeness' of God." *Journal of Biblical Literature* 91 (1972): 289–304.

Miller, Richard W. "Three Versions of Objectivity: Aesthetic, Moral, and Scientific." In Jerrold Levinson (ed.), *Aesthetics and Ethics: Essays at the Intersection*, pp. 26–58. Cambridge, UK: Cambridge University Press, 1998.

Moberly, R. W. L. "To Hear the Master's Voice: Revelation and Spiritual Discernment in the Call of Samuel." *Scottish Journal of Theology* 48 (1995): 443–68.

Modiano, Raimonda. *Coleridge and the Concept of Nature*. Tallahassee, FL: Florida State University Press, 1985.

Moltmann, Jürgen. *Theology of Hope: On the Ground and the Implications of a Christian Eschatology*. London: SCM, 1967.

Moore, James. "Theodicy and Society: The Crisis of the Intelligentsia." In Richard J. Helmstadter and Bernard Lightman (eds), *Victorian Faith in Crisis: Essays in Continuity and Change in Nineteenth-Century Religious Belief*, pp. 153–86. Basingstoke: Macmillan, 1990.

Morasso, Pietro, and Vittorio Sanguineti. "Self-Organizing Body Schema for Motor Planning." *Journal of Motor Behaviour* 27 (1995): 52–66.

Morgan, Alison. *Dante and the Medieval Other World*. Cambridge, UK: Cambridge University Press, 1990.

Morgan, David T. "Benjamin Franklin: Champion of Generic Religion." *Historian* 62 (2000): 723–9.

Morgan, Jamie. "What is Meta-Reality?" *Journal of Critical Realism* 1 (2003): 115–46.

Morgan, Jamie. "Ontological Casuistry? Bhaskar's Meta-Reality, Fine Structure, and Human Disposition." *New Formations* 56 (2005): 133–46.

Morris, Charles William. *The Pragmatic Movement in American Philosophy*. New York: Braziller, 1970.

Mothersill, Mary. *Beauty Restored*. Oxford: Clarendon Press, 1984.

Mühlenberg, Ekkehard. *Die Unendlichkeit Gottes bei Gregor von Nyssa: Gregors Kritik am Gottesbegriff der klassischen Metaphysik*. Göttingen: Vandenhoeck & Ruprecht, 1966.

Munck, Thomas. *The Enlightenment: A Comparative Social History, 1721–1794*. London: Arnold, 2000.

Murata, Sachiko, and William C. Chittick. *The Vision of Islam*. St Paul, MN: Paragon House, 1994.

Murdoch, Iris. "Vision and Choice in Morality." *Proceedings of the Aristotelian Society*, supplementary vol. 30 (1956): 32–58.

Murdoch, Iris. *The Sovereignty of Good*. London: Routledge, 1970.

Murdoch, Iris. *Metaphysics as a Guide to Morals*. London: Penguin, 1992.

Murdoch, Iris. *Existentialists and Mystics: Writings on Philosophy and Literature*, ed. Peter J. Conradi. London: Chatto & Windus, 1997.

Murphy, Nancey. *Bodies and Souls, or Spirited Bodies?* Cambridge, UK: Cambridge University Press, 2006.

Naddaf, Gerard. *The Greek Concept of Nature*. Albany, NY: State University of New York Press, 2005.

Nagel, Thomas. "What is it Like to be a Bat?" *Philosophical Review* 83 (1974): 435–50.

Nagel, Thomas. *The View from Nowhere*. New York: Oxford University Press, 1986.

Nakamura, Jeanne, and Mihaly Csikszentmihalyi. "The Concept of Flow." In C. Snyder and S. Lopez (eds), *Handbook of Positive Psychology*, pp. 89–105. New York: Oxford University Press, 2002.

Narlikar, Jayant V. "The Concepts of 'Beginning' and 'Creation' in Cosmology." *Philosophy of Science* 59 (1992): 361–71.

Nasr, Seyyed Hossein. *Religion and the Order of Nature*. Oxford: Oxford University Press, 1996.

Nebelsick, Harold P. "Karl Barth's Understanding of Science." In John Thompson (ed.), *Theology Beyond Christendom: Essays on the Centenary of the Birth of Karl Barth*, pp. 165–214. Allison Park, PA: Pickwick Publications, 1986.

Neiman, Susan. *Evil in Modern Thought: An Alternative History of Modern Philosophy.* Princeton, NJ: Princeton University Press, 2002.

Neusner, Jacob. *The Rabbinic Traditions About the Pharisees Before 70,* 3 vols. Leiden: E. J. Brill, 1971.

Neusner, Jacob. *The Incarnation of God: The Character of Divinity in Formative Judaism.* Philadelphia: Fortress Press, 1988.

Neville, Robert C. *Behind the Masks of God: An Essay Toward Comparative Theology.* Albany, NY: State University of New York Press, 1991.

Newbigin, Lesslie. *The Open Secret: Sketches for a Missionary Theology.* London: SPCK, 1978.

Newman, John Henry. *Apologia Pro Vita Sua.* London: Longmans, Green, & Co., 1864.

Newman, John Henry. *An Essay in Aid of a Grammar of Assent.* London: Burns & Oates, 1870.

Newman, John Henry. *Fifteen Sermons Preached Before the University of Oxford.* London: Longmans, Green, & Co., 1909.

Newman, Murray. "The Prophetic Call of Samuel." In B. W. Anderson and W. J. Harrelson (eds), *Israel's Prophetic Heritage: Essays in Honor of James Muilenburg,* pp. 86–97. London: SCM Press, 1962.

Nichols, Aidan. *The Word Has Been Abroad: A Guide Through Balthasar's Aesthetics.* Edinburgh: T&T Clark, 1998.

Nichols, Ashton. *The Poetics of Epiphany: Nineteenth Century Origins of the Modern Literary Moment.* Tuscaloosa, AL: University of Alabama Press, 1988.

Nicolson, Marjorie Hope. *Mountain Gloom and Mountain Glory: The Development of the Aesthetics of the Infinite.* Ithaca, NY: Cornell University Press, 1959.

Niditch, Susan. *Chaos to Cosmos: Studies in Biblical Patterns of Creation.* Chico, CA: Scholars Press, 1985.

Niebuhr, Reinhold. *The Nature and Destiny of Man: A Christian Interpretation,* 2 vols. London: Nisbet, 1941.

Nietzsche, Friedrich Wilhelm. *Human, All Too Human: A Book for Free Spirits.* Cambridge, UK: Cambridge University Press, 1986.

Niiniluoto, Ilkka. "Defending Abduction." *Philosophy of Science* 66 (Proceedings) (2000): S436–51.

Noèe, Alva (ed.). *Is the Visual World a Grand Illusion?* Thorverton, UK: Imprint Academic, 2002.

Norris, Christopher. *Against Relativism: Philosophy of Science, Deconstruction and Critical Theory.* Oxford: Blackwell, 1997.

Norton, Robert E. *Herder's Aesthetics and the European Enlightenment.* Ithaca, NY: Cornell University Press, 1991.

Novak, David. *Natural Law in Judaism.* Cambridge, UK: Cambridge University Press, 1998.

Núñez, Rafael E., and Walter J. Freeman (eds). *Reclaiming Cognition: The Primacy of Action, Intention and Emotion*. Bowling Green, OH: Imprint Academic, 1999.

Nussbaum, Martha C. "Beatrice's Dante: Loving the Individual?" *Apeiron* 26 (1993): 161–78.

Nussbaum, Martha C. *Upheavals of Thought: The Intelligence of Emotions*. Cambridge, UK: Cambridge University Press, 2001.

Nygren, Anders. *Agape and Eros: A Study of the Christian Idea of Love*. Philadelphia: Westminster Press, 1953.

Oak, Sung-Deuk. "Shamanistic *Tan'gun* and Christian *Hananim*: Protestant Missionaries' Interpretation of the Korean Founding Myth, 1805–1934." *Studies in World Christianity* 7 (2001): 42–57.

Oakes, Lisa M., and David H. Rakison. "Issues in the Early Developments of Concepts and Categories." In L. M. Oakes and D. H. Rakison (eds), *Early Category Development: Making Sense of the Blooming, Buzzing Confusion*, pp. 1–20. Oxford: Oxford University Press, 2003.

Oakley, Francis. *Omnipotence, Covenant and Order: An Excursion in the History of Ideas from Abelard to Leibniz*. Ithaca, NY: Cornell University Press, 1984.

Obermann, Andreas. *Die christologische Erfüllung der Schrift im Johannesevangelium: eine Untersuchung zur johanneischen Hermeneutik anhand der Schriftzitate*. Tübingen: Mohr, 1996.

Odom, Herbert H. "The Estrangement of Celestial Mechanics and Religion." *Journal of the History of Ideas* 27 (1966): 533–58.

O'Donaghue, Noel. "A Theology of Beauty." In John Riches (ed.), *The Analogy of Beauty: The Theology of Hans Urs von Balthasar*, pp. 1–10. Edinburgh: T&T Clark, 1986.

O'Donnell, John. "The Trinitarian Panentheism of Sergej Bulgakov." *Gregorianum* 76 (1995): 31–45.

O'Donovan, Joan. "Man in the Image of God: The Disagreement between Barth and Brunner Reconsidered." *Scottish Journal of Theology* 39 (1986): 433–59.

O'Donovan, Oliver. "*Usus* and *Fruitio* in Augustine, *De Doctrina Christiana* I." *Journal of Theological Studies* 33 (1982): 361–97.

O'Donovan, Oliver. *Resurrection and Moral Order*. Grand Rapids, MI: Eerdmans, 1986.

O'Donovan, Oliver. "The Loss of a Sense of Place." In Oliver O'Donovan and Joan Lockwood O'Donovan, *Bonds of Imperfection: Christian Politics, Past and Present*, pp. 296–320. Grand Rapids, MI: Eerdmans, 2004.

Okure, Teresa. " 'I Will Open My Mouth in Parables' (Matt 13:35): A Case for a Gospel-Based Biblical Hermeneutic." *New Testament Studies* 46 (2000): 445–63.

Onorato, Richard J. *The Character of the Poet: Wordsworth in the Prelude*. Princeton, NJ: Princeton University Press, 1971.

Orlov, Andrei A. "The Face as the Heavenly Counterpart of the Visionary in the Slavonic *Ladder of Jacob*." In Craig A. Evans (ed.), *Of Scribes and Sages: Early Jewish Interpretation and Transmission of Scripture*, pp. 37–76. London: T&T Clark, 2004.

Osborn, Eric F. *Irenaeus of Lyons*. Cambridge, UK: Cambridge University Press, 2001.

Otto, Randall E. *The God of Hope: The Trinitarian Vision of Jürgen Moltmann*. Lanham, MD: University Press of America, 1991.

Otto, Rudolf. *The Idea of the Holy*. London: Oxford University Press, 1977.

Overgaard, Søren. *Husserl and Heidegger on Being in the World*. Dordrecht: Kluwer, 2004.

Owen, J. Judd. *Religion and the Demise of Liberal Rationalism: The Foundational Crisis of the Separation of Church and State*. Chicago: University of Chicago Press, 2001.

Pailin, David. "Should Herbert of Cherbury be Regarded as a 'Deist'?" *Journal of Theological Studies* 51 (2000): 113–49.

Pals, Daniel L. *Seven Theories of Religion*. New York: Oxford University Press, 1996.

Pannenberg, Wolfhart. *Jesus – God and Man*. Philadelphia: Westminster Press, 1968.

Pannenberg, Wolfhart. "Redemptive Event and History." In *Basic Questions in Theology*, pp. 15–80. London: SCM Press, 1970.

Panshin, Alexei, and Cory Panshin. *The World Beyond the Hill: Science Fiction and the Quest for Transcendence*. Los Angeles, CA: J. P. Tarcher, 1989.

Pargament, Kenneth I. *The Psychology of Religion and Coping: Theory, Research, Practice*. New York: Guilford Press, 1997.

Parker, Richard. "From Symbolism to Interpretation: Reflections on the Work of Clifford Geertz." *Anthropology and Humanism Quarterly* 10 (1985): 62–7.

Parmentier, Richard J. *Signs in Society: Studies in Semiotic Anthropology*. Bloomington, IN: Indiana University Press, 1994.

Partington, V. L. *The Beginnings of Critical Realism in America*. New York: Harcourt, Brace, 1930.

Pater, William. *Renaissance: Studies in Art and Poetry*, ed. Donald L. Hill. Berkeley, CA: University of California Press, 1980.

Pawelski, James O. "Perception, Cognition, and Volition: The Radical and Integrated Individualism of William James." PhD Thesis, Pennsylvania State University, 1997.

Peacocke, Arthur R. *Creation and the World of Science*. Oxford: Oxford University Press, 1979.

Peacocke, Arthur R. *Paths from Science Towards God: The End of All Our Exploring*. Oxford: Oneworld, 2001.

Pearce, Sandra Manoogian. "Edna O'Brien's 'Lantern Slides' and Joyce's 'The Dead': Shadows of a Bygone Era." *Studies in Short Fiction* 32 (1995): 437–50.

Pearce, Spencer. "Nature and Supernature in the Dialogues of Girolamo Fracastoro." *Sixteenth Century Journal* 27 (1996): 111–32.

Pelikan, Jaroslav. *Christianity and Classical Culture: The Metamorphosis of Natural Theology in the Christian Encounter with Hellenism.* New Haven, CT: Yale University Press, 1993.

Pennock, Robert T. *Intelligent Design Creationism and Its Critics: Philosophical, Theological, and Scientific Perspectives.* Cambridge, MA: MIT Press, 2001.

Penrose, Roger. "The Modern Physicist's View of Nature." In John Torrance (ed.), *The Concept of Nature,* pp. 117–66. Oxford: Oxford University Press, 1992.

Penrose, Roger. *Shadows of the Mind.* London: Vintage, 1995.

Penrose, Roger. *The Road to Reality: A Complete Guide to the Laws of the Universe.* London: Jonathan Cape, 2004.

Peterson, Christopher, and Martin E. P. Seligman. *Character Strengths and Virtues: A Handbook and Classification.* New York and Oxford: Oxford University Press, 2004.

Peterson, Gregory R. "The Created Co-Creator: What It Is and Is Not." *Zygon* 39 (2004): 827–40.

Piaget, Jean. *The Origins of Intelligence in the Child.* London: Routledge & Kegan Paul, 1952.

Piaget, Jean. *The Construction of Reality in the Child.* London: Routledge & Kegan Paul, 1955.

Piaget, Jean. "Intellectual Evolution from Adolescence to Adulthood." *Human Development* 15 (1972): 1–12.

Piaget, Jean. "Problems of Equilibration." In M. H. Appel and L. S. Goldberg (eds), *Topics in Cognitive Development,* vol. 1, pp. 3–14. New York: Plenum, 1977.

Pillow, Kirk. *Sublime Understanding: Aesthetic Reflection in Kant and Hegel.* Cambridge, MA: MIT Press, 2000.

Placher, William C. *The Domestication of Transcendence: How Modern Thinking About God Went Wrong.* Louisville, KY: Westminster John Knox Press, 1996.

Poellner, Peter. *Nietzsche and Metaphysics.* Oxford: Oxford University Press, 2000.

Pöhlmann, H. G. *Analogia entis oder analogia fidei? Die Frage nach Analogie bei Karl Barth.* Göttingen: Vandenhoeck & Ruprecht, 1965.

Polanyi, Michael. *Personal Knowledge: Towards a Post-Critical Philosophy.* London: Routledge & Kegan Paul, 1958.

Polanyi, Michael. "Science and Reality." *British Journal for the Philosophy of Science,* 18 (1967): 177–96.

Polkinghorne, John C. *Belief in God in an Age of Science.* New Haven, CT: Yale University Press, 1998.

Polkinghorne, John C. "Physics and Metaphysics in a Trinitarian Perspective." *Theology and Science* 1 (2003): 33–49.

Polkinghorne, John C. *Science and the Trinity: The Christian Encounter with Reality.* New Haven, CT: Yale University Press, 2004.

Porter, Jean. *Natural and Divine Law: Reclaiming the Tradition for Christian Ethics*. Grand Rapids, MI: Eerdmans, 1999.

Posner, Michael I., and Steven E. Petersen. "The Attentional System of the Human Brain." *Annual Review of Neuroscience* 13 (1990): 25–42.

Preus, Samuel J. *Explaining Religion: Criticism and Theory from Bodin to Freud*. New Haven, CT: Yale University Press, 1987.

Price, Daniel J. *Karl Barth's Anthropology in Light of Modern Thought*. Grand Rapids, MI: Eerdmans, 2002.

Priestman, Martin. *Romantic Atheism: Poetry and Freethought, 1780–1830*. Cambridge, UK: Cambridge University Press, 1999.

Prinz, Friedrich. "Die Kirche und die pagane Kulturtradition. Formen der Abwehr, Adaption und Anverwandlung." *Historische Zeitschrift* 276 (2002): 281–303.

Psillos, Stathos. "On van Fraassen's Critique of Abductive Reasoning." *Philosophical Quarterly* 46 (1996): 31–47.

Psillos, Stathos. "Simply the Best: A Case for Abduction." In Robert Kowalski, Antonis C. Kakas, and Fariba Sadri (eds), *Computational Logic: Logic Programming and Beyond*, pp. 605–25. Berlin: Springer, 2002.

Pyle, Andrew. "Introduction." In *The Boyle Lectures (1692–1732): A Defence of Natural and Revealed Religion*. 4 vols, vol. 1, pp. vii–liii. Bristol: Thoemmes Press, 2000.

Räisänen, Heikki. *The "Messianic Secret" in Mark*. Edinburgh: T&T Clark, 1990.

Randall, John Herman, Jr. *The Meaning of Religion for Man*. New York: Harper Torchbooks, 1968.

Rapport, Nigel, and Joanna Overing. *Social and Cultural Anthropology: The Key Concepts*. London: Routledge, 2000.

Rasmusson, Arne. *The Church as Polis: From Political Theology to Theological Politics as Exemplified by Jürgen Moltmann and Stanley Hauerwas*. Lund: Lund University Press, 1994.

Ratzinger, Joseph. "Das Problem der Transubstantiation und der Frage nach dem Sinne der Eucharistie." *Theologische Quartalschrift* 147 (1967) 129–58.

Raven, Charles E. *Natural Religion and Christian Theology*, 2 vols. Cambridge, UK: Cambridge University Press, 1953.

Redwood, John. *Reason, Ridicule and Religion: The Age of Enlightenment in England, 1660–1750*. London: Thames and Hudson, 1996.

Reiter, David. "Calvin's 'Sense of Divinity' and Externalist Knowledge of God." *Faith and Philosophy* 15 (1998): 253–70.

Reno, Russell R. *The Ordinary Transformed: Karl Rahner and the Christian Vision of Transcendence*. Grand Rapids, MI: Eerdmans, 1995.

Rescher, Nicholas. *Process Metaphysics: An Introduction to Process Philosophy*. Albany, NY: State University of New York Press, 1996.

Rescher, Nicholas. *Process Philosophy: A Survey of Basic Issues*. Pittsburgh, PA: University of Pittsburgh Press, 2000.

Reventloh, Henning Graf. *The Authority of the Bible and the Rise of the Modern World*. London: SCM Press, 1984.

Rice, Hugh. *God and Goodness*. Oxford: Oxford University Press, 2000.

Richmond, Alasdair. "Between Abduction and the Deep Blue Sea." *Philosophical Quarterly* 49 (1999): 86–91.

Rief, Josef. *Der Ordobegriff des jungen Augustinus*. Paderborn: Schoningh, 1962.

Robbins, Vernon K. *Jesus the Teacher: A Socio-Rhetorical Interpretation of Mark*, revised edn. Philadelphia: Fortress Press, 1992.

Roberts, Noel Keith. "Newman on the Argument from Design." *New Blackfriars* 88 (2007): 56–66.

Roberts, Tyler T. *Contesting Spirit: Nietzsche, Affirmation, Religion*. Princeton, NJ: Princeton University Press, 1998.

Robertson, John. *The Case for the Enlightenment: Scotland and Naples 1680–1760*. Cambridge, UK: Cambridge University Press, 2005.

Robinett, Richard W. *Quantum Mechanics: Classical Results, Modern Systems and Visualized Examples*. New York: Oxford University Press, 1997.

Roe, Nicholas. *The Politics of Nature: Wordsworth and Some Contemporaries*. New York: St. Martins Press, 1992.

Rolston, Holmes. "Does Aesthetic Appreciation of Landscapes Need to be Science-Based?" *British Journal of Aesthetics* 33 (1995): 374–86.

Rolston, Holmes. "From Beauty to Duty: Aesthetics of Nature and Environmental Ethics." In Arnold Berleant (ed.), *Environment and the Arts: Perspectives on Environmental Ethics*, pp. 127–41. Aldershot: Ashgate, 2002.

Rommen, Heinrich. *Die ewige Wiederkehr des Naturrechts*. Leipzig: Hegner, 1936.

Rorty, Richard. *The Consequences of Pragmatism*. Minneapolis, MN: University of Minneapolis Press, 1982.

Rorty, Richard. *Contingency, Irony and Solidarity*. Cambridge, UK: Cambridge University Press, 1989.

Rorty, Richard. *Objectivity, Relativism and Truth. Philosophical Papers*. Cambridge, UK: Cambridge University Press, 1991.

Rosch, Eleanor. "Principles of Categorization." In Eleanor Rosch and Barbara B. Lloyd (ed.), *Cognition and Categorization*, pp. 27–48. Hillsdale, NJ: Lawrence Erlbaum, 1978.

Rosen, Joe. *Symmetry Discovered: Concepts and Applications in Nature and Science*. Cambridge, UK: Cambridge University Press, 1975.

Rosen, Michael. *Hegel's Dialectic and its Criticism*. Cambridge, UK: Cambridge University Press, 1982.

Rosenberg, John D. *The Darkening Glass: A Portrait of Ruskin's Genius*. London: Routledge & Kegan Paul, 1963; New York: Columbia University Press, 1986.

Ross, Miceal. "Anchors in a Three-Decker World." *Folklore* 109 (1998): 63–76.

Rössler, Roman. *Person und Glaube: Der Personalismus der Gottesbeziehung bei Emil Brunner*. Munich: Kaiser Verlag, 1965.

Rowe, Andrea D., Peter R. Bullock, Charles E. Polkey, and Robin G. Morris. "'Theory of Mind' Impairments and their Relationship to Executive Functioning Following Frontal Lobe Excisions." *Brain* 124 (2001): 600–16.

Rowland, Christopher. *The Open Heaven: A Study of Apocalyptic in Judaism and Early Christianity.* London: SPCK, 1982.

Roy, Louis. *Transcendent Experiences: Phenomenology and Critique.* University of Toronto Press, 2001.

Roy, Louis. "A Clarifying Note on *Transcendent Experiences.*" *Toronto Journal of Theology* 20 (2004): 51–6.

Rudolph, Kurt. *Gnosis: The Nature and History of Gnosticism.* San Francisco: Harper & Row, 1987.

Ruse, Michael. "Is Rape Wrong on Andromeda?" In *The Darwinian Paradigm: Essays on Its History, Philosophy, and Religious Implications,* pp. 209–46. London: Routledge, 1989.

Ruse, Michael. *Evolutionary Naturalism.* London: Routledge, 1995.

Ruse, Michael. "The Argument from Design: A Brief History." In William A. Dembski and Michael Ruse (eds), *Debating Design: From Darwin to DNA,* pp. 13–31. Cambridge, UK: Cambridge University Press, 2004.

Ruskin, John. *Works,* ed. E. T. Cook and A. Wedderburn, 39 vols. London: Allen, 1903–12.

Russell, Bertrand. "On Denoting." *Mind* 14 (1905): 479–93.

Russell, Colin A. "The Conflict Metaphor and Its Social Origins." *Science and Christian Faith* 1 (1989): 3–26.

Ryken, Leland, James C. Wilhoit, and Tremper Longman III (eds). *Dictionary of Biblical Imagery.* Downers Grove, IL: InterVarsity Press, 1998.

Sabin, Marie Noonan. *Reopening the Word: Reading Mark as Theology in the Context of Early Judaism.* Oxford: Oxford University Press, 2002.

Sacks, Oliver. *The Man Who Mistook His Wife for a Hat.* London: Pan, 1986.

Saffran, J., R. Aslin, and E. Newport. "Statistical Learning by 8-Month-Old Infants." *Science* 274 (1996): 1926–8.

Saliba, John A. *"Homo Religiosus" in Mircea Eliade: An Anthropological Evaluation.* Leiden: Brill, 1976.

Salier, Willis Hedley. *The Rhetorical Impact of the Semeia in the Gospel of John: A Historical and Hermeneutical Perspective.* Tübingen: Mohr Siebeck, 2004.

Salmon, Wesley C. "Religion and Science: A New Look at Hume's *Dialogues.*" *Philosophical Studies* 33 (1978): 143–76.

Samuel, Otto. "Der ontologische Gottesbeweis bei Karl Barth, Immanuel Kant und Anselm von Canterbury." *Theologische Blätter* 14 (1935): 141–53.

Samuelson, Norbert M. *Revelation and the God of Israel.* Cambridge, UK: Cambridge University Press, 2002.

Sandner, David. *The Fantastic Sublime: Romanticism and Transcendence in Nineteenth-Century Children's Fantasy Literature.* Westport, CT: Greenwood Press, 1996.

Sanguineti, Vittorio, and Pietro Morasso. "How the Brain Discovers the Existence of External Allocentric Space." *Neurocomputing* 12 (1996): 289–310.

Santmire, H. Paul. "A Reformation Theology of Nature Transfigured: Joseph Sittler's Invitation to See as Well as to Hear." *Theology Today* 61 (2005): 509–27.

Saver, J., and J. Rabin. "The Neural Substrates of Religious Experience." *Journal of Neuropsychiatry & Clinical Neuroscience*, 9 (1997): 498–510.

Scarry, Elaine. *On Beauty and Being Just.* Princeton, NJ: Princeton University Press, 1999.

Schaefer, James. "Appreciating the Beauty of Earth." *Theological Studies* 61 (2001): 23–52.

Schakel, Peter J. *Reason and Imagination in C. S. Lewis: A Study of Till We Have Faces.* Grand Rapids, MI: Eerdmans, 1984.

Scheld, Stephan. *Die Christologie Emil Brunners.* Wiesbaden: Franz Steinbeck, 1981.

Schmemann, Alexander. *The World as Sacrament.* London: Darton, Longman & Todd, 1966.

Schmid, Heinrich H. *Gerechtigkeit als Weltordnung. Hintergrund und Geschichte des alttestamentlichen Gerechtigkeitsbegriffes.* Tübingen: Mohr, 1968.

Schmid, Heinrich H. "Jahweglaube und altorientalisches Weltordnungsgedanken." In *Altorientalische Welt in der alttestamentlichen Theologie*, pp. 31–63. Zurich: Theologischer Verlag, 1974.

Schmidt, James. *What is Enlightenment? Eighteenth-Century Answers and Twentieth-Century Questions.* (Philosophical Traditions, 7). Berkeley, CA: University of California Press, 1996.

Schmidt, James. "What Enlightenment Project?" *Political Theory* 28 (2000): 734–57.

Schneewind, J. B. *The Invention of Autonomy: A History of Modern Moral Philosophy.* Cambridge, UK: Cambridge University Press, 1998.

Schreiner, Susan E. "Calvin's Use of Natural Law." In Michael Cromartie (ed.), *A Preserving Grace: Protestants, Catholics, and Natural Law*, pp. 51–76. Grand Rapids, MI: Eerdmans, 1997.

Schwanz, Peter. *Imago Dei als christologisch-anthropologisches Problem in der Geschichte der Alten Kirche von Paulus bis Clemens von Alexandrien.* Halle: Niemeyer, 1970.

Schwarz, Sanford. "Paradise Reframed: Lewis, Bergson, and Changing Times on Perelandra." *Christianity and Literature* 51 (2002): 569–600.

Schweizer, Eduard. *Ego eimi: Die religionsgeschichtliche Herkunft und theologische Bedeutung der johanneischen Bildreden, zugleich ein Beitrag zur Quellenfrage des vierten Evangeliums*, 2nd edn. Göttingen: Vandenhoeck & Ruprecht, 1965.

Scott, Bernard Brandon. *Hear Then the Parable: A Commentary on the Parables of Jesus.* Minneapolis: Fortress Press, 1989.

Scott, Nathan A. "The Poetry and Theology of Earth: Reflections on the Testimony of Joseph Sittler and Gerard Manley Hopkins." *Journal of Religion* 54 (1974): 102–18.

Scott, William Taussig, and Martin X. Moleski, SJ. *Michael Polanyi: Scientist and Philosopher*. Oxford: Oxford University Press, 2005.

Seeman, T., L. Dubin, and M. Seeman. "Religiosity/Spirituality and Health: A Critical Review of the Evidence for Biological Pathways." *American Psychologist* 58 (2003): 53–63.

Seeskin, Kenneth. *Searching for a Distant God: The Legacy of Maimonides*. New York: Oxford University Press, 2000.

Seligman, Martin. "Positive Psychology, Positive Prevention, and Positive Therapy." In C. Snyder and S. Lopez (eds), *Handbook of Positive Psychology*, pp. 3–9. New York: Oxford University Press, 2002.

Sellin, Gerhard. "Lukas als Gleichniszähler: Die Erzählung vom barmherzigen Samariter (Lk. 10: 25–37)." *Zeitschrift für Neutestamentliche Wissenschaft* 65 (1974): 166–89.

Selvidge, Marla J. *Notorious Voices: Feminist Biblical Interpretation, 1550–1920*. New York: Continuum, 1996.

Shanks, Niall. *God, the Devil, and Darwin: A Critique of Intelligent Design Theory*. Oxford: Oxford University Press, 2004.

Shapiro, David S. "The Doctrine of the Image of God and Imitatio Dei." In Menachem Kellner (ed.), *Contemporary Jewish Ethics*, pp. 127–51. New York: Sanhedrin, 1978.

Sharpe, Eric J. *Not to Destroy but to Fulfil: The Contribution of J. N. Farquhar to Protestant Missionary Thought in India Before 1914*. Lund: Gleerup, 1965.

Sharvy, Richard. "Euthyphro 9b–11b: Analysis and Definition in Plato and Others." *Noûs*, 6 (1972), 119–37.

Sheldrake, Rupert. *The Rebirth of Nature: The Greening of Science and God*. Rochester, VT: Park Street Press, 1994.

Shenk, Wilbert R. "Lesslie Newbigin's Contribution to Mission Theology." *International Bulletin of Missionary Research* 24/2 (2000): 59–64.

Sherry, Patrick. *Spirit and Beauty: An Introduction to Theological Aesthetics*. Oxford: Clarendon Press, 1992.

Shiota, Michelle, Belinda Campos, and Dacher Keltner. "The Faces of Positive Emotion: Prototype Displays of Awe, Amusement, and Pride." *Annals of the New York Academy of Science* 1000 (2003): 296–9.

Shipway, Brad. "The Theological Application of Bhaskar's Stratified Reality: The Scientific Theology of A. E. McGrath." *Journal of Critical Realism* 3 (2004): 191–203.

Shook, John R. *Dewey's Empirical Theory of Knowledge and Reality*. Nashville, TN: Vanderbilt University Press, 2000.

Shore, Bradd. *Culture in Mind: Cognition, Culture, and the Problem of Meaning*. Oxford: Oxford University Press, 1998.

Sibley, Frank. "Aesthetics and the Looks of Things." *Journal of Philosophy* 56 (1959): 905–15.

Sibley, Frank. "Analysing Seeing." In Frank Sibley (ed.), *Perception: A Philosophical Symposium*, pp. 81–132. London: Methuen, 1971.

Siegwalt, Gerard. "Der Prolog des Johannesevangeliums als Einführung in eine christliche Theologie der Rekapitulation." *Neue Zeitschrift für systematische Theologie und Religionsphilosophie* 24 (1981): 150–71.

Silberman, Israela. "Religion as a Meaning System: Implications for the New Millennium." *Journal of Social Issues* 61 (2005): 641–63.

Simon, Yves R. *The Tradition of Natural Law: A Philosopher's Reflections.* New York: Fordham University Press, 1992.

Sittler, Joseph. *Essays on Nature and Grace.* Philadelphia: Fortress, 1972.

Sleeper, R. W. *The Necessity of Pragmatism: John Dewey's Conception of Philosophy.* New Haven, CT: Yale University Press, 1986.

Smart, Ninian. *Choosing a Faith.* New York: Marion Boyars, 1995.

Smart, Ninian. *Dimensions of the Sacred: An Anatomy of the World's Beliefs.* Berkeley, CA: University of California Press, 1996.

Smith, A. J. *The Metaphysics of Love: Studies in Renaissance Love Poetry from Dante to Milton.* Cambridge, UK: Cambridge University Press, 1985.

Smith, Bernard. *European Vision and the South Pacific, 1768–1850.* London: Oxford University Press, 1960.

Smith, Huston. *Cleansing the Doors of Perception: The Religious Significance of Entheogenic Plants and Substances.* New York: Putnam, 2000

Smith, James K. A. *Speech and Theology: Language and the Logic of Incarnation.* London: Routledge, 2002.

Smith, Mark. *The Early History of God: Yahweh and the Other Deities in Ancient Israel.* Grand Rapids, MI: Eerdmans, 2002.

Smith, Ronald Gregor. *The Free Man: Studies in Christian Anthropology.* London: Collins, 1969.

Snodgrass, Klyne B. *The Parable of the Wicked Tenants: An Inquiry into Parable Interpretation.* Tübingen: Mohr, 1983.

Snow-Smith, Joanne. "Michelangelo's Christian Neoplatonic Aesthetic of Beauty in his Early Oeuvre: The *Nuditas Virtualis* Image." In Francis Ames-Lewis and Mary Rogers (eds), *Concepts of Beauty in Renaissance Art*, pp. 147–62. Aldershot: Ashgate, 1998.

Söhngen, Gottlieb. "Rectitudo bei Anselm von Canterbury als Oberbegriff von Wahrheit und Gerechtigkeit." In H. Kohlenberger (ed.), *Sola Ratione*, pp. 71–7. Stuttgart: Friedrich Frommann Verlag, 1970.

Soper, Kate. *What is Nature? Culture, Politics and the Non-Human.* Oxford: Basil Blackwell, 1995.

Soulé, Michael E. "The Social Siege of Nature." In Michael E. Soulé and Gary Lease (eds), *Reinventing Nature: Responses to Postmodern Deconstruction*, pp. 137–70. Washington, DC: Island Press, 1995.

Southall, James P. C. *Helmholtz's Treatise on Physiological Optics*, 3 vols. Bristol: Thoemmes, 2000.

Sperber, Dan. *Rethinking Symbolism*. Cambridge, UK: Cambridge University Press, 1975.

Spilka, Bernard, Ralph W. Hood, Bruce Hunsberger, and Richard Gorsuch. *The Psychology of Religion: An Empirical Approach*, 3rd edn. New York: The Guilford Press, 2003.

Spohn, William C. "Jesus and Christian Ethics." *Theological Studies* 56 (1995): 92–107.

Springsted, Eric O. *Christus Mediator: Platonic Mediation in the Thought of Simone Weil*. Chico, CA: Scholars Press, 1983.

Sproul, Barbara C. *Primal Myths: Creation Myths Around the World*. San Francisco: HarperCollins, 1991.

Stark, Rodney, and Charles Y. Glock. *American Piety: The Nature of Religious Commitment*. Berkeley, CA: University of California Press, 1968.

Steiert, Franz-Josef. *Die Weisheit Israels – ein Fremdkörper im Alten Testament? Eine Untersuchung zum Buch der Sprüche auf dem Hintergrund der ägyptischen Weisheitslehren*. Freiburg im Breisgau: Herder, 1990.

Steiger, Lothar. "Offenbarungsgeschichte und theologische Vernunft." *Zeitschrift für Theologie und Kirche* 59 (1962): 88–113.

Stein, John F. "Space and the Parietal Association Areas." In J. Paillard (ed.), *Brain and Space*, pp. 185–222. Oxford: Oxford University Press, 1992.

Stein, Robert H. "The Genre of the Parables." In Richard N. Longecker (ed.), *The Challenge of Jesus' Parables*, pp. 30–50. Grand Rapids, MI: Eerdmans, 2000.

Steiner, George. *Real Presences: Is There Anything in What We Say?* London: Faber, 1991.

Steinmetz, David C. "Luther and the Ascent of Jacob's Ladder." *Church History* 55 (1986): 179–92.

Stern, David. *Parables in Midrash: Narrative and Exegesis in Rabbinic Literature*. Cambridge, MA: Harvard University Press, 1991.

Stertenbrink, Rudolf. *Ein Weg zum Denken: Die Analogia entis bei Erich Przywara*. Salzburg: Verlag Anton Pustet, 1971.

Stewart, Ian. *Nature's Numbers: Discovering Order and Pattern in the Universe*. London: Weidenfeld & Nicolson, 1995.

Stoeber, Michael. *Reclaiming Theodicy: Reflections on Suffering, Compassion and Spiritual Transformation*. Basingstoke: Palgrave Macmillan, 2005.

Stolz, Fritz. *Homo naturaliter religiosus: gehört Religion notwendig zum Mensch-Sein?* Bern: Peter Lang, 1997.

Stone, Jerome A. *The Minimalist Vision of Transcendence: A Naturalist Philosophy of Religion*. Albany, NY: State University of New York Press, 1993.

Stratman, Thomas B. "St. Francis of Assisi: Brother to All Creatures." *Spirituality Today* 34 (1982): 222–32.

Sturges, Robert S. *Medieval Interpretation: Models of Reading in Literary Narrative, 1100–1500.* Carbondale, IL: Southern Illinois University Press, 1991.

Stuss, D., and V. Anderson. "The Frontal Lobes and Theory of Mind: Developmental Concepts from Adult Focal Lesion Research." *Brain and Cognition* 55 (2004): 69–83.

Suckiel, Ellen Kappy. *The Pragmatic Philosophy of William James.* Notre Dame, IN: University of Notre Dame Press, 1982.

Sullivan, John. *The Image of God: The Doctrine of St. Augustine and its Influence.* Dubuque, IA: Priory Press, 1963.

Sweeney, Eileen. "Anselm's Proslogion: The Desire for the Word." *Saint Anselm Journal* 1 (2003): 17–31.

Swinburne, Richard. *The Existence of God.* Oxford: Clarendon Press, 1979.

Swinburne, Richard. "Natural Theology, its 'Dwindling Probabilities' and 'Lack of Rapport'." *Faith and Philosophy* 21 (2004): 533–46.

Taves, Ann. *Fits, Trances and Visions: Experiencing Religion and Explaining Experience from Wesley to James.* Princeton, NJ: Princeton University Press, 1999.

Taylor, Bron. "A Green Future for Religion?" *Futures* 36 (2004): 991–1008.

Taylor, Charles. *Sources of the Self: The Making of the Modern Identity.* Cambridge, UK: Cambridge University Press, 1989.

Taylor, Charles. *A Secular Age.* Cambridge, MA: Belknap Press, 2007.

Taylor, Claire. *Heresy in Medieval France: Dualism in Aquitaine and the Agenais, 1000–1249.* London: Royal Historical Society, 2005.

Tedsechi, R., and L. Calhoun. *Trauma and Transformation.* Thousand Oaks, CA: Sage 1995.

Tennant, Frederick R. *Philosophical Theology,* 2 vols. Cambridge, UK: Cambridge University Press, 1930.

Tetlock, Philip, and Aaron Belkin (eds). *Counterfactual Thought Experiments in World Politics: Logical, Methodological, and Psychological Perspectives.* Princeton, NJ: Princeton University Press, 1996.

Thagard, Paul R. "The Best Explanation: Criteria for Theory Choice." *Journal of Philosophy* 75 (1976): 76–92.

Thagard, Paul R. "Why Is Beauty a Road to Truth?" In R. Festa, A. Aliseda, and J. Pejnenburg (eds), *Cognitive Structures in Scientific Inquiry,* pp. 365–70. Amsterdam: Rodopi, 2005.

Thayer, H. S. *The Logic of Pragmatism: An Examination of John Dewey's Logic.* New York: Humanities Press, 1952.

Thorner, Isidor. "Prophetic and Mystic Experience: Comparison and Consequences." *Journal for the Scientific Study of Religion* 5 (1965): 82–96.

Thornton, R. K. R. *All My Eyes See: The Visual World of Gerard Manley Hopkins.* Sunderland: Ceolfrith Press, 1975.

Tirosh-Samuelson, Hava. "Theology of Nature in Sixteenth-Century Italian Jewish Philosophy." *Science in Context* 10 (1997): 529–70.

Tolkien, J. R. R. "Beowulf: The Monsters and the Critics." In Christopher Tolkien (ed.), *The Monsters and the Critics and Other Essays*, pp. 5–48. London: HarperCollins, 1997.

Tomasello, Michael. *The Cultural Origins of Human Cognition*. Cambridge, MA: Harvard University Press, 2000.

Torchia, N. Joseph. *Creatio ex nihilo and the Theology of St. Augustine: The Anti-Manichaean Polemic and Beyond*. New York: Peter Lang, 1999.

Torrance, Robert M. *Ideal and Spleen: The Crisis of Transcendent Vision in Romantic, Symbolist, and Modern Poetry*. New York: Garland Publishing, 1987.

Torrance, Thomas F. *Space, Time and Incarnation*. London: Oxford University Press, 1969.

Torrance, Thomas F. *Theology in Reconciliation: Essays Towards Evangelical and Catholic Unity in East and West*. London: Chapman, 1975.

Torrance, Thomas F. *The Ground and Grammar of Theology*. Charlottesville, VA: The University of Virginia Press, 1980.

Torrance, Thomas F. "Divine and Contingent Order." In A. R. Peacocke (ed.), *The Sciences and Theology in the Twentieth Century*, pp. 81–97. Notre Dame, IN: University of Notre Dame Press, 1981.

Torrance, Thomas F. *Divine and Contingent Order*. Oxford: Oxford University Press, 1981.

Torrance, Thomas F. *Reality and Scientific Theology*. Edinburgh: Scottish Academic Press, 1985.

Torrance, Thomas F. *The Christian Frame of Mind: Reason, Order, and Openness in Theology and Natural Science*, 2nd edn. Colorado Springs: Helmers & Howard, 1989.

Torrance, Thomas F. "The Transfinite Significance of Beauty in Science and Theology." In Luz García Alonso, Evanghelos Moutsopoulos, and Gerhard Seel (eds), *L'art, la science et la métaphysique: Études offertes à André Mercier*, pp. 393–418. Berne: Peter Lang, 1993.

Towler, Robert. *The Need for Certainty: A Sociological Study of Conventional Religion*. London: Routledge & Kegan Paul, 1984.

Tracy, David. *The Analogical Imagination: Christian Theology and the Culture of Pluralism*. New York: Crossroad, 1981.

Trakatellis, Demetrios. "Being Transformed: Chrysostom's Exegesis of the Epistle to the Romans." *Greek Orthodox Theological Review* 36 (1991): 211–29.

Tremlin, Todd. *Minds and Gods: The Cognitive Foundations of Religion*. New York: Oxford University Press, 2006.

Troisfontaines, Roger. *De l'existence à l'être: la philosophie de Gabriel Marcel*, 2 vols. Louvain: Nauwelaerts, 1953.

Truchlar, Leo. *Über Literatur und andere Künste: 12 Versuche*. Vienna: Böhlau, 2000.

Tsumura, David T. *The Earth and the Waters in Genesis 1 and 2: A Linguistic Investigation.* Sheffield: Sheffield Academic Press, 1989.

Tuck, Richard. "The 'Christian Atheism' of Thomas Hobbes." In Michael Hunter and David Wootton (eds), *Atheism from the Reformation to the Enlightenment,* pp. 102–20. Oxford: Clarendon Press, 1992.

Tuckett, Christopher M. *The Messianic Secret.* Philadelphia: Fortress Press, 1983.

Turner, Frank Miller. "The Victorian Conflict between Science and Religion: A Professional Dimension." *Isis* 69 (1978): 356–76.

Turner, H. E. W. *The Patristic Doctrine of Redemption: A Study of the Development of Doctrine During the First Five Centuries.* London: Mowbray, 1952.

Tuveson, Ernest Lee. *The Imagination as a Means of Grace; Locke and the Aesthetics of Romanticism.* Berkeley, CA: University of California Press, 1960.

Umbach, Maiken. *Federalism and Enlightenment in Germany, 1740–1806.* London: Hambledon, 2000.

Vanhoozer, Kevin J. *Is There a Meaning in this Text? The Bible, the Reader, and the Morality of Literary Knowledge.* Grand Rapids, MI: Zondervan, 1998.

Varela, Francisco J., Evan Thompson, and Eleanor Rosch. *The Embodied Mind: Cognitive Science and Human Experience.* Cambridge, MA: MIT Press, 1991.

Viladesau, Richard. *Theological Aesthetics: God in Imagination, Beauty and Art.* New York: Oxford University Press, 1999.

Vine, Steve. "Blake's Material Sublime." *Studies in Romanticism* 41 (2002): 237–57.

Vygotsky, Lev S. *Mind in Society: The Development of Higher Psychological Processes.* Cambridge, MA: Harvard University Press, 1978.

Wachtmann, Christian. *Der Religionsbegriff bei Mircea Eliade.* Frankfurt am Main/Berlin: Peter Lang, 1996.

Wainwright, William J. "Jonathan Edwards, William Rowe and the Necessity of Creation." In Jeff Jordan and Daniel Howard-Snyder (eds), *Faith, Freedom and Rationality,* pp. 119–33. London: Rowman & Littlefield, 1996.

Waldenfels, Hans, and Leo Scheffczyk. *Die Offenbarung von der Reformation bis zur Gegenwart.* Freiburg: Herder, 1977.

Walton, Kendall. "Categories of Art." *Philosophical Review* 79 (1970): 334–67.

Wang, Xiaochao. *Christianity and Imperial Culture: Chinese Christian Apologetics in the Seventeenth Century and their Latin Patristic Equivalent.* Leiden: Brill, 1998.

Ward, Keith. *God, Chance and Necessity.* Oxford: One World, 1996.

Ware, Owen. "Rudolf Otto's Ideal of the Holy: A Reappraisal." *Heythrop Journal* 48 (2007): 48–60.

Wassermann, Earl. "Nature Moralized: The Divine Analogy in the Eighteenth Century." *English Literary History* 20 (1953): 39–76.

Webb, Mark O. "Natural Theology and the Concept of Perfection in Descartes, Spinoza and Leibniz." *Religious Studies* 25 (1989): 459–75.

Wee, David L. "The Temptation of Christ and the Motif of Divine Duplicity in the Corpus Christi Cycle Drama." *Modern Philology* 72 (1974): 1–16.

Weikart, Richard. "A Recently Discovered Darwin Letter on Social Darwinism." *Isis* 86 (1995): 609–11.

Weil, Andrew. *The Natural Mind: An Investigation of Drugs and the Higher Consciousness*, rev. edn. Boston: Houghton Mifflin, 1986.

Weil, Simone. *Waiting for God*. New York: Harper & Row, 1951.

Weil, Simone. *On Science, Necessity and the Love of God*. London: Oxford University Press, 1968.

Weiskel, Thomas. *The Romantic Sublime: Studies in the Structure and Psychology of Transcendence*. Baltimore, MD: Johns Hopkins University Press, 1986.

Welker, Michael. "Creation and the Image of God: Their Understanding in Christian Tradition and the Biblical Grounds." *Journal of Ecumenical Studies* 34 (1997): 436–48.

Westerman, Pauline. *The Disintegration of Natural Law Theory: Aquinas to Finnis*. Leiden: Brill, 1998.

Westfall, Richard S. "The Scientific Revolution of the Seventeenth Century: A New World View." In John Torrance (ed.), *The Concept of Nature*, pp. 63–93. Oxford: Oxford University Press, 1992.

Westhelle, Vitor. "The Poet, the Practitioner, and the Beholder: Thoughts on the Created Co-Creator." *Zygon* 39 (2004): 747–54.

White, Stephen K. *Sustaining Affirmation: The Strengths of Weak Ontology in Political Theory*. Princeton, NJ: Princeton University Press, 2000.

Whitehead, Alfred North. *Process and Reality: An Essay in Cosmology*. New York, Macmillan, 1929.

Wierzbicka, Anna. *What Did Jesus Mean? Explaining the Sermon on the Mount and the Parables in Simple and Universal Human Concepts*. Oxford: Oxford University Press, 2001.

Wigner, Eugene. "The Unreasonable Effectiveness of Mathematics." *Communications on Pure and Applied Mathematics* 13 (1960): 1–14.

Wiles, Maurice. *Archetypal Heresy: Arianism Through the Ages*. Oxford: Oxford University Press, 1996.

Willard, Dallas. *The Spirit of the Disciplines: Understanding how God Changes Lives*. London: Hodder & Stoughton, 1988.

Willard, Dallas. "Spiritual Disciplines, Spiritual Formation, and Restoration of the Soul." *Journal of Psychology and Theology* 26 (1998): 101–9.

Williams, Catrin. *I Am He: The Interpretation of 'Anî Hû' in Jewish and Early Christian Literature*. Tübingen: Mohr Siebeck, 2000.

Williams, George C. "Mother Nature Is a Wicked Old Witch!" In Matthew H. Nitecki and Doris V. Nitecki (eds), *Evolutionary Ethics*, pp. 217–31. Albany, NY: State University of New York Press, 1995.

Williams, James G. *Gospel Against Parable: Mark's Language of Mystery*. Sheffield: Almond, 1985.

Williams, N. P. *The Ideas of the Fall and of Original Sin: A Historical and Critical Study*. London: Longmans, Green and Co., 1927.

Williams, R. J. P., and J. J. R. Fraústo da Silva. *The Chemistry of Evolution: The Development of Our Ecosystem*. London: Elsevier, 2006.

Williams, Rowan. "Does It Make Sense to Speak of Pre-Nicene Orthodoxy?" In Rowan Williams (ed.), *The Making of Orthodoxy*, pp. 1–23. Cambridge, UK: Cambridge University Press, 1989.

Willis, David. *Clues to the Nicene Creed: A Brief Outline of the Faith*. Grand Rapids, MI: Eerdmans, 2005.

Wilmer, Clive. "Back to Nature: Ruskin's Aspen and an Art in the Service of the Given." *Times Literary Supplement*, 1 December 1995, pp. 3–4.

Wilson, Edward O. *Biophilia: The Human Bond with Other Species*. Cambridge, MA: Harvard University Press, 1984.

Wilson, Fred. *Hume's Defence of Causal Inference*. Toronto: University of Toronto Press, 1997.

Witczak, Michael. "The Manifold Presence of Christ in the Liturgy." *Theological Studies* 59 (1998): 680–702.

Wojcik, Jan W. *Robert Boyle and the Limits of Reason*. Cambridge, UK: Cambridge University Press, 1997.

Wolf, Ernst. "Zum protestantischen Rechtsdenken." In *Peregrinatio II: Studien zur reformatorischen Theologie, zum Kirchenrecht, und zur Sozialethik*, pp. 191–206. Munich: Kaiser Verlag, 1965.

Wolpert, Lewis. *The Unnatural Nature of Science*. London: Faber and Faber, 1992.

Wolterstorff, Nicholas. *Divine Discourse: Philosophical Reflections on the Claim that God Speaks*. Cambridge, UK: Cambridge University Press, 1995.

Wood, Jim, Teresa Nezworski, and O. Lilienfeld Scott. *What's Wrong with the Rorschach? Science Confronts the Controversial Inkblot Test*. San Francisco, CA: Jossey-Bass, 2003.

Woods, John. *Paradox and Paraconsistency: Conflict Resolution in the Abstract Sciences*. Cambridge, UK: Cambridge University Press, 2003.

Woodward, Thomas. *Doubts About Darwin: A History of Intelligent Design*. Grand Rapids, MI: Baker Books, 2003.

Woolcock, Peter G. "The Case Against Evolutionary Ethics Today." In Jane Maienschein and Michael Ruse (eds), *Biology and the Foundation of Ethics*, pp. 276–306. Cambridge, UK: Cambridge University Press, 1999.

Wordsworth, Jonathan. *William Wordsworth: The Borders of Vision*. Oxford: Clarendon Press, 1984.

Work, Telford. "Advent's Answer to the Problem of Evil." *International Journal of Systematic Theology* 2 (2000): 100–11.

Wright, N. T. *The New Testament and the People of God*. Minneapolis, MN: Fortress, 1992.

Wright, N. T. "'Word of God' and Scripture in the Apostolic Church." In *Scripture and the Authority of God*, pp. 35–44. London: SPCK, 2005.

Wulff, David M. *Psychology of Religion: Classic and Contemporary.* New York: Wiley, 1997.

Wynn, Mark. *God and Goodness: A Natural Theological Perspective.* London: Routledge, 1999.

Yancey, Philip. *Rumors of Another World: What on Earth Are We Missing?* Grand Rapids, MI: Zondervan, 2003.

Yoder, Joella G. *Unrolling Time: Christiaan Huygens and the Mathematization of Nature.* Cambridge, UK: Cambridge University Press, 1988.

Yolton, John W. *Perception and Reality: A History from Descartes to Kant.* Ithaca, NY: Cornell University Press, 1996.

Young, F. W. "A Study of the Relation of Isaiah to the Fourth Gospel." *Zeitschrift für die Neutestamentliche Wissenschaft* 46 (1955): 215–33.

Zachary, Alexander L. "Interpretative Desire: Augustine's Semiotics and the Transcendental Signified." *Columbia Journal of Literary Criticism* 2 (2004): 25–34.

Zachman, Randall. "Jesus Christ as the Image of God in Calvin's Theology." *Calvin Theological Journal* 25 (1990): 46–52.

Zagzebski, Linda. *Virtues of the Mind.* Cambridge, UK: Cambridge University Press.

Zaidel, Dahlia W. *Neuropsychology of Art: Neurological, Cognitive and Evolutionary Perspectives.* New York: Psychology Press, 2005.

Zakai, Avihu. "Jonathan Edwards and the Language of Nature: The Re-Enchantment of the World in the Age of Scientific Reasoning." *Journal of Religious History* 26 (2002): 15–41.

Zaniello, Tom. "Alpine Art and Science: Hopkins' Swiss Adventure." *Hopkins Quarterly* 27 (2000): 3–15.

Zemach, Eddy M. *Real Beauty.* University Park, PA: Pennsylvania State University Press, 1997.

Ziman, John M. *Reliable Knowledge: An Exploration of the Grounds for Belief in Science.* Cambridge, UK: Cambridge University Press, 1978.

Zizioulas, John D. *Being as Communion: Studies in Personhood and the Church.* Crestwood, NY: St Vladimir's Seminary Press, 1993.

Index